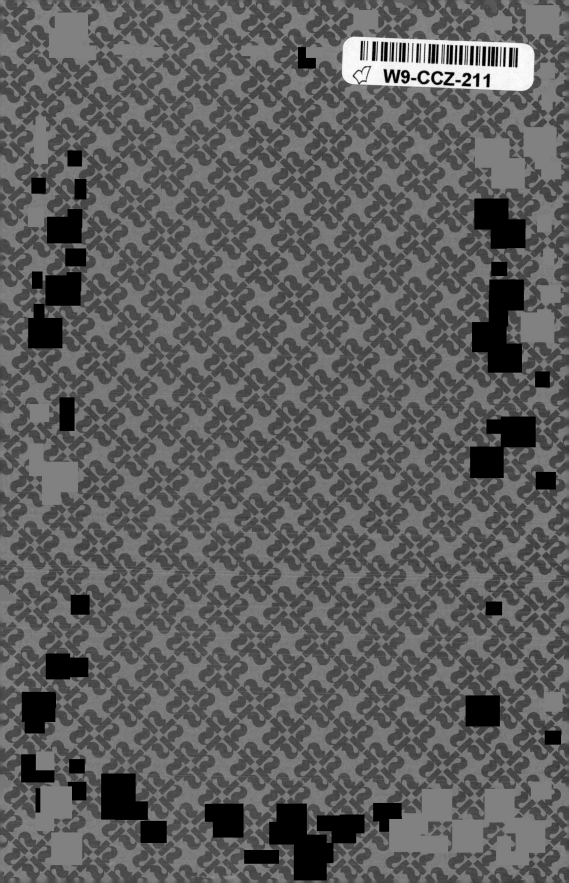

THE SPIRITUAL
CRISIS OF
THE GILDED AGE

THE HADROSAURUS.

*Bone hunters were disclosing to a startled Victorian world the
splendor of the dinosaur.*

THE
SPIRITUAL
CRISIS OF

Paul A. Carter

NORTHERN ILLINOIS UNIVERSITY PRESS
DeKalb : 1971

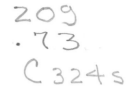
Paul A. Carter is professor of history at Northern Illinois
University, DeKalb, Illinois

Library of Congress Cataloging in Publication Data
Carter, Paul Allen, 1926–
    The spiritual crisis of the gilded age.
    Bibliography: p.
    1. U.S.—Religion—19 century. I. Title.
BR525.C37   209'.0973   72–156938
ISBN 0–87580–026–2 (hbd)
ISBN 0–87580–507–8 (pbk)

Drawings, etchings, and cartoons accompanying the text
are reproduced from *Frank Leslie's Illustrated Newspaper*
of 1878 and 1887; *Harper's Weekly* of 1875; *Harper's New
Monthly Magazine* of 1888; and Alexander Winchell,
*Sketches of Creation: A Popular View of Some of the
Grand Conclusions of the Sciences in Reference to the
History of Matter and of Life* (New York: Harper &
Brothers), 1870.

Published by the Northern Illinois University Press,
DeKalb, Illinois 60115
Manufactured in the United States of America
All Rights Reserved

JULIE, THIS BOOK IS FOR YOU,
WITH ALL MY LOVE AND GRATITUDE

Preface

HE nineteenth century "continually embarrasses us, as a father often embarrasses a son," Basil Willey has written, "by stating with pertinence and superior knowledge positions which we had assumed, without having really examined them, to be obsolete or untenable." This book deals with three decades of that embarrassing century, from around 1865 to, roughly, 1895. (I say "around" and "roughly" in an effort to resist the historian's impulse to "periodize" a span of real time into an abstraction.) These were the years of Gladstone and Disraeli, of the Third French Republic, of Bismarck and Dom Pedro and the Emperor Meiji; they were the time of Tolstoi and Hardy and Flaubert, of Verdi, Wagner, and Brahms. In America they were given a name by two writers who lived through them, in the title of Mark Twain's and Charles Dudley Warner's novel *The Gilded Age*.

Any age men called *gilded* rather than *golden* would be peculiarly prone to historical stereotyping. But historical symposia like H. Wayne Morgan's *The Gilded Age: a Reappraisal* and anthologies of documents such as Ari and Olive Hoogenboom's *The Gilded Age* have recently reminded us of the richness and complexity of a period to which we had hitherto tended to condescend, as one that was at best comic and at worst dreadfully dull. In college-level survey courses in American history, we are now less likely than we were to hear those years treated as a mere interlude, as if the historical process had stopped at Appomattox (except for the *coda* of Reconstruction) and resumed with the Populists and the new overseas imperialism. Vernon L. Parrington's colorful caricature of the times from Andrew Johnson's Presidency through that of Grover Cleveland—a caricature which Parrington himself transcended when he got down to particulars—is yielding to the view that the age, "gilded" or not, had a certain inner logic of its own. Its quaintly antiquarian concerns now begin to sound uncomfortably close to the aspirations, the anxieties, and even the cultural style of our own time.

vii

Can the same be said of the period's religion? The classroom lecturer on the Gilded Age has ordinarily noted that that postwar generation was also the first to come of age after the publication of Darwin's *Origin of Species,* and before proceeding on to the derivative movement usually called *social* Darwinism he has sometimes mentioned in passing that the assimilation of this knowledge gave some church-going people a rather bad time of it. If he has gone further, and taken into account the trans-Atlantic context—the very real crisis of doubt and faith so painfully manifest in the writings of Dostoevski, or in a different fashion in those of Tennyson—he might still have been inclined to discount the significance of those experiences by comparison with the moral and religious revolution our own newest generation has been undergoing. "How can we take seriously the religious qualms of the Victorians," Gertrude Himmelfarb asks, "now that the 'Death of God' has been solemnized on the cover of *Time?*"

Her own excellent study *Victorian Minds* is one answer to that question. Another is suggested in a remark made by Albert Einstein in 1937: "The essential unity of ecclesiastical and secular cultural institutions was lost during the 19th century, to the point of senseless hostility"—long before the day of the God-killers chronicled in *Time,* or even that of the antireligious generation symbolized in H. L. Mencken. Still, Charles Dickens's skeptical caution in the opening paragraph of *A Tale of Two Cities,* "It was the best of times, it was the worst of times . . . ," is applicable here also. In America's Gilded Age "the culture as usual was getting more religious and more secular at the same time and even through the operation of some of the same forces," one historian of the period's religion has written. "Faith *was* both growing and declining; the point is to figure out the special form (if any) in this age, of our perennial paradox."[1] To chart the outlines of that special form is one of the purposes of this book.

Another American historian, upon reading six of these chapters in an earlier draft, raised a different question: "Spiritual crisis for *whom* in a Gilded Age?" Catholics and Lutherans may not have been hit as hard by the religious problems of the era as were Protestants of British-derived denominations, Jews of German-speaking background, and the American-born children of such Jews; "Some orthodoxies disintegrated faster than others." Robert Handy has raised the further possibility of a rural-urban differential in this process: "The 'decay' might be in upper- and upper-middle class faith, while a considerable revival was going on among lower-middle and lower classes of *rural* (though apparently not so much of immigrant and working-class) background."[2]

These points are certainly well taken. Lutherans of several synods in the Eighties were preparing for use a new Hymnal "purged of the errors of Rationalism" (as that book of worship's preface still puts it), and some Roman Catholics in the Gilded Age seem to have operated on the comfortable assumption that loss of faith was something that only happened to persons outside their Church. ("Like most non-Catholic men of his day and generation," ran one line in a story serialized in 1886 in a leading Catholic magazine, "he was a materialist in opinion."[3]) Furthermore there definitely was a "Third Great Awakening" in some quarters in "WASP" Protestantism; both James Findlay, biographer of the great urban evangelist Dwight L. Moody, and Timothy L. Smith, historian of the "holiness" upsurge which led to the founding of the Nazarene denomination (among others), would doubtless go a step further than Handy and say that during those years city as well as country life in America was being religiously stirred. *It was the best of times . . . .*

On the other hand, Robert D. Cross in a major monograph has shown that the emergence of a liberalized Catholicism in the Gilded Age was not achieved without pain and controversy.[4] American Lutheranism, particularly in its Norwegian- and German-speaking ghettoes, may have been relatively sealed off from faith's erosion; still, the very intransigence of men like Carl Ferdinand Wilhelm Walther on such questions as Biblical inerrancy may have been a measure of how formidable they considered the secular foe. As for rural immunity to skepticism and anticlericalism, I suspect that this is largely an invention of urban myth-makers. Men as heterodox as Thorstein Veblen, Edgar Lee Masters, and Carl Sandburg have emerged from rural backgrounds, and they have not always waited until they got to the city to become religiously radical. And for every overt village freethinker there must have been dozens who responded to organized religion in the way of passive resistance. If the author may be permitted a personal note, one of my great-grandfathers, a founder of the Grange in his part of the country in the early, more militant days of that farmers' organization, was also remembered by older members of our family as "a great reader" (a phrase which, in rural Maine idiom, connotes both admiration and mistrust) who, when the preacher came to call, went out and hid in the barn.

Are we left, then, with the inconclusive judgment that "it was the best of times, it was the worst of times," so far as religion was concerned? If no two Gilded-Age Americans balanced their personal equations of doubt and faith in exactly the same way, still there were recurrent rhythms in the way they verbally and emotionally performed these balancing acts. All of them, no matter how far they lived from the population centers, had to reckon with a rapidly industrializing civilization whose transactions increasingly took place on a planetwide scale. All of them, no matter how little might be their own scientific expertise, had to live in the same culture with a burgeoning science and technology that made the most extraordinary claims as to what man could accomplish and know—claims about which men of science nowadays are inclined to be more modest, if not defensive. All of them, no matter how "anti-intellectual" they might be in theory or in practice, were caught up in a rising wave of mass education and university-building which achieved even in the midst of the "lowbrow" Gilded Age a basic and seemingly irreversible intellectualizing of American life, to an extent that the most dedicated efforts of life-adjustment educators and of do-your-thing revolutionaries have not yet been able to undo. These were the parameters for the "spiritual crisis of the Gilded Age" which I have undertaken in the following pages to describe.[5]

Such an undertaking is peculiarly periled by subjectivism, of the kind described by Carl Becker in *Every Man His Own Historian.* Upon re-reading these manuscript pages I am struck by the frequency of allusion, often ironical, to New England and more particularly to Boston. This may be inconsistent with my frequently-expressed view (as in *Church History*, March, 1968) that the writing of American religious history ought to be liberated from its traditional confines on the Northeastern Atlantic seaboard. But in the period under consideration an emphasis upon the scions of the old pre-Revolutionary Protestant denominations perhaps carries with it an important historical insight, whatever distortions of the picture it may also entail.

What gave the spiritual crisis of the Gilded Age a peculiar and personal edge for such people was that it was inextricably linked in their minds with the visible decline of New England—which was beginning to be a region whose most interesting characters, in sharp contrast to the national norm, were its old people. As the Yankee-WASP contemplated his own cultural past in the context of a non-Puritan future of which he took a dim view (see William Dean Howells's jabs at the Boston Irish), it would have been only human for him to have linked the national transformation of religion and culture to his own culture's (and culture-religion's) imminent downfall. But that story achieves a certain poignancy because *his* "old-time religion" had been, theologically at least, liberal by comparison with classic Protestant orthodoxy. His experience, therefore, parallels that of the secular liberal of our own day, who also finds the positions he had defended as *avant-garde* (*e.g.,* in foreign relations and in civil rights) brushed aside by a new generation that has no patience with them. Moreover all America, over against the rising expectations of the rest of the peoples on this planet, may now metaphorically be in a similar position to that of New England *vis-à-vis* the rest of America during the Gilded Age.

*   *   *   *   *

The personal responsibility of an author for any such inquiry as this is his alone, but the insights that give it whatever credence it may win are collective. I have circulated draft chapters among professional colleagues in other universities and in theological seminaries—William A. Clebsch, Robert D. Cross, Robert T. Handy, Richard Hofstadter, William R. Hutchison, Martin E. Marty—and incorporated into the manuscript many of their valuable criticisms. Chapter 9 first appeared an an essay in the *Historical Magazine of the Protestant Episcopal Church* in 1964, and is reproduced in this volume by permission of the editor. I learned much both from its preparation and from responses to it. But the collaborative process had begun much earlier.

The give-and-take between students and professor in a succession of graduate seminars on religion in the Gilded Age, first given at the University of California in 1963–4 and four times since then at Northern Illinois University, was particularly rewarding. Students—Janice Brandon, Allan Eickelmann, Willie D. Gaither, Steven D. Gotham, Evelyn Hubbard, Robert Johnson, Paul C. Kurtz, William Magney, George E. Moore, Vivian Narehood, David Ramis, Betsey Rosten, Peter Slater, Richard A. Taylor, and N. Eugene Tester—whose research papers obviously and materially contributed to my own work will find them cited in the notes to the pages that follow; those not so cited may have equally influenced this book in more intangible ways. Still other students, captive audiences in university lecture-halls, have had raw drafts inflicted on them from the platform, and such guinea-pig listeners performed more of a service than they may have known at the time; for I know of no way for a writer more patently to become aware of his own literary barbarisms than to read them aloud. Before the research embodied in this book was consciously begun, still other students had participated in its germination, as for six consecutive years in a course in American intellectual history at the University of Montana they and I wrestled each winter quarter with the mind and spirit of the Gilded Age.

Students are an instructor's livelihood and, if he be lucky, his joy, but every historian has also to acknowledge that some of his best friends are librarians. The systematic reading that has gone into this study began in the library of the University of California, Berkeley, supplemented by those of the Pacific School of Religion and of the Church Divinity School of the Pacific. It has continued in the libraries of the University of Massachusetts, Smith College, and Mount Holyoke College; the Robert Frost memorial library at Amherst College; the library of the College of Wooster; and especially in the Swen Franklin Parson Library of Northern Illinois University, whose holdings proved unexpectedly rich in bound volumes of nineteenth-century general magazines. For the necessary newspaper-reading, and for unusually inaccessible items—the Spiritualists' *Religio-Philosophical Journal,* for example, and the *Buddhist Ray*— I had recourse to Chicago's Newberry Library, an institution whose life-style and architectural setting, to an *emigré* Yankee, were a nostalgic reminder of Boston. In the summer intervals when the dissociated scraps of this enterprise were being stitched together into a book, the library of the University of Montana was more than hospitable to a former resident and regular user.

Northern Illinois University has been generous without stint. The penultimate draft of the book is being written on a summer grant from its College of Liberal Arts. Course-loads have been lightened or adjusted in the interest of furthering this work, and travel expenses paid; relays of History Department secretaries have worked over successive drafts of these chapters, and borne with surprising patience my marginal scribblings and mysterious emendations. Several colleagues in the Department of History made valuable comments on Chapter 1, an early version of which was presented in our intra-departmental faculty seminar in December, 1968. Emory G. Evans, Chairman, deserves the special thanks of his colleagues for helping to create a scholarly atmosphere in which men write and publish because they feel they have something to say, not because they fear the fall of the executioner's axe if they do not.

Finally, it is the convention at the end of an introductory essay such as this to mention one's wife. The debt I owe mine is no mere convention. She has found or made the time, alongside the claims of four very young and highly active children, to retype the unbelievably illegible first drafts of eight of these chapters into a form which, after still further editing, could be passed along to the university typists, all the while firmly suppressing my inveterate tendency toward Teutonic sentences, pretentious diction, and fascinating tangents that are not really germane. Again and again she has spotted the human import of a document I had been reading essentially from the viewpoint of a bibliophile, and the manuscript has thereby immeasurably been improved. Without this challenge and inspiration, in fact, quite probably this book would never have been begun. Its rightful dedication is therefore inevitably hers.

Paul A. Carter

Contents

1

The Confrontation of
Doubt and Faith

Now faith is the substance of things hoped for,
the evidence of things not seen.

Heb. 11:1 (KJV)

FAITH, n. Belief without evidence in what
is told by one who speaks without knowledge, of things without parallel.

Ambrose Bierce, *The Devil's Dictionary*[1]

FORT Sumter had just fallen. Hundreds of miles away at a prep school in northern Pennsylvania, unaware of the forces just set into motion which would one day sweep him and some two hundred thousand other young men into a maelstrom at Chancellorsville, twenty-year-old Lester Frank Ward bloodied his nose playing football, argued with his fellow students over the rights of Negroes, read Caesar and Cicero, and ardently pursued a girl. During a pause in this busy life one of Ward's teachers came to his room for a long talk about the youth's duty to God. As a result his "heart was very heavy," the young man confessed, so he went to church. When he sat down, as he wrote afterward in his diary, he "could not suppress the tears. . . . I came home and *tried to pray but I did not know how. I cannot say why, but I did not know how.*"[2] A moment later he was writing of a matter more urgently on his mind, but now even the thoughts of a young lover were tinged with a sense of something lost. To think, Ward wrote, that he and his beloved "might be angels, happy in heaven, but perhaps we will never be."

Four dark and terrible years passed. Afterward, the men who had fought, like Ward, Oliver Wendell Holmes, Jr., and Ulysses S. Grant, and those who had stayed at home, like John D. Rockefeller, Grover Cleveland, and William Graham Sumner, moved onstage as actors in a new and disturbingly altered world. Diverse though they were in talents and temperament, in style, methods, and goals, such men in some measure could all share in the spirit of their time.

Lester Ward and William Graham Sumner, for example, would end as irreconcilable antagonists, the former as a proponent of social planning and control, the latter as an advocate of laissez-faire. "Two contemporaries could hardly be more incompatible in every respect," Perry Miller later wrote. And yet, in their shared confidence in science and its methods, and also in the waning of their childhood faith, Sumner and Ward had much in common. Sumner's experience of losing his religion lacked the rhetorical *Sturm und Drang* of Ward's, but the outcome was the same: the Yale professor used to say that he had put his religious beliefs in a drawer and

3

turned the key, and that upon unlocking it many years later he found the drawer empty.[3]

Men who lost their faith in this fashion were not simply spiritual casualties of the war for American union. In contemporary England, where the political and military turbulence that had lately shaken the United States was lacking, Matthew Arnold in his ivory tower could hear the "melancholy, long withdrawing roar" of the Sea of Faith, retreating

>   down the vast edges drear
> And naked shingles of the world.

To describe the attitude of many such men Thomas Henry Huxley invented the word *agnosticism*. John Tyndall doubtless spoke for a good many British scientists in 1875 when he tried to give a concrete definition of the Power he saw manifested in the universe, and found that it eluded him: "I dare not, save poetically, use the pronoun 'He' regarding it; I dare not call it a 'Mind'; I refuse to call it even a 'Cause'."[4] Far more bluntly over on the Continent Ernst Haeckel was preaching an unabashed scientific materialism, preparing the way for the joyous cry of Nietzsche's *Zarathustra*: "God is dead." The religious crisis in America, then, was the reflection of a broader religious crisis in western Christendom.

II   Among the faiths of by-gone years
              Our minds no longer stray,
              But they may guide some wand'ring soul
              To find the broader way.[5]

As the members of the Free Congregational Society of Florence, Massachusetts, dedicated a new lyceum hall in 1874 they sang these new and different words to the old tune "O God Our Help in Ages Past." In the Gilded Age the "broader way" could be very broad indeed. In 1876 one tough old atheist marked the centennial of American independence by asserting: "There are millions in this country who cannot conscientiously support any kind of supernatural religion"[6]—a large claim, in the face of the statistical rise in church membership throughout the nineteenth century, but one that was widely echoed. "It is a generally admitted fact that in these days only a small proportion, even of intelligent and eminently respectable people, are regular attendants on religious services every Sunday," asserted a writer in 1883, under the pseudonym "Non-Church-Goer." "The pulpit is behind the age. . . . Science is today doing more for morals than the church."[7]

An orthodox religious upbringing was apparently no guarantee against the attrition of piety. As early as 1848 Horace Bushnell had warned that "much of what is called Christian nurture only serves to make the subject of religion odious, and that, as nearly as we can discover, in exact proportion to the amount of religious teaching received."[8] Typically William Graham Sumner, whose references to religion throughout his academic career were uncompromisingly naturalistic, began his career as a candidate for holy orders in the Episcopal Church. In like manner the Reverend Joseph Powell, a farmer-preacher in the Wesleyan Methodist Connection, named his second son John Wesley after the founder of the family's faith and then was angered and heartbroken when the youth felt no vocation for the church, having heard a clearer call from fossils and mineral specimens and shells.

After a career as soldier, explorer, scientist, and government bureau chief, John Wesley Powell embraced in his later years a scientific positivism so extreme in its reduction of religious ideas to "ghost-lore" that it prompted one biographer to rank him with the leading freethinker of the day: "Bob Ingersoll was scarcely more an atheist."[9] In similar fashion Mrs. Annis Eastman, a daughter of the manse and an able, effective clergywoman in a time of strong prejudice against women in the ministry, thought and felt her way toward an agnosticism which by 1907 was almost as thoroughgoing as that of her more notoriously radical son.[10]

No region of the United States seemed immune from this tendency. Sumner came from the urban Northeast, Powell from the rural Midwest, Mrs. Eastman from upstate New York. In South Carolina—supposedly the heartland of conservative politics and religion in America—R. Habersham Barnwell, a nephew of the Presiding Bishop of the Episcopal Church in the Confederate States, left the ministry in 1883, a decision he recalled years later in a wistful letter to an older brother who had remained in the Church: "I gave up trying to solve the riddle of the ages some time ago and have felt better ever since."[11]

Those raised in the ancestral faiths who did not find religion "untrue," in the formal sense, might still be inclined to find it irrelevant. In 1868 a character in Harriet Beecher Stowe's book *The Chimney Corner* observed that "the General Assembly of the Presbyterian Church refused to testify against slavery, because of political diffidence, but made up for it by ordering a more stringent crusade against dancing." In accents that call to mind the "revolt of youth" during the 1920's, or still more recently, this fictional spokesman for the post-Civil War younger generation charged that "the only thing the Church has done is to forbid and frown. We have abundance of tracts against dancing, whist-playing, ninepins, billiards, operas, theatres, —in short, anything that young people would be apt to like."[12] In the same booming postwar period James Parton visited some of the fashionable churches on Fifth Avenue, and came away with "the impression . . . that he had been looking . . . not upon a living body, but a decorated image"; he had heard sermons in such churches, "laboriously prepared and earnestly read, . . . from which everything that could rouse or interest a human soul living on Manhattan Island in the year 1867 seemed to have been purposely pruned away."[13] At the opposite extreme from the bloodless gentility Parton found in New York was the raucous huckster Rudyard Kipling listened to thirty years later in Chicago, "with imagery borrowed from the auction-room," who "built up for his hearers a heaven on the lines of the Palmer House . . . and set in the centre of it a loud-voiced, argumentative, and very shrewd creation that he called God."[14]

III   How widespread, and how typical of the period, was the distaste for religion to which such witnesses bore testimony? Were these critics an enlightened (or disillusioned) minority doing battle against a dominant religious conventionalism? William Graham Sumner taught at Yale; Powell, Huxley, Tyndall, and Haeckel were scientists, and thus members of a select group; the aversion of Matthew Arnold, and in a different way of Rudyard Kipling, to mass culture is well known; and even Lester Ward, who is usually thought of as an advocate of a coming popular democracy, had little respect for popular opinion when it clashed with what he conceived of as scientific truth.[15] The German immigrant intellectuals who seeded the Minnesota prairie with freethinking societies were an elite cultural minority, swamped in numbers by the religiously conservative rural German-Americans who surrounded them.[16] And the Free Congregationalists in a small town in western Massachusetts probably thought of themselves as members of an intellectual aristocracy by comparison with Baptist and Catholic believers living nearby.

At the same time many American religious believers would have been innocently unaware of what all those bookish religious liberals were writing and saying. For example, little of the formal conflict between doubt and faith had reached the ear of Charles Marion Russell, the self-taught cowboy artist, as he broke bread in 1881 with a notable circuit-riding frontier preacher on a ranch in a remote corner of Montana Territory. Russell later described this encounter in language as spontaneous and free-wheeling as was his religion.

the eavning you came there was a mixture of bull whackers hunters and prospecters who welcomed you with hand shaks and rough but friendly greetings . . . and when we all sat down to our elk meet beens coffee and dryed apples under the rays of a bacon grease light. these men who knew little of law and one among them I knew wore notches on his gun   men who had not prayed since they nelt at their mothers knee bowed there heads while you, Brother Van, gave thanks and when you finished some one said Amen[17]

Meanwhile, back in the cities, detractors of "the old-time religion" such as those I have quoted were being answered by defenders, who complacently saw the religious life of Americans as yet another Gilded-Age success story. The anonymous "Non-Church-Goer" who asserted that "only a small proportion, even of intelligent and eminently respectable people" were regularly attending church was followed in the same issue (of the *North American Review*) by eighteen pages of vehement rebuttal. "Ours is a church-going people, a church-respecting, a church-honoring people, and never more so than now," a fellow contributor declared, and the statement on church attendance was "palpably untrue." In *Footprints of Four Centuries*, an opulent, "de luxe" popular history of the United States published in 1895, Hamilton Wright Mabie insisted that "religious sentiment, not to say religious principle, has a deeper hold upon the American people than it has ever had."[18] More recently a scholar writing from a longer and wider perspective than Mabie's has concurred. Of the seven meticulously researched volumes in his *History of the Expansion of Christianity* Kenneth Scott Latourette devoted no less than three to "The Great Century," as he termed the years from 1800 to 1914. "The nineteenth century was a time of unequalled expression of the vitality inherent in the Christian faith," Latourette concluded.[19]

Martin Marty, another twentieth-century historian of religion in America, has called our attention to "the extent of the evangelical triumph" during the Gilded Age, and to the awe of foreign visitors at the prestige enjoyed in America by revivalists and other ministers. "Wherever one turned, signs of progress, growth, and success could be documented. . . . All these signs were impressive to partisans of Christianity and seemed oppressive and overpowering to its antagonists." Foes of organized religion who claimed that millions of Americans privately agreed with them may have been indulging in wishful thinking, much in the spirit of the radical intellectual in a conservative era who hopefully imagines that every proletarian is a true revolutionary at heart. Accepting Marty's argument, Richard Hofstadter suggests that real infidelity "was much too weak in America to be of grave importance in itself," and sur-

PRESIDENT HAYES BEING INTRODUCED TO THE GUESTS, AT THE RECEPTION OF THE UNION
LEAGUE CLUB, PHILADELPHIA, APRIL 24, 1878.

vived chiefly "as a scare word in the orthodox sermon and in theological re-
criminations"—in short, as a bogeyman, comparable to the official Soviet
charges in the Thirties that Trotskyism still remained a serious threat to
Stalin's Russia.[20]

But perhaps the historians of the Gilded Age have listened too much to
spokesmen for the literary, educational, and religious Establishments like
Hamilton Wright Mabie, or to twentieth-century Christian apologists like
Latourette, and not enough to the period's gadflies. Seeing that era neither as
a time of vital regenerative faith (as Latourette judged it to have been) nor
as one of heresy and anticlericalism (as the critics I have been quoting attested), many modern students of Victorian America have found its religious
experience conventional, orthodox, and a bit dull. Except for a few "neglected prophets," Henry F. May has written, the 1860's and 1870's were a "summit of complacency" for American Protestantism. Over that summit brooded
spirits such as Lucy and Rutherford Hayes, with their wineless White House
dinners and their Sunday night hymn-sings, recalled by one Congressman's
wife many years later: "the heavy ebony furniture; the potted plants scattered all about the room; the dripping candles; the hot fire, one huge lump
of anthracite! and Lucy Webb Hayes, in hoop-skirted black velvet, illusion,

MRS. HAYES VISITING THE GIRLS' NORMAL SCHOOL, PHILADELPHIA.

and seed pearls, at a gloomy Chickering square piano playing hymns while the guests . . . sang with heart and soul."[21]

Before we jump to the conclusion, however, that the United States was a nation "more devout, more dogmatic, and more conservative" than it had been in earlier years of its history,[22] we must remember that Robert G. Ingersoll was denouncing the Bible with humor and passion—"They may say I will be damned if I do not believe that, and I tell them I will if I do"—before crowds as enthusiastic as those who sang with Mrs. Hayes or with Ira Sankey. The publisher of a collection of Ingersoll's addresses asserted that "these lectures are the most radical ever delivered in the United States" and noted proudly *"Over twenty thousand copies of this book already sold,"* implying from a purely business point of view that Ingersoll had some kind of popular following.[23] In 1876 Ingersoll made the nominating speech for James G.

Blaine, a major Presidential contender, at the same Republican national convention that went on to choose Hayes; can one imagine a serious aspirant for the Presidency even today, when we are supposedly less godly than our Victorian ancestors, inviting so avowed a freethinker to place his name in nomination? Can we conclude a priori that Bob Ingersoll was less representative of Gilded-Age America than was Lucy Hayes?

Some conservatives were alarmed by the secession from the church of a large section of the intelligentsia.[24] But to the historian, sensitive as he must be to broad social currents, what may have been of even greater significance was the movement for secession among all sorts and conditions of men. "There is a more widespread uncertainty, doubt, and unbelief than people imagine," a prominent Anglican priest declared in an 1878 baccalaureate sermon, and in a pastoral letter of 1873 the Northern Methodist bishops warned that "opposition to the truth" (meaning Christian, and more specifically Protestant, orthodoxy) was "not confined to the scientific few"; "the baleful influence of unbelief," as they termed it, was also "found among the common people." And one observer flatly stated in 1888 that "the masses have lost their reverence for the church as an institution."[25]

Religious statistics are notoriously, even outrageously, unreliable, but Henry King Carroll, director of the Division of Churches for the Eleventh U.S. Census, making the most educated guess that he could, estimated on the basis of the population figures for 1890 that "one out of every twelve persons is either an active or passive opponent of religion." To be sure, the Gilded Age had also been a period of enormous growth for the churches, in both wealth and numbers. But instead of drawing an optimistic inference from these figures, Carroll concluded that "we have a problem of sufficient magnitude to engage the mind, heart, and hand of the church for a generation." Whether or not there actually was a general withering of faith, many articulate observers evidently thought there was; "without controversy," declared a writer in *The Forum* for December, 1886, "Christianity appears to many of the wisest to be at the present day in deadlier peril than it has been at any time during the eighteen hundred years of its existence."[26]

IV   Not only the reputation and influence of organized religion were in question, but also the Church's own inner morale. For example, the Gilded Age is often remembered as the great era of the gospel hymn; but—however lustily the crowds at Dwight L. Moody's revivals and the guests at Lucy Hayes's piano *soirées* may have sung them—one leading monthly magazine soberly traced the decline in many churches from singing to mere listening. The change was an inevitable casualty of urbanism, the writer thought; "in the country, where amusements are few," it was feasible for church people to get together to practice singing hymns, but "in the city, where life is full, especially at that season of the year when rehearsals are practicable," a volunteer choir was all but impossible to keep alive. Many downtown churches had therefore abandoned the unequal struggle, and resorted to hiring a quartet. It was all very well in theory to cry with the Psalmist "Let the people praise thee," "if the people would sing, or would take the pains to learn and rehearse; but they do not."[27]

Methodism since hymn-writer Charles Wesley's time had been a singing denomination, but "the singing in many churches," one American Methodist testified in 1875, "is more to show off some prima donna or a fine basso than to worship God in spirit and in truth."[28] Some defenders of the church complacently reasoned that it was as legitimate for a congregation to hire professional singers to lead them in praise as it was to hire a professional minister to lead them in prayer. However, it is but a step from passivity to complete indifference—as many a twentieth-century pastor or choir director could also acknowledge, while struggling to trick or shame his flock into active participation.

The busywork of the church—parish meetings, church suppers, and so on —went on unchecked, conceded the editor of *The Chautauquan* in 1885, but its vital spiritual life seemed on the decline.

> The conversation of Christians is less frequently on religious subjects. . . . We are not made . . . to feel the force and warmth of religious conviction. The sermons are logical, literary, and cold; if there be warmth, it seems to be rather intellectual than religious. The more able religious editors complain that they can not get written for them articles which are at once readable and spiritual.

In fact some of them were saying "that the expression of religious experience has 'hopelessly gone into the keeping of cranks and weak-headed and morally-unsound persons.' "[29] The expression of religious experience could also have been found in the keeping of persons having both dedication and strength, like Dwight L. Moody, Cardinal Gibbons, or Isaac M. Wise; but men of their stature are rare in any age, and even Moody's great evangelistic sermons sometimes got a surprisingly tepid reception. Conceding the excitement of a Moody-Sankey revival—"A great multitude of people always magnetizes itself, and the choral singing of a thousand voices is always inspiring" —the editor of *Harper's* nevertheless found it "impossible to read one of Mr. Moody's sermons . . . and not feel that however earnest and sincere the preacher may be, the hearer may be very easily confused by his words, and mistake a feeling, or a wish, or a nervous emotion for a spiritual spring and revelation."[30]

Alongside those keepers of the faith whose discourse some hearers found earnest but confusing stood those whose remarks were merely superficial. "Take a small quantity of ideas which everybody knows, paste them on a Bible text, put in two or three funny anecdotes, pour on them three or four quarts of filtered words," Isaac Wise wrote in 1878, ". . . throw the whole liquid upon paper, dry it in the moonshine of sentimentalities, then cut it in slices of equal size, and you have a sermon which will hurt nobody." Rabbi Wise's witty warning to his own seminary students on "How a Bad Sermon Is Made" should remind us also that the decline of deep religious devotion was not felt by Christians alone. "We must . . . confess that as a general rule the synagogue fails to have an abiding influence upon the worshiper," one American Jewish journal charged. "The charm has been snapped. Some of our congregations compete like rival tradesmen; each wants to outdo the other in . . . the splendor of its choir, the resonance of its organ, the voice of its reader, the drawing qualities of its preacher. Synagogues have grown to be business corporations." Quoting this diatribe, a leading Protestant weekly commented that the picture might well be copied for the benefit of Gentile congregations as well.[31]

Such congregations may have been subtly aware that the paralysis of doubt had reached into the pulpit itself. Thus in the midst of a ringingly affirmative sermon on "The Light of the World" the popular preacher Phillips Brooks admitted that "a sense of foreignness and unnaturalness and strangeness lies like a fog across the entrance of the divine country." Some of his hearers might have been shocked that the author of the much-loved Christmas carol "O Little Town of Bethlehem" could thus refer to "the obscurity, the feebleness, the vague remoteness of religion," and wonder whether he, as a man, had any business there at all; but this kind of honest admission was an integral part of Brooks's conception of the minister's task.[32]

In his essay "The Pulpit and Popular Skepticism" the same distinguished churchman referred to the "terrible . . . glimpses that we get occasionally into a minister's unbelief," and—much in the spirit of Emerson addressing the young divinity graduates at Harvard forty years before—he warned the readers of the eminently orthodox *Princeton Review* that members of a congregation had every right to know about such qualms. "Let their doubts know that you have doubted and their wonder feel that you have wondered," the Sage of Concord had said, and Phillips Brooks warned that the pastor who tried "to make people believe that which he questions, in order to keep them from questioning that which he believes" would bring on among his hearers the very skepticism against which he was trying to guard. "The most pitiable and powerless of all preachers," Brooks thought, was the one "who tries to preach doctrine which his own soul does not really believe and use."[33] Not everyone put it so charitably. Thomas Paine had declared in *The Age of Reason* that to profess what one did not really believe was a form of "mental lying," and a century later Robert Ingersoll was preaching anticlerical sermons on the same theme.

Many of Ingersoll's clerical opponents conceded, publicly or privately, that the charge was just. "Many facts about the Bible are known by intelligent ministers of which their congregations do not hear," Washington Gladden observed in 1891, attributing this silence to "an anxious and not unnatural feeling . . . that the faith of the people . . . would be shaken if the facts were known." Phillips Brooks acknowledged that "almost any company of clergymen . . . talking freely to one another" would express opinions which would "greatly surprise and at the same time greatly relieve" their parishioners, but he thought that not only preachers but also a great many parents and teachers were thinking and living in this same evasive way. Having "started with a great deal more belief than they have now . . . they think that their children, too, must start believing so much that they can afford to lose a great deal and still have something left, and so they teach these children what they have themselves long ceased to believe."[34]

It would be easy to dismiss such a position as a typical and deplorable example of Victorian hypocrisy, but the enlightened twentieth-century reader is reminded that as recently as 1963 a poll of the students attending a mixed batch of American colleges and universities—Sarah Lawrence, Williams, Yale, Marquette, Boston University, Indiana, South Carolina, Howard, Reed, Davidson, Brandeis, and Stanford—disclosed that substantial proportions of them were determined to raise their own children in traditional faiths which they themselves had largely ceased to accept.[35] These findings, and the subsequent uproar over the controversial opinions of Bishop James A. Pike, suggest that this is a continuing and perennial issue. "It is not so much that he denies things which church people believe to be true," one of his contemporaries wrote of Pike, "but that his candor violates the understanding that a clergyman . . . has with churchgoers: the understanding that the clergyman shall assert certainty about matters which the intelligent layman considers highly doubtful."[36]

V   "With the decay of the traditional faiths the younger generation"—meaning the generation that was young in the Nineties—"was left to wander as best it might upon the bleak table-lands of impersonal energy," Vernon Louis Parrington wrote in his unfinished fragment "The Darkening Skies of Letters."[37] But why were the traditional faiths in decay? Parrington found the main reason for what was happening in the natural sciences, with "the discovery of a vast impersonal cosmos that annihilated the petty egocentric world of good and evil postulated by the theologians."

Scientific investigation as an enemy of religion was a common theme in the Gilded Age. A Catholic writer warned in 1888 that "heresy and rational-istic philosophy" were no longer "the most formidable antagonists to be encountered" by defenders of the faith: "the really dangerous foe is a form of unbelief which professes to be science."[38] Advocates of science often reciprocated this hostility, urging that we cleanse ourselves of "the leprosy of the miraculous which taints men's minds." The *Popular Science Monthly* —then a far more formidable intellectual organ than the hobbies-and-car-repair magazine it has since become—editorially attacked the "groveling anthropomorphism" of believers who thought of God "as watching from on high with special solicitude the doings of Moody and Sankey. . . . Men who look upon the universe as science has disclosed it cannot much sympathize with this view of the Deity and all that it implies." When a conflict arises be-tween religion and science, argued such men as John Burroughs and Andrew Dickson White and Edward L. Youmans, science is always right.[39]

Still, if genuinely "popular" skepticism existed in the Gilded Age, it would have been found among many people who had never heard of physiological psychology or the conservation of energy. "More people, in this western land, are led away from God by a sort of every-day materialism than by scientific doubt," James DeKoven insisted.[40] In fact the "bleak table-lands" Parrington referred to and the "every-day materialism" which DeKoven mentioned probably had a more direct and dynamic relationship than stu-dents of the Gilded Age have always been aware of. On another occasion DeKoven said that the two great preoccupations of his day were "material development" and "the study of nature," and in a sermon preached in 1874 he linked them together: "The soul, engrossed in earthly pursuits, scouts all mysteries. It wants its religion to be as practical as its business."[41]

The Reform rabbi Isaac M. Wise thought the "old-time-religion," in both its Jewish and its Christian forms, was in part a victim of the impressive tech-nology in which those earthly pursuits were visibly embodied, although Wise did not himself pursue this insight to its logical conclusion: "Like rabbinic Judaism, dogmatic Christianity was the product of ages without typography, telescopes, microscopes, telegraphs and the power of steam," Wise wrote in 1874. "These right arms of intelligence have . . . conquered and demolished the ancient castles, and remove now the debris" from the site upon which the new temple of humanity would be constructed.[42]

The dogmatic scientism (and "gadgetism," to coin a word) of the Gilded Age may also have been aggravated by the anti-aesthetic philistinism rampant in that era in both America and England, symbolized here by the sarcastic descriptions of the dingy old art treasures of Europe in Mark Twain's *The Innocents Abroad*, and in the old country by the caricatures of Wilde and Swinburne in Gilbert and Sullivan's comic opera *Patience* (1881). James DeKoven's argument that the materialism of the marketplace counted for more than the materialism of the laboratory in leading people away from the faith of their fathers might therefore mean that religious aspiration would be scoffed at not only as "bad science" but also as "mere poetry."

Consider for example the dilemma of a poet trying to write for modern nineteenth-century readers on the doctrine of the bodily ascension of Christ:

> Gone up! But whither? To a star?
> Some orb that seems a point of light?
> Or one too infinitely far
> For our fond gaze beneath the night?
> Some fairer world, to which our own,
> With all its vastness, is a grain?
> ·　·　·　·　·　·　·　·　·
> Let science coldly sweep away
> A fancied Eden here and there
> From out the starry space, and say
> 'Tis *all* brute matter—crude and bare . . .

Still, the traditional dogma insisted,

> God is man for evermore . . .
> As man was born, and died, and rose . . .

and, out there in temperatures approaching zero on the Kelvin scale, this risen God still has a body,

> And still he wears it in the skies—
> Matter in place . . .
> 　　　　[in] the bright Elysian home
> His own primeval word had wrought.

To the Catholic poet who wrote these lines, they were a perfectly valid response to the challenge of writing a poem suitable for the Feast of the Ascension in the year of our Lord 1876. But the trouble with this kind of answer to the questions raised by post-Newtonian astronomy was that a literal-minded reader reflecting upon these verses might be impelled to become more skeptical, rather than less. "We still tell the child, 'Heaven is up in the sky,' " the Congregationalist Newman Smyth wrote in 1879.

> But the sky nowhere gives to our astronomy the faintest suggestion of a place for heaven. . . . There is iron, and sodium, and heated hydrogen, and other earthly elements to be found among the stars—nothing else. This visible universe is made throughout of the same perishable stuff; it is of one piece, and it is growing old.[43]

Smyth tried to salvage something of the old faith by arguing that Heaven is not somewhere else, in a spatio-temporal sense; it is "in the Unseen." But the times were not appropriate for reliance upon Unseens and Unknowables. In 1906 Thorstein Veblen, in an essay "The Place of Science in Modern Civilization," would argue that the culture of modernity had become "peculiarly matter of fact." The growing body of impersonal factual knowledge plus the insensate discipline of the machine increasingly gave industrial man a worldview in which intangible reality had no place. The new world of human experience was, to use Veblen's arresting adjective, opaque. And the Anglo-Catholic apologist James DeKoven anticipated the great Norwegian-American renegade by a generation: "The visible encroaches on the invisible," DeKoven confessed in 1878. "Between us and God appear to come laws, and forces, and powers, the duration and extent of which we can grasp and measure. . . . What, then, if these laws begin to take to us the place of God?"[44]

Some could of course get along in their religious life without the Visible. For men of a certain temperament it would suffice if God existed "in, with, and under" the phenomena of Nature, truly present to the believer and yet vanishing into air when the phenomena were tested and measured; such seems to have become the personal stance of many of the radical theologians of our own day. But to the Victorian Age with its wholistic conception of truth with a capital T, and the ever-increasing "matter-of-factness" which Veblen later noted, such evasion was intolerable. No *mysterium tremendum* here; poetic indirection, or mythic metaphor, or intuitions of the Divine would not serve the age of iron and steam. "If God is only to be left to the gaps in our knowledge, where shall we be when these gaps are filled up?" asked the visiting British evolutionist and theist Henry Drummond in his

Lowell Lectures of 1894. "And if they are never to be filled up, is God only to be found in the disorders of the world?" Those who sought for such gaps, "gaps which they will fill up with God," Drummond saw as men in quest not of knowledge but of ignorance, men "whose daily dread is that the cloud may lift, and who, as darkness melts from this field or from that, begin to tremble for the place of His abode."[45]

VI   For many of the advocates of science the Visible held no terrors. The vast universe opening before modern man was not a "bleak tableland" under "darkening skies," but a high and healthful plateau under the cheering light of day—an illumination which might indeed call forth poetic raptures more satisfying than those evoked by a small-scale cosmos inhabited by stars that marched over Bethlehem and angels with feathered wings.[46] In 1882 Albert A. Michelson, whose invention of the interferometer was helping to smash through the science of the Gilded Age and lift it to a still higher and more rarefied plateau, told some reporters who asked him why he was measuring the velocity of light: "Because it is such fun." Perhaps this answer smacked too much of Veblen's "instinct of idle curiosity" for the busy workaday world of the late nineteenth century, and so in 1899 Michelson put his aspirations into less playful form for an audience in morally serious Boston."If a poet could at the same time be a scientist," he told the Lowell Institute, "he might convey to others the pleasure, the satisfaction, almost the reverence, which the subject of light inspires."

Many a clergyman actively joined in Michelson's reverent and joyful scientific quest, and the thought that the laws they were discovering might become a barrier between themselves and God does not seem to have spoiled their fun. The physicist Michelson was a freethinker, but the chemist Edward W. Morley, his colleague in the great experiment that bears their names, retained the religious values of his Congregationalist ministerial training and preached regularly in the college chapel at Western Reserve.[47] Many other ordained ministers found time to pursue science as an avocation and to make solid contributions; the number of Reverends and D. D.'s who appeared in the pages of the *Popular Science Monthly*—alongside the writings of other men who attacked their faith!—is impressive. These men of the cloth might have been less surprised and upset than many a liberal arts professor in the twentieth century would be at the thought of heart transplants and DNA; their spirit was more like that aged heretic Ralph Waldo Emerson, who was able in 1871 to contemplate with equanimity the prospect of man's creation of life itself.

I do not know that I should feel threatened or insulted if a chemist should take his protoplasm or mix his hydrogen, oxygen, and carbon, and make an animalcule incontestably swimming and jumping before my eyes. I should only feel that it indicated that the day had arrived when the human race might be trusted with a new degree of power.[48]

Evidently, if "the visible encroaches on the invisible," some religious believers were ready to accept whatever came to light, and praise it as the handiwork of God. But mixed with their hobby-interest may have been a more anxious concern that they keep up with the scientific Joneses, lest "the intelligent part of society go past us." As Henry Ward Beecher said in his famous Yale Lectures on Preaching (1872). "The providence of God is rolling forward a spirit of investigation that Christian ministers must meet and join. There is no class of people upon earth who can less afford to let the development of truth run ahead of them than they."[49] And so, in the Old Chapel at Yale in the Eighties, on the Sunday evenings when Professor James Dwight Dana told the students that the theory of evolution did not overthrow the story of creation as found in the first chapter of Genesis, "except perhaps in one or two details," the college pastor listened with approval and then dismissed the congregation with a scientific benediction: "You see, gentlemen, that when the right kind of a man of science and the right kind of a theologian come together there is no dispute between science and religion."[50]

The trouble with this kind of "peaceful coexistence" proposal was that the scientists and the popularizers of science would not let the theologians alone. To one clergyman's denial in 1876 that there was any conflict between "true" science and "true" religion Edward L. Youmans, *Popular Science Monthly*'s crusading editor, replied that the clash was "natural and inevitable." "That the antagonism continues," Youmans reasoned, "is not because of the wrongheadedness of a few partisans who are bent on stirring up strife, but because science is driving on . . . regardless of anything but the new truth it aims to teach, while the religious world is full of anxiety and dread about what is going to happen as a result." *Popular Science* had been happy to print a lecture by the prestigious pastor of Plymouth Church in Brooklyn, but Henry Ward Beecher's offer to meet science half way was implicitly rejected. The only terms Youmans offered to churchmen were unconditional surrender; peace could be purchased only at the price of "the entire indifference of religious people, *as such*, to the results of scientific inquiry."[51] To such a partisan it was a case simply and starkly of order against disorder, of painful knowledge or else willful ignorance.

In our own time this kind of conflict is sometimes muffled by relativism:

you may be right, I could be wrong, so if you don't criticize my faith, I won't find fault with yours. In his more genial moods H. L. Mencken sometimes masked his basic hostility to religion by a kind of personal tact: "We must respect the other fellow's religion, but only in the sense and to the extent that we respect his theory that his wife is beautiful and his children smart."[52] In the Gilded Age it was less possible to let well enough alone in this fashion. The thought of the nineteenth century was still monistic; the truth of the marketplace and the truth of the laboratory were assumed to be one and the same. It followed that the defender of the truth must combat the purveyor of falsehood, come what may. The unbeliever could not simply quietly go fishing on Sunday; he had to challenge the believer's reasons for going to church instead.

Just as the evangelist urgently felt the duty of asking anyone he met "Have you been saved?" rather than tactfully letting him go his own way, so also a freethinker like Ingersoll quite naturally carried the fight into the enemy camp: "The agnostic does not simply say, '*I* do not know.' He goes another step, and he says, with great emphasis, that *you* do not know."[53] Thus people on both sides of these controversies felt a crusading commitment which a later age may find hard to understand. At the beginning of the decade we misname the "gay Nineties" Hugh Miller Thompson, a member of the Anglican episcopate, told a college audience at Ann Arbor that the time in which they were living was "the most serious and sadly earnest age that the earth ever saw." "We have had none of the frivolous unbelief or frivolous skepticism of the last century," Bishop Thompson asserted. "Where doubt exists in the nineteenth century it is deeply and profoundly earnest."[54] The rejection of traditional religion had itself, paradoxically, become "religious."

This kind of judgment was not to be confuted by casuistry—by merely "puzzling back again into orthodox speciousness the minds that have already been puzzled away with the speciousness of science," as Phillips Brooks once put it.[55] The truth of religion could not be "proved" with finality in any event; otherwise, the greater the intellect the greater the chance of being religious, which in the 1870's clearly was not the case. "The invisible must not simply be proven, it must be seen," James DeKoven argued; a modern preacher of the same intellectual and emotional outlook might say "known existentially." And when, DeKoven asked his hearers, had they known or seen the Invisible?

> Was it when your mother or your father died? Was it when you were sick? . . . Was it before the altar when the Mystical Presence flashed upon you? Was it in the stillness of the night, or at some time when nothing masked it except that He was there?

The problem for people who made this kind of feeling the basis for their religious experience, as DeKoven himself admitted, was that "there was never an age of the world when the visible seemed to possess such claims in our thoughts as now."[56] Here the full impact of the bleak new world which Veblen and Parrington described and which the Gilded-Age generation experienced becomes apparent. Parrington's "tablelands" had to be crossed, and the cold winds would not cease to blow if men changed the subject of conversation.

2

The Ape
in The Tree
of Knowledge

"But if human conceit was staggered for a
moment by its kinship with the ape, it soon
found a way to reassert itself. . . . A process
which led from the amoeba to Man appeared to the philosophers to be obviously
a progress—though whether the amoeba
would agree with this opinion is not known."

Bertrand Russell[1]

I HE self-love of mankind has "been three times severely wounded by the researches of science," said Freud. It suffered the first blow when men learned that their small planetary home was not the center of the universe; the second, when the presumed gulf between themselves and the rest of the animal kingdom was bridged by the theory of evolution; the third, when sleuths like Freud himself showed them that the ego was not master even in its own house. With a certain professional bias, perhaps, the Viennese doctor declared the third of these shocks to have been probably the most severe;[2] but he would have been the first to acknowledge that Nicolaus Copernicus and Charles Darwin had also taken their historic toll.

The new astronomy of the seventeenth century prompted Blaise Pascal to exclaim: "The eternal silence of these infinite spaces frightens me," and the new biology of the nineteenth century, writes one leading cultural historian, "seemingly made final the separation between man and his soul."[3] Small wonder, then, that some who heard this dismal news fell back upon the most traditional means available for the defense of human dignity. "When you read what some writers say about man and his bestial origin your shoulders unconsciously droop. . . . Your self-respect has received a blow," wrote Dyson Hague, Professor of Liturgics in Wycliffe College, Toronto, around 1909. "When you read Genesis, your shoulders straighten, your chest emerges. You feel proud to be that thing that is called man."[4]

With any trauma, according to Freud, goes repression; the victim is naturally inclined to forget how deep these cultural shocks were. The humiliation implicit in civilized man's discovery that he is just another of the animals may have been dispelled for many by the comfortable words of Dr. Benjamin Spock, whose well-thumbed baby book has within the past decade begun to rival the Bible in sales; certainly it has been read by many a woman of child-rearing age with more attention than she had free to devote to Scripture. "Each child as he develops is retracing the whole history of mankind, physically and spiritually [sic]. . . . A baby starts off in the womb as a single tiny cell, just the way the first living thing appeared in the ocean. Weeks later . . . he has gills like a fish," et cetera.[5] To the twentieth-century American mother as she anxiously watches her one-year-old "celebrating that period millions of years ago when man's ancestors got up off all-fours," the theory of evolution is not exactly news; in fact, if she has time to reflect, she is likely aware that the good doctor's version of the doctrine that ontogeny recapitulates phylogeny is somewhat inaccurate and out of date.[6]

Nevertheless, viewers of the National Geographic Society's 1966 television documentary on man's lowly origins may have squirmed a bit as the homely likeness of Zinjanthropus swung into focus before the camera. Desmond

THE LATE CHARLES HODGE, D.D., LL.D.,
OF PRINCETON, NEW JERSEY.

What is Darwinism? It is Atheism.

Morris's book *The Naked Ape* made the best-seller lists in 1968 partly because its subject matter, man, still seemed a bit scandalous under that title; and at some showings of Stanley Kubrick's remarkable motion picture *2001* the physically and morally ugly ape-men depicted in its opening "dawn of man" sequence drew an audience response of nervous laughter. Freud's "wound," however forgotten it may sometimes seem at the conscious level, is an historical reality. As for its implications for religion, a graduating high school senior in Grafton, Ohio, in 1964 said to his teacher: "I suppose that if you really think about it, you can't believe in God and evolution at the same time. We just don't like to think about it."[7]

In the 1920's the edges of the wound were more raw. " 'Close your eyes and think of some muddy gutter or frog pond full of stagnant water with a scorching sun glittering down on the green slime'," one Fundamentalist leader cried, quoting from a pamphlet he had found in the hands of a twelve-year-old boy. " '. . . Those cesspools, geologists tell us, were the cradle of life on earth'." Outraged at this "sample of the stuff some of our children are getting," he urged the church to do something about it—which indeed it did.[8] In the same spirit Alfred W. McCann in his prosecutor's brief *God—or Gorilla?*, published in 1922 and illustrated with vivid photographs of unattractive anthropoids, denounced Darwinism as "this new 'chemic creed,' that out of the lowest clod man has developed in common with the toad and the cockroach." Such a creed was a denial of civilization, of conscience, of manhood itself: "For what law, except the law of fear, shall this soulless THING have respect?"[9]

Forty or fifty years earlier some Americans had found little difficulty in reconciling respect—sometimes exaggerated respect— for conventional morality with the belief that man had sprung from more lawless breeds. Kinship with toad and cockroach could be taken not only as a reminder of how humble man's poor relations were but also as an assurance of how far above their social level he had climbed, in the spirit caricatured by Gilbert and Sullivan in the haughty Pooh-Bah, who was proud to claim that he could trace his family tree back to a "protoplasmal primordial atomic globule." "People who get up in the world are sometimes ashamed of their parentage," conceded the American Unitarian Minot J. Savage, but "since my line runs back millions of years, and ends in God, I see no good cause for being ashamed of the long and wondrous way by which it has come." He was not half as anxious to find out that he did not come from an ape, Savage declared, as he was to know that he was not traveling toward one.[10]

Father John Augustine Zahm, professor of physics at Notre Dame University, pointed to the precedent of Saint Francis of Assisi, who had called creatures even humbler than the primates his brothers; "whether he was correct, either theologically or zoologically, he was plainly free from that fear of being mistaken for an ape which haunts so many in these modern times."[11] The fears of theologians lest Darwinism shatter their souls were likened by one British writer to the panic of a man who clings to a precipice all night and

then, his strength failing, lets go—only to learn that his feet have been hang-
ing within a few inches of the ground all the while.[12] In other words Darwinian evolution, rationally considered, was not really a crippling wound to
the human ego at all, but only a bad scare.

II   But to some evolutionist Victorians in England and
America such an answer smacked less of science than of Christian science.
At the very least, the blow struck at man's self-esteem had been experienced
as if it were real. "The fears that were felt when the doctrine of evolution was

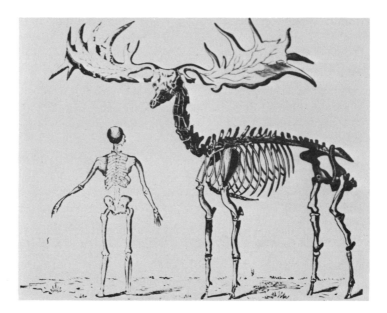

SKELETON OF EXTINCT GIANT ELK (MEGACEROS HIBERNICUS) OF
IRELAND, COMPARED WITH MAN, FROM AN IRISH LITHOGRAPH.

first offered to the world were not unnatural," wrote Theodore T. Munger in
1886. When a new doctrine with revolutionary implications for the nature
and destiny of man is put forth, this Protestant liberal acknowledged, "there
is an intuitive wisdom or instinct of self-preservation in man that prompts
him to turn on it with resentment and denial." Freud of course would have
called this the ego's refusal to believe and accept the awful truth. But since
evolution, rightly understood, was (in John Fiske's words) "God's way of
doing things," and therefore was an exalting, not a humbling, doctrine, it fol-

lowed that "if we shrink from linking our nobler faculties with preceding orders, it is because we have as yet no proper conception of the close and interior relation of God to all his works," preached Munger. "Let us be thankful for existence, however it came about, and let us not deem ourselves too good to be included in the one creation of the one God."[13]

And yet, even though man ought not to regard himself as "too good" to be only a part of God's whole world, the acceptance of evolution on terms such as these betrayed a subtle man-centeredness nevertheless. While some of the religious liberals did not shrink from linking their nobler faculties with preceding orders, it was often at the price of sentimentalizing those more distant animate cousins into a spurious resemblance to man. "Have Animals Souls?" asked James Freeman Clarke in the *Atlantic Monthly* for October, 1874. He testified that he himself owned a horse that he believed could distinguish Sunday from the other days of the week, and that had shown "a very distinct feeling of the supernatural." The other animals are "made 'a little lower' than man," Clarke concluded, "and if we are souls so surely are they."[14] Still, even with souls, they were lower than man, and in the theological tradition of Genesis 1:28 they had to be kept firmly in their place. We can "adore the directing Power and delight in His method" while we study the developing animal forms in the evolutionary series, Theodore Munger wrote in *The Appeal to Life*, "but the feeling of reverence only possesses us as we discern that creative process issuing in man as a moral being."[15]

High religion had once known reverence elsewhere. "Hast thou entered into the springs of the sea? or hast thou walked in the search of the depth?" the Voice out of the Whirlwind asked Job; and, viewing with awe the mighty works of Yahweh, the Psalmist cried "What is man, that thou art mindful of him?" Or, as a reflective conservationist in the last half of the twentieth century like Joseph Wood Krutch might have said, Who is man, to be so little mindful of his environment? Must modern man save his sense of awe for himself as made in God's image, sharing a little of it perhaps with a few of the lesser species that are safely housebroken? Or might he share with Blake in the *mysterium tremendum*, as he contemplates the

Tyger, Tyger burning bright
In the forest of the night,

and then shudderingly asks

Did He who made the Lamb make thee?

If the creative process is only worthy of reverence when it issues in man as a moral being, may one then experience no sense of wonder at solar flares, or the weird behavior of Helium II, or the craters of the moon?

Measured by standards such as these, Theodore Munger's cosmos turns out after all to be a remarkably impoverished one, precluding any religious dimension to the vast remainder of the universe which is left over after we have discovered man and morality in one cozy corner of it. Comfortable in its narrow confines, a defender of that rather dowdy faith would have been able to concede Freud's point but deny its significance. The human ego turns out once more to be remarkably adaptable; in the words of the modern humorist James Thurber "The noblest study of mankind is Man—says Man."[16]

Some of the Gilded-Age liberals went even further, arguing that Darwinism had left man more at home in the universe, not less.[17] Only ten years after *The Origin of Species* Alexander Winchell, a professor of geology, zoology, and botany at the University of Michigan and director of that state's geological survey, published his *Sketches of Creation*. Ambitiously subtitled "A popular view of some of the grand conclusions of the sciences in reference to the history of matter and of life, together with a statement of the intimations of science respecting the primordial condition and the ultimate destiny of the solar system"—the work assumed throughout that this vast panorama of natural wonders confirmed its author's faith that "science prosecuted to its conclusions leads to God."[18] Far more cautiously, but with equal religious serenity, the great American botanist Asa Gray found his way back to theism. Darwinism itself prosecuted to its conclusions might not lead inevitably to God. "Darwinian evolution . . . is neither theistical nor nontheistical," Gray asserted, but the alternative to a belief in a Divinely based order in nature was a belief in chaos, a belief which for both the religionist and the materialist in the Gilded Age would have been difficult to accept;[19] and Gray's own option was for God.

Arguments like these by scientists were quickly seized upon by liberal clergymen. The first tendency of Darwin's hypothesis had indeed been "toward infidelity and skepticism," wrote a theological professor in 1889 in the *Cumberland Presbyterian Review*. But with greater familiarity, placed alongside the researches of Newton, Copernicus, Laplace, and Lyell, "it has ceased to be atheistic, and is likely to become itself one of the arguments of natural theologians."[20] Washington Gladden, the kindly minister of the Social Gospel, found in the doctrine of evolution "a most impressive demonstration of the presence of God in the world." And in any event, Gladden wrote to Lyman Abbott, if we can't lick them we will have to join them: "Our theology

HAUNTS OF THE PTERODACTYL.

Did He who made the Lamb make thee?

PRE-HISTORIC MAN.

The hypothesis of evolution must stop short of man.—A. F. Hewitt, O.S.P., 1887.

must adjust itself to evolutionary conceptions; we can not now think in any other terms."[21]

III   Other inquirers, seeking out the fuller meaning of the logic and grammar of science, were disinclined to let these ministers of reconciliation get away with it. "Those scientific men who have sought to make out that science was not hostile to theology have not been so clear-sighted as their opponents," declared the cantankerous Charles Sanders Peirce in 1878.[22] The same could have been said of many of their allies among the clergy. When Theodore Munger, for example, argued that "evolution not only perfects our conception of the unity of God, but . . . strengthens the argument from design," he ignored an evolutionary mechanism (random variation of individuals) and method (the struggle for existence) which logically seemed not to strengthen the design-argument but to shatter it.

"Certain theories"—for example, "that matter has within itself the potentiality of all terrestrial life, and goes on in its development alone, and by its own energy"—would be grounds for the fears some had voiced about evolution, Munger admitted, but only if such theories "were to be accepted as settled." He clearly implied that they were not. "But that *is* 'evolution'!" one reader of this defensive essay exclaimed. The uncompromising materialism which Munger claimed was only one theory among many "is the definition of evolution given by the most conspicuous scientific men on that side of the question," including Thomas Henry Huxley, whose definitive *Britannica* article on the subject could hardly have been classed as (in Munger's words) " 'an outcast in the world of thought' "![23]

Those who rejected the whole proposition, asserting that if evolution were true then theism was false, had at least the virtue of consistency. Furthermore, as Edward Lurie has pointed out, judging solely on the character of the evidence available in 1859 when *The Origin of Species* first appeared it was respectably possible to disagree with Darwin.[24] Edward Youmans of the *Popular Science Monthly* had to defend himself and his magazine from attacks for his "strong bias . . . as an evolutionist" not only by clergymen but also by the prestigious *Scribner's Monthly*, which editorially declared in 1872 that "the doctrine of Evolution, with its offspring, Darwinism, is nothing more than a provisional hypothesis, based upon *a priori* reasonings, and not on any valid induction of facts." Youmans gave a good account of himself in reply, reviewing the scientific evidence for evolution and then advising the editor of *Scribner's* to "stick to his fiction and his verse-making."[25] Such arguments continued, however, to the joy and solace of distressed churchmen.

They were particularly comforted by Louis Agassiz, who brought his meticulous Swiss mind and the prestige of Harvard to bear against Darwinism to his dying day, and by such lay partisans as the proprietors of the New York *Tribune* when they inserted an advertisement in the *Nation* proclaiming " 'the Darwinian theory utterly demolished' (or words to that effect) 'by AGASSIZ HIMSELF!' "[26] The year before Darwin's *Origin of Species* appeared, Louis Agassiz had published two massive volumes of *Contributions to the Natural History of the United States of America,* in which he argued that the relationships of life-forms man finds were a witness not to the random selection of a blind mechanical process but to the deliberate intent of the Hand that had made them; God the Creator was also a professor of taxonomy, grouping species and genera together into larger units of classification in order that men might learn clues of His overall plan for the universe. "If we can prove premeditation prior to the act of creation, we have done, once and forever, with the desolate theory which refers us to the laws of matter as accounting for all the wonders of the universe, and leaves us with no God," Agassiz wrote in the opening pages of this work. Reviewing it for the *Atlantic Monthly,* Oliver Wendell Holmes, Sr., was "thankful that so profound a student of nature as Mr. Agassiz has tracked the warm foot-prints of divinity throughout all the vestiges of creation."[27]

Having taken this stand, the formidable Swiss scientist never budged. "Darwin's theory, like all other attempts to explain the origin of life, is thus far merely conjectural," Agassiz concluded in his last, posthumously published article, and Darwin had "not even made the best conjecture possible in the present state of our knowledge." The Harvard biologist based his case strictly on the evidence from embryology, paleontology, and comparative anatomy, kept God out of the argument until the closing paragraphs, and brought in a convincing verdict of "Not Proven."[28] Quite understandably an obituary in a leading Methodist weekly summed up Louis Agassiz's lifework as "a demonstration of the baselessness of all atheistical philosophy."

Two years after the death of Agassiz a contributor to *Scribner's Monthly* returned to the attack: "The truth is more in danger in our day from the prejudice that accepts without question the new, than from that which unreasonably holds to the old," J. B. Drury declared. Like Agassiz, this opponent of the new theory addressed himself primarily to the scientific issues, although Drury also argued that Darwinism left "no room for providence, prayer, or redemption." But what seems to have bothered him even more was that the doctrine of evolution pointed toward some rather horrible consequences for human society, along with its merely biological humiliations.

Darwinism in deriving man from the brute, making him an improved ape, rather than a fallen spirit, at one blow robs morality of its sanctions. . . . Might, and cunning, and whatever tends to advance self-interest, will more and more tell in the struggle for existence, and be the goal of human progress. The Christian virtues of self-denial, thoughtfulness for others, care for the infirm, the destitute, and the aged . . . must, under such evolution, be eliminated.[29]

The Reform rabbi Isaac Mayer Wise, striking his own balance between science, philosophy, and religion in a book entitled *The Cosmic God* (1876), called Darwinism "Homo-Brutalism," and condemned it as a doctrine of might makes right.[30] Some of Darwinism's defenders, including T. H. Huxley and Darwin himself, were worried about the possibility of this same conclusion being drawn,[31] and they therefore argued that man—naked ape or not—was somehow *ethically* different from other species. But their logic was inconsistent, argued the American Catholic writer John S. Vaughan in 1890. If conscience itself should turn out to be no more than a product of trial-and-error (of evolution, that is to say, by Darwin's definition), so that "virtue" meant only whatever traits or practices had proved "most serviceable" for "groups of human animals" struggling to survive, and "vice" merely "that which is disadvantageous to the race," then why should man not engage in morally repugnant but racially enhancing practices such as eugenic infanticide? And from an evolutionary standpoint why had such policies once adopted, as in Sparta and ancient Rome, not spread throughout mankind by "natural selection" and become universally accepted practice?[32] (We may add that in the cruel twentieth century certain "Aryan" post-Darwinists did ask "Indeed, why not?")

Alas, the mere unpleasantness of an idea is no guarantee of its untruth. As late as 1889 so notable an American cleric as Cardinal Gibbons could call Darwinism "an unproven and disproven theory that will soon be forgotten to give place to some other phantom of a futile brain,"[33] and Isaac Wise continued into the Nineties to hold fast to his earlier belief that "the gorilla theory is a dream without a foundation in science."[34] But sadly for those who would refute evolution on such grounds a rising generation of younger Darwinists had been busy replacing that theoretical phantom with solid flesh.

John Wesley Powell's spectacular boat trip down the canyon of the Colorado in 1869 and the quiet eloquence of his *Geology of the Uinta Mountains* both dramatized convincingly the uniformitarian geology of Sir Charles Lyell. A vast Western land required a vast time scale for its making, vast enough to meet the requirements for evolution, rather than the cramped six thousand years called for by Archbishop Ussher's Biblical chronology. Man himself had been on this stage long before 4004 B.C.; "The great antiquity of mankind upon the earth," said the anthropologist Lewis Henry Morgan in the preface to his pioneering and widely influential study of *Ancient Society* (1877), "has been conclusively established."[35] Judging from the Eohippus fossil sequence which the Yale paleontologist O. C. Marsh convincingly assembled (to Thomas Huxley's delight), man's perennial companion the horse had been around even longer. And in the great Cretaceous beds of the Rocky Mountain West a host of bone hunters were disclosing to a startled Victorian world the splendor of the dinosaur. On the strength of these and other discoveries one of those hunters, Marsh, told the American Association for the Advancement of Science: "To doubt evolution today is to doubt science, and science is only another name for truth."[36]

IV   By that time the battle lines had shifted. With the publication in 1871 of Darwin's *The Descent of Man*, the argument begun over *The Origin of Species* moved from the evolution of life in general to that of man in particular. Conceding to science the geological time scale and the evolution of life, some of the defenders of Genesis 1, 2, and 3 drew the line at Adam and Eve.

Reviewing the evidence, pro and con, from stratigraphy, paleontology, geography, physiology, morphology, and embryology, the Rev. A. F. Hewitt, a founder of the Paulist order, concluded in 1887: "The hypothesis of evolution must stop short of man." This was an echo of what soon became—and, technically, still remains—the official position of the Roman Catholic Church on evolution. In post-*Kulturkampf* Germany the scientist-politician Rudolph Virchow, physical anthropologist, physician, and distinguished lecturer at the University of Berlin, drew the line against the new doctrines at the same point. Opening an international scientific congress in Moscow in 1892, Professor Virchow told his professional colleagues: "There exists a definite barrier separating man from the animal, which has not yet been effaced."[37] Most other scientists hopefully focused their attention on the word "yet," but Virchow was more pessimistic or, in terms of Freud's argument, optimistic. He concluded that all the studies undertaken with the purpose of discovering biological continuity between the other animals and man had been a failure: "There exists no *proanthropos*, no man-monkey, and the 'connecting link' remains a phantom."

Twenty and thirty years later American Fundamentalists girding themselves for the Scopes Trial would still be clinging to Virchow's words.[38] But it was an increasingly untenable position. In 1857 Virchow had pronounced Neanderthal Man not to be an ancient human fossil at all, but a relatively modern man whose bones had been shaped not by evolution but by rickets, arthritis, and heavy blows on the skull. *One* Neanderthal Man might have been such a fluke, but could the same be said of the dozens or hundreds of fragments that later came to light, not only in Europe but in the Near and Far East? Even though Virchow had been only thirty-six years old at the time of that first discovery, his expert opinion on that first Neanderthal skull has been judged "a masterpiece of senile resistance to new ideas."[39]

As the nineteenth century rushed on toward its end, the mounting scientific consensus in favor of evolution, including that of man, became an embarrassment for men like Cardinal Gibbons, who was having trouble enough as it was reconciling his own Church with the American cultural ethos, and like Phillips Brooks, who bravely preached that "the Church . . . will have nothing to do with the false awe of the *Credo quia impossibile*." For such men, to reject the evidence of all the patient investigators in the field solely because it conflicted with dogma was out of the question. "The truths of Heaven and the truths of earth are in perfect sympathy; every revelation of the Bible is clearer the more it is to be found in the speaking conscience, or in the utterance of history, or in the vocal rocks," Brooks insisted. In fact, far from contradicting the Darwinian hypothesis, declared the Southern Presbyterian chemist and theologian James Woodrow, if rightly interpreted "the Bible, implicitly yet distinctly, teaches the doctrine of Evolution."[40]

Even before Lyell's time the theologians had begun to make this adjustment, allowing that the Hebrew word ordinarily translated "day" might in fact allude to periods millions of years long, punctuated not by "the evening and the morning" as in Genesis 1 but by intervals of mountain-building. Now, in Darwin's era, biology as well as astronomy and geology came under the tent. In the pages of *Popular Science Monthly* for January, 1874, George Henslow argued that the very grammar of the Divine commands (as in verse 21, "Let the waters bring forth") was consistent with an evolutionary origin for marine life: "The use of the imperative mood can only signify an agent other than the speaker," an agent corresponding to "natural law, which, after all, is but a synonym for the will of God." Theodore T. Munger reasoned, "When there is such an accumulation of knowledge and of evidence against the apparent meaning" of a passage in the Bible "that the mind cannot tolerate the inconsistency, it must search the text to see if it will bear a meaning . . . consistent with ascertained facts."[41]

But was this not twisting the words of Scripture in the manner of Humpty

Dumpty, to make them mean whatever the apologist wanted them to mean? "Let the waters bring forth abundantly" might be stretched into consistency with man's fragmentary factual knowledge about the rise of life in the ocean, but what of the astronomical havoc wrought by having the sun and moon wait in the wings until the fourth day (Gen. 1:16–19)?[42] One pious Prussian professor, who believed in the literal truth of the Bible but who also believed that a day really meant a day, told his class that the chronology of creation was unfortunate; God ought logically to have begun with those cosmic time pieces, since without them "the first three days, vaguely composed of morning and night," saw no real order and discipline in the world!

Sometimes this puzzling passage has been made to read that God "caused the sun and moon to appear," *i.e.*, break through the clouds; but pretty quickly one is torturing the text as with Shakespeare's plays, in order to make them yield Baconian cryptograms. For the more literal-minded of the harmonizers of science with Scripture, "the accommodation was often grotesque, resulting in a strained 'reconciliation' of Biblical passages to make the facts of evolution fit them," George Daniels has written, and "most modern readers will be inclined to think that if the Bible is as wondrously plastic" as such interpreters assumed, "there is little meaning in the claim that it is 'inspired truth.' "[43] We are reminded further that in scientific investigation, or any other kind, a hypothesis becomes suspect the moment it stops explaining things and starts explaining things away.

And it was all so futile, for the same spirit of inquisitive investigation which was pushing back the mysteries of geologic time, of life, and of man, had been turned also to the study of the Bible. The book of Genesis itself was seen as the product of historical evolution, composed and collated over a span of centuries.[44] In that case, what did it matter how much one stretched and shuffled the "days of creation" to make them fit the researches of Lyell and Darwin if those days turned out to have been not part of the original story at all, but interpolations by a later Hebrew editor into a more primitive narrative in order to make it square with a Babylonian calendar chronology? The new mode of Biblical criticism made it even more painfully evident that some critics of Darwin were not so much arguing a theory as making excuses.

V   Early in the debate over *The Origin of Species* William North Rice, a devout bearded Methodist who bicycled over the Triassic sandstones of Connecticut in search of dinosaur tracks and who taught geology to several generations of students at Wesleyan University, expressed regret "that the discussion of this question has often assumed a character rather theological than scientific." "The shameful retreat of the church from point to point, after each vain endeavour to check the progress of science," he thought, was "as prejudicial to the interests of religion, as it is contrary to the spirit of science." Many "noble minds" had been "driven into infidelity, not by the supposed infidel tendencies of science, but by the folly of Christian teachers" who had engaged in this kind of intellectual trench warfare, Rice wrote.[45] He might have added that this negative defense of the faith, yielding one position after another to science without creating any kind of positive counter-strategy, opened religious apologists to devastating attack.

"In the history of modern natural science, God is treated by his defenders as Frederick-William III was treated by his generals and officials in the Jena campaign," Friedrich Engels wrote in the *Dialectics of Nature*. "One division of the army after another lays down its arms, one fortress after another capitulates before the march of science, until at last the whole infinite realm of nature is conquered by science, and there is no place left in it for the Creator." And of course from a Marxist point of view the "harmonizers" of religion with science were no better than the out-and-out reactionaries. "God is nowhere treated worse than by the natural scientists who believe in him," Engels gibed, tracing the humiliating retreats of God's defenders from Newton to "his last great Don Quixote, Agassiz," and ending with Tyndall, who "forbids Him any entry into nature and relegates Him to the world of emotional processes, only admitting Him because, after all, there must be somebody who knows more about all these things [nature] than John Tyndall!"[46]

Moreover, the question can be legitimately raised of whether the compromise positions to which some of these apologists had come were altogether sincere. A prominent Unitarian leader, William Channing Gannett, wrote a hymn in 1888 whose first line reads "God laid the rocks in courses," seemingly an attempt to reconcile the earth sciences with theism; yet three years earlier Gannett had privately questioned whether a member of his denomination need believe in God at all.[47] The stanza remained in Unitarian hymnals down to modern times, even after the agnostic humanism a few of its members were beginning to embrace had become far more widespread in the denomination.[48] When such humanists sang that hymn on a Sunday morning, did they reflect that the Divine Bricklayer was only Gannett's literary invention, and that the word *God* ought to have stood in quotation marks?

From the perspective of more conservative (but not Fundamentalist) twentieth-century religious thought, all this logic-chopping was unnecessary. A confessional stance far more "orthodox" than Theodore Munger's "New Theology"—Karl Barth's, for example— could be perfectly consistent with a far more thoroughgoing radicalism toward the text of Scripture than the Victorian harmonizers had any stomach for. From such a standpoint, the truth of the Bible consisted in its totality, not in the "truths" of its several parts, least of all in its artificially-divided "chapters" and "verses." The Bible as a whole was the outcome of an encounter between God and man, with the dazzlement of man's senses by that experience recorded as truly as his enlightenment. Taking care not to dogmatize too much as to which part of that record was God's and which was man's, such a theology could say the Creed far more comfortably than could the religious liberals of the Gilded Age and yet go far beyond them in taking the word of science for whatever it was worth.[49] But many in the soberly literal nineteenth century would have taken any such "existential" or "dialectical" interpretation of the Word of God merely as clever casuistry.

Sensus literalis unus est, the Lutheran exegetes had traditionally said, which is one reason why Lutherans in America have been more resistant than some other Protestants to accepting the (so-called) "higher" kind of Biblical criticism; for many of them, then, Genesis 1 is either literally true, or it is altogether false.[50] The Lutheran Church—Missouri Synod adopted a resolution as recently as 1965 affirming that Adam and Eve were real, historical personages, and the delegates narrowly defeated an amendment which would have declared that "God created heaven and earth . . . in six solar days and not in immense periods of time."[51] Only a decade earlier a professor of biology in a Lutheran teachers' college wrote a five hundred page textbook based upon antievolutionary premises for use in Missouri Synod parochial schools, and conceded to the evolutionists only such claims as were fully compatible with Genesis. Well-illustrated with the same kinds of photographs and drawings that are found in conventionally Darwinian books of the same type, this work denied all the essential Darwinian conclusions, even with the modifications of Mendel and DeVries. On the crucial point of the origin of man, the author weighed the fossil evidence in the balance and found it wanting: "Man was created by God perfect and sinless," the chapter on fossil man concluded. "We have not had evolution in man but we have had degeneration and deterioration." As for living things other than man, the author believed "that evolution in the generally accepted sense of the term has not taken place."[52]

Lutheranism in the United States during the Gilded Age was a largely immigrant and foreign-language faith, to some extent outside the evangelical mainstream. But English-speaking Protestantism in America was tempted to the same simplistic cutting of the knot. Sprawled over the vast spaces of the New World, cut off from any normative tradition by which Scripture itself might have been measured, and too busy filling up those spaces to have evolved such a tradition themselves, American Protestants were driven to the doctrine of Scriptural infallibility almost by a *force majeure.*

That unique sociological invention the "denomination," neither a "church" nor a "sect" in the European sense, could give shape and discipline to the anarchic distortions of the Bible's meaning which often resulted from the eccentric exercise of purely private judgment only by agreeing, in effect, with Lutheran orthodox scholasticism that *scriptura scripturam interpretatur.*[53] In the revivalistic anti-intellectualism which had suffused Protestantism since the death of Jonathan Edwards, American Protestants could not very well do as some of the Germans had done and reconcile the contradictions between Biblical antiquity and the modern world through the consolations of idealistic philosophy.[54] People like John Fiske and T. T. Munger did have a following, but in the American cultural environment a great many troubled believers felt they were forced to choose between flatly insisting, as one staunch Protestant evangelist did in 1889, that "the Bible nowhere teaches what is scientifically false," and is therefore a treasure trove of accurate factual knowledge in every field from astronomy to zoology —or of agreeing with Charles Darwin that the Old Testament was "no more to be trusted than the sacred books of the Hindoos."[55]

They might have yielded a point or two in matters of diction, as when the Biblical writers had used the words "sunrise" and "sunset" in their ordinary colloquial sense, instead of referring to the earth's motion; after all, the astronomer himself does the same. And they might have conceded that some of the seeming contradictions between science and the Scriptures could be the result of incorrect translation; the word "firmament," for example, interpreted as a solid physical barrier between Heaven and earth. But apart from semantics, where there was clear conflict over matters of fact then either the Scriptures or the scientific investigators must be wrong. "Reasons that have no connection with astronomy or geology force me to accept the Bible as a revelation from God," one believer affirmed in 1878, "and hence, *prima facie,* I accept that first chapter of Genesis even though I may not wholly understand it."[56] *Credo quia impossibile!*

VI   In sheer desperation some believers would escape from the terrible intellectual choice seemingly being forced upon them by flight into sheer sentimentalism, like the Methodist prelate who "once told a preachers' meeting that the Mosaic authorship of the Pentateuch had been settled for him by a trip through the Red Sea; as he had looked off toward the purple mountain peaks to the east, the conviction had been born in his soul that Moses had written the books that bear his name." Of course, the literal-minded side of the nineteenth century would never have bowed to such whimsy, even from "an enthusiastic orator, in the ecstasy of one of those emotional climaxes in which the speech organs function automatically" —especially when the man later denied that he had ever said anything about the effect of the Red Sea trip on his religious convictions.[57]

Anglicanism, settling its differences "through creative tension between varying shades of mellowed reasonableness," may have escaped some of these anxieties. By agreeing to ordain Charles A. Briggs as an Episcopalian after he had been tried as a heretic by the Presbyterians for questioning the Mosaic authorship of the Pentateuch, the reigning Bishop of New York (H. C. Potter) is said to have "settled an issue that has never been officially raised: that the literal inerrancy of the Scripture is not an official doctrine of our church." However Bishop Potter was quick to depose one of the clergy-men in his diocese who moved beyond Darwinism to radical anticlerical socialism.[58] And although the Roman Catholic Church was having its own difficulties over evolution, Roman Catholics, like the Anglicans, had certain advantages in this debate: unlike many Protestants they were not forced to center their source of final religious authority in the pages of a book. In the hermeneutical tradition of their Church they were not bound by *sensus literalis unus est*; or as H. L. Mencken would one day put it, the Catholic Church had always known the wisdom of keeping the Bible in its place.[59]

Line-by-line translations of Genesis into a scientific treatise on evolution were therefore unnecessary, and both the emotional flights of fancy like that of the Methodist orator contemplating the Red Sea and also the more elegant "harmonizations" attempted by science-minded religious liberals were alike irrelevant. More sophisticated than sheer Biblical literalism though this approach undoubtedly was, it did not always avail to keep the Catholic savant out of trouble with his own Church. John Augustine Zahm's har-monizing tract on *Evolution and Dogma* suffered the rebuke of official sup-pression by Rome, even though Father Zahm was careful to write that "between the brute creation and man there is an impossible chasm."[60]

But a Catholic humanist had yet another defense to fall back on, of a sort which might not be so readily available to his Protestant contemporaries with their letter-of-the-law tradition. He could translate the whole controversy from the direct statement of evidence and axioms into an indirect statement of intuitions and metaphors. And so, while one writer in the *Catholic World* in 1886 was dismissing one of John Fiske's prestigious *Atlantic Monthly* essays on evolution as " 'dude' metaphysics," a few pages further on another contributor to that magazine had a go at reconciliation between science and religion in a fashion quite unlike the matter-of-fact approach which so often characterized the mind of the Gilded Age: he wrote a poem.

In these imaginative "Days of Genesis," verse 2 of the original, when "the earth was without form and void; and darkness lay over the face of the deep," became a time when

> . . . blind forces drove or drew
> By laws which even dull inertia knew

—a description not very far from science's own characterization of the Azoic Age. Though Father Walworth used the words "waste of waters," in his poetic context the great deep clearly was a metaphor for interstellar space; and, after the command *fiat lux,*

> The eddying atoms rolled in wreaths of light,

much as they continue to do for Mr. Fred Hoyle.[61] As the *Proem* to these verses makes clear, this was no mere adjustment of the ancient Hebrew writers' speculations to the findings of Darwin, Lyell, Asa Gray, and O. C. Marsh.

> Deem not these days primordial spanned by time.
> Range not the bells of Genesis to chime
> With science . . .

Days, years, or geological ages, to the prophetic eye of the Biblical writer, were only means

> To teach high law and holy truth to man.

The Prophet, then, did not so much count the days of Creation as chant them.

> . . . and from inspired tongue
> Burst this grand burden in a solemn song,

With intervals of choral praise;
And the intervals are days.[62]

Nineteenth-century reductionist scholarship had assumed that the Genesis 2 account of creation differs from that of Genesis 1 because they are from different documentary sources several centuries apart in composition. But certain *avant-garde* Biblical critics of the 1960's, especially in the Church of Norway, have rejected the "documentary hypothesis" of the origin of the Pentateuch in favor of a "cultic chant" theory quite close to the one the priest-poet Walworth implied: these two creation-stories differ in detail for the same reasons that govern the statement and restatement of a theme in music. Should this turn out eventually to be the consensus of Biblical scholarship, it would make Clarence Walworth's intuitive shot in the dark hit uncannily close to the mark—and foreclose the whole line of historical investigation which had aroused the Biblical literalists' anxieties in the first place. But in the Gilded Age, such an interpretation was neither anthropology nor philology, as it is today; it was poetry.

As was intimated in the previous chapter, in that period such a solution to a religious problem would not do. Divorced from both scientific and philosophical rigor, it all but reduced religion to aesthetics. Isaac Mayer Wise, for example, believed in the Mosaic authorship of the Pentateuch as firmly as did that anxious touring Methodist—but not on the grounds of a visit to the Red Sea! Wise was never more a citizen of Gilded-Age America than when he wrote: "If there is no salvation in truth, there is certainly none in fiction."[63]

Still, salvation by fiction had its adherents. Andrew Dickson White, who probably did as much as any one man in the United States toward routing orthodoxy in the name of science, retained enough of his dignified Anglican upbringing to advise others on the correct technique for chanting the Psalter; and on visits to European churches he was properly repelled by "perfunctory performances of the service, both Protestant and Catholic." He found the Order for Holy Communion in his own denomination "calm, comprehensible, touching," and he "more than once lingered to see it"—although he never partook of it himself. A modern student of White has concluded that little was left of the Cornell educator's original faith except ethics, dignity, and acoustics.[64]

This is not very far from the point of view which a university wit once attributed to George Santayana, namely that "there is no God, and Mary is his mother." In the following century Walter Lippmann would have the chilly last word. Santayana's view that we should not argue about religion because "we never argue with a lover about his taste," Lippmann declared, was the expression of ultimate unbelief. "For what would be the plight of a lover, if we told him that his passion was charming?—though, of course, there might be no such lady as the one he loved."[65]

3

Of Sin
and Freedom

"We acknowledge and bewail our manifold
sins and wickedness, which we, from time to
time, most grievously have committed, by
thought, word, and deed, against thy Divine
Majesty, provoking most justly thy wrath
and indignation against us. We do earnestly repent, and are heartily sorry for these
our misdoings; the remembrance of them is
grievous unto us; the burden of them is
intolerable."

The Book of Common Prayer

"I think I could turn and live with ani-
      mals, they are so placid and self-
      contained;

   .   .   .   .

They do not sweat and whine about their
      condition;
They do not lie awake in the dark and
      weep for their sins;
They do not make me sick discussing
      their duty to God;

   .   .   .   .

Not one kneels to another, nor to his kind
      that lived thousands of years ago;
Not one is respectable or industrious over
      the whole earth."

Walt Whitman[1]

I   🌀HE day was fine and bright, and would have been far better spent out of doors, but the calendar and Aunt Sally said it was Sunday. So the small boy perched on an uncomfortable pew in the stuffy church, squirming through lengthy prayers and an even lengthier sermon. "It was an argument that dealt in limitless fire and thinned the predestined elect down to a company so small as to be hardly worth the saving." But by the grace of God the unwilling young listener had in his pocket a sharp-pincered beetle. In the midst of the pastor's discourse the insect and an inquisitive puppy made each other's acquaintance, and thereafter the sermon's homiletic effect on the congregation was somehow not the same. The event may not have happened just as the boy from Hannibal, Missouri, remembered it, but when he grew to man's estate he took a still more elaborate revenge on that kind of religion: the episode became the fourth chapter in *The Adventures of Tom Sawyer*.

Actually, Americans had been hammering away at the kind of religious attitudes that Mark Twain satirized for quite some time. The dark doctrines of total depravity and double predestination had suffered blows as early as 1713, when the Reverend John Wise reminded his fellow-Puritans that in spite of what had happened in the Garden of Eden man "remains at the upper end of nature, and as such is a creature of a very noble character"; however corrupted he may be from Heaven's point of view, "he is the favorite animal on earth."[2] In 1828, in the full tide of the Romantic movement, William Ellery Channing took a further leap and preached of man's "likeness to God."[3]

In much of nineteenth-century America the fear of damnation still drove people weeping and groaning to the mourner's bench, but in Puritanism's own heartland less of the old hellfire spirit remained, even among those who did not follow the more radical paths of Channing and Emerson. By Horace Bushnell's time, Barbara Cross has written, "The terrible *deus absconditus* of Calvinism had become genial, rational, and reliable."[4] Those who could not thus rationalize God into a proper Bostonian sometimes left the church altogether; Phillips Brooks reported in 1878 that he constantly heard in New England "the lamentations of men . . . who say, 'Oh, if I had not had the terrors of the Lord so preached to me when I was a boy . . . I should be

THE CHRISTMAS DINNER WAITS.

Perched on an uncomfortable pew in the stuffy church, squirming through lengthy prayers and an even lengthier sermon.

religious today'."[5] In the literary imagination of the elder Oliver Wendell Holmes, the elaborate intellectual structure which the New England theologians had built to celebrate the majesty of God and the littleness of man became only a wonderful one-horse shay. It held together "a hundred years and a day" (dating from the publication in 1755 of that other "deacon's masterpiece," Jonathan Edwards's treatise on *Freedom of the Will*); and then, on a day which the good doctor placed in 1855, it collapsed into dust.

The rigorous old doctrines continued to have their defenders, for example the formidable Hodges—Charles and Archibald—of Princeton Theological Seminary;[6] but as the nineteenth century came near its end Washington Gladden declared that what some Presbyterian divines continued to call Calvinism was "no more the Calvinism of Calvin than the astronomy which is taught in our colleges today is the astronomy of Ptolemy."[7] Gladden's own view of the matter had gone on record a quarter-century earlier. "To claim scriptural authority for the doctrine that a just God punishes a person for the sins of his ancestors," he wrote in 1873, "is to say that the Bible clearly teaches a monstrous lie."[8]

To many Americans in the generation of Mark Twain and Oliver Wendell

Holmes, the dark theology of their fathers was not only a tissue of strained logic but was downright immoral. "If a created being has no rights which his Creator is bound to respect, there is an end to all moral relations between them," said the elder Holmes in 1870.[9] Mary Baker Eddy recalled her own spontaneous reaction as a child to her parents' religious teachings: a God Who would not forgive you when you were sorry was not as good as her own mother.[10] Father Isaac Hecker, a former associate of Emerson and the Brook Farmers who knew his cold roast Protestant Boston at first hand, thought it would be better to embrace "the paganism which universally pervades our era" than to return to "the withering, soul-destroying horrors of Calvinism" which had done so much toward creating "all that is repulsive and hard in the Yankee character."[11] Some Protestants concurred, and Henry Van Dyke probably summed up the judgment of many in his generation when he wrote the following in *The Gospel for an Age of Doubt*.

> The idea of an irresponsible God ruling by an eternal and inflexible *fiat* over responsible men is a moral nightmare. . . . Between the unknowable God of agnosticism and the unlovable God of absolutism there is indeed little to choose. But the choice, such as it is, lies on the side of agnosticism.[12]

The great Reform rabbi Isaac Mayer Wise would have agreed that this was a grievous choice, but Wise argued that it was a choice forced only upon Christians. Judaism had always had a less dismal conception of human nature than had Christianity: "The history of mankind teaches that man was not as wicked as he was foolish"—a remarkably charitable judgment if one considers Israel's centuries of experience with oppression and terror, from which a survivor might well have inferred the depravity of mankind. But the fate of humanity was not decided in some long-lost Eden, said Wise; man's will is free, and he does have the capacity in this life to achieve the good: "Ignorance is the original sin and stupidity the original depravity, of which man must be redeemed."[13] Far from disputing this opinion some Christian apologists tried to transfer the credit or blame for "Calvinist" doctrines to other shoulders than their own; the "fall of Adam and the imputation of his guilt to all posterity," thundered Henry Ward Beecher, "was a bastard belief of the Jews."[14]

II   Twentieth-century thought both religious and secular, conditioned by Auschwitz and Hiroshima, has rediscovered merit or at least plausibility in the doctrine of the Fall of Man. As a result, neo-orthodox Protestant and Conservative Jewish theology professors and seminarians in

America during the 1950's were prone to fault the religious liberals of the 1880's (and of the 1920's) for having been "shallow," "falsely optimistic," "utopian," and perhaps above all for having been so hopelessly middle class. "The real basis for all the errors of liberalism is its erroneous estimate of human nature," Reinhold Niebuhr characteristically wrote in 1934.[15] Even Franklin Roosevelt, a liberal whose estimate of human nature was alternately cynical and sunny, allowed one earnest young curate in wartime Washington to instruct him in the newly fashionable theology of Kierkegaard. The experience did not noticeably alter FDR's assessment of the nature of man in America, but it did prompt him to say that the tormented Dane's dark view of man had made it easier to understand how the Nazis, at least, could act that way.[16]

On the other hand surviving liberals like Harry Emerson Fosdick, who entered theological training in 1900 and studied under the great systematizer of the liberal position, William Newton Clarke, considered the adverse neo-orthodox judgment on the liberal position as unfair to the point of caricature. "Sentimental man-worship . . . was part of the *Zeitgeist*" when his generation came to maturity, Fosdick conceded, "and certain extreme forms of religious liberalism were infected by it"; but in the half-century he had spent in the ministry "no evangelical liberal I ever knew would have consented to it," the veteran pastor testified. In any event, at the end of the Gilded Age when men like Fosdick were launching their careers, the sophisticated dialectics of Niebuhr and Tillich and Barth were simply not available. The alternatives to the compromise faith the liberals of the Eighties and Nineties adopted seemed to be either antireligious radicalism, or a return to the gloomy faith from which they had so painfully freed themselves.

Fosdick himself, born in 1878, was in the late Eighties "a sensitive boy, deeply religious, . . . morbidly conscientious." Seventy years afterward he still could "vividly recall weeping at night for fear of going to hell, with my mystified and baffled mother trying to comfort me," and he remembered also believing his grandmother when she told him that if he did not believe literally in the story of Jonah and the whale he must logically give up his religion altogether. His subsequent battles with religious conservatives had therefore a quality of irony: "The fundamentalists in later years have hated me plentifully, but I started as one of them." In his autobiography, *The Living of These Days* (1956), the minister-emeritus of Riverside Church testified that, for him at least, the espousal of an evolutionary theological liberalism had not been a Pollyannish escape from the ugly reality of human nature but an inescapable existential choice, in the spirit of Luther's "God help me, I can do no other."

> What present-day critics of liberalism often fail to see is its absolute necessity to multitudes of us who would not have been Christians at all unless we could thus have escaped the bondage of the then reigning orthodoxy. Of course the revolt was not the whole answer! Of course it left out dimensions in Christian faith which would need to be rediscovered! Despite that, however, it offered to a generation of earnest youth the only chance they had to be honest while being Christian.[17]

The currents of doubt in the Gilded Age may have flowed in two directions. Conceivably, if the impact of science transformed some men of faith into unbelievers, moral aversion to a cruel and life-denying theology may have blocked some scientists from becoming men of faith. One theistic evolutionist in America attributed the agnostic tendencies in Darwin himself to rebellion against an orthodox upbringing: "The freedom which he found everywhere in nature did not accord with the Calvinistic idea of fatality."[18] On the other hand, Isaac Wise thought Darwin's rebellion against his orthodox upbringing had not gone nearly far enough. "It took a Christian savant," brought up in Christianity's "pessimistic and degrading estimate of human nature," to come up with so debased an idea as that of "man's descent from a brute," Wise wrote in 1889.[19]

But the scientists and their allies had scientific as well as ethical reasons for rejecting the concept of original sin. The same great investigative breakthrough which had overthrown the Biblical account of man's creation had also overthrown the Biblical idea of man's "fall." "Important evidences have been found of upward evolution in his family, social, moral, intellectual, and religious relations," argued Andrew Dickson White in his monumental *History of the Warfare of Science with Theology in Christendom.* Man had not come down from the high and fertile plateau of Eden into a Slough of Despond; quite the contrary: "The consenting voice of unbiased investigators in all lands has declared more and more that the beginnings of our race must have been low and brutal, and that the tendency has been upward."[20]

If there had been no Fall, what became of the classic doctrines of sin and redemption? Could man be led inevitably into temptation if, as one theistic professor of biology put it, "persistent variation toward evil is in time weeded out by natural selection"?[21] Bob Ingersoll had, of course, no doubt whatever on the matter: "You cannot harmonize evolution and the atonement. The survival of the fittest does away with original sin."[22] Many who refused to follow the Great Infidel into the camp of outright irreligion were able to agree with him wholeheartedly on this one crucial point: eating the fruit of the Tree of Knowledge had led men to a glorious ascension rather than to a fall. Much as William Newton Clarke tried to retain something of the traditional concept of sin in his *Outline of Christian Theology* (1898), he concluded nevertheless that "humanity certainly is by nature a slowly rising race, with a native tendency to outgrow faults"[23]—a thought which must have rested disturbingly on the mind of a worshiper trying sincerely to recite those terrible words in the prayer of general confession according to the Lutheran liturgy: "We know that we are by nature sinful and unclean."

The Lutheran response was often one of rejecting the theory of evolution, as we have seen. Moreover, just at the moment when Calvinist predestination was fading out of most "WASP" (British-derived) denominations, something very like it was entering one powerful branch of American Lutheranism for the first time![24] And the theistic evolutionists themselves were troubled by one aspect of their own doctrine. Man's origins had been "low and brutal," and since his appearance on this planet his moral tendency had been upward, said Andrew Dickson White. How, then, could the persistence in modern man of bad temper, arrogance, meanness, or lying be scientifically accounted for? Not to mention murder, arson, rape, slavery, and war? Somehow, in the nineteenth century as in the first, Paul's despairing cry still seemed to ring true: "For the good that I would I do not: but the evil which I would not, that I do. . . . Who shall deliver me from the body of this death?"

III   Short of denying the existence of evil altogether as an error of the imagination, as did the Christian Scientists, the answer that most easily satisfied the equation for many of the liberals was to declare that *sin is animality*. "Original sin," John Fiske stated, "is neither more nor less than the brute-inheritance which every man carries with him, and the process of evolution is an advance toward true salvation," toward an ultimate social state in which "the ape and the tiger in human nature will become extinct." Lyman Abbott wrote, "Every man falls when, by yielding to the enticements of his lower, animal nature, he descends from his vantage-ground of moral consciousness to the earthiness out of which he had begun to emerge." Abbott enlarged upon this argument in *The Theology of an Evolutionist* (1897).

We carry the animal with us. When we indulge our appetite, or our greed, or our covetousness, or our pride, or our vainglory, or our selfishness, we are falling back into the animal. . . . Every man is two men,—a centaur, part animal, part man.[25]

Lyman Abbott hedged a little in the direction of tradition by the caveat that while "development" (*i.e.,* evolution) may cure crudeness, only redemption can cure sin; but another Protestant evolutionist of that day, Theodore T. Munger, went even further than Fiske in translating the entire Christian drama of man's moral quest into a struggle against his animal self. "Sin, repentance, conversion, regeneration, aspiration, and struggle after the highest; . . . all of these turn on, and have their meaning in, a yielding to the animal nature or a striving after the spiritual nature," Munger wrote. Man as an individual re-enacts the history of his species, and at both levels his quest is successful; "The animal is kept down and crowded out."[26] Translated into the terms of biological evolution, the personal struggle of the spirit to subdue the flesh becomes also the conflict of the ages.

This identification became popular with others besides theologians. At least as early as 1871, the year Darwin published his *Descent of Man,* the argument had found its way into the pages of a best-selling novel. Like many another fictional hero before and since his time, young Ralph Hartsook in *The Hoosier Schoolmaster* was required at one point in the plot to struggle with his conscience—"the same battle," commented the book's author, "that Paul described so dramatically when he represented the Spirit as contending with the Flesh. Paul also called this dreadful something the Old Adam, and I suppose Darwin would call it the remains of the Wild Beast."[27] The equation between the Old Adam and the Wild Beast far antedated Darwin; indeed, the notion that the soul (or the mind) is good and that the animal body (or matter) is evil antedates Christianity. In the Christian era this traditional antithesis between "spirit" and "flesh" had become axiomatic for many religious believers—who were forgetful, perhaps, that when Saint Paul drew this distinction he listed among the "works of the flesh" such predominantly mental activities as idolatry, witchcraft, seditions, and heresies, sins no ordinary animal was capable of committing (Gal. 5:20, KJV).

Thirty years before *The Origin of Species* appeared, William Ellery Channing had said: "Man has animal propensities as well as intellectual and moral powers. He has a body as well as mind." To a being so constituted, "religion, or virtue, is a conflict, requiring great spiritual effort."

Channing of course was an early spokesman for Brahmin Boston, mentally liberal but socially proper, "where ideas were generously entertained but where Margaret Fuller's costumes were deemed bizarre."[28] But spokesmen for the Catholic culture, which after the Civil War was beginning to displace Yankee-WASP gentility from power in Boston and elsewhere in America, were prone to this same disjunction between virtue and animality. "Man is rational, but he is a rational *animal*," A. F. Hewitt noted in the *Catholic World* for December, 1887. "His spiritual part is substantially united to a gross, material, corruptible body, which is gradually developed from a germ"—a germ which, thinkers in that Church were beginning to concede, might have a material pedigree antedating Adam and Eve. But in the meantime, "as a spiritual being, and as an animal, [man's] inclinations and impulses are conflicting."

Hence this Roman Catholic writer saw the development of intelligence, the overcoming of the passions, the directing of actions toward good ends, and the like, in semi-Puritan terms as self-mastery, as a triumph of the will, much as did his ex-Calvinist Congregationalist and Unitarian contemporaries. But in a Catholicism which knew not the theistic evolutionism of Teilhard de Chardin—Hewitt wrote his essay when Teilhard was six years old—there was little room for the kind of optimism expressed by Lyman Abbott: "The individual man is partly the animal from which he has come, and partly the God who is coming into him; but God is steadily displacing the animal."[29] Unlike many liberal Protestant evolutionists of the Gilded Age, a Catholic critic like Father Hewitt had no illusion that the natural process—or God—would one day weed the vulgar beast out of man altogether.

Of course not all the liberal theists went so far as Abbott and Munger in their reasoning. Joseph LeConte, the theistic professor of geology at the University of California, cautioned that "the struggle for mastery of the higher spiritual with the lower animal is often so severe that the latter seems to many as *essential evil* to be extirpated, instead of a useful *servant* to be controlled." But LeConte's attempt at a "middle-of-the-road" position between the ethic of spirit and that of flesh—"All evil consists in the dominance of the lower over the higher; all good in the rational use of the lower by the higher"—conceded too much to the power of the rational will to commend itself either to the traditionalist or to the psychoanalytically-oriented modern.[30]

It should be noted in all fairness that religious apologists were not the only persons subject to the kind of squeamishness I have been describing.

"In general," writes Gertrude Himmelfarb in her study *Victorian Minds,* "a major complaint against orthodox religion was the physical, corporeal, and therefore degrading character of such doctrines as baptismal regeneration, the resurrection, or the eucharistic sacrifice," implying that the "super-stition" the emancipated Victorian associated with such doctrines repelled him less than did their material grossness. Some philosophical materialists, especially since Freud, have preached a gospel of libidinal release, which accepts and rejoices in man's animality; but one disciple of "Darwin, Huxley, Tyndall, Spencer, and Haeckel," writing in 1919 when Freudianism was just coming into vogue, warned a friend against letting "too much *emotion,*" that animal-linked quality, into his personal philosophy: "It involves the play of nervous tissue far less evolved than that wherein true intellection resides." Culturally there may have been an echo of traditional religion in this counsel since the writer, Howard Phillips Lovecraft, was by inheritance a scion of Puritan New England, but intellectually there was not a scrap. In the very brain which undertook to give or to follow this advice there was nothing remarkable, Lovecraft paradoxically added; "We know more about it because we possess it, yet actually it is no more than a clumsy device for the redistribution of energy in a blind and purposeless cosmos."[31]

IV   "We must be born again," affirmed Theodore T. Munger in 1883, " not merely because we are wicked, not because of a lapse, but because we are flesh."[32] Man may be "the final form in creation," Munger wrote in 1887, but man as we find him is no pure spirit. "The habits and motives of the animal world linger within him. . . . The appetites and passions and tempers of beasts still assert themselves in him, even as we name them—beastly." Yet, as was noted in the preceding chapter, on another occasion Theodore Munger urged his fellow-creatures not to be ashamed of their brute ancestry! Was he here being inconsistent? Not from an evolutionary standpoint, he might have answered: when I was an animal, I understood as an animal; but when I became a man, I put away my animal nature (compare I Cor. 13:11). That was the way Professor John M. Tyler of Amherst College resolved the paradox of man as ape and angel; "To attempt to go backward to a plane of life once passed is to surely degenerate. . . . If [man] seeks to be an animal rather than a spiritual being, he becomes not an animal but a brute; and the only genuine brute is a degenerate man."[33]

All very logical; but maturation brings its own physical complications.

Yield not to temptation,
For yielding is sin,

admonished Doctor of Music Horatio Richmond Palmer in a hymn widely used among Protestants of the YMCA variety during and since the Gilded Age.[34] Recent generations of theological students have gratefully recovered the ancient Hebraic view of man and creation in which the fleshly appetites are seen as a God-given power and blessing, subject to misuse but not evil in themselves; but even today in less sophisticated circles one kind of temptation, and one only, is meant when such a hymn is sung. To "Victorians," in the ordinary meaning we give to that word, the most spectacularly animal trait in man, and the most likely to overwhelm his rational self-control, was sex.[35] It does not require any recondite Freudian analysis to suggest that to preach to an over-inhibited and, by the same token, sex-obsessed generation that sin was "a relapse into animal appetite and passion, in which man betrayed the rationality the race had so hardly won," was to flirt with psychological and cultural disaster. If in America's Gilded Age "the most representative Christian liberals firmly believed that the corrupting effects of sin have been carried down the stream of life through biological reproduction,"[36] such thinkers, instead of helping the troubled believer come to terms with modern science, may only have added to the burden of civilization and its discontents.

The Christian liberals' task of harmonizing evolution with both religious dogma and social convention was not made any easier by the arch-evolutionist himself. "Of all the causes which have led to the differences in external appearance between the races of man, and to a certain extent between man and the lower animals, sexual selection has been the most efficient," Charles Darwin wrote in *The Descent of Man*. In the struggle for existence that he had earlier described in *The Origin of Species,* the trappings of sex—brilliant plumage or great spreading antlers—were actually a hindrance; they gave away one's camouflage or they got caught in the bushes. Darwin therefore deduced that sexual selection was an independent variable, and he went on for four hundred pages (more than half the book) to trace the trail of sex in evolution from lobsters and centipedes through insects, cold-blooded vertebrates, birds (four chapters), mammals, and man.

No doubt civilized man was outgrowing his lustful simian ancestry, but Darwin hinted that this might not be altogether a good thing. As William Irvine has epitomized *The Descent of Man,* sexual selection in evolution had given to man courage, intelligence, and vigor, and to woman tenderness and unselfishness, "thereby proving once more that biology was a soundly Victorian science."[37] Moreover sexual selection would have been a stronger element in man at an early stage in his evolution "than at a later period, when man had advanced in his intellectual powers but had retrograded in his instincts," and as a result, said Darwin, he would not have practiced such relatively civilized refinements as infanticide, wife-enslavement, or betrothal during infancy. In that far-off time when man was "guided more by his instinctive passions, and less by foresight or reason," our ancestors (in contrast to our own bourgeois selves) would have chosen "their partners not for mental charms, or property, or social position, but almost solely from external appearance"; and between the lines of this proper Victorian gentleman's prose there is a strong suggestion that his barbarous ancestors were better at making this sort of choice than were his contemporaries.[38]

Even if theistic evolutionists did not go so far as to commit the venerable heresy—heretical from either the authentic Judaeo-Christian or the orthodox Freudian point of view—of saying that sin is sex, and sex is sin, there were psychic strains inherent in their position. Freud, in his discussion of the three "wounds," astronomical, biological, and psychoanalytic, to the mental security of modern man was careful to point out that the rejection of man's animal heritage is culturally conditioned. Children, he argued, had no inherent aversion to kinship with animals, as evidenced by their fascination with the talking animals in their fairy tales; and primitive man had adopted a beast or bird as his tribal totem with pride, not shame.[39] As was shown in our previous chapter the damage to man's self-respect could be grievous even when he saw his primeval ancestry merely as an embarrassment, like the black sheep whose picture one passes quickly over in displaying the family album. Some of the religious Darwinists now proceeded to rub salt in the wound, by affirming that man is an animal, just as Darwin said, and then arguing that the admission of this fact is automatically a confession of sin!

> Shun evil companions,
> Dark passions subdue,

Horatio Palmer's hymn-stanzas continued; and Sigmund Freud would have had some things to say not only about the state of mind of such men but also about the means by which they proposed to get themselves out of it.

V   There is a further paradox in the position of men like Lyman Abbott and Theodore T. Munger: their effort to rescue their articles of faith from extinction by translating them into scientifically acceptable categories, in this case redefining "sin" as "animal inheritance" and "redemption" as "evolution," may have inadvertently destroyed more of their religious heritage than they were able to save. If in Abbott's words "God is steadily displacing the animal" in man, or if, as Munger more daringly put it, man had "come to the verge of matter" and was now destined to "drop what senses we have, and go off into that world of the spirit . . . and explore it simply as minds,"[40] then what was the point in repeating an historic creed that closed by affirming "the resurrection of the body"? Is it any wonder that this same period saw the rise of Christian Science, which resolved the conflict by denying the existence of the body, and of matter itself?

In 1889 a scholar of the Church of England, Charles Gore, preached a sermon at Cambridge University in which he blocked this exit, explicitly rejecting any identification of "sin" with "flesh" or "matter." Such a view of man's nature did not give him a more "spiritual" tone, Gore argued; quite the reverse. To represent "goodness and badness in men as the simple product of natural forces," which one then struggled to overcome, if one were a Christian evolutionist, or to exorcise, if one were a Christian Scientist, was in fact to fall into a kind of moral materialism. "It is common to all the anti-Christian views of sin that at the last resort they make sin natural, a part of nature. It is characteristic of Christ's view of sin—of the Scriptural view of it—that it makes it unnatural."

Liberal theists in both England and America who were striving to reconcile Darwinism with Christianity might have been disconcerted to hear themselves called "anti-Christian," particularly by a man who insisted he was as committed to the new scientific world-view as they were. For there was nothing in the Bible basically incompatible with the theory of evolution as applied to man, Gore insisted. Indeed, "The Scriptures stand alone among ancient literatures in presenting the idea of gradual progress, gradual education, movement onwards to a climax. The Bible is the book of development," and *development* in the thought of Charles Gore and his contemporaries was synonymous and interchangeable with *evolution*. "All that we are led to believe is that the historical development of man has not been the development simply as God meant it. It has been tainted," and the taint is not of a kind that fades away in time as man moves further away from his animal ancestry. "The state of things as they were in days of savagery, or as they are in days of civilization, are a *parody* of the Divine intention for the childhood and manhood of the race."[41]

The classic doctrine of the Fall, a doctrine to which "Christianity appears to be bound," was "a view that . . . brings us into no conflict with scientific discovery," Gore claimed, provided only that one did not stumble into the trap of prosaic Scriptural literalism, as both liberals and conservatives were so prone to do. Thomas Huxley, Darwin's doughty champion, had attacked one of the Genesis stories dealing with man's temptation and fall by asking, "What sort of value as an illustration of God's method of dealing with sin has an account of an event which never happened?" To which Gore replied, "Has the story of the rich man and Lazarus any value as an illustration of God's method of dealing with men?" Here a nineteenth-century Oxford don anticipated exactly the twentieth-century "neo-orthodox" way of coping with such problems, as for example in Reinhold Niebuhr's influential essay "As Deceivers, Yet True." "What we have in Genesis is a tradition used as a vehicle for spiritual teaching," Gore wrote. "As the story is told, it becomes, like that of Dives and Lazarus, a typical narrative of what is again and again happening."[42]

Against this kind of religious and moral argument, Charles Gore implied, the natural sciences as such can have little to say. Quite the reverse, according to J. F. Illingworth, a co-author with Gore and other Anglican scholars of the important theological treatise *Lux Mundi;* the naïvely evolutionist view of man as preached by men like Lyman Abbott and T. T. Munger, namely that "what had been called his fall was in reality his rise," could be challenged as "unscientific," on empirical grounds. Moral evil, or sin, was "a fact of experience. . . . We breathe it, we feel it, we commit it, we see its havoc all around us," and "when we are met by an appeal to experience," *i.e.,* to scientific induction, "it is necessary to insist that no element of experience be left out."[43]

There were Gilded-Age Americans, also, who had their doubts that the tragedy of human moral failure could be reduced to an accident of animality. A merely evolutionary explanation of sin is "infantile," declared Borden P. Bowne in 1887. Sin could not be simply equated with brute instinct, asserted Lewis F. Stearns; "natural man becomes no nobler in the process of evolution." William Newton Clarke, despite his insistence that "nature is favorable to goodness," admitted that "the higher part of man has capabilities of moral evil far greater than the brute element ever possessed," and he explicitly rejected any definition of sin as "the dominion of the body over the spirit," as "a mere incident of growth," or as "a mere misfortune, like a disease."[44]

The "old-time religion" had been morally and psychologically dreadful, Mark Twain, Robert Ingersoll, Henry Ward Beecher, and Phillips Brooks all agreed, but its ethic had had a certain austere dedication which a more autonomous and permissive morality was in danger of losing. Better even "the most material notions of eternal penalty," Phillips Brooks declared, than the new theological liberalism, if the latter would only "make life seem a playtime and the world a game." It was well that the New Theology had mitigated the old terrors of hellfire and predestination, thought Brooks, but nevertheless "we ought to be afraid of any theology which tampers with the sacredness of duty and the awfulness of life."

The Broad Church Episcopalian Phillips Brooks had ancestral roots in seventeenth-century Massachusetts Congregationalism, and he was not the only "Victorian" in whom the traditional Puritan assertion of an imperious will to inner righteousness underlay the ethos of the Gilded Age, and in fact may have helped to redeem it from the hypocrisy and cant with which the period so often has been associated. For all his robustly modern-minded conviction that the natural condition of man is goodness,[45] Phillips Brooks regarded sin as "a dreadful, positive, malignant thing" from which man could not simply trust that he would evolve away. "What the world in its worst part needs is not to be developed, but to be destroyed."[46]

This was, of course, a stance which could be shared with non-Puritans, and even with infidel scientists. By 1892 no less a "modernist" than T. H. Huxley (who was himself something of a secular Puritan) had come to agree that the old doctrines of predestination, innate depravity, and original sin seemed "vastly nearer the truth than the 'liberal' popular illusions," such as "it is given to everybody to reach the ethical ideal if he will only try."[47] By that time, ironically enough, the march of science itself had raised the very ghost the liberals thought they had forever exorcised: that of moral determinism.

VI   Latent in the scientific world-view of the eighteenth century had been the conviction that if stars and apples obey the inexorable decrees of mathematics, so also must man. "It would be very singular that all nature, all the planets, should obey eternal laws, and that there should be a little animal, five feet high, who, in contempt of these laws, could act as he pleased, solely according to his caprice," wrote Voltaire.[48] The atheist *philosophe* Baron D'Holbach declared that "free will is an idle fancy," supporting his argument by a chain of logic which startlingly resembles that of Jonathan Edwards in his famous treatise *Freedom of the Will*;[49] and indeed Edwards gave renewed intellectual strength to Calvinism in eighteenth-century America very largely by uncovering in the new psychology and astronomy of that day the deterministic implications which Locke and Newton themselves had overlooked.

The physics of the nineteenth century seemed to point in the same de-terministic direction. The great Clerk-Maxwell, whose equations seemed to many to have bound the physical and electromagnetic worlds into a grand and terrible unity, saw among his professional colleagues a "prejudice in favor of determinism," although he himself did not share it. The researches of Willard Gibbs, the greatest American physicist of the Gilded Age, one day would help to undercut "the almost Calvinistic determinism so prevalent in the scientific thinking of the nineteenth century"; but among the general public and even in the scientific community of that time the argument for free will implicit in Gibbs's highly abstruse mathematical work was all but unknown.[50]

Nineteenth-century research into the physiology of the nervous system also seemed to confirm Voltaire's doubt as to the real freedom of the mind. While insisting that the same amount of molecular movement in the nervous centers did not produce the same degree or quality of mental activity in a sot as in a Shakespeare, Doctor Oliver Wendell Holmes in 1870 nevertheless described memory as a material record traced on the brain,[51] the flow of thought "like breathing, essentially mechanical and necessary," and con-versation itself (in an amusing aside) as sometimes no more than a biological and automatic flow. Publicly, as we have seen, the Autocrat of the Breakfast Table argued for freedom of moral choice, like a good anti-Calvinistic Bostonian. But in a private letter to President Porter of Yale in 1879 Holmes admitted that "in the matter of predestination he came nearer the old re-former" (Calvin) than he did in such comparatively less important matters as the New England Sabbath, although he deduced from the doctrine certain corollaries that Calvin would never have accepted.[52] And much of Holmes's novel *Elsie Venner* was a subtle argument for a kind of medical equivalent of Calvinism.[53]

Where did Darwin's *Origin of Species* and *Descent of Man* fit into the age-old debate between determinism and freedom? At first reading, the doctrine of the survival of the fittest had seemed a vindication of Emerson's doctrine of "self-reliance" in its most crass, post-Civil War form. But as paleontology and biology fitted themselves into a broader context of math-ematics and chemistry, evolution began to seem but one more way the reliant self got pushed around.

"The advance . . . represented by the intellectual and social distance between . . . the lowest existing types of humanity and the highest," wrote Benjamin Kidd in 1894, "is the result . . . of . . . certain elementary biological laws . . . which have controlled and directed it as rigidly as the law of gravity controls and directs a body falling to the earth." So too with man's "rational moral nature," or his "personality," which he liked to think of as autonomous; its existence was "the result of the last and longest step toward and in conformity to environment," Professor John Tyler reasoned. In short, it too had come into being in the same evolutionary fashion as had man's hands, his vermiform appendix, and his brain.[54] Early studies in anthropology, as for example the pioneering work of Lewis Henry Morgan, seemed to offer man no more freedom than did the other sciences: "Through the pages of *Ancient Society,* which recognized few deviations from its pattern of evolution, man stalked as John Calvin might see him, bound to assent to the laws of the universe."[55] Relatively an innocent in the field of scientific knowledge, Harriet Beecher Stowe was able in 1869 to intuit what was coming: "Nature in her teaching is a more tremendous and inexorable Calvinist than the Cambridge Platform."[56]

For men who were striving both to reject Calvinism and to embrace science —indeed, to reject the Calvinist concept of the nature of sin in the very name of science—this was a melancholy outcome. Later, in the twentieth century, some of the theologians were going to start taking determinism rather more seriously, and some of the scientists (as Gibbs and Clerk-Maxwell already foresaw) were going to start treating it rather less so. But for the time being the theistic and the naturalistic liberals had come to a parting of the ways— a parting which rendered the conflict between religion and science still more grievous by making it seem also a choice between optimism and pessimism.

William James, scientist and pragmatic theist, had already written his essay "The Dilemma of Determinism," in which he argued that a universe without freedom of moral choice was "a place in which what ought to be is impossible,"[57] and his progressive Christian and Jewish contemporaries perforce concurred. "We know that we have the power to choose the better life and to struggle toward it," Washington Gladden cried. "Even if we are crippled by heredity and borne down by a hostile environment, we can turn our faces upstream and swim against the current."[58] "Free-will is essential to man," summed up William Newton Clarke in his *Outline of Christian Theology*. ". . . Take it away, and man is a mere machine. Every man knows that he decides his own action, and would not be a man if he did not."[59]

Exactly so, replied the aged Mark Twain in his last bitter catechism: man is a machine. The barrier between man and animal is nonexistent; "Fleas can be taught nearly anything that a Congressman can." And man and beast are alike automata. "One is a complex and elaborate machine, the other a simple and limited machine, but they are alike in principle, function, and process."

Then what became of the freedom of man to make a moral choice, as at the inspiring climax of *Huckleberry Finn*? The man "did not make the choice, it was made for him by forces which he could not control." The rest was casuistry: "Free Will has always existed in *words*, but it stops there, I think—stops short of fact."[60] In the name of science, the boy from Hannibal who had rebelled against predestination tamely surrendered to Jonathan Edwards.

4

Fiction
and Faith in an
Age of Fact

"Guilt and innocence, the mystery of
iniquity—most of our present-day writers
are not in any orthodox sense religious . . . ,
but almost all of them feel that there are
deeper perceptions of man's plight than
the brash optimism of a Rousseau."

Leslie A. Fiedler[1]

"But it is not only that the novelist of
today, in "our expanding universe," is
embarrassed by the insignificance . . . of
his finite world. A greater problem is
that he cannot quite believe in it."

Mary McCarthy[2]

63

I   IT was the night's pause between two days of
slaughter which the history books would dignify as the Battle of Pittsburg
Landing, or Shiloh, but which has been more accurately described as a conflict of two armed mobs. Between Owl Creek and a bend in the Tennessee
River the exhausted troops stood to arms in a torrent of rain, while fresh
levies of frightened men were marched in. "Very often we struck our feet
against the dead," wrote one of these newcomers, a sergeant-major with the
Ninth Indiana Volunteers, in a memoir published long afterward; "more
frequently against those who still had spirit enough to resent it with a moan."
In the morning his company took up a position in a clearing, and then the
forest in front of them "seemed all at once to flame up and disappear with a
crash." Far off to their right at about the same time another Indiana volunteer, this one a division commander who had spent most of the previous day
marching his men down the wrong road, was giving the order to open fire at
Confederate forces dug in at the top of a bluff, and the day's work was begun.[3]

Mass armies notoriously bring together the most radically diverse sorts of
men, but in the American Civil War surely no such fortuitous and temporary
comradeship in arms was more striking than the one between these two Indiana volunteers. Son of a former Indiana governor and Congressman, General "Lew" Wallace saw and reported an officer's horseback war quite
different from the enlisted men's grimy trudge that Ambrose Bierce, an em-
bittered child of poverty and failure, would remember and record. In the
"gilded" postwar years the gulf between them yawned wider, as Wallace, the
two-star general, became famous for writing *Ben-Hur: a Tale of the Christ*,
while Bierce, the sardonic sergeant-major, was earning a different kind of
reputation as the compiler of *The Devil's Dictionary*.

"O, Lord, who for the purposes of this supplication we will assume to have
created the heavens and the earth before man created Thee. . . ." Robert
Ingersoll himself, who had also been at Shiloh, could not have written copy
more savagely anticlerical than what Ambrose Bierce began in 1868 to turn
out regularly as a columnist for a San Francisco newspaper. "In consideration of the fact that Thou sentest Thy only-begotten Son amongst us, and
afforded us the felicity of murdering him," this mock prayer by the "Town
Crier" went on, "we would respectfully suggest the propriety of taking into

heaven such of us as pay our church dues. . . . We ask this in the name of
Thy Son whom we strung up as above stated. Amen."[4] Like Ingersoll, too,
was the valedictory and credo Bierce wrote in 1872 before going off for a
whirl at the literary and bohemian life in London: "Be as decent as you can.
Don't believe without evidence. Treat things divine with marked respect—
and don't have anything to do with them." Curiously, at that time this might
also have been the creed of Lew Wallace, who later professed to have been
"not in the least influenced by religious sentiment" when he set out to write
Ben-Hur.[5]

The novelist seems to have chosen the birth and death of Jesus as thematic
material for the most crassly commercial of reasons: the best-seller of all
times was based upon them. But then, on a night train bound for a soldiers'
reunion, by chance Wallace met Ingersoll. They talked religion until they
rolled into the passenger terminal at Indianapolis, and then Wallace, shun-
ning the street cars, walked the long way to his brother's house northeast of
town, thinking. That, he testified in *Harper's Weekly*, was the beginning of
his own religious conversion.[6] (In an account written for the *Youth's Companion*, Wallace mentioned the long midnight walk but protected the innocence of his young readers by making no mention of the Great Infidel.)
Ingersoll may have consoled himself with the thought that you can't win
them all.

Whatever suspicion a disenchanted twentieth-century mind might enter-
tain regarding the novelist's underlying motives, General Wallace had most
certainly gauged a national mood. *Ben-Hur* was no ordinary best-seller, hailed
today and remaindered tomorrow; it reached people who had never read novels before.[7] Proper Boston received it coldly; at receptions for the author
there and in Cambridge Doctor Holmes, William Dean Howells, and James
Russell Lowell were conspicuously absent. The *Atlantic Monthly*, the authoritative spokesman for the Hub of the Solar System, warned its readers of
"the imminent danger which the book is always in of dropping into the habits
of the dime novel," as for example the author's device of tacking on a conventional happy ending immediately after having described the Crucifixion.[8]
But elsewhere in the republic the book was received with more warmth.

The President of the United States (another Shiloh veteran!) sat up until
two in the morning reading *Ben-Hur*, wrote Wallace a letter of thanks, and
decided to send him as minister to Turkey, where he would be able to draw
inspiration and do research for his next book. President Garfield's expectations for Wallace were only partly fulfilled, for the new novel was to enjoy
nowhere near the success of its predecessor, but by the time *The Prince of*

India appeared in 1893 it hardly mattered; *Ben-Hur* had already outsold *Uncle Tom's Cabin.*[9] In the following decade Wallace's best-seller spawned a host of imitators, with titles like *The Gladiators, The Court of Pilate, Saul of Tarsus,* and *Titus, a Comrade of the Cross*—a trend which has continued to the present day.

At the end of the Nineties *Ben-Hur* was adapted for the theater, and in that form it was if anything an even more smashing success than the novel had been. Opening in New York late in 1899, it played to packed houses from Broadway to Drury Lane, from San Francisco to Sydney, for twenty-one consecutive years. At one time no fewer than five road companies, each with its stable of real horses for the chariot race, were on tour.[10] The first actor on stage in the role of Messala (the rival charioteer to Ben-Hur, and the villain) was William S. Hart, who today is better remembered for his work in early silent films such as *The Great Train Robbery*; the choice was unconsciously prophetic. In the Twenties *Ben-Hur* itself was successfully translated to the screen (Ben-Hur played by Ramon Navarro and Messala by Francis X. Buschman), and a modern wide-screen Technicolor remake in 1960 continued to draw the crowds.[11] What Lew Wallace had done was not so much a case of novel-writing as of popular myth-making. Although the novel is dated by the cultural values of the time when it was written, so that Ben-Hur himself seems at times no more than a Horatio Alger boy in Biblical costume, the soldier-novelist had evidently started something which far transcended the historical horizons of the Gilded Age.

II   In the biographical preface to one modern edition of *Ben-Hur*, brought out to coincide with the latest of the motion picture versions, Ben Ray Redman contended that the "religious element that initially attracted many of Wallace's readers" was really incidental; "Ben-Hur is an overwhelmingly worldly tale if there ever was one."[12] This may have been a salesman's argument, playing down that "religious element" in order to sell more copies of the book to readers in the (presumably) more worldly twentieth century. But it can also be taken as an oblique comment upon religion in America, in the Gilded Age or at any other time. The very act of reaffirming "old" cultural and religious values, in literature or in the theater, may be a concession to the fact that change is taking place.[13]

A modern student of the mass media who takes the trouble to read the 1881 original of *Ben-Hur* may be struck not so much by its outmoded nineteenth-century literary conventions as by its startlingly "cinematic" quality. In scenes like the Roman galley's sea fight with the pirates, or the betting in the Circus just before the chariot race, and especially at the Crucifixion, Wallace handles his crowds more in the manner of D. W. Griffith or Eisenstein than of Dickens or Bulwer-Lytton. Cecil B. DeMille had not yet made his momentous discovery that "Bible and bubble-baths are an unbeatable box-office combination,"[14] but through the book's veil of Victorian reticence the Egyptian siren, Iras, seems predestined for portrayal by a motion-picture sex queen, and the familiar miracles of the Gospel sometimes ring more of Hollywood than they do of the interpretations attributed to Saints Luke and Matthew. The Star of Bethlehem in *Ben-Hur* is a Christmas card in Technicolor, "a roseate electrical splendor" that fans out to rest upon a mountain skyline, before the camera cuts away (so to speak) to the people on rooftops and in courtyards, their awestruck faces made luminous by its rays. And whereas the Biblical writers were decently vague about what an angel of the Lord looks like, Wallace gave the one who announced the Nativity to the shepherds real wings, that "stirred, and spread slowly and majestically, on their upper-side white as snow, in the shadow vari-tinted, like mother-of-pearl." When they were fully expanded the angel "arose lightly and, without effort, floated out of view, taking the light up with him"—a very nice process shot indeed; and after his departure the chorus (may one say the sound track?) swelled into a *Gloria in excelsis Deo*.

Like Hollywood, too, was the meticulous technical accuracy that went into the depiction of costumes, weapons, dining arrangements, localities, buildings—everything, in short, except what really mattered.[15] Wallace wrote the novel with a map of ancient Palestine always propped up in front of him, a painstaking German creation that showed all the towns, the holy places, "the heights, the depressions, the passes, trails and distances"; on one occasion, the author declared, he had gone to Washington and then to Boston "for no purpose but to exhaust their libraries in an effort to satisfy myself of the mechanical arrangement of the oars in the interior of a *trireme*."[16] But the theologians and Biblical commentators, those dry-as-dust fellows, Wallace did not consult, and in terms of what he was trying to accomplish in the book this may have been just as well.

The real problem with his mass audience was not presented by the scenes of Roman orgies or of Jewish family life but by the ones dealing specifically with the life of Christ. "The Christian world would not tolerate a novel with Jesus Christ as its hero, and I knew it," Wallace confessed. He was reluctant to allow the work to be adapted for the stage at all, and consented only on the condition that the person of Christ be represented not by an actor but by a shaft of light. In the novel he kept the Founder of Christianity backstage, yet to be seen, most of the way through the book, and he was careful to allow the spoken words of Jesus to be heard only in the exact language of the King James Version—a convention which, again, Hollywood has almost always followed.[17]

It was probably inevitable, therefore, that the physical Christ of the novel would have "the delicacy of the nostrils and mouth . . . the pallor of the complexion, the fine texture of the hair, and the softness of the beard" that belong to the sweet and ineffectual Jesus of American Protestant churchianity. Strength of a sort—"strength to bear suffering oftener than strength to do" —the author did concede; but "never a soldier but would have laughed at him in encounter," Wallace, the ex-soldier, wrote. Five years after his first literary description of the Man of Nazareth, Wallace wrote a short story speculating on "The Boyhood of Christ" which carried this familiar stereotype to the point of travesty. Profusely illustrated with engravings of a goody-good Sunday-School boy of the sort Mark Twain loved to caricature, wearing his halo even while he tended sheep or learned his *aleph-beths* at his mother's knee—with prompting from angels, Wallace said, when she or his synagogue teachers ran out of ideas—the story was the featured item in the Christmas number of *Harper's Monthly* for 1886.[18]

In other times, Christians had attributed to the mother of Jesus a rather subversive prayer, still chanted by some of them, which praises God because "he hath filled the hungry with good things; and the rich he hath sent empty away." But the Holy Family depicted for *Harper's* subscribers in the Gilded Age was staunchly middle class. Wallace theorized that Mary and Joseph had received enough treasure from the Wise Men on the child's behalf to leave them comfortably well off, in "exactly the condition to allow our Saviour a margin of time in which to taste something of natural boyish freedom; to have little playmates, run races with the youngest of the flocks, deck himself from the anemone beds in the hills, and watch the clouds form slowly about the summit of old Hermon." But not too much of this sort of thing, of course, since the promised Messiah would have been precocious and therefore "preternaturally serious." Indeed, as if baffled by the problem of describing plausibly for nineteenth-century Americans a boy who was not also a bit of a scamp, Wallace's fictional narrator lamely concluded that for all practical purposes "Christ had no boyhood at all." (The face of this boy-god was, of course, "oval and delicate," and his hair, in violation of all the ethnic probabilities, was blond.)

Both in this saccharine Christmas tribute and in *Ben-Hur*, Lew Wallace may well have been an archetype of the virile American man-of-the-world

"LISTENING FOR VOICES."

Profusely illustrated with engravings of a goody-good Sun-day school boy of the sort Mark Twain loved to caricature, wearing his halo even while he tended sheep. . .

firmly putting Christ and religion in their place. The eyes of this Man-God, "softened to exceeding tenderness by lashes of the great length sometimes seen on children, but seldom, if ever, on men" might be both adored and at the same time subtly condescended to, in much the same way Victorian men adored and condescended to their women. Of course, another available way of putting the Prince of Peace in His place in that era would have been to go to the other extreme of "muscular Christianity," and praise Him as the greatest of combat infantrymen.[19] The bloody Battle of Allatoona Pass, an incident of Sherman's march to the sea, inspired the religious songwriter Philip

MARY TEACHING JESUS THE ALPHABET.

P. Bliss in 1870 to compose words and music for a gospel hymn, "Hold the Fort, for I Am Coming,"[20] and in Victorian England Sir Arthur Sullivan turned aside from his catchy orchestrations for the Gilbert and Sullivan operettas to write out the martial cadences of "Onward, Christian Soldiers."

Since the First World War, for many moderns, neither the meek-and-pallid nor the blood-and-glory stereotypes of Christ have seemed altogether palatable.

III   In the summer of 1888 the author of *Ben-Hur* took time out from his work on the forthcoming *Prince of India* to write a campaign biography of Benjamin Harrison, and to get himself elected head of the Indiana chapter of a Civil War veterans' association for officers, the Loyal Legion. Out in San Francisco that same year Ambrose Bierce was also thinking wistfully of their war of a quarter-century before. He could not attend the reunion of the Ninth Indiana Volunteers, he wrote regretfully in response to their invitation—but he could get the reminiscences out of his system in another way. On March 11, 1888, George Hearst's San Francisco *Examiner* ran a short story by Bierce with a Civil War locale. Others soon followed, in spite or because of dire personal tragedy in his immediate family the year afterward.[21] In 1891 they became a book, *Tales of Soldiers and Civilians.* Reprinted in England a year later under the title *In the Midst of Life,* it established its author at once as the literary arbiter of the West Coast, a more regional and raffish version of the role played in Boston by Howells; but the Eastern literary establishment ignored Bierce even more pointedly than it had ignored Wallace.[22]

"The 'old soldier' is beginning to outline himself upon the public mind as a distinct character in American life," wrote Charles Dudley Warner (Mark Twain's collaborator on *The Gilded Age*) soon after this book of war stories had appeared, but "literature has not yet got hold of him," as Hugo and Balzac had gotten hold of the veterans of Napoleon's campaigns. Perhaps, thought Warner, this was because a quarter-century was not enough time for the process to take effect by which the survivor from the war "eliminates himself from the mass, and begins to take, and to make us take, a romantic view of his career." If romance was the natural outcome of this process it is small wonder that Warner overlooked *Tales of Soldiers and Civilians.*

Ambrose Bierce was a "romantic" of sorts, but it was a strange, black kind of romanticism. He captured the pain, cruelty, terror, and sheer physical ugliness of war with the authority of a Remarque, and organized his visions around a personal judgment that life was at once iron-bound in determinism and capriciously coincidental. This point of view was, as Larzer Ziff has noted, "a natural outgrowth of a personality so shocked by war that it held itself together only by the compulsive demonstration that meaningless slaughter contained all the meaning there was."[23] Cumulatively these tales added up to a very different world from the moral universe of Lew Wallace, where heroes die happy and rich while only villains are mangled under chariot wheels.

In Bierce's bleak cosmos, for example, a soldier knowingly kills his own father in order to preserve an army's tactical surprise. A six-year-old child gleefully watches many men "playing horsie," unaware that they are crawling away from a field of battle horribly wounded. A fat and pompous state governor goes into a war zone and blunders into a retreating rearguard, led by a man whom in civilian life he has cuckolded; he is rescued at the cost of that officer's life. And in perhaps the sharpest contrast of all with Lew Wallace's *Weltanschauung*, a lone scout goes forth to draw the fire of a concealed enemy, thereby sparing the loss of an entire skirmish-line: " 'Let me pay all,' says this gallant man—this military Christ," giving his life as a ransom for many, and then, in absolute futility, the skirmishers charge out to avenge him and are slaughtered anyway. Of such is the kingdom of earth that Ambrose Bierce preached, and as for heaven, the reader of these bitter vignettes of war will not be surprised that in his *Devil's Dictionary* Bierce would define "Extinction" as "the raw material out of which theology created the future state."[24]

"You can hang me, General, but there your power of evil ends," declares a captured spy in one of these tales; "you cannot condemn me to heaven."[25] It is a measure of the paradoxical variety of American culture in the Gilded Age that during the same generation in literature a character in one story could have uttered such a cry of defiance while in another story a fictional Balthasar, the last surviving Wise Man, interrupted the action to lecture Iras and Ben-Hur on the hope of the world to come. In the spectrum of attitudes toward Being or Non-Being taken by American men of letters in the years following the Civil War, Lew Wallace and Ambrose Bierce, the ex-officer and the ex-enlisted man, the novelist for the masses and the writer for a coterie, the believer and the cynic, may be taken as polar extremes.

Somewhat to Bierce's right was Mark Twain, who for most of his life suppressed the more caustic of his religious views out of deference to his female relatives (a kind of deference which Bierce, notoriously, never showed[26]), and somewhat to Wallace's left was Elizabeth Stuart Phelps (Ward), whose pioneering "social gospel" novel *The Silent Partner*, an exposé of living conditions in a Massachusetts factory town, showed an acute compassion for people caught under the chariot wheels of the modern world. ("It ain't a rich folks' religion that I've brought to talk to you," cries a street-corner evangelist in her closing pages, in striking counterpoint to Lew Wallace's suburban

Sunday-school lesson on the boyhood of Christ; ". . . the religion of Jesus Christ the Son of God Almighty is the only poor folks' religion in all the world."[27]) But in 1871 Miss Phelps's novel—in the present writer's judgment a better book, incidentally, from a literary standpoint than those later, better-known tracts of this type, *In His Steps* and *If Christ Came to Chicago* —was historically premature. It was well received, as "a terribly needed lesson, if one-half her picture is to be accepted as true—a lesson that not only the mill-owners of New England but, if the ominous signs of the times are not false prophets, the mine-owners of Pennsylvania, need to consider too";[28] but the field of Elizabeth Phelps's greatest popularity, and of her own greatest literary energies, as a writer of religious fiction lay in quite a different direction.

Born in 1844, Miss Phelps was of an age with the young men who marched off to fight the Civil War, and her first novel was prompted by the one kind of war experience she knew at first-hand. What impressed Bierce and, in a different fashion, Lew Wallace was the shock and pageantry of battle; what affected Elizabeth Phelps was a more quiet kind of reality: "The regiments came home, but the mourners went about the streets."[29] A man she had loved died at Antietam,[30] and it does not take very much psychological probing to find the connection between that personal loss and the short story she published in January of the bitter year 1864, "A Sacrifice Consumed." Its simple and familiar theme of love and death in wartime ends with a scene which in real life has been re-enacted countless thousands of times, from the wars of the cavemen down to the wars in Southeast Asia: the embarrassed buddy trying to explain to the fallen soldier's girl just how it happened.

Society honored as heroes the men who willingly offered up their lives, "all bright with dreams of an unknown success, or joyous with tender loves," Miss Phelps concluded, but there were "martyrs at humble firesides" who gave up even more.[31] For Lew Wallace's characters, death in battle—or in any other manner—was but a passage between "this human life, so troubled and brief," and "the perfect and everlasting life designed for the Soul." Even for Ambrose Bierce's fallen combatant, "his clothing defiled with earth, his face covered with a blanket or showing yellow and claylike in the rain," at least death had been the end of suffering.[32] But for the soldier's widow and his orphan it was frequently only the beginning.

IV   Three years after the pounding of the guns had finally stopped, in the midst of the sentimentality, pretension, and sheer escapism we usually associate with the Victorian era, twenty-four-year-old Elizabeth

Stuart Phelps opened her novel *The Gates Ajar* with a passage, timeless in its honest, unadorned pain, which could have voiced the bereavement of any survivor in any war.

> They tell me that it should not have been such a shock. "Your brother has been in the army so long that you should have been prepared for anything" . . . . and a great deal more that I am afraid I have not listened to. I suppose it is all true; but that never makes it any easier.
>
> The house feels like a prison. I walk up and down and wonder that I ever called it home. . . . Something ails the voices of the children, snowballing down the street; all the music has gone out of them, and they hurt me like knives. . . . It seems to me as if the world were spinning around in the light and wind and laughter, and God just stretched down His hand one morning and put it out.[33]

From that point onward, however, *The Gates Ajar* turned into a sermon. Eschewing the more dreary doctrines of the New England theology in which she had been raised, and rejecting also the traditional imagery of heaven in terms of thrones and harps and crowns, the young author discoursed on the resurrection of the body and the life everlasting in a way that would have shocked Jonathan Edwards, but that she thought might have pleased Martin Luther.[34] Heaven was a logical and natural extension of life on earth. Not only would God give back to a woman her loved ones, but also "He would give back a poet his lost dreams"—and would even do something for "that scrap of a boy who lost his little red balloon the morning he bought it, and, broken-hearted, wanted to know whether it had gone to heaven."

"Ben-Hur" Wallace, when he wrote on personal immortality, was more cautious than Elizabeth Phelps: "Shall I dispute with myself or you about the unnecessaries—about the form of my Soul?" Balthasar asks Ben-Hur. "Or where it is to abide? Or whether it eats or drinks? Or is winged, or wears this or that? No. It is more becoming to trust in God. . . . I leave to him the organization of my Soul, and every arrangement for the life after death." But the author of *The Gates Ajar*, like her New England contemporary Emily Dickinson, seemed seized by an almost Faustian urge to know what it is like on the other side. At a breakfast in 1880 honoring the elder Oliver Wendell Holmes she contrasted the guests who were less than fifty years old—nervous, restless, "full of the stir of ambitions satisfied or thwarted, . . . of the jar of *doing*, not the calm of done!"—with the senior persons present, "already set apart from us by an invisible line as silent as death"; had they already taken on some of the qualities of the next world? the thirty-six-year-old novelist wondered.[35]

In one of her short stories Miss Phelps took the logical next step, of attempting to describe the subjective experience of death itself. It is instructive to compare this story, "Since I Died," with a similarly speculative tale by a writer with a far more powerful imagination but with far less sensitivity to the human overtones, Edgar Allan Poe. In "The Colloquy of Monos and Una" Poe described, in an eerie, curiously plausible fashion, what happened to the physical senses of a person once dead, whereas Miss Phelps was concerned with the anguish felt by the decedent because he sees, but cannot reach and reassure, the person who mourns him.[36] As Emily Dickinson put it,

> Parting is all we know of heaven,
> And all we need of hell.

In 1883 came a sequel to *The Gates Ajar,* dedicated "to my brother, Stuart, who passed beyond, August 29, 1883." The earlier novel had been in the form of religious and philosophical discussion of death by the living; *Beyond the Gates* was told entirely from the point of view of the dead. The protagonist, a clergyman's daughter, aged forty, living in a Massachusetts factory town—in short, a person very like the author herself—succumbs to illness in the first chapter. Her father, who had preceded her in death many years before, comes to fetch her home to heaven, which turns out to be a place very like Boston and vicinity, except for the climate. There are mountains, mists, showers, rainbows, seashores; there are trees, grass, four-leafed clovers, brooks, fruits (edible), and birds—one of which is heard singing a *Te Deum.*[37] There are cities and suburbs, with libraries, museums, clean streets, public gardens, and a symphony hall where Beethoven conducts a new oratorio he has just composed. People go on journeys, commute regularly to their work, or do research.

It is indicative of the author's human compassion that in this busy and productive heaven there seems one ineradicable flaw: as in the story "Since I Died," the dead must suffer the pain of not being able to comfort those who remain alive. But eventually the determination of this active Protestant ghost breaks even that final barrier, and she is able to reach through to her mother on earth by a vague form of telepathy. A more complicated problem arises when the heroine is found by the one man she had loved on earth, who has also died. The hosts of heaven discreetly retire so that they may be alone to talk, and the dialogue is pure soap opera. She speaks first, in italics: "*Where is she?*" "Not with me," the man answers. The Other Woman is "on earth, and of it;" his place there with her has long since been taken by another man.

And now Christ Himself appears to the reunited lovers and blesses them, and they walk off through the Elysian Fields hand in hand. Ducking the thorny practical question of what happens when the other woman (and the other man!) eventually die and join them,[38] the author very soon thereafter brings the book to a close.

Even more than *The Gates Ajar, Beyond the Gates* would seem fair game for the satirist.[39] But nothing daunted, Elizabeth Phelps wrote two more novels in the same vein, *The Gates Between* and *Within The Gates*, and—with her husband, Herbert D. Ward, whom she married in 1888—*Come Forth*, a Biblical romance in the *Ben-Hur* tradition, the subject of which was Lazarus, the brother of Martha and Mary, whom Jesus raised from the dead (John 11:1–44). It would be easy for a bleak-minded modern to condescend to all this sort of thing as "wish-fulfillment" of a peculiarly petty kind.[40] Better to face up to the reality of extinction, said Freud, than to live psychologically beyond one's means in the attempt to deny it; "To endure life remains, when all is said, the first duty of all living beings. . . . If you would endure life, be prepared for death."[41] And yet the extraordinary popularity of *The Gates Ajar*—a first printing of four thousand exhausted in a matter of weeks, and fifty-four more printings between 1869 and 1884—attested to the heart-hunger of the postwar generation to and for whom it spoke. "So long as there are death and bereavement in this world, and the necessity for books of consolation, it will have a permanent, intrinsic value," declared a reviewer for San Francisco's *Overland Monthly*. "In regard to heaven, we probably *know* as little of it as Miss Phelps does . . . but . . . if [she] has, with womanly tact, worked up some half-truths into pleasantly delusive perspective, who shall blame her?"[42]

V   Other writers discovered this popular subject, enough of them that Horace Scudder in 1884 wrote a review article for the *Atlantic* entitled "The Annexation of Heaven." But he was inclined to regard this kind of speculative writing with a cold eye. "If literature is ever to engage in the occupation of the other world, it must believe in it, and then use its imagination," Scudder wrote. "If it merely hauls into boundless space the baggage of this world, it is pretty sure to lose its way."[43] By contrast with these novelists of the afterlife Walt Whitman, whose style is so easy to parody because he hauled so much baggage into his poetry when he sang of this world, took care to use his imagination in describing the next, "where neither ground is for the feet, nor any path to follow."

No map there, no guide,
Nor voice sounding, nor touch of human hand,
Nor face with blooming flesh, nor lips, nor eyes, are in that land.

Life after death, which was for Elizabeth Phelps a comfortable prospect of Beethoven matinées and toy balloons, and for Lew Wallace a pious vagueness to be talked of in the tents during pauses between love and chariot racing, seemed to Whitman something wholly mysterious.

. . . all is a blank before us,
All waits undream'd of in that region, that inaccessible land.[44]

For writers still less orthodox than Whitman, the "blank before us" might seem just that, a nullity. The human wreckage strewn over Ambrose Bierce's fictional battlefields would obviously never rise again. Yet even Bierce could not completely escape the concerns of "an age morbidly preoccupied with belief in personal immortality,"[45] as the nineteenth century so markedly was.

If the Confederate general in "Parker Adderson, Philosopher" could not condemn the Federal spy to go to heaven, neither could he forbid his ghost to walk on earth. Bierce had been interested in occult or paranormal phenomena long before he wrote those stories; he could relate a few "psychic" experiences of his own, one of them involving communion with a friend who was dead.[46] The war stories in his *Tales of Soldiers and Civilians* stayed well within the limits of Bierce's darkly antireligious creed; such "hauntings" as are to be found, in "An Occurrence at Owl Creek Bridge," for example, are entirely subjective. But the civilian adventures in the same volume included some memorable encounters with ghosts.

Bierce was ambivalent about the "reality" of his supernatural phenomena, as many good ghost-story writers are. "Perhaps it was a phantasm of a disordered mind in a fevered body," one of these tales concludes, but on the other hand "perhaps it was a solemn farce enacted by pranking existences that throng the shadows lying along the border of another world."[47] In *Can Such Things Be?* a second collection of Bierce's short stories, the supernatural element became even more explicit, in the military as well as the civilian episodes (see "A Resumed Identity"). Apparently, then, the weakening or outright rejection of traditional religion did not necessarily carry with it a corresponding rejection of supernaturalism in literature. "Sometimes a curious streak of fancy invades an obscure corner of the very hardest head," wrote a more modern practitioner, H. P. Lovecraft; "so that no amount of rationalisation, reform, or Freudian analysis can quite annul the thrill of the chimney-corner whisper or the lonely wood."[48]

But chimney-corner whispers were distinctly a minor theme in the railroad hustle-bustle of the nineteenth century. It was this world, at least as much as the next, that attracted the writers of the Gilded Age, and alongside the novels of Bible times like *Ben-Hur* and the tracts on the next world by Elizabeth Phelps (and, *malgré lui*, Ambrose Bierce), there were numerous descriptions of religious life in the here-and now.

Thus in one serial which ran in the *Catholic World* a young doctor and a veteran priest who have been laboring together during an epidemic in a poverty-stricken "river suburb" come from an all-night vigil at a deathbed and argue the immortality of the soul. The dialogue is a bit textbookish, but the working-class Irish milieu is realistically done.[49] In E. P. Roe's best-selling *Barriers Burned Away*, the recent Chicago Fire (1872) was used as the setting for another fictionalized conflict between doubt and faith.[50] William Dean Howells quietly but effectively portrayed the theological and personal inadequacies of one fictional Gilded-Age clergyman in *The Minister's Charge*.[51] Satire, as in the corrupt Senator Dilworthy's speech before his old Sunday School in Twain's and Warner's *The Gilded Age*,[52] alternated with straight reporting, of the sort Harriet Beecher Stowe attempted in her novel *Oldtown Folks*: "Though Calvinist, Arminian, High-Church Episcopalian, sceptic, and simple believer all speak in their turn, I merely listen, and endeavor to understand and faithfully represent the inner life of each."[53] In one respect these Victorian novelists were precisely the reverse of their heirs in the twentieth century; they wrote with reticence about sexual relations and with easy familiarity about people's most intimate religious beliefs, whereas the moderns write with belligerent frankness about sex and with downright embarrassment about God.[54]

A favorite device in the Gilded Age was the representation of the religion of a generation just prior to one's own. Remembered vividly enough for plausibility of detail, the near-past was distant enough to be worked over with aesthetic control. Anchored in a local geography which the author knew at first hand, novels dealing with religious practices in various parts of the country were also a contribution to a growing literature of regionalism. At the same time, since they chronicled past and, therefore, to some degree rejected religious views, these regional novels contributed in their own way to the religious debate going on in Gilded-Age America at the national level. They suggest moreover, writes Robert T. Handy, that "a period's religious premises may be deeper than what organized religion expresses."[55]

Admittedly some of this fictional regionalism may have been a subtle form of advertisement for oneself. Since the days of Mrs. Stowe's *Oldtown Folks* (published in 1869), wrote a reviewer in *The Forum* for February, 1892, the minute study of provincial character had been pursued by writing women, until there was hardly a county in New England which lacked its own special novelist. "They still read these tales up there"—*The Forum* was published in New York, which had already begun to put on airs as against poky old Boston—"with avidity; it is the food of that sort of vanity which likes to contemplate its own photograph." But modern criticism has taken these tales more seriously. Vernon Louis Parrington, certainly no lover of New England, praised Mrs. Stowe's work in particular as foreshadowing the greatness of Sarah Orne Jewett's *Country of the Pointed Firs*, as well as the realistic New England regionalism of Mary E. Wilkins Freeman and, in some of her moods, Edith Wharton.[56] In much the same way Edward Eggleston's *The Hoosier Schoolmaster*, chronicling the religious and secular folk-life of frontier Indiana, has been rediscovered by American literature specialists as something more than a book intended primarily for children.

VI   It is easy for the reader today to miss altogether the significance of what such writers were doing. They loved their childhood religious milieux far more than they hated them, and so their criticisms of ancestral faiths lack the antireligious bite of an *Elmer Gantry*. Edward Eggleston's *The Circuit Rider* recaptured a Methodist frontier culture which he remembered with respect and affection, even though he satirized its excesses, and Harriet Beecher Stowe found in New England's "constant wrestling of thought with infinite problems which could not be avoided" the source of that region's strength and independence of character, even though she also "conceded that these systems . . . had, on minds of a certain class, the effect of a slow poison, producing life habits of morbid action."[57] But precisely because these religious portraits were not one-sided caricatures they may have been all the more effective as religious criticism. No civilized essay in rebuttal to the more primitivist excesses of American religion could have had the concreteness of the chapter on "The Hardshell Preacher" in *The Hoosier Schoolmaster*, a passage which even today can be hilarious if read aloud,[58] and no formal confutation of the tenets of Calvinism could have outdone Mrs. Stowe's simple and graphic descriptions of Calvinism's effect upon people who had to live under it.

Not all who turned their hands to this kind of reminiscence were able to bring it off. Henry Ward Beecher was as unhappy with the doctrines of total depravity, infant damnation, and so on as was his sister, Mrs. Stowe, and—perhaps because of James Russell Lowell's praise of *The Minister's Wooing* moved to a snap judgment that anything his kid sister could do he could do better[59]—the pastor of Plymouth Church also turned to novelistic dramatization of his religious views. If Harriet would write of how a constant exposure to the King James Bible during childhood "insensibly wrought a sort of mystical poetry into the otherwise hard and sterile life of New England," then her brother would attempt in his own fiction "to obtain the full flavor of a New-England Sunday."[60] Quite surprisingly, since in the pulpit Beecher was a raconteur of no mean ability, this attempt at persuasion in the guise of entertainment was a failure; even by the standards of literary criticism in the Gilded Age, so vastly different from our own, Harriet won the competition hands down. William Dean Howells was as kind to the prestigious son of Lyman Beecher as he could be, quoting generously from the Yankee dialect of the quaint minor personages in Beecher's *Norwood; or, Village Life in New England* for three of the *Atlantic Monthly*'s fine-printed double-columned pages, but in the end Howells's honesty overcame his Bostonian tact; he found it "quite impossible to describe the ruthlessness with which the author preaches, both in his own person and that of his characters."[61]

In stark contrast to Henry Ward Beecher's heavy-handed tract was Margaret Deland's quite remarkable narrative *John Ward, Preacher*, first published in 1888. The more theologically liberal among these Gilded-Age novelists often cast the religious controversies of their day and the day before as a conflict between older and younger generations. Mrs. Stowe wrote about the effect of the sulphurous old doctrines taught in one fictional New England town which caused the children who suffered under such teachings to "consider religion, and everything connected with it, as the most disagreeable of subjects, and to seek practically to have as little to do with it as possible."

> There was among the young people a great deal of youthful gayety and of young enjoyment in life, notwithstanding the preaching from Sunday to Sunday of assertions enough to freeze the heart with fear. Many formed the habit of thinking of something else during the sermon-time.[62]

Mrs. Deland put the conflict between the old religion and the new into a sharper and more anguished form, forcing it upon fictional characters who could not escape its demands by thinking of something else; she made of it an issue between a husband and wife.

John Ward believes in, and preaches, a literal Hell; Helen Ward instinctively and indignantly rejects it. And both of them stick by their guns. Helen, like many wives in any age, is prepared to humor her husband's quaint notions: "It does not make any difference to me what you believe . . . you were

born a Presbyterian, dear; you can't help it." But John will not have it so.
Not only does her view that "doctrine is of little importance . . . for belief is
a matter of temperament" violate his own sense of intellectual integrity, but
also, for him, the soul of the woman he loves is at stake. He actually goes to
the point of preaching an impassioned sermon on Hell and addressing the
climactic altar-call to his wife! Whereupon the choir and congregation join
heartily in singing:

> 'Tis boundless, 'tis amazing love,
> That bears us up from hell.

Needless to say, Helen, who has been "sitting in the dusky shadow by the
open window, her face a little averted, and her firm, sweet lips set in a line
which was almost stern," does not get the message.[63]

Of all the religious novels of the Gilded Age this may be one of the most
difficult for the modern reader. It would be easy to take a scene such as the
one just described as the ravings of a moral monster, like many of the preacher characters in twentieth-century anticlerical novels; it is not. ("Perhaps you
need the sternness and the horror of some of the doctrines as a balance for
your gentleness," Helen tells him. "I never knew any one as gentle as you,
John.") Nor is the clash sentimentalized, as is the debate between the (mo-
mentarily) unbelieving Christine and the believing Dennis in Roe's *Barriers
Burned Away*; it is tragic. That two normal, nonfanatical people in love could
come to shipwreck over a matter of mere religious dogma may seem highly
implausible to the reader in what is sometimes called our "post-Christian"
era; there must have been something else the matter, he may reason in his
Freudian wisdom, or "they would have worked it out somehow." But there
wasn't, and they don't. The preacher sends his wife away in the hope she will
think it over and come around, which, of course, she does not. In the end,
in what is less of a concession to Victorian sentimentalism than it sounds,
John dies of a broken heart.

Only in the political realm could some moderns find a really persuasive
analogy; perhaps a determined civil-rights integrationist married to a convinced racist, or an active "hawk" married to an equally militant "dove,"
might have undergone a like fate in more recent years. Yet the conflict of
Helen and John as depicted by the author of *John Ward, Preacher* makes
realistic psychological and dramatic sense, and one realizes with a shock that
the conversations Mrs. Deland set down in this novel, like the vivid marital
quarrels of Carol Kennecott and her doctor husband in Sinclair Lewis's *Main
Street*, almost certainly mirrored conversations in the real world. Reading

such a novel one realizes that, at the personal level, the emotional stakes of the religious debate in the Gilded Age were just as high as the scientists and the preachers said they were.

One realizes something else also. The clash between the modernist and the traditionalist in religion is often seen, especially by liberal intellectuals, quite simplistically as a clash between enlightened rationality and bigoted anti-intellectualism. On the contrary, argued Mrs. Ward, the whole trouble with the "old-time religion," at least in its New England version, was that it contained too much intellectualism, rather than too little. John Ward was a good man in the grip of a bad creed. Helen Ward was appealing to him to turn from his grim religion of the head to a warm and loving religion of the heart; and so too, in their respective media, were Henry Ward Beecher and Harriet Beecher Stowe.

It is easy to condescend to the "gospel of love" that was preached from liberal pulpits in the 1870's as sheer Victorian gush, inadequate to the real industrial and social problems of the times; but preached to persons reared in a creed as angular and unloving as John Ward's—as the children of old Lyman Beecher knew all too well!—it was about the most relevant and liberating message they could have heard. Only one step beyond the protest of Helen Ward was that of the novelists of the Social Gospel in the next generation, condemning the old orthodoxy not only for its theological inhumanity but also for its social regressiveness. John Ward died of a broken heart, fictional ministers in other books published at about the same time as *John Ward, Preacher* were resigning, or being ousted, from their pulpits to devote themselves fulltime to relief work in the slums.[64]

5

"If a Man Die, Shall He Live Again?"

"The Infinite always is silent:
It is only the Finite speaks.
Our words are the idle wave-caps
On the deep that never breaks.
We may question with wand of science,
Explain, decide, and discuss;
But only in meditation
The Mystery speaks to us."

John Boyle O'Reilly,
journalist and political reformer (1844–1890)[1]

"While medical experts injected brandy
into Grant's veins, Newman seized a bowl
of water and baptized the unconscious
man according to the rites of the
Methodist Church. As the patient revived,
the cleric exclaimed: 'It is Providence!
It is Providence!' 'No,' replied the
scientist, 'it was the brandy!' "

William B. Hesseltine,
Ulysses S. Grant: Politician[2]

85

    I   ARLY in 1962, the year of John F. Kennedy's dramatic nuclear confrontation with Nikita Khrushchev, an editorial in an American theological monthly noted a strange paradox: contemporary man, more capriciously threatened by death than at any time since the Black Plague, seemed almost less concerned about it personally than he was about his professional status, his sex life, or the revolutionary disruption of his society. "Whether from cancer, cardiac causes, or nuclear attack, death tends to become a technical matter, representing more the issue of a struggle between the physician and the mortician than between life and death."[3] The writer may not have spoken for all of his contemporaries, in that era of the seat belt, of the warning on the cigarette package, and of the movement to abolish capital punishment as "cruel and unusual." Still, it is possible that one reason why religious radicals of the day were able so comfortably to proclaim God's death was that man had come to think and feel differently about his own.

A class in philosophy at an American Catholic university, asked in 1968 to write "an essay on death: what they had been taught, and how much of it they now found convincing," expressed considerable hostility to the whole idea of life after death. "The day I was born I was given a command to *live* in this world, not sit around and wait in a church for the next," one student wrote. Another objected to the traditional imagery of *requiem aeternam dona eis domine*, repeated six times in the Burial Mass, whereby the believer came to think of the afterlife as rest, stasis, "the place where there are no more choices to be made"—an intolerable idea for the activist existential consciousness of the youth-culture. "To the young, such a Heaven is precisely a Hell."[4]

Hostility to a religion of stasis and repose was of course no new thing in the United States. The Gilded Age in its own way had had an activist consciousness also. To affirm the continuity of human existence as a plausible and natural expectation, one popular preacher in that period felt he had also to affirm that "the world beyond Death will seem to be one with the life on this side of it," and, by inference from the pace of the life on this side, Phillips Brooks wrote in 1882, "the activity of the Eternal Life must be intense."[5] Yet even the most militant and "muscular" of Christians preached, usually, a gospel of activity in this world and of rest in the next. The same generation that wrote activist hymns like "Stand Up, Stand Up For Jesus" and "Work, For the Night Is Coming"[6] also wrote "We Are Going, We Are Going to a Home Beyond the Skies" and "In the Sweet By and By." Protestant Christians in America, if they were black, sang,

> Soon I will be done with the troubles of the world,
> Going home to God,

and if they were white, they sang "Softly and Tenderly Jesus Is Calling," with its echoing refrain,

> Come home, come home,
> Ye who are weary, come home,

or, in the somewhat more genteel environs of Lake Chautauqua, they sang,

> Day is dying in the west,
> Heav'n is touching earth with rest.[7]

The kinds of heavens men hope for can be taken as unconscious commentary on what they cherish or regret in this world. "We build heaven out of our joys, out of our sufferings, out of our griefs, out of our experiences, taking the best and noblest things, and arranging them so that they shall fill the imagination," Henry Ward Beecher declared. "Thus we construct our heaven to suit our personality."[8] Some of his contemporaries visualized heaven as a very "homey" place indeed; Washington Gladden for example looked forward to "landscapes like these we here look upon—hill and valley, . . . verdure and blossoms, sunny skies and smiling fields," and among these scenes Gladden envisioned songbirds, squirrels, crickets, cattle, and even "lambs skipping upon the hillside," a picture of heaven much like that of Elizabeth Stuart Phelps, surveyed in the previous chapter. Others were more cautious in their expectations. Preaching on Rev. 20:12, "And I saw the dead, small and great, stand before God," Phillips Brooks rejected the literalness of that text's image in favor of a metaphor: the dead stand before God in the same sense that "the poet stands before nature . . . the philosopher stands before . . . abstract truth . . . the artist stands before beauty."[9] But whether the promised Kingdom were to be taken literally or metaphorically, it was a hope that had to be consciously asserted against "a theory," as the novelist Miss Phelps put it, "which shuts us into our coffins, screws the lid down, and says, 'Now get out if you can!'"

Perhaps people burst into gospel songs in order to drown with music the doubts and disagreements they could not have harmonized by the exchange of words. Personal immortality, wrote Professor Charles Briggs in 1889, was an issue upon which "the consensus of Christendom is little, the dissensus is great, the questions undefined greater still." We have already noticed the wretched inability of many believing Americans to cope with Genesis in the light of evolution, and they seem to have been similarly helpless before this ultimate question. Elizabeth Phelps thought in 1886 that the tide was beginning to turn back toward hope for the world to come, but she conceded that "it has been the great effort of the time to establish a mathematical equation between an instructed mind and an abandoned faith."

> We learned that we were not men, but protoplasm. We learned that we were not spirits, but chemical combinations. We learned that we had laid up treasure in the wrong places. We learned that the drama of Hamlet and the Ode to Immortality were secretions of the gray matter of the brain.[10]

If Darwin seemed to be reducing man's soul to the caperings of a naked ape, Wundt seemed to be reducing it to the electrochemical discharges inside man's skull. In 1904 Sir William Osler somewhat regretfully summed up a half-century's research: "Modern psychological science dispenses altogether with the soul." Such phenomena as "the slow decay of mind with changes in the brain" gave pause to any scientific student trying to conceive of consciousness as existing without a corresponding material basis.[11] Long after the Gilded Age was over,[12] it remained possible to conclude from the physiological evidence that "clear-cut atheism and materialism" had become "the only tenable hypotheses" for modern rational man. As that tireless letter-writer Howard Phillips Lovecraft put it in 1921:

> You speak of immortality as if one's personality were something apart from his material structure, yet when we analyse personality we can trace every quality to the atoms and electrons of the body. Certainly, these electrons were never thus assembled until the body in question took form; and equally certainly they will never be thus assembled again. When a man dies, his body turns to liquids and gases whose molecules soon enter into an infinitude of new combinations— there is nothing left. Haeckel has dealt so clearly with this subject in *The Riddle of the Universe* that it is really superfluous for me to repeat the arguments here.[13]

II   When a distinguished philosopher like Paul Carus undertook to replace the old religion of "superstition" with a new "religion of science" he sometimes seemed to hold out the hope that science itself would vindicate man's belief in an afterlife. "The preservation of soul-life after the death of the individual is not an assumption, nor a probability, nor a mere hypothesis, but a scientific truth which can be proved by the surest facts of experience," Carus wrote in 1893. But upon examination this continuing soul-life turned out to be the evolutionary continuance of the individual's ideas, which in the monistic universe assumed by men like Carus would be interchangeable with those of anyone else, and of his actions, understood behavioristically: "Deeds live on, and what are we but the summation of our deeds!" In practice Carus's religion of science annihilated the individual ego as thoroughly as did Buddhism: "As soon as we rise above the pettiness of our individual being, the boundaries of birth and death vanish, and we breathe the air of immortality."

The dynamic sociologist Lester F. Ward played a similar game of words with the doctrine of an afterlife. "Science is not skeptical as to the immortality of the soul," Ward asserted, but he evidently did not mean the word "soul" in the Church's traditional sense: "Science postulates the immortality not of the human soul alone, but of the soul of the least atom of matter." Was this enough as a replacement for the age-old hope of religion? Ward believed so; "It is something to have learned that there exist, have always existed and will ever continue to exist, the indestructible and unchangeable elements and powers out of which, through similar processes, equal and perhaps far superior results may be accomplished." *As it was in the beginning, is now and ever shall be, world without end, Amen.*

It was a tremendous act of abnegation for a man who on the eve of the Civil War had sadly wondered whether he and his bride-to-be would ever be together in heaven. The mature Ward, like Carus, ended by concluding that all such desires as he had once confided to his diary were both illusory and egoistic.[14] His was the self-transcending ethic expressed in a poem by George Eliot, of which many thoughtful agnostics have been fond.

> Oh may I join the choir invisible
> Of those immortal dead who live again
> In minds made better by their presence: live
>
>   ·   ·   ·   ·   ·
>
>   . . . in scorn
> For miserable aims that end with self,
>
>   ·   ·   ·   ·   ·
>
>   So to live is heaven,
> To make undying music in the world.[15]

"When we attain the realization that death finishes the story, we know the worst," Corliss Lamont wrote in 1935. "And that worst is not really very bad." The author of *The Illusion of Immortality* was not the first American thus to depreciate the dread of personal cessation. Out of his experiences as a physician in a Confederate prison camp in the autumn of 1864, where men had perished in wartime misery at the rate of four hundred a week, Junius Henry Browne testified a quarter-century later that he could "not recall a single instance of a man who was troubled with doubt or alarm. . . . They were not concerned about the future, but about the past and present, leaving messages and mementos for the near and dear, and passing away gently and in peace." But what we can not know from such testimony is what proportion of these men were dying in calm certainty of the absoluteness of what was ending for them—and how many were letting go their hold on life while keeping a grip on the traditional comforts of religion. We do know that in the American Civil War the armies on both sides were periodically swept by religious revivals; that Robert E. Lee was not above dismounting from his horse and doffing his hat to pray with his men; and that an Ozark folksong celebrating one of the worst battles of that war ended with a prayer

> . . . to God my Saviour, consistent with His will,
> To save the souls of them brave men who fell on Shiloh's Hill.[16]

Radical anticlericals in the postbellum years sometimes conceded that belief in immortality was a great deterrent to the overthrow of orthodoxy. One such skeptic considered that particular doctrine "the great bulwark of the church, and the standing obstacle in the way of all organized movement against her." It was all very well for Emerson bravely to say "Of immortality, the soul, when well employed, is incurious," but testimony such as his would "not satisfy the mind of average humanity, which shudders at the thought of dissolution."[17] Moreover, were the survivors of all those young men fallen in battle expected stoically to affirm that the worst is not really very bad?

We have already heard the heartbroken cry that the Civil War wrung from Elizabeth Stuart Phelps, and in peacetime Phillips Brooks, that most serenely optimistic of men, spoke in one sermon of "the sadness, which no faith in immortality can dissipate, belonging to the death of those who die in youth, the sense of untimeliness which we cannot reason down." Brooks's Anglican colleague James DeKoven preached, "Beside some silent form, the quiet stillness of the dead, we stand and ask . . . where is he now? . . . Tell me not of physical laws and the workings of disease, of forces, and gases, and currents.

Philosophy and science and culture have no words warm enough to comfort me. O Cross of Christ! Cast thou thy shadow on my breaking heart."[18]

The trouble with the consolations of science was that for many they were not really very consoling. A correspondent of the Providence *Journal* wrote sarcastically of the thin substitutes which science and philosophy were offering in place of the supreme hope of religion.

> Before long we shall become so scientific and so well-informed that when a person dies there will be no funeral services. Some one will read comforting passages from the Transactions of the American Scientific Association, and the mourners will go about with small hammers in their hands, chipping the rocks and assuaging their anguish by proving the antiquity of creation. . . . We have traded off all simple religious faiths for a few meagre scientific facts; but there may come that day, when we think of bestowing our patronage on some under-taker, that we shall wish to trade back again, and in something of a hurry. . . . Darwin's greatest work is the last book we should want to read the last evening we spent on this earth.[19]

Charles Darwin himself was not happy with some of the comfortable words put forth in his name. "Believing as I do that man in the distant future will be a far more perfect creature than he now is, it is an intolerable thought that he and all other sentient beings are doomed to complete annihilation," Darwin wrote. "To those who fully admit the immortality of the human soul, the destruction of our world will not appear so dreadful." A distinguished survivor from the Gilded Age echoed these words of Darwin as recently as 1956: "With the planet's perishing, the last Robinson Crusoe on this wandering island in the sky will be finally dead, and nothing will be left, no value conserved, no purpose fulfilled from all that was endeavored and done on earth," wrote Harry Emerson Fosdick in his autobiography *The Living of These Days*. "My faith in immortality has been mainly a corollary from my faith that creation cannot be so utterly senseless and irrational."[20] Not all men of Fosdick's generation drew this corollary; compare the tragic naturalism of Bertrand Russell's *A Free Man's Worship*. But Russell and Fosdick would have agreed with Darwin that there is one fatal drawback in joining George Eliot's "choir invisible": one day, thanks to the Second Law of Thermodynamics, the chorus is going to have to stop singing. The poetess herself conceded the point:

> That better self shall live till human Time
> Shall fold its eyelids, and the human sky
> Be gathered like a scroll within the tomb
> Unread for ever.

Some contemporaries of Paul Carus and Lester Ward therefore considered their ethical conclusion that "the only worthy immortality is survival in the remembrance of one's fellow creatures" as little more than "a travesty and a trick." John Fiske cried, "If the world's long cherished beliefs are to fall, in God's name let them fall, but save us from the intellectual hypocrisy that goes about pretending we are none the poorer!" The argument that a person should be glad to lose his individual voice in the Choir Invisible because it is egoistic to desire the survival of one's own psyche is self-defeating, Theodore Munger added; if I cease to exist, I cease being able to give and serve. "It is one thing to see the difficulties in the way of immortality, but quite another thing to erect annihilation into morality, and . . . to claim for such morality a superiority over that of those who hope to live on."[21]

Some of those who hoped to live on may simply have been reviving Pascal's old argument for the necessity of the Wager: "If you gain, you gain all; if you lose, you lose nothing." If God and the afterlife are real, you gain immortality by gambling on their existence; if they are illusory, your consciousness will not survive to feel the humiliation of having been proved wrong. The skeptic's option, of refusing to call the toss of the coin at all, is not really available, since all men in their concrete decisions in life will act as if they believed in ultimate Being or in ultimate Nothingness. "And, thus," concluded that seventeenth-century mathematician and mystic, "when one is forced to play, he must renounce reason to preserve his life."[22]

III   Life is a narrow vale between the cold and barren peaks of two eternities. We strive in vain to look beyond the heights. We cry aloud, and the only answer is the echo of a wailing cry. From the voiceless lips of the unreplying dead there comes no word; but in the night of death hope sees a star and listening love can hear the rustle of a wing. He who sleeps here, when dying, mistaking the approach of death for the return of health, whispered with his latest breath, "I am better now." Let us believe, in spite of doubts and dogmas, and tears and fears, that these dear words are true of all the countless dead.[23]

It is not surprising that words like these were spoken at a funeral in the emotionally effusive Victorian Age, but on first reflection it is astonishing that they should have been spoken by Robert G. Ingersoll. Did the eloquent freethinker quail away from the courage of his convictions when he was burying his own brother? Admirers of Ingersoll have had trouble with this paragraph. One biographer, pondering the "rustle of a wing" passage, became convinced that these were no more than "the words of Ingersoll's agony. He may have found relief in the phantasm of the words but only while he said them."[24] But

personal crisis was not the only occasion on which this crusading anticleric
considered the ultimate question and came out with a tentatively affirmative
answer. Ingersoll often delivered funeral orations, and they seem genuinely
to have comforted the bereaved.

The comfort was sometimes ambiguous; "We do not know whether the

FORECASTING THE FUTURE. ORTHODOX DOMINIE.—"NONE OF THAT,
COLONEL! WE HAVE ENOUGH OF YOU WHILE ALIVE, AND WON'T WISH AN
ENDLESS REPETITION OF YOU HEREAFTER."

*Can we conclude a priori that Bob Ingersoll was less representative
of Gilded-Age America than was Lucy Hayes?*

grave is the end of this life or the door of another," Ingersoll admitted. Many
of his beloved dead he commended, "without assurance, and without fear,"
to a half-personified Nature: "With morn, with noon, with night; with changing clouds and changeless stars; with grass and trees . . . with leaf and bud,
with flower and blossoming vine . . . we leave our dead"—hinting perhaps

at a Romantic pantheism, or perhaps at Spinoza's austere *natura sive deus*; or he may merely have meant that to mingle obliviously with the earth was better at any rate than consciously to endure the fatuous heavens or gross hells of tradition. He wrote with especial tenderness in 1885 to a bereaved mother, brought up in Calvinism and distraught to the point of insanity by the fear that her unconverted son was suffering in Hell, to tell her that if God existed her own heart, which "could never send your boy to endless pain," was the best revelation of Him.

> After all, no one knows. The ministers know nothing. . . . Creeds are good for nothing except to break the hearts of the loving. . . . Listen to your heart, be-lieve what it says, and wait with patience and without fear for whatever the future has for all. If we can get no comfort from what people know, let us avoid being driven to despair by what they do not know.[25]

Much of this was compatible with pure naturalistic humanism, but unlike most other naturalists Ingersoll always left a door open. The Great Infidel did not brush aside the notion of personal survival after death as egocentric fantasy; whatever else might be thought of the concept, it had for him at least the legitimacy of naturalness. "The idea of immortality . . . was not born of any book, nor of any creed, nor of any religion," Ingersoll said in one of his lectures. "It was born of human affection, and it will continue to ebb and flow beneath the mists and clouds of doubt and darkness as long as love kisses the lips of death."[26] In a letter to his wife in 1879 he voiced the hope that in the earth "my dust may mingle with yours. Even this hope gives a glow to the cheek of death. . . . We will keep to-gether until every passion dies, and then through the shadows of death, we will exchange dim looks of love."[27]

Was this sheer Victorian sentimentalism? Could one give full allegiance to the monistic world-view which typified the science of the Gilded Age and still indulge in a fancy as capriciously personal as this, except on what William James might have called a "moral holiday"? Only if personal hope could somehow be squared with impersonal conviction. Ingersoll was an orator, not a laboratory researcher, and his own answers to the question of immortality were expressed as platform or even graveside eloquence rather than as scientific reports (which is not to deny their intuitive integrity). But there were others who took a more theoretical and experimental approach to the problem.

"Immortality came under question simply because science could find no data for it," wrote Theodore T. Munger in 1885, but it was not thereby necessarily disproven. Personal immortality might therefore turn out to be not a mysterious disclosure of God's grace, to be accepted on faith, but a hitherto unrecognized natural phenomenon, to be measured like any other. Even in the matter-of-fact nineteenth century not all occult beliefs had turned out upon careful examination to be superstitions; hypnotism, wrote Minot J. Savage in 1889, had once been investigated and pronounced fraudulent, and clairvoyance and telepathy might now be going through the same process of rejection, examination, and eventual acceptance. "In a universe the size of this, a modest scientific man will hesitate about declaring as to what is or is not impossible."[28] Perhaps the persistence of personal identity after death is not, by the usual definition, "supernatural" at all.[29]

Some Victorian thinkers were already aware that the palpable material world upon which so much of their science seemed to rest was not so much a fact of experience as a mental construct. The quest for a tangible, measurable reality knowable by "common sense" had led unexpectedly instead to such notions as that of a "luminiferous ether," surely an idea as intangible, abstract, and contrary to common sense as Thomas Aquinas's angels dancing on the point of a pin. Noting as early as 1873 the overthrow of what had been classic textbook distinctions between "substances" that could be weighed and those more imponderable "substances" such as light, electricity, and magnetism, E. A. Sears wrote: "Matter has no ultimate units, but is divisible to the point where it vanishes from human perception." Hence, this religious apologist argued, "the best scientific research and progress do not tend downward toward a grosser materialism, but away from it." (Such reasoning has not been unknown in the twentieth century among theistic scientists, to the annoyance of many among their professional colleagues, as when Sir James Jeans concluded in 1931 that "the universe begins to look more like a great thought than like a great machine.")[30] If a dying God, or some semblance of Him, might be resuscitated by such argumentation, thought some in America's Gilded Age, so might man's own immortal soul.

IV   Two lines of attack commended themselves to such inquirers. Assuming as many of them did a universe governed by natural causation rather than by miraculous fiat,[31] and knowable by empirical inquiry rather than by transempirical revelation, they had to locate human immortality within such a universe. The investigator might find it in space; if people do not go off at once to a "hell" or a "heaven" (which, as was seen earlier, raises the difficult question "Where?"[32]) then they may still be among us, engaging in activities which can be objectively measured. This was the method of "psychic research" and of Spiritualism. Or, he might find it in time; life after death is a natural inference from Darwinism. In his book *Old Faiths in New Light* (1879) Newman Smyth suggested that the human brain might not be the last step in evolution, but the first: "The brain may be only the embryonic condition of the matter of mind"—and the transition to an afterlife would then seem to be a natural process, "a conceivable and fitting termination of the whole course of nature."[33]

Going much further than this modest inference, Thomson Jay Hudson argued in *A Scientific Demonstration of the Future Life* (1895) that evolution did not merely permit immortality, it required it. Natural selection, by definition, never produces a physical or mental trait without some legitimate adaptive function, and yet there are depths of human consciousness which can in no sense be explained merely as a means for coping with man's natural environment. Therefore, Hudson reasoned, since the human psyche was endowed "with faculties that perform no function in this life," that fact constituted "demonstrative evidence that the subjective mind was created, *ab initio*, with special reference to a future life."[34]

The British lecturer on evolution Henry Drummond, who was enough of a scientist to have gone on geological expeditions in the Rocky Mountains and enough of an evangelist to have traveled with Dwight L. Moody, took a somewhat different tack.[35] He believed that the partition between the water-tight compartments labeled Science and Religion showed signs of giving way; that generalizations about natural phenomena, such as the theory of evolution, could be extended into the "supernatural," which would be shown eventually to be governed by the same kinds of laws that prevailed in the "natural" world; and therefore—a very long inference indeed!—that observed natural processes could be used by analogy to explain the Unseen. The organisms formerly limited to an ocean habitat which had evolved into air-breathing forms that conquered the land could thus become a metaphor for the transition from this world to the next: "Is the change from the earthly to the heavenly more mysterious than the change from the aquatic to the terrestrial mode of life?"[36]

This tempting, but logically shaky, mode of reasoning was common among liberal theists in the Gilded Age. Contrast "the headless mollusk glued to rock in a world of water, and an antlered deer in a world of verdure"; contrast the dinosaur with man; these were transformations no more startling than the leap from death to the afterlife, Theodore Munger argued. "There is a reason why the reptile should become a mammal; it is more life. Is there no like reason for man? Shall he not have more life?" But there were hazards in this method of defending the faith. The trouble with "religious"

Darwinism was that, like "social" Darwinism, it was equivocal; diametrically opposite conclusions could legitimately be drawn from the same scientific premises. The British agnostic Leslie Stephen warned hopeful believers that the fact of evolution could also be used as evidence against life after death.

> Does not the new theory make it difficult to believe in immortal souls? If we admit that the difference between men and monkeys is merely a difference of degree, can we continue to hold that monkeys will disappear at their death like a bubble, and that men will rise from their ashes?

If, on the other hand, this difference between men and monkeys was one not of degree but of kind, so wide a gap would be a serious blow at the continuity inherent in a strict Darwinian view of the evolutionary process. To be consistent, Stephen argued, we must either endow animals with "some kind of rudimentary souls," or deny the soul to man.[37]

Eventually, of course, the religious Darwinists could have answered arguments like Stephen's by citing further advances in evolutionary theory. Already scientists were beginning to doubt that Darwin's gradual and random "natural selection" was sufficient to account for the phenomena observed. By the mid-1880's Hugo DeVries was looking for a scientifically respectable way of viewing the development of life on earth as discontinuous, and in 1900 the rediscovery of Mendel's mutation theory gave this hypothesis empirical foundation.[38] It might then have been in order to interpret immortality as "discontinuous," that is, as a mutation which entered the natural order for the first time with man. Developments in physics as well as in genetics seemed to permit the same general conclusion: "With every new form of force, with every new birth of the universal energy into a higher plane, there appear new, unexpected, and, previous to experience, wholly unimaginable properties and powers," Joseph LeConte asserted. "Why may not immortality be one of these new properties?"[39]

This would still have left unanswered the question of which "men" first acquired this new power. Did Neanderthal Man, who was physically more primitive than modern man but who laid out his dead with their tools and other possessions (an act having clearly religious implications) possess a soul, whereas the primeval hominid in Kenya who initially stumbled upon the use of tools lacked one? In any case, such a approach compromised the integrity of the religious apologist's entire position. Impelled toward skepticism by what seemed one inescapable inference from science (continuity, in the classic Darwinist version of the evolutionary hypothesis), and then propelled toward faith by what seemed another (genetic discontinuity, as in the mutation theory), he would have been forced to measure the validity of his doctrines by their scientific plausibility rather than by their intrinsic merit as religious ideas—exactly as positivists like E. L. Youmans were demanding that he do.

Furthermore, to have claimed that man's immortal soul was a mutation rather than an adaptive progression would have been only a temporary victory for religion. Just around the corner as the Gilded Age ended was the science of Dirac and Heisenberg and Bohr, which one after another would overthrow the traditional dichotomous pairs—"space/time," "matter/energy," "wave/particle," "mind/body"; perhaps one day the "life/death" antithesis might also have to be discarded. Such an outcome would hardly have satisfied the conventional wisdom of the Gilded Age, although it might have pleased Mary Baker Eddy, whose *Science and Health* (first published in 1875) did seem to argue that whether an individual be considered "living" or "dead" is largely a matter of one's point of view. More congenial to the kind of vision in that period that has been described as "matter-of-fact" or "opaque" would have been the approach to immortality which sought for the afterlife neither in the temporal unfolding of evolution nor in a Heaven above our heads, but in opaque and matter-of-fact phenomena such as tables, trumpets, slates, noises, and voices.[40]

V   "It is twenty-five years since the tiny raps at Hydesville, New York, ushered in the grandest movement of all the centuries," President Victoria Claflin Woodhull told the American Association of Spiritualists as she took the chair at their 1873 annual convention. "Led by heartless science, the world was fast declining into the blank of Atheism, but the dawning of the light of Spiritualism has driven doubt back . . ."[41] Stimulated by the religious ferment of the 1840's, particularly by Universalism whose denial of the doctrine of eternal punishment opened the way to a revolutionary new concept of the hereafter, and by Swedenborgianism with its unorthodox portrayal of the invisible world, Spiritualism attracted a respectable following in the United States; Adin Ballou became a convert, and William Lloyd Garrison and Horace Greeley both flirted with the movement. In the Fifties the cult spread to England, where it attracted attention both among the credulous and among the more cautious—men, for example, like the mathematician Augustus De Morgan, co-founder (with Boole) of symbolic logic and modern algebra; Sir William Crookes, a pioneer in experimental physics; and Alfred Russell Wallace, co-discoverer with Darwin of the principle of natural selection.[42] From time to time revelations of fraud checked the growth of the movement,[43] but faith has often outlived fraud.

As the modern reader scans news stories in a leading nineteenth-century Spiritualist weekly with headlines like "Remarkable Seance: Instantaneous Transference of a Skeptical Gentleman from Within a Locked Room to a Distance of One Mile and a Half," he can readily see why, in an era that was as science-minded in its own way as ours, the movement was greeted in some quarters with a loud chorus of ridicule. "We are asked to believe in ghosts because in every age there have been ghost stories," wrote William Jay Youmans in the *Popular Science Monthly* (1893). "But would it not be more natural to suppose that in every age the human mind has been subject to aberration?" Since ghosts, "such as they are," had been coming and going for some thousands of years, if they had anything important to say it was high time they said it; meanwhile, since all we know has been gained from "patient study of the laws of Nature," Youmans editorialized, "we prefer to stand in the paths that Science has worn and work at the tasks she assigns." *Harper's Weekly,* commenting in 1875 on one striking "manifestation" which had lately been discredited, pointed to a fatal weakness in the Spiritualists' methods:

> The difficulty has always been that the machinery is precisely that which fraud requires. The "conditions," as they are called, . . . dark rooms, cabinets, joined hands, things in the air and things under a table, covers and veils of every kind, . . . have always been such as to suggest imposture. . . . Nor is there any record of any wise word said, or noble thing done, or of any service to humanity, in all the jumble of revelations and appearances . . . that compose what is known as spiritualism.[44]

Like the editorial writer for *Harper's,* John Fiske was bothered not only by the lack of credibility in the Spiritualist revelations but also by their banality: "We have nothing to say to gross materialistic notions of ghosts and bogies, and spirits that upset tables and whisper to ignorant vulgar women the wonderful information that you once had an Aunt Susan," Fiske wrote in 1876. The unseen world he believed in, this Brahmin theist affirmed, was not connected with our material universe by the kinds of bond which would allow "Bacon and Addison to come to Boston and write the silliest twaddle in the most ungrammatical English before a roomful of people who have never learned how to test what they are pleased to call the 'evidence' of their senses." This was, and remains, a standard rebuttal to Spiritualism;

"SPIRITS" AND THEIR MANIFESTATIONS. AN EVENING SEANCE.

We have nothing to say to gross materialistic notions . . . of spirits that upset tables and whisper to ignorant women the wonderful information that you once had an Aunt Susan.—John Fiske.

as Robert Peel has written, "The ghostly small-talk of departed spirits seemed to promise a beyond which reproduced most of the drearier features of the here."[45]

Fully aware of such criticisms, the more responsible of the Spiritualists sought to distinguish the significant spirit messages from the trivial,[46] and the serious investigator from the charlatan. From two hundred sittings over a period of sixteen months Robert Dale Owen tried, in the manner of Dr. Rhine in our own time with his ESP cards, to quantify his findings, and Owen was quick to disavow results which he himself discovered to be imposture.[47] The Spiritualists' *Religio-Philosophical Journal,* along with its accounts of psychic phenomena it believed to be genuine, ran accounts of the exposure of fraudulent mediums.[48] The possibility of serious investigation of this kind eventually led hard-headed men like the astronomer Simon Newcomb, the psychologist G. Stanley Hall, and J. P. Langley of the Smithsonian Institution to found the American Society for Psychical Research, as an offshoot of a British parent body whose president, Henry

Sidgwick, William James described in 1892 as a man "known by his other deeds as the most incorrigibly and exasperatingly critical and sceptical mind in England."[49]

The psychic researchers had, moreover, a comeback for critics such as the Youmans brothers: not to investigate such phenomena was to engage in unscientific behavior. When the physiologist Wilhelm Wundt, in an essay published in translation in *Popular Science Monthly,* told investigators of "psychic" manifestations "Even if your phenomena are real they are not entitled to the attention of science, since they are prejudicial to the moral development of man," a Spiritualist editor attacked this judgment, logically enough, as showing "contempt for the scientific method." He charged that *Popular Science* editor Edward Youmans by endorsing Wundt's argument was rejecting empirical evidence, not in the skeptical spirit necessary for proper scientific inquiry, but rather from a prior subjective bias against findings that "seem to conflict with his own preconceptions as to what nature ought to do, or ought not to do!" Less bombastically, William James warned that any psychic investigator had to cope with the bias of the scientific Establishment.

> Orthodoxy is almost as much a matter of authority in science as it is in the Church. We believe in all sorts of laws of nature which we cannot ourselves understand, merely because men whom we admire and trust vouch for them. If Messrs. Helmholtz, Huxley, Pasteur, and Edison were simultaneously to announce themselves as converts to clairvoyance, thought-transference, and ghosts, who can doubt that there would be a prompt popular stampede in that direction?[50]

If there was orthodoxy in the conventional scientific reaction to Spiritualism, conversely there was unorthodoxy in Spiritualism's judgment on conventional Christianity. With the shrewdness which so often underlay his long-winded manner the elder O. W. Holmes observed that this particular way of affirming human immortality was also "quietly undermining the traditional ideals of the future state." Holmes saw eternal punishment doctrines as especially hard hit, but he implied that the movement also entailed a kind of desupernaturalizing of the whole concept of an afterlife. Summing up the results of his own investigations as a Spiritualist, Robert Dale Owen began one of his many *Atlantic Monthly* articles with a declaration that "throughout the civilized world the reign of the Miraculous is gradually losing power and prestige, superseded by the reign of law." The Spiritualist rejected—for the same reasons, said Owen, as any other believer in the reign of law—not only original sin and election but also the Devil, the inerrancy of Scripture, and the divinity of Christ.

In as radical a "demythologizing" of the Gospels as the most severe German critics have been able to accomplish, Owen concluded: "Either the wonderful works ascribed by the evangelists to Jesus and his disciples were not performed, or else they were not miracles." Christ did not overcome Death for all mankind by a mysteriously divine act of resurrection; quite the contrary. His post-Crucifixion appearances among His followers, "the doors being shut, or walking to Emmaus with two of them and vanishing from their sight," were no more supernormal than a thousand such incidents reported (and, in Owen's judgment, sufficiently documented) by mediums and psychics of a later day. Spiritualism appeals "by adducing what *must* win the credence of mankind at last, the evidence of our senses," and Owen saw no strong reason for disbelieving that doubting Thomas actually saw his risen Lord, "seeing that, in a lighted room and with the doors so securely closed that entrance or exit was impossible, I have myself seen a materialized form, that had spoken to me a few minutes before, disappear under my very eyes, then reappear and walk about as before."[51] If Spiritualism was right, Christ's advice to Nicodemus (John 3: 3–8) became irrelevant; salvation was not a matter of being "born again," but only of learning a new technique.

VI   Considering its methods and subject matter, Spiritualism was rather less "otherworldly" than many another religious movement of the nineteenth century. Andrew Jackson Davis, a Spiritualist leader whose life (1826–1910) spanned both the Transcendentalist era and the Gilded Age, considered his belief in Spiritualism as enabling him to accept the various social reforms of his day—abolition of slavery, women's rights, temperance, world peace.[52] Robert Owen, Sr., was a veteran Socialist and a major figure in the history of that movement; and Robert Dale Owen, his son, shared his father's socialist faith and considered Spiritualism necessary to trigger a revival of the other kinds of reform. Orthodox religion whether Protestant or Catholic, "based on infallibility and backed by wealth," could not do the job; it had had three hundred years in which to try.[53]

The Owens were not alone in this fusion of Spiritualism with social action. That son of the middle border Hamlin Garland, whose compassion for the poor erupted into novels, articles, and a six-act play denouncing the machinations of capital and defending the economic heresies of Henry George, was also a student of the Unseen. His romantic novel *The Tyranny of the Dark* (1905) was written from a pro-Spiritualist point of view, with a cast

A Sunday morning in the Spiritualists' meeting-house at Boston—exercises for
the children.

of characters drawn from both sides of the veil, and Garland's own obser-
vations of paranormal phenomena were later summed up in a book entitled
Forty Years of Psychic Research.[54] William Dean Howells, whose mild
Boston-accented social criticism reached people who might have been deaf
to the appeals of a Populist Midwesterner like Hamlin Garland, fellow-
traveled for a time with the movement. His *The Undiscovered Country*, published in 1880, showed a keen eye for the mediumistic fakery in Spiritualism
and could just as well have been written by a skeptic, but after the death of a
daughter in 1889 Howells for a time took psychic research quite seriously.[55] And Benjamin O. Flower, whose magazine *The Arena* was the first
successful "muckraking" journal in America, found in his Spiritualism a
powerful support for his program of social reform.[56]

   Addressing the Spiritualists' national convention in 1873, Mrs. J. J.
Severance noted that their movement was divided into radical and conservative wings, but expressed a hope that the majority of the delegates
would "decide that Spiritualism is broad enough, high enough, and deep
enough to take in all the reform movements of the day—to take in everything

that shall make of us better men and women here and hereafter." At that convention very little was said about spirit-writing and table-lifting, and a great deal about the rights of children and women, the necessity for separation of church and state, and the religious bigotry of clergymen. Some of the speakers sounded as radical as Ingersoll;[57] one delegate proudly referred to the movement as "we anti-Christians," and another urged Americans to work "to maintain our present Godless constitution and Christless institutions," and offered a resolution—which was carried—"that the clergy are a source of danger to the American republic." Speaking against a well-financed and highly-publicized national drive to write Sabbath-day observance into the Federal Constitution, Anna E. Hinman cried: "It is Christianity against liberty, and if Christianity threatens to destroy liberty, then we must take care of it and render it powerless to do so!" *Écrasez l'infâme!*

Under the formidable leadership of Victoria Woodhull—Spiritualist, suffragist, and avowed champion of free love—the American Association of Spiritualists directed its fire also against conventional morality. Delegate D. W. Hull displayed his license as a Spiritualist minister, authorizing him to preach, marry, and bury, and tore it up; "I have never tied anybody together so that they could not be cut apart, and I do not think that I have any authority to do so." In pungent language delegate Benjamin Todd demanded an end to the rule of "Mr. Law, Mr. Gospel, and Mrs. Grundy." After minor amendment, a proposed resolution "that the community has no right to enact laws impairing either the physical, intellectual, moral or sexual liberty of the individual" was adopted by a heavy majority. A minority report which would have specifically repudiated free love was tabled 113–28, and in the balloting for President of the Association the next day the mover of that report, Judge E. S. Holbrook, received only one vote, as against three for the militant Mrs. Severance and one hundred and fifteen for the super-militant Mrs. Woodhull. About the only "spiritualist" manifestation in these proceedings was a message from one in the spirit world (relayed by a live delegate) congratulating the President on her election to a third term.[58]

A Victorian backlash was inevitable. Outside the movement, The Woodhull's manifestoes were cutting most uncomfortably into the religious and secular power structure, most specifically through her references to the Reverend Henry Ward Beecher.[59] Within the movement, the *Religio-Philosophical Journal* vehemently attacked "Woodhullism": "Be assured we shall perform our whole duty in rolling back the black pall of sensualism now overshadowing our heaven-born philosophy." The magazine claimed that Mrs. Woodhull and her followers had unrepresentatively taken over the

Association (in the fashion radicals so often do), and made it a mere splinter of "the great mass of Spiritualists," who "were *shocked* at the thought of giving countenance to such a movement" as the Association had become. Shortly before his humiliating defeat at the 1873 convention Judge Holbrook wrote an open letter urging that Spiritualists stick to their haunted furniture and musical instruments, saying, in effect, they had enough opposition as it was without taking on free love as well.[60]

Within two years Victoria Claflin Woodhull herself had retracted her *avant-garde* views, leaving the field of heavenly philosophy to more strait-laced investigators.[61] The novelist of the afterlife Elizabeth Stuart Phelps, for example, whose vision of the next world had so often been criticized as grossly physical, made it clear that her vision of this world was not. In a *Forum* article "The *Décolleté* in Modern Life" (1890) she condemned not only the dress styles current in high society but also salacious literature (as an example of which she offered Tolstoi!); the nude in art; the custom of women visiting doctors of the opposite sex; current standards in the theater and in ballet; and ballroom dancing. "The groves of Ishtar were more frank about it. . . . Any fashion which gives to a *roué* the right to clasp a pure woman in his arms and hold her for the length of an intoxicating piece of music, is below moral defense."[62]

Still, for the three years of Mrs. Woodhull's presidency, the Spiritualist movement had succeeded in touching a raw nerve in the culture, which some of America's Victorians would have preferred to leave anesthetized. And if heresy be defined as an overemphasis upon a part of the Creed which orthodoxy had been neglecting, these Spiritualist heretics with their physical ghosts and their sexual assertiveness may have been striving, however crudely, to recapture an essential Judaeo-Christian insight. For "the specialty of Christian eschatology lies precisely in its rejection of the Platonic hostility to the body and to 'matter'," writes a radical Freudian critic of our own day, Norman O. Brown. "Hence the affirmation of Tertullian: *Resurget igitur caro, et quidem omnis, et quidem ipsa, et quidem integra*—the body will rise again, all of the body, the identical body, the entire body."

In this sense Victoria Woodhull and Robert Dale Owen may have been more "orthodox" than their more conventional contemporaries, some of whom worshiped a "God everlasting, without body, parts, or passions" and took that definition of Him literally as a model for their own behavior.[63] Those liberal Protestant and Jewish believers in immortality who abandoned the idea of a physical resurrection, as many of them felt they had to in order to come to terms with modern thought,[64] may only have abetted the historic confusion between Biblical faith and Greek philosophy. Inconsistently, some who rejected bodily resurrection became involved in a somewhat morbid debate over the merits of burial versus cremation,[65] a debate the emotional overtones of which suggest that after all it was the material body, not an immaterial soul, whose preservation a great many people really cared about. "Never has the tenement from which vitality has escaped been held so precious as it is to-day," wrote Junius Henri Browne in 1874. "We make a fetish of it. . . . We perpetuate our wretched vanity in housing insensate dust, and carve marble with sonorous fiction to hide the sordid facts of life."[66] The last word on this point had been said a long while before: "Where your treasure is, there will your heart be also."

6

God and Man
in Brooklyn:
The Reputation of
Henry Ward Beecher

"Above all, I was held spellbound by the
last of a series of "protracted meetings" in
the church when the new converts related,
so far as they might desire, the story of
their sinful lives, not forgetting the sins
they had seen committed by others. If
they did not tell everything, they told
enough for a boy to understand what kind
of lives were being lived by some men and
women in the community. . . . It is clear that
in these early formative years I had developed very little interest in religion except
for the light it threw upon secular matters."

Wilbur L. Cross,
reminiscing of the 1870's[1]

"Let the world know this. The Church
looks at the world with profound understanding, with sincere admiration and
with the sincere intention not of conquering it, but of serving it, not of despising it,
but of appreciating it, not of condemning
it, but of strengthening it and saving it."

Pope Paul VI[2]

109

I   HE death of Henry Ward Beecher on March 8, 1887 was front-page news. The President of the United States telegraphed his condolences. The London *Standard* marked the passing of "one of the comparatively few Americans who enjoyed a world-wide reputation"; a visitor from Europe to the United States might have omitted making his pilgrimage to Concord, and left his letter of introduction to Longfellow undelivered, the British newspaper declared, "but to have failed to 'sit under' Mr. Beecher at Plymouth Church would have been like missing Niagara or neglecting to dine at Delmonico's." One Americanized European, Edward Bok, got up at once a memorial volume of tributes from people as diverse as Edwin Booth, the Shakespearian actor; Charles Parnell, the Irish nationalist; seven surviving Civil War generals, both Union and Confederate; the antibusiness critic Henry George, and the business leader Andrew Carnegie; the raw spoilsman Roscoe Conkling, and the impeccable statesman Hamilton Fish; religious leaders ranging from a member of the Shaker sect to the roaring freethinker Bob Ingersoll; and such assorted notables as Mark Hopkins, Edward Eggleston, Louis Pasteur, Elizabeth Blackwell, Alexander Graham Bell, and Anthony Comstock of the New York Society for the Suppression of Vice.[3]

Mindful that this deceased clergyman had shared a platform with Frederick Douglass in his own fashionable Brooklyn church at a time when that militant black leader was being slighted and snubbed in the North, and that he had campaigned not only against slavery in far-off Kansas but also against segregated omnibuses in nearby Manhattan, the Negro clergy of New York City paid tribute by marching in his funeral procession en masse.[4] One nationally prominent rabbi, at the Sabbath-eve services next after his Protestant colleague's passing, further noted that "when anti-Semitism threatened to take hold of certain circles in America [Beecher] championed the cause of the Jews . . . almost alone among the Christian clergy."[5] "A great army would attest," exclaimed the author of the *Battle Hymn of the Republic,* Julia Ward Howe,

To the succor that he gave
To the poor God loveth best,
To the woman, to the slave![6]

111

THE DEATH AND OBSEQUIES OF HENRY WARD BEECHER. THE
FUNERAL PROCESSION ON ITS WAY TO PLYMOUTH CHURCH. THE
13TH REGIMENT SALUTING THE REMAINS OF ITS DECEASED CHAP-
LAIN AT HIS LATE RESIDENCE.

Here and there in this chorus of praise a sour note was sounded. At their
regular weekly meeting on March 7, 1887 the Congregational ministers of
Chicago passed a resolution to send condolences to Mrs. Beecher by so
narrow a margin (18-15) that the mover withdrew his proposal, on the
ground that "an expression of sympathy which was opposed by so many of

the members of the association would fail in its object." (Opponents argued that such a dispatch would commit their group to an endorsement of Beecher's "dangerously heterodox" religious views; they specifically mentioned the Brooklyn pastor's teachings on evolution and on Hell.) But this mean-spirited decision was exceptional. The Methodist ministers of the same city sent a properly compassionate message to the Beecher family, and the secular press denounced the Congregationalist Chicagoans for their display of bigotry: "It had been supposed that even 'Christians' ceased hating each other at the grave, but it would appear from yesterday's proceedings . . . that such is not always the case," said the Chicago *Times*. Far more typical than that discordant wrangle beside Lake Michigan was the handsome encomium which appeared in the *National Cyclopedia of American Biography* six years after Henry Ward Beecher's passing: "It is safe to say that no man, unless it be George Washington, has ever died in America, more widely honored, more deeply loved, or more universally regretted."[7]

Had Beecher died twenty or thirty years earlier, the honors and regrets might have been something less than universal. If British subjects visiting America in 1887 felt that a pilgrimage to Plymouth Church was a "must," other Britons reacted quite differently in 1863 when the pastor of that church visited England. "MEN OF MANCHESTER, ENGLISHMEN!" shouted one of the wall posters that greeted Beecher when he came to that city to lecture for the Union cause. "What reception can you give this wretch, save unmitigated disgust and contempt? His impudence in coming here is only equaled by his cruelty and impiety."[8] In that situation such words may only have reflected the bias of Southern sympathizers; but one of Henry Beecher's fellow veterans of the antislavery crusade, Jonathan Blanchard, was equally harsh: "The history of this extraordinary person, when faithfully written . . . will show him to the coming age, merely as a resplendent and crafty leader of the degeneracy and corruption of his own," Blanchard prophesied in 1872.

For Jonathan Blanchard, who had taken part in Beecher's ordination to the ministry, anger was made keener by personal disappointment. "I loved him as a brother. I admired his genius . . . I was proud of his early successes," the Midwestern educator and religious journalist confessed. But now, as he saw Beecher "sweet and lovely upon a roystering, Christless multitude, dealing out the love of Christ to sinners with the indiscriminate fondness of a successful prostitute who loves everybody who does not condemn her trade," Blanchard recoiled from the man upon whose head in apostolic succession he had once laid his own hands: "The American churches have drunk and are still drinking the poison of his teachings, and their ministry is being debauched by his terrible example."[9]

The same deep loves and hearty hatreds that swirled around Beecher's public activities warmed and stained his private life also, and for one long and painful year—from the summer of 1874 through the summer of 1875— the public and the private controversies merged. "We can recall no one event since the murder of Lincoln that has so moved the people as this question whether Henry Ward Beecher is the basest of men," said the New York *Herald* on July 23, 1874, and "this question" had nothing to do with Beecher's Republican politics, nor his views on the South and slavery, nor his judgment on labor unions, nor even his cautious endorsement of Darwinism; it was whether or not he had committed adultery with the wife of Theodore Tilton.[10]

II   Like a fire that works quietly and long in the sub-surface humus before exploding into the trees, the Beecher-Tilton gossip smoldered in the immediate neighborhood of Plymouth Church for several years before erupting into a national scandal. It flared in September of 1872 in the unlikely environment of Proper Boston, where Victoria Claflin Wood-hull, in the course of reelection to her second term as President of the As-sociation of Spiritualists, poured out before that assembly the whole story, as she understood it, of the Beechers and the Tiltons.[11] It blazed again two months later when *Woodhull & Claflin's Weekly* spread the circumstantial story all over New York.[12] For the moment, the fire was quenched by Anthony Comstock, who hustled Victoria and her sister off to jail for sending obscene matter through the mail; but the story would not down. When the Spiritualists met the following year in Chicago to choose The Woodhull for a third term as their president, many of them also endorsed her charges against Henry Ward Beecher. The convention had not been in session for more than a few minutes when Mrs. Rhoda Loomis, a delegate from Battle Creek, Michigan, rose to read a poem entitled "Progression; or, I Wish It Were Respectable." Much of this was a versified Ingersollish attack on Biblical orthodoxy, aimed at such favorite targets as Elijah and his chariot, Eve and her apple, and Jonah and his whale; but the reader soon modulated from satire on religious belief in general to strong hints about one religious leader's practice in particular.

I wish it were respectable for ministers of grace,
If they have loved another's wife, and *kissed* her out of place,

To be no coward at their posts, but own the truth as well;
And let the world say what it will, and send them straight to Hell.[13]

Then in 1874 Plymouth Church excommunicated Theodore Tilton from membership for slandering his pastor, and Tilton replied by publicly charging the pastor, on the 10th of October, 1868, with having seduced his wife. The scandal was now out in the open, and "through all the offices of the City Hall and County Court House, in the shops, saloons, street cars, parlors, kitchens . . . ," in the overgrown village which was Brooklyn a century ago, one heard of "nothing but Beecher and Tilton, Tilton and Beecher, the livelong day and far into the night."[14] When the Manhattan papers took up the tale they fairly drenched their readers in it. During the second half of the year 1874 the New York *Times* alone ran one hundred and five stories and thirty-seven editorials on the scandal; Tilton and Beecher made Page One seventeen times. Other newspapers carried comparable amounts of copy. The *Times* was restrained in its discussion, perhaps from a sense that this time all the news really was not fit to print; some of the other papers

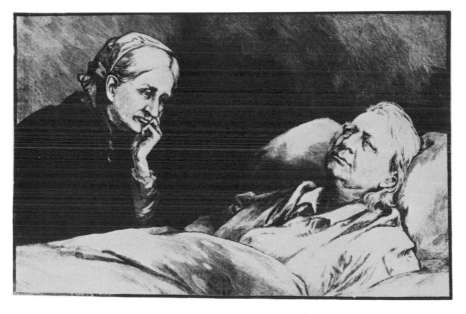

PLYMOUTH'S DYING PASTOR—A FAITHFUL WIFE'S UNTIRING VIGIL.

The same deep loves and hearty hatreds that swirled around Beecher's public activities warmed and stained his private life also.

had fewer inhibitions, and the *Times* itself had a tendency somewhat hypo-critically to wring its editorial hands over the "wild stories" being hawked about by the other papers—and then, on the facing page, repeat them.[15]

It did not remain a neighborhood quarrel for long. Chicago papers had given the Spiritualists' meeting in their city a rather bad press,[16] but they thoroughly discussed this new phase of the controversy, and two of them— the *Inter Ocean* and the *Tribune*—dug back into Beecher's Midwestern career prior to his coming to Brooklyn and broke stories having an important bearing on the case. After *Tilton* v. *Beecher* had gone to formal trial, a monthly in San Francisco, considered the end of the earth in those days, ran an account by E. P. Buffett vividly describing for West Coast readers the end of a typical afternoon in the Brooklyn courtroom as "the curtain drops on the closing scene of a Tilton-*versus*-Beecher matinée." The writer enlarged the actors in the drama into characters Cruikshank might have drawn for a Dickens novel. Tilton looked "like a tiger at bay," Beecher like "a well-to-do farmer," and William R. Evarts, who had successfully defended President Andrew Johnson against the impeachment charges of 1868 and who now was but one of a battery of high-powered lawyers defending Beecher, was "a thin attenuated individual . . . in a black broadcloth dress-suit, which depends from the skeleton it incases as if it had been hastily hung there to be dried after exposure to a sudden shower."[17] Actually it was not necessary for journalists to embroider in this fashion; the words and actions of the principals themselves contained melodrama enough. To study the proceedings of that court is to realize that Mark Twain was less the writer of comic burlesque and more an exact reporter of life than the modern reader sometimes supposes; for the real people involved in *Tilton* v. *Beecher* talked like the fictitious people involved in the Laura trial in Volume II of *The Gilded Age,* published two years earlier. Perhaps it was another case of life imitating art.

By the time it got into Judge Nielson's courtroom, *Tilton* v. *Beecher* had received such a barrage of colorful and contradictory publicity that it had become an impossible case to try. "It would seem difficult in the present universal reading of papers to find any human being, able to spell, who had not read some journal containing portions of the Beecher and Tilton controversy," one of the more responsible of those papers conceded. If a prospective juryman had been following the story regularly he would likely be dismissed for having formed an opinion on the case; "or if he, having been blessed with eyes, had not read anything," he would not be believed. Again and again in the impaneling of a jury the attorneys' questions came down to "Is your opinion formed on what you read in the newspapers?" and again and again, except for one venireman who had been abroad when the scandal broke, they all answered "yes."[18] One splendid comic moment came when a German immigrant, whose only regular newspaper fare was the *New Yorker Presse,* was questioned closely as to his ability to follow the fine shades of meaning which the lawyers were going to torture out of the already ambiguous language in certain letters which had passed between Henry Beecher and Elizabeth Tilton. First they asked him if he had read Schiller, Goethe, Heine, or Lessing, and then if he had read any "English literature—works of English writers."

A. Yes, sir, that is so.
Q. What works were they?
A. Some of them in the fire insurance business, and I get
   some papers from lawyers.

Explaining that that was not what was meant, the examiner asked:

Q. What is literature?
A. I thought you meant a letter.
Q. Do you know what the word "condone" means?
A. Yes, sir; it is a part of a country—condone—county;
   you could not expect that I am a lawyer over here.

After some wrangling the bewildered new citizen was excused.[19]

Under the circumstances they got a jury with commendable speed, but six months later when the trial finally came to an end the jurors debated for eight days, taking fifty-two ballots, and then told the judge they were unable to agree, a verdict which satisfied nobody.[20] As the twentieth-century reader wades through the attacks and rebuttals, the theories and countertheories, as to what Beecher and Tilton and Mrs. Tilton had or had not done, he may find himself as confused about the facts as their contemporaries were, and if he long persists in his search through the bulky bound volumes of newspapers and the fading fine print in the pamphlets and books he may react exactly as the Chicago *Tribune* did when the story flared up again briefly in 1878: "The people are tired of [Tilton]. . . . the people are tired of [Mrs. Tilton], they are tired of Moulton, of the mother-in-law, and of every man, woman and child who has had connection, direct or indirect, with this miserable old scandal."[21] Suiting action to words, the *Tribune* pushed the latest developments in the case off Page One to make room for one of Cook County's more spectacular mass executions.

Paxton Hibben, whose biography of Beecher remains a standard account in spite of its outdated "debunking" approach and inner-monologue style, believed that all the national attention focused on the case was escapist, diverting Americans' attention from their "real" problems: "The nation, still in the grip of the panic of 1873, rendered captious and disillusioned by the discovery of a seemingly unending succession of frauds in municipal, state and national government, gave itself up to the Beecher Scandal as to an anodyne." It was not the fault of the newspapers, thought Francis D. Moulton, one of the leading witnesses, when a reporter interviewed him in 1878; "The public has no morals. It wants all this sort of thing you can give 'em, and the newspapers would be voted a box" if they did not give their readers scandals "with spice and excitement. . . . That is the weakness of the nineteenth century."[22]

But even allowing for the prurience of readers in that Victorian age (or any age), and for the financial lust of publishers to sell newspapers, it is quite possible that in *Tilton* v. *Beecher* certain "real" problems for Americans of that day were indeed on trial. This great bundle of editorials, personal interviews, public statements, reports of how Mrs. Beecher looked and what Tilton was wearing, and the endless rehashings of evidence to which nothing really new was added after the first few weeks, seems to me to have an obsessive, even a compulsive quality, and it is a truism in psychology that an obsession tells us something about the person or persons obsessed. Conceivably *Tilton* v. *Beecher* was one of the great symbolic trials, like those of Bukharin or Dreyfus or Alger Hiss—the kind in which in the minds of partisans the accused must be guilty or must be innocent because of larger issues that turn upon that guilt or innocence.

III   In his opening address for the plaintiff Samuel D. Morris told the jury: "Upon the result of your verdict, to a very large extent . . . will depend the integrity of the Christian religion." Counsel for the defense Benjamin F. Tracy in his own opening statement twisted this remark into a concurrence, and then went on to make his own point: "The questions here involved . . . go down to the very foundations of our social, moral, and religious life." This was no mere matter of deciding whether Tilton had suffered a wrong at the hands of Beecher entitling him to compensatory damages, Tracy argued; "Look at it as we may, it is impossible to separate the defendant from his representative character."[23]

Eventually the Establishment would realize the bind it had gotten itself into by this kind of reasoning. The New York *Times* in its obituary editorial of 1887 found the formula: "It may be said that his [Beecher's] personal conduct was in a sense independent of his work."[24] It was the same kind of disjunctive value judgment that had been made in the meantime on Grover Cleveland's Presidential candidacy: if Cleveland's private life were profligate and his public life above suspicion, whereas with his opponent it was the other way around, then, reasoned one political strategist in 1884, "we should elect Mr. Cleveland to the public office which he is so admirably qualified to fill and remand Mr. Blaine to the private life which he is so eminently fitted to adorn."[25] But this formula does not always work, even with politicians, and for a nationally-known WASP clergyman such a resolution of the difficulty would be out of the question even today.

The trial of *Tilton* v. *Beecher* in short had exposed a flaw endemic in America's entire Puritan-Protestant tradition. Theologically speaking, the more liturgical churches have an "out" in a situation of this kind: if one posits at the outset an objective Sacrament, it follows logically that a bad priest can say a good Mass. But in Puritanism, which had made the forms incidental and the inner experience decisive, this relief was not available; if the minister be corrupt his ministry will be corrupt also, and a church which supports and extenuates him will be in the position of accomplices. Some commentators made a more specifically sectarian point out of this. *El Diario* of Havana devoted a short article to the Beecher-Tilton scandal and expressed the opinion that the affair would "redound to the benefit and progress of Catholicism in the United States." The American Catholic apologist Isaac Hecker agreed, as he called a plague on both Beecher and Tilton: "If the Congregational pastor of Plymouth Church affords a sad example of the impotence of emotional pietism, the unfortunate plaintiff in the lawsuit against him is no less a melancholy instance of the aberrations of the last phase of American Protestantism." As evidenced by "developments such as Mormonism and the Oneida Community [and] the increasing frequency of divorce," the editor of the *Catholic World* concluded, "the morality of Protestantism offered no assistance to the individual in this conflict between reason and the excesses of that instinct which is at once the most necessary and at the same time the least governable."[26]

Moreover, as the Chicago *Tribune* editorialized, "Mr. Beecher has been a kind of Pope among Protestants. . . . He is known and read in England, in Switzerland, in Germany, in France. His influence for good or evil is co-extensive with his reputation." Some rigorous souls therefore drew the logical conclusion; if the minister were guilty, the Church would be better off without him, regardless of injury to what we would nowadays call its "image"; *if thine eye offend thee, pluck it out.* Beecher should either "refute the charges against him," the *Tribune* continued, or else he should "come forward, confess his guilt and retire from a position which no one but a pure man should fill."[27]

On the other hand, even that belligerent newspaper had noted that it was the accused clergyman's reputation, rather than his character, upon which rested his influence for good or evil. Hypocrisy has been defined as the tribute vice pays to virtue, and the nagging pressure of a Victorian culture may therefore have suggested quite another answer to the question. Beecher should not merely be given the benefit of the doubt and assumed to be innocent until proven guilty; for the sake of the Church, and therefore of society as a whole, he should be considered innocent even if in fact he were proven guilty. In the words of a letter to the editor of the New York *Herald*:

> I can only deplore that one who has been a shining light to his fellows for so many years should have been placed before the tribunal of censure and criticism from any *real or imaginary* acts of his own. . . . For the good of humanity and all future religious teachers I pray that he may come out unscathed. . . . To err is human, to forgive divine.

But this amounted to saying that there was one standard of justice for all sorts and conditions of men, and quite another for the clergy. The French and American Revolutions had presumably been fought to get rid of that sort of thing. A member of one much-maligned lay profession wrote an indignant rebuttal, also printed in the *Herald*: "If it was an actor or an actress . . . how they would investigate, how they would point to it as an awful warning to those who visit places of amusement." He made bitter reference to the ministers of Manhattan, who had refused Christian burial to one veteran actor "not for any crime of his own . . . but because he belonged to a profession which they, in their sanctity, were pleased to outlaw."[28] It was particularly ironic that this comment should have been made in a discussion of Henry Ward Beecher, the author of a famous thundering paragraph against show business: "If you would pervert the taste—go to the Theatre. If you would imbibe false views—go to the Theatre. . . . If you would be infected with each particular vice in the catalogue of Depravity—go to the Theatre!"[29]

To its great credit, most of the secular press declined to accept a double standard for ministers and laymen in its coverage of the Beecher-Tilton scandal. "The maintenance of justice, blind to all distinctions of wealth, intellect, or position, is of much greater importance to a nation than the preservation of any individual reputation, however valuable that reputation may be," stated the New York *Times.* The Hartford *Courant* had "never been required to perform a sadder or more distasteful" duty than that of printing Tilton's statement of the charges—"Mr. Beecher has been such a power for good," et cetera—but "the whole truth must be known," whatever it may be. If professional churchmen were worried lest a black mark against the good name of so eminent a colleague might rub off on all of them, said the Springfield *Republican,* they should have thought of that sooner; "The fact is that the newspapers have kept silent about it for six years, and never would have mentioned it if it had not been forced upon them by the clerical professors and by the religious press."

"We know this to be true," the New York *Times* agreed, "for we have ourselves suppressed hundreds of 'statements' and letters which have been sent to us on this subject." They had sat on the story as long as they decently could, and had refrained from printing any of this undocumented gossip. But then Theodore Tilton himself had forced the issue by making a formal accusation, detailing actions, dates, and places; now, suddenly, there were sworn statements, "public documents such as a newspaper has no right to suppress," said the *Times,* "even though the scandal will do more to injure the young, and weaken the cause of religion in the eyes of the unthinking, than anything which has happened for many a long day."[30]

IV   Once the ice had been broken, the newspapers speedily began to choose up sides.[31] Paxton Hibben has noted that as the scandal and the trial wore on the evenly balanced scale began to tip, as one by one the major newspapers—Samuel Bowles's Springfield *Republican,* Joseph Medill's Chicago *Tribune,* Charles Dana's New York *Evening Sun*— dropped away from Beecher.[32] But Hibben neglected to add that several influential journals of news and opinion stood by the Plymouth pastor to the bitter end. "The real result is not to be found in the formal verdict of the jury, but in the general impression," said *Harper's Weekly,* "for as the evidence in no cause was more universally read, so the verdict in every man's breast was never more entirely independent of that of the court-room"— and that independent verdict was for acquittal. The editor of *Scribner's Monthly* agreed: "That he has been washed clean by the waters up through which he has come is the verdict, at last, of the majority of the American people."[33] In short, the partisans of Henry Ward Beecher said in effect, "In your heart you know he's right," no matter what the lawyers say.[34]

At an earlier stage in the proceedings Theodore Tilton's own little paper, the *Golden Age,* conceded that "there is scarcely a man or woman in America but hopes [Beecher] is innocent . . . , and tries to believe him so in spite of circumstantial evidence confirmed by his own course."[35] Facing the most prominent preacher in the United States, backed by an affluent congregation prepared to cover most of Beecher's trial expenses by voting him a salary for that year of $100,000 (a vote "without any parallel in the history of a religious or secular body," said *Harper's Weekly*[36]), Tilton must have felt at times as if he were not the plaintiff but the defendant.[37] Facing the widely-held belief that an attack on that preacher was an attack on the whole Church in America, Tilton's attorney's tried to counter with the equally sacrosanct American principle that the law is no respecter of persons, even when the person in question is named Henry Ward Beecher. But six months before the opening of the trial this clear-cut course of action was fatally compromised by one unpremeditated outcry of Tilton's own.

Under cross-examination before the Plymouth Church's own investigating committee (hand picked by Beecher himself), and goaded by the attempt of his questioner—Benjamin Tracy, one of the same attorneys whom he would later face in court—to shift public attention from the pastor's amours to Tilton's own, the tormented husband cried:

> Thank God, I am not a minister! I want you to put that down, Mr. Stenographer. . . . I love God, but I despise the Church. I saw the cowardice of the Church in the great anti-slavery fight, and it has always been false. But Elizabeth has always had a reverence for the Church. . . I had to reject [some of its teachings] and it disturbed her very much.[38]

The outburst was humanly understandable, especially under those circumstances. But the battle was thereby joined at an emotional level such that it made an objective trial of Tilton's cause all but impossible. Tilton's admission when the chips were down that he despised the Church was the last straw, from the standpoint of orthodoxy, and as a matter of fact Tilton's heterodox statements before that Plymouth Church committee—"I do not believe in one of the thirty-nine articles, nor in either of the catechisms, nor in the divine inspiration of Scriptures, nor in the divinity of Christ," and so on[39]—became an integral part of Beecher's attorneys' argument against Tilton at the trial.

In one powerful oratorical burst Benjamin Tracy called the jury's attention to the "startling likeness" between the features of Tilton's key witness, Francis D. Moulton—"the red matted hair, the low forehead, the sharp, angular face, the cold and remorseless eye"—and those of the Judas in Leonardo's painting of the Last Supper! At this incredible bit of demagoguery, said the *Times* reporter, "the Plymouth Church portion of the audience broke out in a round of applause," which was at once suppressed by Judge Nielson.[40] We have seen in the previous chapters that in America's Gilded Age the decline of faith was a matter for considerable public and private anxiety, and an astute trial lawyer always knows the general temper of his audience; still, from the standpoint of twentieth-century judicial construction of the First Amendment's "establishment clause," it is a wonder that Tilton did not take an appeal on constitutional grounds.

Counsel for the plaintiff foresaw this line of attack and tried to anticipate it, both in their own oral arguments and earlier while they were impaneling the jury. So we find them asking a prospective juror "Do you consider that the interests of Christianity are involved in this trial?" "Do you conceive that the character of the Christian ministry is involved in this trial?" "Do you take a religious newspaper?"—and getting "no's" on all three before accepting him.[41] But the precautions were insufficient. Shoddy though it sounds to modern ears, Beecher's attorneys got a great deal of mileage out of the argument that they were not lawyers pleading for a client but soldiers of Christ defending the faith.

The irony in all this is that in some quarters Beecher himself was considered dangerously destructive of the ancestral pieties. A minister of the African Methodist Episcopal Church, interviewed by the New York *Herald* in 1874, praised Beecher's actions for racial justice and stoutly defended his innocence in the Tilton scandal, but added, "I am not a Beecher man. . . . For me he has never preached the Gospel enough."[42] Another incident from the trial will further illustrate the irony. Francis Moulton was an avowed freethinker, and Beecher's counsel therefore not only compared his physiognomy with that of Judas Iscariot but also tried to impugn his testimony, which was most damaging to Beecher, on the ground that "a man who . . . scoffs at the idea of future accountability" cannot be trusted under oath; why should he tell the truth if he does not believe God is going to punish him after death if he lies? Yet Beecher himself in a sermon on "Future Punishment" had already rejected most of the specific imagery ("fire and brimstone, darkness or lurid light, the sword, scorpions, gnawing worms") as poetic embroidery, and two years after the trial he publicly and explicitly rejected any belief in Hell.[43]

To be sure, Henry Ward Beecher's heterodoxies were carefully attuned to the sensibilities of his hearers. Even in the antislavery movement he had been something of a Johnny-come-lately; his archcritic Jonathan Blanchard, himself a veteran of that movement, noted in a long obituary editorial on Beecher that at a time when "Garrison was mobbed—as we all were at that day—Lovejoy, a Congregational minister, was shot at Alton; Amos Dresser, a tract missionary was whipped five hundred lashes in Tennessee; . . . and George Storrs, a Methodist preacher, was dragged from his knees while praying in an abolition meeting in New Hampshire," Henry Ward Beecher had preferred to "observe from a distance when the popular tide should turn."[44] As for the new heresy of Darwinism, Beecher told Herbert Spencer in 1882 that he had been a "cordial Christian evolutionist" for twenty years, but in 1874, while embroiled in a public struggle for existence of his own, he hedged. "You know very well that I do not believe in the technical theology that man fell from a state of perfection, because he never had such a state to fall from," he told his congregation on July 5, 1874, two Sundays after Tilton had formally charged him with adultery. "I believe that he began at the bottom . . . and that he has been working his way up all the time since." But the pastor covered himself at once by saying "I do not mean to give in my faith to the theory that man ever was a brute absolute," even though Darwin's *Descent of Man* had been in print already for three years.[45]

V   Paradoxically, Beecher's other-directed opportunism may have made him more effective as a bringer of new ideas into the church than outright and honest religious radicalism would have been. To a really rigorous champion of orthodoxy, a man like Beecher was far more dangerous than an avowed infidel like Robert Ingersoll,[46] because he promoted his heresies in the guise of the old-time religion. "When Henry Ward Beecher is about to assail some fundamental truth, held and suffered for by the Puritans, he always begins by proclaiming himself their descendant," wrote Jonathan Blanchard in 1872. Some liberal rationalists of the period found the Plymouth pastor's preaching enthralling for the very reason Blanchard and other religious conservatives found it objectionable. He might conduct his church services "upon the ancient model, and chiefly in the ancient phraseology," James Parton reported in 1867, but "from the moment when Mr. Beecher swings from the moorings of his text and gets fairly under way, his sermon is modern. . . . His text may savor of old Palestine, but his sermon is inspired by New York and Brooklyn." Beecher was thus able to preach, in a way that pleased both the liberal and the orthodox, "sermons which Edwards and Voltaire, Whitefield and Tom Paine might have enjoyed."

This kind of popular preaching was of course open to the same criticism that in a later day has been leveled at television: if it had something for everybody it had not much for anybody. (That may be why these sermons have proved so ephemeral; both Edwards and Paine are still intensively studied, but who reads Beecher today?) And not even Henry Ward Beecher could be all things to all men all the time. There were some wild inconsistencies in the pastor's discourse, Parton admitted; some of his own "thorough-going friends" wanted to know how a man could prove that the fall of rain was governed by pure cause and effect, and then "finish by *praying* for an immediate outpouring upon the thirsty fields?" But to James Parton, objections of this nature were beside the point. In the transition that American religion was then going through even Beecher's contradictions and vagueness were helpful. Quoting with approval Lecky's dictum that old dogmas do not die because they are refuted but fade away because they are neglected, Parton concluded: "Mr. Beecher has helped himself to such beliefs as are congenial to him, and shows an exquisite tact in passing by those which interest him not, and which have lost their regenerating power."[47]

So exquisite was Beecher's tact in passing over the beliefs which did not interest him that in 1879 a Jewish lecturer, attacking "dogmatic Christianity" for its inherent illiberalism and uncharitableness, made an exception in favor of what it was the fashion for some Christian ministers to preach to their flocks and call orthodoxy: "I do not refer, for instance, to that Christianity so called which the Rev. Mr. Beecher preaches."[48] This, even though Beecher was the author of a *Life of Jesus, the Christ*! Joseph Brandon intended his remark as a tribute to Beecher's lack of theological intolerance, and of the unconsciously insulting judgment on Judaism from which even the best-intentioned of Christians find it hard to escape; but the compliment can also be taken as a comment on the fuzzy quality of what Beecher had to say. It is a familiar intellectual dilemma for Americans: the achievement of charity at the price of clarity.

Should the Plymouth pastor have taken sides in any clear-cut way "with either the death or the resurrection that is going on in his own unconscious entrails," wrote one reviewer of Beecher's *Lecture-Room Talks* in 1870, "his providential significance would at once subside into the measure of his intelligence, which is by no means a large measure." His function as a broker of ideas was legitimate and important, but an originating thinker he was not. He might indeed be a "golden chrysalis" between "the base grub of men's servile ritual devotion" and "the soaring butterfly of their emancipated scientific hopes," but pupation is not a process requiring intellectual endeavor. Or to change the metaphor, "Mr. Beecher is at most the friendly duck that incubates the egg of destiny; he is not for a moment to be mistaken for the royal bird that lays it."[49]

But such traits in the pastor of Plymouth Church, taken by themselves, do not go very far toward explaining the emotional heat generated by the Tilton-Beecher scandal. If mere logical vagueness were a crime, few Americans would go unpunished! The trouble was that "infidelity" in the strictly theological sense—that is, unbelief—had always been rhetorically confused with the more popular usage of that word; in our own century, "adultery" and "want of belief in (a certain) religion," along with "breach of trust," all remained acceptable dictionary definitions.[50] If Henry Ward Beecher was vague and self-contradictory in the way he defended the old-time religion, was he also vague and self-contradictory in his practice of the old-time morality?

Here and there a worldly-wise soul declined to take the whole matter with such intense seriousness. When Theodore Tilton publishd his formal charge a prominent layman of another denomination noted the fact in his diary, but added: "Probably Beecher . . . went in merely for a little pious evangelical flirtation and fun."[51] In the reign of Queen Victoria—and morally she reigned at least as effectively in America as in England—so flippant a judgment would itself have seemed shocking. "We rely on the continence of clergymen and physicians," wrote one reader of the New York *Herald,* "we trust them implicitly with our wives and daughters, of whom we are fiercely jealous in other men's cases." Damage to the Church's reputation or no, "if there be offence in this matter in a congregation it must be purged out." And let it not be supposed, this correspondent went on, that clergymen were peculiarly immune to the temptations which beset other kinds of men.

> The mistake is to suppose that a theological curriculum or the ministerial profession roots out the old Adam. Clergymen are a little better than most other men, but not so very much. . . . To men who know the world the continence of popular preachers is a wonder. They are tried to the utmost, especially if young, good looking and what the world calls "magnetic".[52]

Beecher was no longer young, nor would that fleshy Tweedledum figure have been accounted good-looking by the streamlined standards of a later age; perhaps we may concede the magnetism. As for his having been "tried to the utmost," Beecher's defenders—with the unhelpful exception of Victoria Woodhull, who argued that the Plymouth pastor by his actions had lent his great influence to the cause of free love[53]—denied it as a matter of course. "His bearing . . . has been that of a man who knew that the dark shadow in

which he moved was that of slander, not of guilt," *Harper's Weekly* declared,[54] and Beecher himself played to a hilt the role of the winsomely innocent man.

On July 5, 1874, two Sundays after the story broke, he preached the
usual farewell sermon preceding his summer vacation, as scheduled, and
according to the New York *Herald* his discourse "was in the jubilant, confident, earnest, hearty strain of Mr. Beecher's best days, and showed that
recent outside troubles had disconcerted him but little." Following the
sermon Beecher administered communion and afterward shook hands with
the members of the congregation; "Mr. Beecher was the happiest counte-
nanced man of the assembly," the *Herald's* reporter concluded, "and pre-
served his characteristic self-composure throughout this very severe ordeal."[55]
Again, the following January, soon after the opening of the trial, he told
his regular Friday night prayer meeting that he was "placed now in a position
which might be called a new ordination, or imposition of hands. . . . Instead
of being a suffering creature, I am probably the happiest man in the whole
nation." Was this the testament of an untroubled spirit, or was it all a
consummate actor's bluff?

With the evidence in the case so hotly controverted, Beecher's demeanor
was really about all the man in the street had to go on, and on the whole the
performance was impressive. But now and again he behaved in a manner
suggesting that a mask had slipped. For example, two Sundays after the
"happiest man" remark a hearer with any knack for sensing psychological
overtones, who listened to the cadences of Beecher's pastoral prayer in an
analytical rather than a devotional mood, might pardonably have wondered
just how close the preacher was sailing to the wind: "Thy ways seem strange
because we are so unpracticed in spiritual things. We are constantly measuring life by the measure of the body," the accused minister cried. "Our minds
are now clear and now clouded again by our passions; but our reliance is
in thy steadfastness . . ." The *Times* man said, "Mr. Beecher had gradually
warmed in the fervor of his delivery, and the last sentences sounded like a
despairing cry for succor." Then he preached on Philippians 4:11, "I have
learned in whatever station I may be placed to be content," and shortly he
was back in his usual form; the newspaper's account of the sermon itself
was punctuated nine times by "[Laughter]".[56]

VI   The inability not to crack a joke, in that humorless
situation, may have contributed in large measure to Beecher's undoing. A
troubled theologian in Bonn University who had heard him preach thought

that such polemical value as these sermons might otherwise have had was blunted by the Plymouth pastor's little pulpit jokes, which broke the force of his thrusts by provoking the assembly to mirth: "Under the influence of these witticisms impressions of sin and wrong are soon forgotten. Edification gives place to entertainment."[57] Popular preacher though Henry Ward Beecher was, many in that morally solemn age considered such conduct in church altogether unseemly. If Phillips Brooks thought Beecher "the greatest preacher of America and of our century," Brooks's own father did not agree: "Do you suppose [Beecher's] congregation go to hear him as a Christian minister?" William Gray Brooks wrote in 1864 to his son. "No, it is all for his allusions and quaint expressions . . . and they are followed up by *applause*. It is sad to see the house of God and the pulpit so debased."[58] Whatever Henry Ward Beecher had once said about the dangers of going to the theater, wrote George Templeton Strong, "A capital low comedian was lost to mankind when he [Beecher] 'professed religion.' "[59]

But at least a preacher who joked about sacred things was better than one who moaned over them, Beecher's defenders might have replied. "It is the misfortune of the world to have it understood that righteousness is sad and painful, and that joy and hilarity are to be sought for in an unspiritual life," he preached on that same memorable Sunday just before his 1874 summer vacation. The Christian religion had come down to modern man "stained through and through with the ascetic element," from which it ought to be purged; the gospel of Christ rightly understood was one of joy, not gloom. Much of the spiritual wrestling traditionally associated with Judaeo-Christian religion was unnecessary, Beecher thought; as he had remarked a decade and a half earlier, "There are many troubles which you can't cure by the Bible and Hymn-book, but which you can cure by a good perspiration and a breath of fresh air."[60]

Under Beecher's tutelage "religion seemed a natural experience, something for every-day use, something to be enjoyed." He read from the Bible with the same naturalness, "utterly avoiding the professional 'holy tone' but developing the spirit and meaning of the passage . . . precisely as he would have done a passage from any other book," and those Friday night prayer meetings seem to have been marked by a pleasant informality and a psychological tact rare indeed in the pushing, hard-sell, "have-you-been-saved-brother" tradition of American evangelism.[61] Beecher's admirers were inclined to see him as a man with "a hearty, joyous nature, touching human life at every point . . . at home in streets and towns; . . . jumping on the street-car in motion"—in short, as a man in harmony with the things of this world, *just as his opponents said he was.* With rare candor, Henry Ward Beecher once explained why he and the evangelist Dwight L. Moody "could not work together": "Mr. Moody thinks this is a lost world, and is trying to save as many as possible from the wreck; I think Jesus Christ has come to save the world, and I am trying to help him save it."[62]

THE REV. HENRY WARD BEECHER, PASTOR OF PLYMOUTH CHURCH, TAKING THE INSTALLATION OATH AS CHAPLAIN OF THE 13TH REGIMENT, N.G.S.N.Y., AT THE REGIMENTAL ARMORY, FULTON AND FLATBUSH AVENUES, BROOKLYN, MARCH 1ST.

Beecher's admirers were inclined to see him as a man . . . in touch and harmony with the things of this world, just as his opponents said he was.

To the liberal Christian of a later day, striving to accept and embrace "the secular city," such preachment might sound old hat; but in Beecher's time it came to many of his hearers as the height of heresy. Methodism since its inception had gone on the assumption that "between true Christians and the world, with its fashions and lusts, there was a very wide chasm, without any middle ground," declared the influential Methodist weekly the *Christian Advocate* (of New York), in an editorial printed shortly before Theodore Tilton made public his charges. "It is only when the heart is without the rich consolations of religion that it hungers and thirsts after the pleasures of the world," that leading denominational paper said, in response to one reader, a loyal Methodist for fifty-eight years, who had written to inquire of its editorial opinion on "worldly amusements." "Ministers especially should act with great circumspection in these things," the *Advocate* explained.

> Playing at some few of the least exceptionable kinds of popular games may not be absolutely incompatible with soul-saving; but it must be in very peculiar and rare cases that the two can be made to work together to advantage. The act of the minister that seems entirely harmless, and perhaps is so as to himself, may afterward bear its fruit in another person in all the horrors of dissipation and debauchery.[63]

The potentially corrupting pastime about which the aged reader had made worried inquiry was croquet!

In the context of a Christianity so scrupulously self-denying as this, Henry Ward Beecher's portrayal of religion as "a natural experience, something for everyday use, something to be enjoyed" must have come to many with liberating force. It is curious that in a pleasure-loving modern America trying to shake off the last of what it calls the "Protestant work-ethic" in favor of a "fun morality" this aspect of Beecher's ministry has received so little attention. In spite of all those laudatory obituary notices, the twentieth-century consensus on Beecher has been generally adverse.[64] At best, writes Robert Handy, Beecher was merely a man with a genius for expressing "to perfection what his huge congregations were thinking."[65] But if Beecher's huge congregations were thinking about religion as something natural and joyous, then by implication their own life-style was something radically different from what we have been taught was typical of Gilded-Age America. What Henry Ward Beecher preached was a kind of qualitative hedonism,[66] and that may very well have been what was really on trial in Brooklyn in 1875.

Ordinarily we have followed Sinclair Lewis in attributing much that was meretricious and even positively harmful in the United States in the twentieth century to the influence of the pastor of Plymouth Church, Brooklyn: "Though we speak with the brisk quack of the radio, our words are still too often the lordly lard of Henry Ward Beecher."[67] But the ever-perceptive

Vernon Louis Parrington managed (perhaps by a rhetorical trick) to link Henry Ward Beecher's discourse with Walt Whitman's, in a paragraph describing the rise in the Gilded Age of "a youthful paganism, lusty, and vigorous," which proclaimed "a glorification of the physical that put to rout the traditional Hebraisms."[68] Coming from Parrington, in the light of what he had written earlier about those "Hebraisms" (by which he meant America's entire Puritan heritage), this assessment of Beecher can be interpreted as rather high praise. It would make the Plymouth pastor an ancestor not of bigotry and reaction in the Twenties, as Paxton Hibben and Sinclair Lewis assumed, but rather of the mental and moral liberations we ordinarily associate with those same years.[69]

There is another, and in terms of the moral flux of our own day a fascinating, possibility. Lyman Abbott, Henry Ward Beecher's successor as pastor of Plymouth Church and editor of the *Christian Union*, recalled that he had once asked Beecher to give him "an article on how to keep well. 'There are but three rules,' he replied: 'Eat well, sleep well, and laugh well.' " "And love well?" a speculative contemporary might have completed that quotation. Frank Moulton's testimony, purporting to tell what Beecher, man-to-man, had confided to him about his relationship with Elizabeth Tilton, refused to type-cast the pastor of Plymouth Church according to the two-valued moral logic of Victorianism, according to which Beecher must be either the suffering innocent or the remorseful transgressor; instead Moulton made him sound like a pioneer of what we now call the "New Morality" who did not quite have the courage of his convictions. "I think God will not blame me for my acts with her," Moulton said Beecher had said. "I know that at present it would be utterly impossible for me to justify myself before man."

Beecher's and Moulton's flamboyant contemporary Victoria Claflin Woodhull expressed the same idea with considerably more verve. "I ask you to be happy, and then you will be virtuous," that radical feminist cried in her moment of triumph before the Spiritualists' Chicago convention of 1873. "You have the right to love one woman or forty women, and nobody has any right to say no. And no one has the right to exercise any tyranny over my sexual organs any more than they have over the processes of thought in my brain." As for Henry Ward Beecher, she declared in her initial blast for *Woodhull & Claflin's Weekly*, he had "permitted himself . . . to be over-awed by public opinion. The fault with which I . . . charge him is not infidelity to the old ideas, but unfaithfulness to the new."[70]

The New York *Times* rejected Moulton's testimony as a "disgusting series of prurient innuendoes," and, like the American press generally, treated "The Woodhull" with a mixture of alarm and scoffing contempt. But that news- paper did dimly perceive the danger, from the standpoint of a Victorian culture, of holding up as a model a man who preached a gospel of exuberance, of spontaneity, of loving overflow—and who seemed to some of his con- temporaries to be also a man who lived that way. It was an ambivalence characteristic of Gilded-Age America, if not of Western Civilization as a whole at that time: the freewheeling, untrammeled individual is good for society, but the full use of that freedom is dangerous; Nietzsche is the alter ego of Ralph Waldo Emerson. "There is only one good result which can possibly follow from this exposure and trial," said the *Times* after the jury's disagreement. "It may lead people in Brooklyn and elsewhere to distrust the new Gospel of Love."[71]

7

The Mammon of Unrighteousness

He doth execute the judgment of the
fatherless and widow, and loveth the
stranger, in giving him food and raiment.
Love ye therefore the stranger: for ye
were strangers in the land of Egypt.

Lev. 10:18–19 (KJV)

I   ⊚ HANKSGIVING Day in America has been more often than not an occasion for vulgar self-congratulation, and the ordinary Thanksgiving sermon is one of the dreariest specimens of the homiletic art.[1] But once in a while a searching and prophetic judgment does break through, even in such an unlikely place as a handsome Romanesque church facing on Boston's Copley Square. There, on Thanksgiving Day, 1888, Phillips Brooks preached to his well-fed parishioners in Trinity Church not of the blessings they should count, but of the widespread "fear that the world we live in is growing to be a sadder world, that happiness is less spontaneous and abundant as the years go by." Seeking to explain this malaise, Brooks touched on "the vague way in which our complicated life puts us in one another's power," and on the presence of terror in men's lives because "vast, unmeasured forces hold us in their hands"; he spoke of

> the larger view of the world, the clearer atmosphere, so that we hear the groans of misery in Mexico or Turkey. The curtain has fallen between the rich and the poor; the poor look into our luxurious homes with their haggard faces, and we eat and talk and sleep in the unceasing sound of their temptation and distress.[2]

Rich Americans in the Eighties ate and talked and slept in the sound of poor Americans' distress—and of their anger. "Lean Starvation glares greedily at rotund Plenty, and Despair scowls at self-satisfied Sanctity crossing the church-door," said the *Catholic World* in 1886, the year of the Haymarket bombing. "The blessings we boast of—with more pride than gratitude —have not been equally distributed, or have been diverted from their original destination by cunning hands, and the voices of millions of our fellow-men cry out against us."[3] In that same year of Haymarket the humane-hearted Reverend Washington Gladden, mindful though he was of optimists' assurances "that there was no such thing as a labor question except in the minds of a few crazy agitators," looked out at the combinations and countercombinations of pyramiding monopolies against the armies of the discontented, at strikes and lockouts and rioting, at "children's faces pale with hunger, and women's sunken eyes," and concluded: "The state of industrial society is a state of war, and the engagement is general all along the line."[4]

Of course there had been outcries like this in America from churchmen before. H. L. Hastings wrote during the Civil War that men were growing "rich in multitudes," sometimes by "open, honest, and energetic toil" but more often by "secret craft, or damnable fraud, or open war"; by slave trading, by pushing opium, by kidnapping coolie labor, by exploiting the peoples of India. They grew rich "amid the rattle of machinery, where thousands toil for scanty graves," and the world grew no better for it. Quite the reverse; the piling up of wealth was not a signal of progress but a "sign of the times" (Matt. 16:1–3), forecasting the last days of the wrathful judgment of God. In 1865 the Anglo-Catholic priest James DeKoven, at the opposite pole in his theology from the millennialist Hastings, painted an almost equally dark picture of modern society, burdened with the guilt of exterminating the American Indian, plagued with racial inequality in spite of the technical emancipation of America's slaves, and ravaged by the strange and terrible weapons which had displaced knife and club in the waging of civilized warfare. To remedy these dreadful evils the palliatives of personal good will and the traditional charities of the Church were altogether inadequate; "philanthropy" DeKoven likened to "a kind-hearted but ignorant nurse, who watches by the bedside of one ill of some mortal disease."[5]

When it came to practical attacks on the evils they described, such men had less to say. To a critic like Hastings, there seemed little reason to attempt repairs to damaged social machinery if the world was coming to an end anyhow. Like some young dissenters a century later, who would also judge The System so corrupt that the only valid protest was to "turn off" or "drop out" of it altogether, this dissenter of the 1860's cried out: "Now is our time to sever our connection with the governments of this world." To a High Churchman like DeKoven, the only real solution to "the problems which arise from inequality of race and condition" was the unity of mankind in a universal church, and the coming of such a unity must be more God's doing than man's: "The American mind may believe in a self-made man, but never in a self-made church"—a striking reversal of Tom Paine's sturdy judgment that a man's true church is his own mind.[6]

But at least Hastings and DeKoven were willing to call a spade a spade. In contrast, the overwhelming majority of American clergymen of their day, far from diagnosing the evils of the times as evils, either denied or ignored them (personal "sins" excepted); the existing social order was either irrelevant to the religious man or it was an unmitigated blessing. For Protestantism in particular this period was a time when the gospel of Christ was felt to be in full harmony with the Gospel of Wealth.[7] In certain other directions the clergymen of the Seventies did wrestle with the problems of modernity, as we have seen; but their acceptance of the challenges from biology and geology may have actually inhibited their response to the challenges of industrial society. If the mounting skepticism toward the Bible was undercutting the literal face value of stories like that of Joshua making the sun stand still, it undercut the literal face value of everything else in Holy Writ as well—including such admonitions as "Go and sell that thou hast, and give to the poor."

The Social Gospeler, as we should now call him—the person who believed that his religious concerns necessarily involved action within the social order —seems by comparison with the general run of Gilded-Age individualists to have been an avant-gardesman, looking forward to the collective and reformist temper of a later day. But judged on the basis of what claimed to be the most up-to-date scientific knowledge of the 1870's, his moral condemnation of monopolistic wealth and the exploitation of labor might have sounded a bit archaic and naïve. The Hebrew scriptures, considered as a serious account of the history and destiny of man, were a literary fossil, quaint but irrelevant. Darwinism had explained how man got from the slime to where he now is, and social Darwinism explained how all things work together for the common good, including the Erie Railroad and Standard Oil, with every man—mansion dweller or slum inmate—getting exactly what he deserves.[8] Therefore, to have applied literally to the high and mighty of Washington and New York and Chicago the attacks by the prophets of Yahweh upon the high and mighty of ancient Israel would have seemed like sentimental nonsense.[9]

Herbert Gutman has shown that the pages of labor newspapers in the Gilded Age were filled with what amounted to a Social Gospel, denouncing the Mammon of Unrighteousness, likening the trade union movement to the hoped-for brotherhood of man under the laws of God, and holding up the model of Jesus the Carpenter, Who chose his followers from among workingmen like Himself and Who was blacklisted and at last judicially murdered by "the conservative goody good people" for "disturbing the national order of things." Metaphors were found in the Old Testament also; under God's command an "attempt at organizing labor" was carried out by " 'the Walking Delegates,' Moses and Aaron, for the purpose of redeeming Israel from Egyptian task-masters."[10] (Negro activists, of course, had long used this same kind of imagery.)[11] But how potent would such arguments have been for people who were sensitized to the more radical kinds of German Biblical criticism, which cast doubt on the very existence of Moses, and in its most extreme form even of Christ? Science-minded members of the comfortable classes could thus have discounted as uneducated any labor leader or union member who offered a "social gospel" based literally upon the Bible, and thereby dismissed his legitimate economic grievances as well. Religious and political enlightenment, which the liberal intellectual is prone to think go hand in hand, seem in the Gilded Age to some degree to have worked at cross purposes.

II   The social Christianity preached by trade unionists seems to have had little or no formal connection with "the more widely known and well-studied social gospel put forth by middle- and upper-class religious critics" of Gilded-Age society; "the two groups . . . rarely addressed each other and usually spoke to different audiences," Gutman writes. In Henry May's view, the affluent constituents of Phillips Brooks and Washington Gladden were awakened at last to the needs of America's poor by the great social earthquakes—the "Molly Maguire" violence in the Pennsylvania coal mines, the nationwide railroad strike of 1877, the Haymarket episode—that rocked the nation in the Seventies and Eighties.[12] But one writer, C. M. Morse, thought in 1889 that these troubles might be having exactly the reverse effect; instead of bringing the Church to a greater consciousness of its social responsibility, the class cleavages of the Gilded Age might be driving it further into reaction.

> Intensifying social struggles are working a transformation in the character of the church, [which] is manifest from the new terminology coming into general use, such as "star preachers," "first-class churches," "wealthy congregations," and "our poor charges." The obverse of this is found in the expressions of the working-men: "We can't dress well enough to go to church"; "your leading members don't notice us on the street"; "your preachers run after the rich"; "the ministers side against us in the matter of strikes."

The author concluded that "the churches, slow to accept . . . reform, have reached the last stage of conservatism." In the meantime, Morse argued, the workingmen's own religious faith was being ground down by the wheels of industry.

> By stress of circumstances, individuals are compelled to seek bread and butter first, and that secured, they are too weary and discouraged to think much about the crown laid up for the faithful. There is more anxiety about securing a home here, than about winning a title to "the home over there."

Perhaps these developments were inevitable. "It may be . . . that the old conception of a Christian church, as the one place where all sorts and conditions of men came together . . . , is not adapted to modern society," James Parton wrote in 1867. "It may be that never again, as long as time shall endure, will ignorant and learned, masters and servants, poor and rich, feel themselves at home in the same church." The cultural differential might be even more crucial than the fiscal one: "What form of service can be even imagined, that could satisfy Bridget, who cannot read, and her mistress, who comes to church cloyed with the dainties of half a dozen literatures?"[13]

That such a form had been devised centuries before, and was even then satisfying both well-read ladies and their illiterate servant girls, in New York quite as much as in Dublin, seems altogether to have escaped this Brahmin Bostonian observer. Understandably, therefore, American Catholic writers attacked Protestantism for its lack of social as well as of theological universality. "Would it be prudent for the Protestant Church here in America to wage war against wealth or its unjust acquisition?" asked H. P. Smyth in the *Catholic World* for April, 1886. "Its ministers . . . are supported by their congregations. These congregations are voluntary associations, chiefly of rich people. If a rich man is offended in church he can take a change of venue without qualm of conscience . . . and the good preacher is so much the poorer, without accomplishing anything." A decade earlier the same journal editorially argued that the Roman Catholic Church was peculiarly well suited to the cultural diversity—"the organizing power of the Latin races, . . . the fire and enthusiasm of the Celtic, . . . the solidity of the Germanic and the imagination of the Orientals"—which was to be found in America; the journal strongly implied that Protestantism was not so suited.[14]

These were points that WASPS themselves sometimes conceded. Commenting upon the high salaries of the ministers of New York, Jonathan Blanchard's *Christian Cynosure* taunted: "With a $10,000 gag in his mouth, a man must be a rare prodigy of faith if he can speak otherwise than gingerly of the sins of the donors." That was in 1872, and quite probably the writer had Henry Ward Beecher and his wealthy congregation in mind. But on March 1, 1888, *The Independent,* a paper which had been founded originally to air Beecher's own social and religious views, found statistical evidence in the strife-torn city of Pittsburgh to support the same harsh judgment. Surveying the church population of the steelmakers' community, *The Independent* found that 60 percent of the Protestants were "capitalists, professional men, lawyers, physicians, teachers, salaried men, clerks, etc." One American Catholic clergyman read this article in *The Independent* and hastened to pass along its substance to his coreligionists. "Of the many thousands of wage-earners in Pittsburgh, but one in ten is a Protestant church-member," Father Patrick McSweeney wrote in 1888.

This might not have been so bad; in a time when the power of American capitalism went all but unchallenged, a Social Gospel preached to people in a position to do something about social miseries might have been pragmatically more effective than a Social Gospel preached to the sufferers themselves. What was damning in *The Independent's* attitude was not its statistics but its complacency about them. If Protestantism had lost most of its working-class membership, this prestigious Protestant journal seemed to be saying, then so much the worse for the working class: "Either the Protestant denominations should have the credit of training their members to be thrifty, intelligent, and influential or they attract this class to them." Father McSweeney's response was quick and barbed.

> If two-thirds of the Protestants of Pittsburgh and Alleghany are of the wealthier or higher class, it is not because the Protestant Church has made them any better than their neighbors. The possession of great wealth does not mean that, and often means the opposite. (Matt. xix:24) . . . We must choose rather the other part of the dilemma of the *Independent* and say that Protestantism attracts the worldly.[15]

Some irritated Protestants replied that they really did strive to preach the Gospel to every creature, and if the masses did not respond it was their own fault. (Towns like Pittsburgh were not the place in which to find salvation in any case. "Great cities are the great corrupters of the morals of mankind, like lewd women to whom they are compared by the sacred writers of both Testaments," one Disciples journal declared; and besides, said another, they were hotbeds of Catholicism.[16]) In one attempt to refute the charge that the laboring classes were being estranged from the churches the Reverend Alexander M. Proudfit asserted: "I have every Sunday of my life, in the city of Baltimore, tramps sitting in the best pews of my church—men without a linen collar and without a whole coat—although my ushers bring them in and seat them comfortably, yet I get very few of them." If they stayed away, therefore, it was by their own preference; their alienation was of a kind "which nothing but the work of the Holy Spirit in their hearts will cure"—and besides, this cleric added in further extenuation, "They are wrapped up in worldliness, many of them, and in sinful pleasure."

The condescension of such a judgment is matched only by its human insensitivity. Little wonder that some Catholics questioned whether ruggedly

THE INSPECTION BY THE SUMMER CORPS OF THE BOARD OF HEALTH OF THE CONDITION OF THE POOR—A SCENE IN AN ALLEY IN MULBERRY STREET WITH THE THERMOMETER AT NINETY-SIX DEGREES IN THE SHADE.

individualistic American Protestantism was capable of a truly "social" Gospel at all: "An unjust man," Isaac Hecker wrote near the end of the hellroaring Grant era, "can console himself, when transmitting his dishonest gains to his descendants, that he is to be justified by faith alone." But some Protestant churchmen refused to interpret Luther's great doctrine of justification by faith in so self-serving a way. James McCosh, President of Princeton University, who is remembered today as one of the reconcilers of Darwinism with divinity, sought also as a churchman to reconcile the classes with the masses, when he warned his fellow American Protestants: "We must beware of turning our churches into mere middle-class institutions." The Princeton educator replied directly to the Reverend Mr. Proudfit's condescending testimony with an anecdote of one newspaper reporter who had dressed as a "decent laborer" and gone to each of the principal churches in an American city. Some of them had greeted him with "cold politeness," others had shown him "positive rudeness," and "only one or two gave him a cordial and, even then, a somewhat surprised welcome. . . . You who sit in these cushioned pews put money in the plate to send the gospel to Timbuctoo," McCosh cried. "Do you send it to that man who lives next door to you?"[17]

III[18]   When Washington Gladden's pioneering Social Gospel tract *Applied Christianity* first appeared in 1887, a Roman Catholic reviewer acknowledged that its author "really knows and seems to appreciate the state of antagonism between the owners of money and the owners of labor." Between the lines of this judgment we may read an inference that this Yankee "WASP" was belatedly discovering facts of economic and social life which any Catholic citizen, given his Church's immigrant working-class constituency, would have known all along. But even if all Protestants had been as well intentioned as Gladden, the reviewer doubted that Protestantism was organizationally capable of effective social action: "Beyond the private action of single men and separate churches, Protestantism can hardly extend its influence upon the people generally, for its lacks the power of a great public organism." This argument that Catholic cohesiveness had more to offer in curing American society's ills than had Protestant individualism was an old theme with Isaac Hecker, the founder of the Paulists, who noted in the U. S. centennial issue of the *Catholic World* (July, 1876) that "the Catholics were the only religious body in the United States not torn asunder by sectional strife during our civil war." Father Hecker concluded that "as our numbers grow and our influence increases, we are destined to become more and more the strong bond to hold in indissoluble union the great American family of States." Roman Catholic citizens must therefore prepare themselves "to enter more fully into the public life of the country; . . . to grapple more effectively with the great moral evils which threaten at once the life of the nation and of the church."[19]

It was a plausible argument, but Catholic social criticism in America had one built-in limitation. In their desire to live down the charge of "un-Americanism" which had been hurled at them for so long by Protestant militants, some Catholic Americans were prone to go to the other extreme of a total and uncritical acceptance of "the American way of life." War service in 1862 as chaplain to the Fifth Minnesota Volunteer Infantry and a long peacetime career at the cathedral church in St. Paul so Americanized John Ireland, for example, that he could make the eagle scream as fiercely as any nationalistic Protestant.

America, rising into the family of nations in these latter times, is the highest billow of humanity's evolution, the crowning effort of ages in the aggrandizement of man. Unless we view her in this altitude we do not comprehend her; we belittle her towering stature, and hide from ourselves the singular design of Providence in creating her.

. . . In the solution of social and political problems, no less than in the development of industry and commerce, the influence of America will be dominant among nations. There is not a country on the globe that does not borrow from us ideas and aspirations. The spirit of America wafts its spell across seas and oceans, and prepares distant continents for the implanting of American ideas and institutions. . . . The center of human action and influence is rapidly shifting, and at no distant day America will lead the world.[20]

John Ireland was named Bishop of St. Paul in 1884, the same year in which James G. Blaine, known to millions of his countrymen as "the continental liar from the State of Maine," for his unconvincing public defenses against charges of political corruption, came within a few thousand votes of being made President of the United States. It was a time not only of public corruption but of private misery; a time of crop failures, mortgage foreclosures, labor unrest, and suffering in the slums. Eight years later in Omaha delegates to the national convention of a fighting new third party heard Ignatius Donnelly, a son of John Ireland's home state of Minnesota, declare that the nation was at "the verge of moral, political and material ruin," and thereafter a crescendo of social protest was capped in 1896 by William Jennings Bryan's cry that the business and banking interests of the East should not "crucify mankind upon a cross of gold." Under such circumstances, it may be argued that what Americans needed from the Catholic Church was not congratulation but chastisement; that Archbishop Ireland's call to Catholic priests and laymen to "go into the arena" of public and political life, there to "seek out social evils, and . . . speak of vested wrongs," and later on his condemnation of the war with Spain, spoke more directly to the needs and condition of the United States in the Gilded Age than did his pledge of heart and life to the American flag.[21]

In teaching "his fellow Americans . . . some salutary lessons in patriotism,"[22] Ireland may inadvertently have caused some hearers of the lessons to draw the wrong moral. It did not become a people riding a wave of pride and complacency to be told by a distinguished Catholic prelate that their nation was "the highest billow of humanity's evolution"; Protestants and secularists had told them quite enough of that sort of thing already. Archbishop Ireland may have withheld his critical fire (except on certain key issues such as temperance) in accordance with his own warning that to "belittle" America was to "hide from ourselves the singular design of Providence in creating her." But the Reverend Josiah Strong demonstrated in his book *Our Country,* published at the very height of the Gilded Age (1885), that it was possible to combine a fierce patriotism with a prophetic and critical attitude. Strong certainly agreed with Ireland's judgment that "this is a providential nation,"[23] but he was careful to balance such a view with the warning that an America fit for a nationalistic mission in the world must be mindful of the parable of the mote and the beam.

In an era of virulent anti-Catholicism, Ireland may have felt that Catholic criticism of the evils of secular America had a lesser priority for a responsible churchman of that faith than the overthrow of the "un-American" stereotype of the Catholic in the United States, although the *Catholic World* suggested in 1885 that it might no longer be necessary for a Catholic cleric to "run scared" in this fashion: "Anything worthy the name of an enemy the Catholic Church has not had in North America since before the Declaration of Independence."[24] But in aligning himself with the political party which had held the White House for most of the Gilded Age, accepting that party's philosophy that " 'respect' for capital . . . 'must be supreme,' " and writing an open letter to St. Paul businessmen against Bryan of which "his Republican colleagues . . . ordered a quarter of a million copies for general distribution," John Ireland may have lost more for the Church, in the long run, than he gained.[25] "The working class, we may say, is the nation," wrote Patrick McSweeney in 1888, and "the church, which these masses of men find suitable and in which they feel at home, must be the church of the nation sooner or later.[26] In Ireland's time, under the high-tariff and immigration-restrictionist tutelage of men like Samuel Gompers, many of these masses of men were voting Republican, as Archbishop Ireland was urging that more Catholics should do; but after another half-century under the tutelage of Al Smith and Franklin Roosevelt most of them would find a more comfortable home within the ranks of the New Deal.

IV   By the later 1880's the comfortable classes were beginning to be more sensitized to the cries of the poor. Comfortable Protestants had to listen to the strictures of Dr. Gladden as he denounced monopoly and called for such heresies as progressive taxation and government ownership of the railroads. Comfortable Jews had to face the challenge of the "Pittsburgh Platform" of 1885 to "participate in the great task of modern times, to solve . . . the problems presented by the contrasts and evils of the present organization of society." Comfortable Catholics already had a few prickly individuals to contend with like Father Edward McGlynn, a defender of the fiscal radicalism of Henry George; and shortly they would have to reckon with the call for social justice embodied in the great encyclical *Rerum Novarum*.[27] And all comfortable Americans had to listen to the Old

School Presbyterian who was President of the United States as he delivered what a modern historian has called "one of the most radically leftist annual messages ever to come from the White House . . . a violent attack upon the power elite of the nation."[28] What Reform Jews called the "Social Justice Movement,"[29] or what Protestants called the "Social Gospel," would be as typical of America's next religious generation as May's "summit of complacency" had been of the generation of the Seventies.

But social religion in the United States from the beginning was vulnerable to attack, and vulnerable in a poignantly American way. "As [the church] invaded the social and economic fields," Henry Steele Commager has written, "it retreated from the intellectual"—or, more accurately, continued a retreat which had begun with the first warm surges of popular revivalism. Sidney Mead has rightly noted that the early Social Gospel was a movement in search of a theology, which it did not find until 1917; in the meantime it was a pragmatic, even "issue-oriented" approach, in which "romantic liberal" and "scientific modernist" theologians fellow-traveled happily, avoiding the embarrassing question of whether the basic beliefs that underlay their common work might be incompatible.[30] The Christian call to mission in the slums attracted types as diverse as Anglo-Catholic mystics and Salvation Army volunteers. Indeed, prior to 1920 the churches would be far more ready to find common ground for social action ("life and work," in Ecumenical Movement jargon) than they would be to compose their theological differences ("faith and order"). Spokesmen for the Social Gospel, typically of American reform causes both religious and secular, seemed to be saying: Forget the wordy chatter and metaphysical speculations which have divided Europe's energies for centuries, and let's get on with the job.

But as many critics, Marxist and otherwise, have observed of this strain in the American character, sooner or later the activist and reformer must stop and ask, to what purpose? One Gilded-Age labor leader told a Senate investigating committee inquiring as to the ultimate ends sought by the American Federation of Labor, "We have no ultimate ends," and that very attitude has often been seen as a symptom of what was historically the matter with the A. F. of L. Similarly, Catholic social actionists and Protestant Social Gospelers and the pioneers of the Jewish Social Justice movement, like the secular Progressives of a slightly later generation, were longer on diagnosis than on prescription.[31] That socially concerned churchmen in America lacked a theological consensus may not have been a handicap; given their long tradition of intersectarian sniping it may even have been an advantage. But this same lack of focus extended to their social concern itself.

Phillips Brooks, Washington Gladden, Dwight L. Moody, Edward McGlynn, and the founders of what was to become the Church of the Nazarene[32] in their different ways all expressed compassion for the downtrodden poor. But from what, and *for* what, were these huddled masses to be saved? Were they to be saved from hunger? From urban dislocation? From capitalism? Or merely from sin?

"Our poor do not need largesses of corn, as old Rome thought," wrote the Reverend J. C. Armstrong in 1888, "but the Word of God, which is able to make them cleanly, independent, healthy, and righteous." Someone who knew the horrors of Chicago might pardonably have reacted with cynicism to this remark by the Superintendent of the Chicago City Missionary Society; the Wobblies would one day sing "Pie in the sky bye and bye." Indeed, were missions of this type intended primarily to rescue the poor, or to rescue middle-class WASP America from the poor? "The very destitute in the centre of our city are uncared for," the same church official had written four years earlier, and among them lurked "the same dynamite element" who had been involved in the 1877 labor troubles. Quite devoid of cynicism, apparently, Superintendent Armstrong set down his dictum that "it is far cheaper and wiser to go to them with the gospel, than to have them come to us with fire and sword."[33]

"Why does crime increase?" asked the *Christian Evangelist* for May 28, 1885. Because "the laboring classes of the great cities are largely irreligious. . . . These all have loose ideas of the rights of property, [and] openly preach the right to take whatever is wanted, and to burn, blow up and destroy." Some persons outside the city seem to have reasoned along the lines of the isolationists prior to the Second World War, on the premise that "urban churches were generally polluted by their environment rather than being a purifying source within it"; far better to wash one's hands of the mess that existed in what William Jennings Bryan would one day come to call "the enemy country."[34] Others responded to the challenge of the city, arguing that their religious organization in the future would not be much of a church if they did not. Dwight L. Moody and his associates, bothered by the fact that the academies he founded in the early Eighties, Mount Hermon and Northfield, seemed to be evolving into typical New England prep schools, saw to it that the Moody Bible Institute which opened its doors in Chicago in 1889 was dedicated to the training of workers specifically for urban evangelism. "Either these people are to be evangelized," said Moody in March, 1886—two months before Haymarket—"or the leaven of communism and infidelity will assume such enormous proportions that it will break out in a reign of terror such as this country has never known."[35]

Of course a Social Gospel pioneer like Washington Gladden went a good deal further than Superintendent Armstrong and, in some respects, than Moody's "Gap-Men." Rather than attempting to solve on an individual or a case-by-case basis what was essentially a collective problem, or, worse, trying to brainwash the rejects of society into acceptance of their lot, Gladden wanted to attack the central problem itself. But Gladden's approach had certain inherent middle-class limitations almost as inhibiting as Superintendent Armstrong's. If industrial society was in a state of war, as Gladden maintained, then aid to individual casualties of that conflict could no more settle the basic issue than Red Cross work on a battlefield could stop the fighting itself—however much of an improvement this work was over what had been done in previous wars.[36] Gladden saw this part of the problem clearly enough, but he did not perceive with the same clarity that if the giver of aid to the wounded could not bring an end to the conflict, neither perhaps could the negotiator of cease-fires.

V   Gladden assumed that since the state of war between organized business and organized labor was abnormal, a consequence of the growth of corporate monopoly, then it should be possible to compose their differences in a normal, *i.e.*, nonviolent, fashion. In 1893 he predicted: "We are steadily traveling toward an industrial order which will identify the interests of employer and employed."[37] But in the year of Haymarket another American critic saw the rival parties preparing for strife more bitter than the gentle Gladden could imagine, strife of a kind that could not be ended by the act of sitting down at a table. "Wealth, arrogance, and pride are on one side, and widely prevailing poverty, ignorance, bigotry, and a keen sense of injustice are on the other. Both, impelled by selfish motives, are now organizing their forces all over the civilized world."

The rich had their self-justifications: the iron law of supply and demand, the inevitability of wealth and poverty in the world, and their own right to a return on an investment of skill, risk, and effort. And the poor had theirs: technological unemployment, the widening gap between luxury and squalor, and the inflation of prices by corporate middlemen, in particular those favorite Gilded-Age and Progressive culprits, the railroads. But unlike most Gilded-Age and Progressive prophets, the writer mentioned above was pessimistic that anything could or would be done about the situation. Some among the men of wealth were "fully in sympathy with the laboring classes, and would be glad to act out their sympathy" by such actions as raising wages or shortening hours, but they were powerless to act lest their competitors undersell and ruin them. On the other side of the battle line the wage workers would be able to "organize and unify their interests, but selfishness will destroy the union." Then, as trade unions escalated their demands, this writer made the following prediction.

> Capitalists will become convinced that the more they yield the more will be demanded, and will soon determine to resist all demands. Insurrection will result; and in the general alarm and distrust capital will be withdrawn from public and private enterprises, and business depression and financial panic will follow. Thousands of men thrown out of employment in this way will finally become desperate. Then law and order will be swept away.

Law and order would temporarily be restored, but these catastrophic collisions would recur, and "each time these labor pangs of the new era come upon the present body politic, her strength and courage will be found less, and the pains severer." Remedial measures (New Deals?) would be attempted, but "many of society's physicians would be totally ignorant of . . . the necessities and urgency of the case." Instead of dealing with "the real ailment" they would "undertake repressive measures"—but these measures, too, would fail.

> The efforts of the masses for deliverance from the grasp of Capital and machinery will be *immature*; plans and arrangements will be incomplete and insufficient, as time after time they attempt to force their way. . . . Each unsuccessful attempt will increase the confidence of Capital in its ability to keep the new order of things within its present limits, until at length the present restraining power of organizations and governments will reach its extreme limit, the cord of social organism will snap asunder, law and order will be gone.

The parallel with revolutionary Marxist prophecy and even with anarchist rhetoric is striking, but the writer—Charles Taze Russell, founder of the Jehovah's Witnesses movement—was no Marxist, nor a Christian Socialist, nor even a Social Gospeler. The passages just quoted from "The Present Situation" in his volume *The Divine Plan of the Ages* were not a prelude to a call for revolution. Quite the reverse; "the wage-working masses, beginning to think that laws and governments were designed to aid the wealthy and to restrain the poor, are drawn toward Communism and Anarchy . . . not realizing that the worst government, and the most expensive, is vastly better than no government at all." The class struggle is real, and given the nature of the economy—and of man!—inevitably must be violent, Russell wrote, "but the saint should take no part in that struggle." His living example of "contentment and joyful anticipation, and a cheerful submission to present trials in sure hope of the good time coming," would both witness to his faith and serve as a "valuable lesson for the world."[38]

Eleven years later, convinced that secular events were proving his point, Russell wrote *The Battle of Armageddon*. The years between these two tracts had seen the bloody Homestead and Pullman strikes, the excitement over free silver and Bryan, the Cuban Insurrection, and a near-collision between the United States and Britain over the Venezuela boundary. In the later work Russell dealt at far greater length with the injustices of his times than he had in his first volume, devoting literally hundreds of pages to the "discontent, hatred, friction preparing rapidly for social combustion," and including this time in his analysis the rising international militarism which in the twentieth century was going to make the Jehovah's Witnesses' forecast of holocaust all too plausible. After "the inevitable leveling of society which will be accomplished by the anarchy of the Day of Vengeance," the writer forecast a day when not only would "the banking and brokerage business and other like employments . . . no longer have a place; . . . and private capital and money . . . be things of the past," but also would "the manufacture of munitions of war and defense cease, and armies be disbanded."[39] But this state of affairs, although peaceful and brotherly (for the survivors!) would of course be neither anarchism nor socialism; the Kingdom of God on earth would be an absolute monarchy, with authority delegated to Christ as vice-regent.

In a sense Pastor Russell stood still further to the Left in social criticism than Bakunin or Karl Marx. The proletarian revolution they had predicted would confound and overthrow the bourgeois world order, and then in turn be confounded and overthrown when the angel blew the trumpet and Yahweh rolled the heavens away. If the Witnesses' prognosis for the outcome of the class struggle in America contrasted sharply with the smug chamber-of-commerce outlook of the middle-class "mainstream"—those for whom "the basic Christian conception of crisis was smoothed over by the softer idea of progress," as C. H. Hopkins put it[40]—still their assessment was pessimistic rather than revolutionary. Longer and perhaps more realistic on social analysis than some of the more genteel Social Gospelers and Social Justice men, the Jehovah's Witnesses have been even shorter, and more negative, on what to do now about injustice, poverty, and war: one may resist Caesar's claim to absolute power and refrain from committing idolatry by refusing to salute the flag.[41]

VI   The hardest task of all would be to apply the "Social Gospel" principle to the submerged tenth of America's population. When Pastor Russell wrote *The Battle of Armageddon,* the farmer and the working-man and even the immigrant slum dweller were beginning to find a political voice, and it would be possible for George D. Herron and Father John Ryan, for Walter Rauschenbusch and Rabbi Stephen S. Wise to find and express religious equivalents of the same concerns. But in the midst of all the agitation of the Nineties the voice of the Negro was drowned out.

While white men struggled to restrain the oppressions of the railroads, using the new instrument of the Interstate Commerce Commission, black men knew the humiliation of newly enacted Jim Crow laws; while rural southern poor whites challenged the corporate control of their states, in the process they sacrificed the rights of rural southern Negroes. The nascent civil rights movement of the Radical Reconstruction years was forgotten and even repudiated,[42] even in those white northern churches that had labored directly in the postwar years to help the freedman.[43] In the Nineties as throughout the Seventies and Eighties, white men would be locked in political battles with other white men over issues which the Negro, neglected or mistreated by both sides, could not have cared about less. Bishop Henry M. Turner of the African Methodist Episcopal Church asked in 1892:

> What does the Negro race care about tariff reform, while discrimination prevails against him on the railroads, and while he is compelled to ride from the Potomac to the Rio Grande, without a mouthful to eat, unless he goes in through the back door of the eating-houses and buys a lunch from the kitchen; and if he wants a cup of tea, he must take his own tin cup to get it in, and stand out in the yard and eat and drink on the head of some old, dirty barrel?

From the fragmentation of the new civil rights movement a century later, the white man has learned that the black man can respond to this kind of mistreatment in at least two quite radically different ways. One is the way of integration, of fighting for the right to go in through the front rather than the back door; the other is the way of "black nationalism," of (in effect) building his own eating-houses, to which in return "Whitey" is not welcome. The kinship between the integrationist approach and a Social-Gospel concept of religion is clear; Negro clergymen have indeed played a major, perhaps the decisive, political and social role in that kind of civil-rights activity. But "black nationalism" has a religious dimension also. Recently it has been "Muslim," but at one time it too was Christian, and a black-nationalist Social Gospel was fully manifest in America by the end of the Gilded Age.[44]

Occasionally this was sensed by a white churchman. Reflecting on the task of evangelizing the blacks of his region, a Catholic prelate in the South, Francis Janssens, wrote in 1887:

> The colored race, though living harmoniously with the white race, mistrusts anything carried on for their benefit by the whites, unless the colored men are themselves allowed to act the principal part. They think they can manage their own affairs; they . . . reject anything whatever that bears any semblance of tutelage of the white race over them.

For that reason, Janssens argued, his Church would do well to seek out Southern black youths having a priestly vocation; "There are numbers of bright colored boys that have more than sufficient intelligence to become priests."

But this judgment was ambiguously shrouded in racism; ignoring the realities of the post-Reconstruction era, Father Janssens contended that politically speaking the blacks were not desirous of autonomy at all. "Lack of civilization, a reckless carelessness as to the manner of living, and consequent lack of interest in politics" made them content to "leave most of the civil offices in the hands of the white population."[45] It is not from white, and usually racist, clergymen that one learns of the extent of black separatism in the Gilded Age. It is from the black religious leaders themselves, even though a generation of black historians and sociologists had taught us to regard most of them as willing collaborators with the system of Jim Crow.

A favorite legend among Biblical literalists had made the sons of Noah the founders of the three branches of mankind that re-peopled the earth after the Flood: Shem (Jews and Arabs), Ham (Egyptians and Negroes), and Japheth (the primitive Aryans). Defenders of slavery in antebellum days had seriously argued that God had punished Ham and his descendants by giving them all black skins. Some militant Negroes in the Gilded Age put the shoe on the other foot. Bishop Jabez Campbell reversed this familiar white-supremacist canard when he wrote: "Though Japheth had so far exceeded his brothers in the race for dominion and wealth Ham and Shem had determined to overtake him somewhere and make him disgorge his gains. They had caught him in America and he is now disgorging."[46]

But Campbell's colleague in the A.M.E. Church episcopate, Henry Turner, had his doubts that Japheth could be made to disgorge—at least in America. From the late 1870's onward Bishop Turner voiced a conviction that the only workable solution to the problem of the Afro-American lay in return to Africa. In 1892 his denomination's General Conference named Turner to spearhead its board of foreign missions, and its Council of Bishops called for a major missionary effort concentrating on (but not limited to) "Africa and the Islands of the Sea, where the people of our race are found in large numbers." Seeing an opportunity to advance his own plan for the emancipation of the American Negro, Turner readily fell in with the A.M.E. Church's argument that the best way to Christianize Africa was to plant colonies of Christian Negroes from America on the Dark Continent.

Pausing in London in the spring of 1893 en route to Africa on a visit of his own (his second), Turner told the Westminster *Gazette* that of the eight million Negroes in America two million were "ready to go at once if they had the opportunity." Why should Negroes leave America? the interviewer asked. Had they not full civil rights there? "They have in name, but they can not exercise them," the American Negro bishop replied. "In every State the governing power is against the black man." So were the mass media, "always ready to publish anything that may tell against the [N]egro," as for example accounts of crimes of violence involving Negroes, particularly rape; "but if a charge turns out to be baseless they would not correct it for a thousand dollars." Returning to Atlanta from his African journey that summer, Turner proposed a national Negro convention to further what he called "repatriation or Negro nationalization," declaring: "I do not believe that there is any manhood future in this country for the Negro."[47]

Meanwhile the African Methodist Episcopal Church's nationwide Easter offering to raise money for the work in Africa had failed.[48] Undaunted, Bishop Turner ran an editorial in his *Voice of Missions* telling black Americans how to get there on their own, and that church paper continued to carry advertisements, as it had from its first issue, for a proposed Afro-American Steam Ship and Mercantile Company, a striking anticipation of Marcus Garvey's ill-fated "Black Star Line." Issuing the formal call for his proposed national convention of American Negroes, "for the purpose of crystallizing our sentiments and unifying our endeavors for better conditions in this country, or [for] a change of base for existence," Henry Turner made it plain that he preferred the latter alternative, although the convention, when it met, overwhelmingly chose the former.[49]

Only two years later, in his "Atlanta Compromise" of 1895, Booker T. Washington would declare that "the wisest among my race understand that the agitation of social equality is the extremest folly."[50] As of 1893, black nationalism as a major overt expression of the hopes of black Americans seemed historically premature. Bishop Turner's discourse would have sounded wildly overstated to the white America of Grover Cleveland but would have a more ominous, possibly prophetic ring seventy-five years later. "Unless this nation . . . awakes from its slumbers and calls a halt to the reign of blood and carnage in this land," Turner told the National Council of Colored Men when it convened on November 28, 1893, "its dissolution and utter extermination is only a question of a short time." Without a radical change of program, the United States would not live to celebrate another centennial.

> A Negro is a very small item in the body politic of this country, but his groans, prayers and innocent blood will speak to God day and night, and the God of the poor and helpless will come to his relief sooner or later, and another fratricidal war will be the sequence though it may grow out of an issue . . . far from the Negro.[51] . . . For this is either a nation or a travesty. If it is a nation, every man east and west, north and south, is bound to the protection of human life, and the institutions of the country; but if it is a burlesque or a national sham, then the world ought to know it.[52]

One day Social Christianity and Social Judaism in America would face a more grievous challenge than any Washington Gladden or Isaac Wise had anticipated. Could the gospel of love become so irrelevant when carried from white man to black that a white civil rights worker could best express his love for his black brother by withdrawing from the movement entirely? Did a "nonviolent" activist need to be willing to take whatever actions seemed necessary, knowing that violence must result from them? Should a black Christian make overtures of love to "Whitey" and break ranks with those who sought black power as a precondition of justice? More broadly, in a state of social war, was the churchman's responsibility to bring it to the conference table as Gladden suggested, or to wait it out in Gospel hope as Pastor Russell advocated—or, as Bishop Turner implied, to fight it out to its bitter conclusion? As of 1971, in the burning light of Watts and Detroit and Chicago, there had been found no answer, and the next centennial of American independence was only a few years away.

8

Progressive Pilgrims and Immovable Saints

"Be eloquent in praise
Of the very dull old days
Which have long since passed away;
And convince 'em, if you can,
That the reign of good Queen Anne
Was Culture's palmiest day.
Of course you will pooh-pooh
Whatever's fresh and new
And declare it's crude and mean,
For Art stopped short
In the cultivated court
Of the Empress Josephine."

Gilbert and Sullivan,
Patience (1881)

155

$\mathcal{A}$ I   T least since the Renaissance, the idea of progress—the belief "that civilization has moved, is moving, and will move in a desirable direction"—has been a powerful stimulus to self-congratulation. "We are constantly being surprised that people did things well before we were born," remarked the American humorist Robert Benchley, reacting to a newspaper caption: "Remarkably Accurate & Artistic Painting of a Goose . . . Drawn 3300 Years Ago." ("Why should we be surprised that the people who built the Pyramids could also draw a goose so that it looked like a goose?" Benchley wanted to know. "They may not have known about chocolate malted milk and opera hats, but, what with one thing and another, they got by.")[1] Famine, pestilence, war, and death to the contrary notwithstanding, generation after generation of modern men have felt themselves to be living in a "brave new world," not with the overtones Aldous Huxley gave that phrase but in the dewy-fresh accents of Shakespeare's Miranda. To be sure, with equal regularity age and envy have reviled the falling standards of the younger generation, and a minority has always lingered on to lament the passing of the House of Stuart, or of the antebellum South, or of the Hoover Administration. But the consensus at any given present moment has ordinarily been that what's past is (merely) prologue.

Especially the Victorian Era, or Gilded Age, was characterized by emphasis on growth, development, and "progress," at times almost to the exclusion of all other values. Darwin and Darwinism were but one manifestation of a more general spirit, ranging from the positivist scheme of history as a hierarchy ranging from "superstition" through "metaphysics" to science, and the more subtle dialectical historicism of Hegel and Marx, to the excuses put forth by American businessmen to justify the "natural" growth of small enterprises into large monopolies, and the promotional literature put forth on behalf of World's Fairs. "All educational inquiries assume," Edward Youmans confidently declared in 1867, "that man is individually improvable, and therefore collectively progressive." An occasional skeptic might cavil—"I've seen th' shackles dropped fr'm th' slave, so's he cud be lynched in Ohio," mused the irrepressible Mr. Dooley—but sour notes like these were easily lost in a noisy chorus of national self-praise.[2]

Significantly, when Englishmen and Americans embraced the theory of evolution—on the face of it "a neutral, scientific conception," upon which, as J. B. Bury was to point out, "a theory of pessimism may be built up as speciously as a theory of optimism"—they used it as the clinching argument for progress. Darwin himself so far forgot his scientific caution as to declare, in bringing *The Origin of Species* to a close, that "as natural selection works solely by and for the good of each being, all corporeal and mental environments will tend to progress toward perfection." Darwin's fellow-travelers were sometimes even less cautious, as when Herbert Spencer cried: "The ultimate development of the ideal man is logically certain."[3]

It was characteristic of literary Darwinists and progressives in the nineteenth century, as of literary Marxists and Freudians in the twentieth, that on behalf of their favorite dogma they claimed a great deal. Even the fine arts were pressed into service in its support, as when Andrew Dickson White stated that "the history of art . . . gives abundant proofs of the upward tendency of man." Present-day art criticism is more cautious. "It is hard indeed to say whether the so-called 'primitive' peoples . . . have really lagged behind the 'civilized' races in their manner of experiencing the world within and around them," a standard art encyclopedia of our own day characteristically concludes.[4]

Of all people, White, who was comprehensively aware of ongoing research into human antiquity, ought to have known better. The Paleolithic cave paintings of Altamira were uncovered in 1879, and the Spanish scholar who first examined them, far from dismissing them as an interesting example of a "lower" art out of which "higher" forms had evolved, is reported to have exclaimed: "I know of no living painter who could achieve such work."[5] So generous a view of the artistic achievement of men who had not progressed as far as our own enlightened condition may have been more typical of nineteenth-century Spain than of Gilded-Age America. Mark Twain's *The Innocents Abroad,* with its endless Philistine comments upon the "overrated" Old Masters—whose paintings were dusty and cracked and whose statues lacked heads and arms—was probably all too representative.

Theologians as well as art critics were urged to judge their subject matter by the same crassly positivistic canons. "The history of their own faith attests that religious ideas are a growth, and that they pass from lower states to higher unfoldings," E. L. Youmans told them in a typical *Popular Science Monthly* editorial. If advocates of modern ideas were called "atheists" for upsetting old notions of the cosmos and of animate nature, Jews and Christians under the Roman Empire had been called "atheists" for upsetting still older notions. Yet Judaeo-Christian ethical monotheism, revolutionary for its day, had been "neither the final step" in the development of man's highest ideas of divinity "nor the last experience of disquiet and grief at sundering the ties of old religious associations." Summon the strength to bear such mental pains, Youmans admonished; "remembering that human nature is religiously progressive," do not "copy . . . the bad example of narrow-minded heathen thousands of years ago, who treated the Christians very much as many Christians now treat those who are devoted to the gospel of science."

Unfortunately it was not all that simple. To project the whole of human history as a linear extension on the long upward curve of biological evolution was an embarrassment to men who preached "the Faith once delivered to the saints," with emphasis upon the word "once." Whether such a world-view as theirs can coexist with a secular world-view which remains even today in a sense evolutionary and cumulative is an open question. We may have rejected the more simplistic evolutionism of the nineteenth century, but the concept that reality is essentially flux, change, process— if not necessarily progress— seems to have become a permanent part of the intellectual furniture of modern man. It is not the *fact* of "progress," but the notion that it is unambiguously a *value*, that has tended to drop out of the discussion after two global wars waged with highly evolved technologies.

The high moral seriousness characteristic of the Victorians at their best (and worst) intensified the terrible burden of conflict between innovations which they prized and traditions which they cherished. As George Santayana mockingly summed up the aspirations of Gilded-Age Boston, "If evolution was to be taken seriously and to include moral growth, the great men of the past could only be steppingstones to our own dignity. . . . Undoubtedly some early figures were beautiful, and allowances had to be made for local influences in Palestine, a place so much more primitive and backward than Massachusetts."[6] For men who were trying to be up-to-date moderns and at the same time to revere ancient Palestine as The Holy Land, the dilemma was indeed awkward. Mark Twain's *Innocents Abroad*, triumphantly putting down the barbarous and undemocratic past all the way across Europe only to tiptoe through the holy places of Jerusalem with Sunday school awe, are a case in point. Were the local influences in ancient Palestine something that a modern man had to take seriously? And if he did, what became of his progressivist theorem that later-is-better?

II   At the two ends of the religious spectrum—unbending orthodoxy and uncompromising positivism—the answer was relatively easy.

For the latter, any of those "local influences" found to be in conflict with modern knowledge would simply have to be set aside as childhood dreams that must be sacrificed to progress. And for the former, the doctrine of progressive improvement in religious ideas was simply false; the Faith had been "once delivered," and that was all there was to it. Religious institutions that catered to the spirit of the age were being false to their own highest values. The Church did owe something to the era in which she lived; "There is no cry of our poor humanity . . . which it is not her part and duty to answer and to remedy," preached James DeKoven on All Saint's Day of 1866. "But she never does it simply by reflecting the tone of the times." In fact, DeKoven declared in another sermon, she could not even if she would, for "in all periods the times are evil and good. There are two currents, the one toward regeneration, the other toward destruction; and the true character of an age is the resultant of them both."

The first-mentioned of these sermons was preached in the midst of the abysmal domestic failures of the Andrew Johnson Administration; the tone of the times was indeed hard to rationalize in progressive terms. A decade afterward lay as well as religious observers were commenting on the irony of the centennial of American independence: we had started with George Washington and ended with Ulysses Grant, whom Henry Adams sourly saw as a living rebuttal to Darwinism. "Suddenly acquired wealth, decked in all the colors of the rainbow, flaunts its robe before the eyes of labor, and laughs with contempt at honest poverty," lamented the Chicago *Tribune* in its Fourth of July editorial for 1876. "Great in all the material powers of a vast empire," the United States was entering its "second century weak and poor in social morality as compared with one hundred years ago."[7] The year 1876 was the year of the final failure of the postwar drive for racial justice in the South, and also of the one Presidential election in all American history that by common consensus has been considered stolen; it was a year of hardship and want, with revolutionary class struggle seemingly just around the corner— hardly a time to make a convincing argument for the doctrine of historical progress.

Faced with such evidence, the progressive had either to respond in the blindly optimistic manner satirized by Voltaire in *Candide*, compelled by the challenge of catastrophe "to welcome as good that which he had only shortly before denounced as evil,"[8] or else he had to look the unpalatable facts in the face with whatever ideological adjustment this might require. Such was the bitter choice facing Isaac Hecker, the distinguished Catholic convert and

UNCLE SAM BEATS ALL CREATION.

apostle to the Americans. Under his editorship the *Catholic World* greeted the first centennial of American independence with mixed feelings. Empirically, as they traced their own history in this country from 1776—when even in colonies as tolerant as Maryland and Pennsylvania "the existence of the Catholic families . . . was looked upon as an anomaly, an anachronism, which, from the nature of things, most soon disappear"—to the immense growth of Catholicism in America in the nineteenth century, American Catholics at least as far as their own Church was concerned could hardly be anything else but progressive. And yet, as he looked around the contemporary secular scene, Hecker had his qualms.

"Has our progress in the higher aims of life, in civilization, morality, and religion, kept pace with our extraordinary increase in wealth, population, political power, and material development?" Father Hecker asked. Surveying the corruption rampant in the United States, not confined to Grant's henchmen in Washington nor to Tweed's henchmen in New York but having a nationwide existence "in every circle of society," he concluded: "To deny that there is a pronounced, marked, and universal decadence . . . is simply to . . . contradict the testimony of every sense." The future was by no means a progressive certainty; unless there were "complete and radical reform" of the situation, the second century of American independence would witness "a condition far worse than the enemies of this country have ever yet predicted."

Like most Catholic apologists Hecker assumed that Protestantism had had its day as a vitalizing force in American life. The positivistic liberalism which some progressives saw as reigning in its stead he saw as equally doomed: "The 'positive stage of development,' as it is styled by a certain class of modern writers, is an age of decrepitude. If the analogy be true which they hold to exist between the life of man and the development of a race, we must expect death as soon as the 'positive' era has been attained." And if the nation could be raised "from the slough in which it seems about to settle" neither by Protestantism, the traditional American faith, nor by "paganism," by which Father Hecker seemed to mean a scientized secular humanism, he was also skeptical of its being saved "by the infusion of fresh blood, as was the ancient world according to some ingenious writers. The Hun and Vandal and Goth would never have changed their originally savage state had they not met in the world that they destroyed . . . the power of [Catholic] Christianity."

Implicitly this argument could still, in some sense, be considered "progressive"—but the progress was conditional upon America's turning Catholic. Father Hecker concluded his Fourth of July jeremiad with an optimistic prophecy: "Gradually the church and the republic are approaching each other, and . . . in God's providence they are destined to be united." On this condition only, America would be spared the dire fate which would otherwise befall her, and "out of this divine wedlock will spring forth children . . . whose civilization will be the most glorious development of God's kingdom on earth." But this held out small comfort to the progressive non-Catholic, for whom Catholicism stood for all that was reactionary and oppressive, and

Hecker's solution was not even acceptable to all Catholics. At the time he wrote those editorials it was only twelve years since the Roman pontiff had authoritatively been declared in eternal opposition to "liberalism, progress, and modern civilization."[9]

But Protestantism contained its own animus against "progress" and "modern civilization," and in some of its forms also against "liberalism." Against their ancient foe, to be sure, Protestants in America were perhaps overfond of quoting from the inquisition of Galileo or the Syllabus of Errors in order to imply that the Church of Rome was "superstitious," "medieval," or, in progressivist terms, "backward."[10] And yet in another mood the Protestant could speak of "New Testament" or "Apostolic" Christianity, see the intervening Catholic centuries as aberrations, and urge that men go back to the first century as a model for their faith rather than ahead toward the twenty-first. Just as a Catholic spokesman could argue "progressively," as when Archbishop Ireland affirmed in 1889 that "it will not do to understand the 13th century better than the 19th,"[11] so a Protestant could speak "conservatively" when he asserted that even the thirteenth century was too late a date to use as the norm; that the purpose of the Reformation had been to purge the Church of all its historical excesses, and get back to the "pure" religion of Christ.

This may be more true of American than of European Protestantism, which both in its Anglican and its dominant Continental forms retained a sense of continuity with its medieval Catholic past. Sidney Mead in an influential essay has pointed out "the sectarian tendency of each American denomination to seek to justify its peculiar interpretations and practices as more closely conforming to those of the early Church as pictured in the New Testament than the views and policies of its rivals." For the Baptists in America, theological developments during the first half of the nineteenth century strengthened rather than diluted this tendency,[12] and one denomination indigenous to America, the Disciples of Christ, stressed what may be called a Protestant "primitivism." "The loudest call that comes from heaven," declared a prominent Disciples leader, J. W. McGarvey, in 1868, ". . . is for warfare, stern, relentless . . . against everything not expressly or by necessary implication authorized in the New Testament."[13] This was a pervasive and widespread ideology, manifested both in the boisterous exercises of the camp meeting and in the quiet quest of the Friends' Meeting.[14] The Channing Unitarians were also influenced by it (Unitarianism was really the religion of Jesus; Trinitarian orthodoxy was a corrupt production of his followers, among whom the special culprit was St. Paul). Even so antimedieval and insistently modern-minded a man as Thomas Jefferson, responding to one of the many attacks on him by the clergy, hoped that Christianity, "when divested of the rags in which they have enveloped it," could be "brought to the original purity and simplicity of its benevolent institutor."

If first-century Christianity were still the norm for the nineteenth century, it was difficult to see how the years between could be interpreted "progressively." Had not the Gospel writers who reported the life and teachings of Christianity's founder really told us all we need to know? "Since the days of John the Apostle," wrote L. T. Townsend in 1889, "there has been revealed to the race, in the field of pure theological truth, not a particle of new subject-matter." The blows dealt to orthodoxy by Galileo, Newton, Darwin, and Wundt—these "wounds" Freud would later speak of—were shrugged aside by this nineteenth-century writer with the manly contempt of a Victorian bare-knuckle boxer: "Science, philosophy, archeology, and all the correlated sciences, have added not one new fundamental truth to our theological knowledge, and have changed nothing." By the direct inspiration of God the authors of the Scriptures had found out so much of divine truth that there was essentially nothing new to discover, and thus theology in the very nature of the case could not be a "progressive science." Its terminology might be refined and made more precise, but otherwise "modern skill and wisdom can, in these matters, go no farther."[15]

III   For all the hostility that traditionally had been felt by Fundamentalist Protestants toward the Church of Rome, a Catholic writer of the period, H. H. Wyman, in an essay "Creeds, Old and New," came to essentially the same conclusion as theirs about the finality of divinely revealed truth. The idea that the traditional creeds could be progressively overhauled and brought up to date was opposed "to the very idea of Christianity as a system of objective truths and facts." Replying to a paper by Daniel Curry in the *Methodist Review* for September, 1886, "On Present Necessity for a Restatement of Christian Doctrines," Wyman quoted the Methodist writer's remark that Protestantism had been an "unstable equilibrium from the beginning," and he drew the usual Catholic polemical conclusion: Protestantism is not long for this world. "Perpetual creed-evolution," as Wyman labeled it, was directly destructive of faith, "which can only have certainty as its basis."[16]

Exactly so, said the more radical American Unitarians, the ex-Transcendentalists who founded the Free Religious Association, the ex-Reform Jews who went into Ethical Culture, and the assorted free-thinkers still further to the left; and that was exactly what was the matter with "faith" as traditionally defined.[17] In 1838 Ralph Waldo Emerson had managed to get himself declared persona non grata at Harvard for his Divinity School Address, in which he announced: "The stationariness of religion; the assumption that the age of inspiration is past, that the Bible is closed, . . . indicate with sufficient clearness the falsehood of our theology." There was, in short, no such thing as a "faith once delivered to the saints." In 1869 Francis Ellingwood Abbot, spokesman for a younger generation of Boston radicals and a cofounder with Emerson of the Free Religious Association, carried on in the same progressivist vein: "Christianity is not adapted to the present as it has been to the past. . . . A deeper, broader, and higher faith is to-day silently entering the heart of humanity."[18]

This progressive gospel was preached not only in the accents of Concord and Beacon Hill but also in those of German Cincinnati. "Before our very eyes the world moves onward into the golden age of redeemed humanity and the fraternal union of nations," Isaac Mayer Wise preached in 1875. "This century settles old accounts. It is progressive." "The religion of the future generations," Wise prophesied on another occasion, would be ". . . humane, universal, liberal, and progressive; in perfect harmony with modern science, criticism, and philosophy"[19]—and if Christianity did not fill the bill, some Reform Jews argued, Judaism might. "Judaism, its ceremonial past excepted, is not alone the religion of the Jews, but of all intelligent men in the world who have the moral courage to make themselves independent of inherited superstitions," Wise maintained as early as 1854.[20] Contrasting Judaism's traditional hospitality to science and learning with "the countless miracles, the childish legends, [the] groveling credulity" of medieval and modern Christianity, Joseph R. Brandon concluded that the religion of Israel was better adapted for survival in the modern world than was its venerable persecutor. Not only was Judaism a religion which "in an age of skepticism and inquiry" could be accepted intellectually, without "the *ipse dixit* of the priest," Brandon told the San Francisco Y.M.H.A. in 1879, but it also contained "the elements and principles of that rational religion which will eventually embrace within its fold all mankind."

Far from shying away from this kind of argument as anti-Christian, the Christian often appropriated it. Just as Joseph Brandon dismissed the miraculous element in the Hebrew Scriptures themselves as "word paintings perhaps done in the childhood of our nation," the Congregationalist Washington Gladden referred similarly to the childhood of the Church: "We are doing a great many things to-day that those Christians of the first centuries never dreamed of doing; we ought to have a much larger conception of the meaning of Christianity than they ever had."[21] In 1872 Henry Ward Beecher, in his *Life of Jesus the Christ*, discreetly raised the same point in the form of an inverted rhetorical question: "Has the world . . . no experience . . . which shall fit it to go back to the truths of the New Testament with a far larger understanding of their contents than they had who wrote them?" This was not necessarily a position inherently in conflict with orthodoxy; it was essentially the argument of John Henry Newman in his *Essay on the Development of Doctrine,* for example, and also that of the Anglo-Catholic scholars who wrote *Lux Mundi.* Still, it is interesting that this passage in Beecher's biography of Jesus was marked for reference in a copy owned by Mary Baker Eddy, who was working out the philosophy of religion soon to be set forth in *Science and Health.* Thus the belief that we know more about the truths contained in the New Testament than did the men who wrote it could logically lead not only to positivist liberalism but also to Christian Science; both equally far removed, most orthodox Christians would say, from "the faith once delivered to the saints."

"It is . . . said, 'Are we wiser than the Apostles were?' I hope so. I should be ashamed if we were not. 'Are we better preachers than they were?' Yes, we ought to be better preachers in our time than they would be."[22] In Henry Ward Beecher, who was perhaps as "present-minded" a preacher as America has ever produced, this viewpoint is understandable. But the same bias could subtly influence even the most determinedly "past-minded" of American Protestants. Religious conservatives who rejected Darwin were, for example, often ardent proponents of evangelizing the world, and they asked for contributions to their foreign missions as a way of bringing "backward" peoples into the orbit of a "progressive" western civilization, an argument which if applied to themselves and their own "backward" beliefs they would have rejected. A Presbyterian missionary to India, watching a rival denomination outdo his own in the competition for heathen souls, reacted naturally with a metaphor from contemporary Gilded-Age technology: "You Methodists are reaping by steam." And on the home-mission frontier in the Nineties the technology itself was pressed into service, as Northern Baptists found a new way to carry the Gospel into unchurched whistle-stop towns: they deployed a fleet of seven completely equipped railroad chapel cars.[23]

Even a denomination consciously built around a "restorationist" ideal, such as the Disciples of Christ, was not entirely immune from the appeal of progressivism. "Our work is the same as that of the venerable Thomas Campbell, the cherished Alexander Campbell; . . . the recovery of primitive Christianity from the rubbish of ages and its re-implantation in society in this 19th century," mused the *Millennial Harbinger* in 1868. "But even since those masters began their work, an entire age and more of human years has gone slowly down the abyss of time. . . . We must live in this present active world and not in the world which died with our fathers." And Herbert L. Willett, the Biblical scholar who became the head of Disciples Divinity House at the University of Chicago in 1893, frankly scrapped the denomination's entire primitivist tradition: "Restoration of the conditions prevailing in the Apostolic churches is both impossible and undesirable. . . . The movement of the church is forward, not backward."[24]

IV   William R. Hutchison has rightly criticized the "chastened liberals" of more recent years for the caricature they have generally drawn of their former liberalism. To believe that the movement of the church (or of society) is forward did not mean, necessarily and in all cases, to believe naïvely that it is automatic or easy; "forward movement" concretely experienced is quite often neither, as many a survivor of military service can attest. "Nothing is more deplorable than the shallow optimism that pictures this world as sailing over summer seas to blessed isles, if only men would believe it to be so," wrote Edward Mortimer Chapman, author of *A Modernist and His Creed*, in 1897.[25] Another who sensed and articulated the limitations inherent in the term "progress", and who nevertheless did not therefore revert to a restorationist or primitivist philosophy, was Alexander Viets Griswold Allen, whose lectures on "Religious Progress" delivered at Yale Divinity School in 1894 would have given comfort neither to the defender of a static "faith once delivered" nor to the advocate of the positivist doctrine that the latest is, by definition, the best.

Allen, who seven years afterward would publish a three-volume hero-worshipping *Life and Letters of Phillips Brooks*, understandably began his lectures on religious progress with a quotation from his idol: "We rejoice in life, because it seems to be carrying us somewhere, because its darkness seems to be rolling on towards light, and even its pain to be moving onward to a hidden joy." Allen knew that in the lifetime of the late rector of Trinity Church, Boston, and Bishop of Massachusetts this affirmation had been widely shared: "If there is one conviction, one word, which more than another is characteristic of the nineteenth century, it is progress." But Allen soon went on to express some judgments about the idea of progress with which his mentor possibly might not have agreed.

Allen was aware that the definition of "progress" was ambiguous: "Its power as a word is all the greater because its meaning is vague or indeterminable; indeed, in its vagueness consists its power." He was aware of the suspicions of those who doubted "whether every change is an improvement, who recognize[d] that our complicated civilization involves greater evils than the simpler forms of earlier ages," and also of those who had metaphysical objections to the concept; Schopenhauer, for example. He was aware of the differential between scientific or industrial "progress" and aesthetic or moral "progress," citing with some approval the judgment of Lord Macaulay: "In the Book of Job, they talked with as much skill about the problems of life as they do to-day." He was also aware of the difference between revolutionary progress, "the impulse . . . to reject the old belief or practice in order to further the reception of some new truth"; evolutionary progress, according to which "the old should grow evenly and naturally into the new" so that there is no "violent break with the past"; and even "the conception of progress implied in conservatism," noting that the viewpoint even of an extreme Tory "is not incapable of receiving new truth; only, when it does so it immediately proceeds to call it old."

All three of these modes of "progressive" thought Allen regarded as legitimate, and also as insufficient. As he passed from his first lecture, on "Religious Progress in the Life of the Individual," to his second, on "Religious Progress in the Organic Life of the Church," it was apparent that Allen's own conception of progress was not linear, as it was for many in that "ascent-of-man" era, so much as it was dialectical. Perhaps an echo of Emerson's Yankee intuitions about "polarities" sounded quietly beneath the Episcopalian professor's words: "It is a lesson which we are slow to learn, that opposites are closely, even vitally related; that hostile attitudes which seem irreconcilable may both be true." The most future-minded "progressive" calls upon that future to judge and set aside the historical accidents which are the burden of the present; the most past-minded "restorationist" invokes that past to condemn and cleanse the corruptions into which the heritage of that past has degenerated—and both speak and act in the name of the timeless and unbounded. "The reactionary ecclesiastic, declaring that variation is the badge of error, while sameness is the mark of the truth, is not so far away, as to the principle at issue, from a religious agitator like Theodore Parker, who began his career as a reformer with his sermon on the 'Transient and the Permanent in Religion'."

It would seem to follow, in Allen's view, that both the reactionary ecclesiastic and the radical like Parker are necessary in the scheme of things, and necessary in a sense quite unlike the twentieth-century social analyst's pallid gambit that "we have something to learn from each other." It is not simply that the reactionary and the radical enlarge, revise, and correct each other's positions; that would be too cerebral, too purely verbal a way of describing such a relationship. Nor is it that at some level the advocates of opposite extremes share some watery lowest common denominator with "all right-thinking men"; that would be a hapless vulgarizing of *Quod semper, ubique et ab omnibus, creditum sit*—which Allen called "that wonderful motto, which attracts us while it also repels." It is rather that each party to the dispute, considered in abstraction, is wrong; but put them together and somehow both, in their respective kinds of wrongheadedness, are caught up in Truth. In Allen's hands the cozy Anglican concept of the *via media* has insensibly turned into something quite different; dialectically, two wrongs do make a right.

Allen gave many examples of this process, of which one of the most startling, for that anti-"papist" era in America, was his appraisal of Roman Catholicism: "To secularize the divine is the policy of Rome; to divinize the secular is the motive of its most extreme antagonist. But if one is true, so also is the other. The reconciliation lies in adopting both; then they modify each other, with the result of a larger, completer truth.[26] This sounds like Victorian cant until one substitutes a logical synonym for "most extreme antagonist." Would the "reconciliation" then lie in adopting both Catholicism and, say, Marxian socialism? Even today, when the post-Johannine Roman Church has formally entered into dialogue with religious unbelievers,[27] including Communists, this would be advanced doctrine. With the fragmentation of the nineteenth century's various and competing monisms into the cultural relativism of our own time, the intellectual temptation has become to distort such dialogue into syncretism, or else into a not quite sincere "peaceful coexistence." At the really crucial philosophical points—form versus spontaneity, social responsibility versus individual self-expression, public political consciousness versus private aesthetic vision—there has been no "meeting of the minds" at all. Apollo dismisses Dionysus as beneath contempt, and vice versa. Can the disciples of both meet in the Eucharist?

V   Some religious conflicts of the Gilded Age were beyond resolution by even the most subtly "dialectical" of theologians. "The crown of the long process in this world is a spirit, intelligent, emotional, purposeful, moral, responsible, creative," wrote William Newton Clarke in his influential *Outline of Christian Theology*—"capable of indefinite intellectual and spiritual progress."[28] The kinship of this argument with the

COMPULSORY EDUCATION—THE SAFEGUARD OF FREE INSTITUTIONS.

evolutionary rebuttal of Original Sin described in a previous chapter should
be clear. But put into terms of historical progress rather than of biological
development it raised a logical question even more awkward for traditional
belief than the overthrow of Adam: "Is not Jesus himself also a product of
evolution?"[29]

Of course this question had been raised implicitly before. "One man
was true to what is in you and me," Emerson had said; and, still more unequivocally, "If a man is at heart just, then in so far is he God." To his

epigoni in the post-Transcendentalist era the Sage of Concord bequeathed an embarrassing conclusion indeed. At the second annual meeting of the Free Religious Association in 1869, the aged Emerson rejoiced that modern society contained "a class of humble souls . . . who do not wonder that there was a Christ, but that there were not a thousand."[30] If the upward progress that began with the dawn of civilization has continued since the Crucifixion, does it not follow that modern man is in some measurable way "better" than Christ? Santayana phrased the question with his characteristic irony: "Jesus was a prophet more winsome and nearer to ourselves than his predecessors; but how could anyone deny that the twenty centuries of progress since his time must have raised a loftier pedestal for Emerson or Channing or Phillips Brooks?" No proper Bostonian would have put it quite that way; "It might somehow not be in good taste to put this feeling into clear words," the philosopher admitted, adding with feline savagery that "one and perhaps two of these men would have deprecated it; nevertheless it beamed with refulgent self-satisfaction in the lives and maxims of most of their followers."[31]

From this logical deduction Christian orthodoxy quite understandably recoiled—and found itself impaled on the other horn of the dilemma: how to reconcile the historical philosophy of "onward and upward" with the slogan "Jesus Christ, the same yesterday, today, and forever." How grievous a problem this was felt to be can be judged from the desperation of some of the attempted solutions. Lyman Abbott was conscious of the difficulty: "If the Christian evolutionist regards Jesus Christ as a product of spiritual evolution, he gives up Christianity," Abbott wrote in 1892. "If on the other hand he declares that Jesus Christ is an exception to the law of evolution, he gives up evolution." Abbott's resolution of the dilemma was to argue that by evolutionary progress we shall all achieve on some far-off day what the founder of Christianity accomplished in history. "The consummation of evolution, the consummation of redemption," Abbott wrote in *The Theology of an Evolutionist* (1897), ". . . will not be until the whole human race becomes what Christ was, until the Incarnation so spreads out from the One Man of Nazareth that it fills the whole human race. . . . What Jesus was, humanity is becoming."[32] *As God once was, man now is; as God now is, man will some day become.* This idea had been heard in America before, but well outside the "mainstream" of classical Christian theology; it was and is one of the distinctive doctrines of Mormonism!

Occasionally one of these post-Emersonians took the dilemma firmly by the horns, as when James Whiton asserted in 1892 that Jesus Christ had "no advantage of indwelling Deity that is essentially impossible to us."[33]

But most of the Protestant divines who were sometimes called "New Theologians" in their day, and "Christocentric Liberals" by more recent scholarship, were far more circumspect. William Newton Clarke's discussion of "Christ" occupies more than one hundred of the 482 pages in his *Outline of Christian Theology*, and a major part of it seems to me to be an evasion of Santayana's logic. At times, like Lyman Abbott, Professor Clarke employed quasi-L.D.S. reasoning, saying of Christ, "The best part of humanity has slowly advanced toward him in moral and religious life, but he still moves on as leader"; but thirty pages further on Clarke protected the Divine dignity by declaring: "The relation between God and man is not such that man by growing can become God."

In the intervening pages Clarke tried both to accept and to "modernize" such traditional theological mysteries as the Virgin Birth, the divine and human natures, and the Resurrection. For a philosophic and scientific monist who sought logical unity as well as progressive fulfillment it was an unhappy situation. "It is necessary that an incarnation of God should not appear to us to be a denial of nature," Clarke was obliged to say out of metaphysical consistency.[34] Washington Gladden concurred: "The incarnation of the son of God is not, then, and cannot be any unnatural event, any interruption or dislocation of the natural order" because it has to fit somehow into "the agelong process of evolution."[35]

Some did perform the intellectual acrobatics necessary to harmonize the seemingly irreconcilable. "The world begun by Nature is finished by the Supernatural—as we are wont to call the higher natural," wrote Henry Drummond. "The goal of Evolution is Jesus Christ." The theistic professor of geology Joseph LeConte at Berkeley solved the equation in somewhat the same way. Newman Smyth, in his book *Old Faiths in New Light* (1879), reconciled the Incarnation with historical progress by making the coming of Christ "the great surprise of human history," unaccountable for by the laws of heredity. Dwelling upon His uniqueness and originality, Smyth anticipated Teilhard de Chardin by saying that Jesus has somehow to be the end of creation.[36]

VI   There remained of course one classically acceptable way out of this difficulty: to take at face value the doctrine of the Second Coming. There could then be no logical problem of the kind with which the evolutionary liberals were wrestling. "The faith" could in a sense be "progressive" and "once delivered" at the same time; "once delivered" as wrapped up in an infallible Scripture, and "progressive" in that man looked forward, not back, in time for the faith's consummation. However, this was not so much a manifestation of "progressivism" in religion as it was a symptom of what Mr. Toynbee would call "Archaism-and-Futurism," and to the liberals this remedy was worse than the disease.

"No visible return of Christ to the earth is to be expected, but rather the long and steady advance of his spiritual kingdom," William Newton Clarke typically wrote. But outside the walls of liberal seminary classrooms there were many voices preaching the Second Coming. In 1878 a group of American clergymen called an International Prophetic Conference in New York at which, notes one modern scholar, "a considerable body of respected American and European support was rallied behind premillennialist beliefs."[37] Other such conferences were held periodically through the remainder of the Gilded Age, at which speakers not only affirmed the Second Coming of Christ as imminent but also denied the Darwinism which had posed the theological problem in this form in the first place. As George H. Needham told one such conference in Chicago in 1886, "Brethren, premillennialism pure and simple forms a breakwater against every advancing tide which would throw upon the clean beach of a God-given theology the jelly fish theories evolved out of man's erratic consciousness, pride, and self-will."[38]

That same year Charles Taze Russell appeared on the scene with his volume *Millennial Dawn*, and shortly the Jehovah's Witnesses—a group curiously neglected by both church and secular historians[39]—were putting Pastor Russell's prophecies into the hands of everyone they could reach. They expressed a rigorous primitivism, rejecting every insight since the time of the New Testament: "The testimony of modern theologians has been given no weight, and that of the so-called Early Fathers has been omitted." At the same time they were in a sense "progressive," as Russell predicted that history's dark night would soon be followed by a new day which would "dispel the noxious vapors of evil, and bring life, health, peace and joy."[40]

It was a far cry from the reformist optimism of Washington Gladden, for example, who agreed with Russell that Christians should "listen once more to the voice of our great Leader and Captain, as he cries, 'Repent, for the kingdom of heaven is at hand' "; but who crucially disagreed as to the role in this world that the repentant believer ought to play. Russell, as was shown in the previous chapter, contended that the saint should live as an exemplary witness to his faith and take no part in the struggle; whereas Gladden proclaimed that "to help in the utterance of that message, in the fulfilling of

MEMORIAL SERVICES OF THE GRAND ARMY OF THE REPUBLIC FOR DECEASED
COMRADES, AT FORD'S OPERA HOUSE, BALTIMORE, JUNE 4TH.

that promise, is the high calling of the Christian man," who as a good progressive must act on the conviction that his was "no quixotic undertaking";
that the goal of universal peace was no mere Christmas-Eve dream;

> that this great realm of natural powers can be christianized; that its worst abuses
> can be corrected; that its mighty forces can be sanctified; that industry and
> trade can be so transformed by humane motives that they shall be serviceable
> to all the higher interests of men. . . . Faint signs are even now visible in our
> sky of the dawning of a day when business shall be to many men the high call-
> ing of God and the medium through which unselfish spirits shall pour out their
> energies in ministries of help and friendship; when political office shall be re-
> garded as a solemn trust held for the welfare of the whole people; when the
> creatures who live by corrupting and despoiling their fellows shall seem to
> men's thought almost as fabulous as the dragons and vampires of mythologic
> lore.[41]

But just around the corner in the twentieth century new dragons and
vampires were lurking. Prescient writers looked into man's future and found
terror. In England in 1898, in the magazine-serial version of *The Time
Machine,* H. G. Wells imagined a horrid caricature of the Utopian dream;

and Mark Twain's *A Connecticut Yankee in King Arthur's Court* (1889) sustains a "progressivist" tone only until the catastrophe of its final chapter, when the hopes of Sir Boss are confounded in a hurricane of technological slaughter, and the "progressives" perish amid the stench of the "reactionary" knights they have just slain with electricity and Gatling guns.[42] The progressivism so typical of the late Victorian Age was punctuated at times by a kind of eschatological minority report; among secular thinkers, there was apprehension that the coming century might not be a time of peaceful democratic progress but of dictatorship and wars, and among religionists, that it might not be an evolutionary advance of the Kingdom but a catastrophic final judgment. Sometimes in an odd way religious and secular apocalypse were fused. The Jehovah's Witnesses, in picking an exact date for "the final consummation of the age" when the terrible prophecies of the Book of Revelation would begin to be fulfilled, hit upon October, 1914, and they could hardly have chosen a more plausible year. Events since that time have seemed only to confirm their expectations; even the comparatively placid Eisenhower years were filled with enough turmoil that one "eager young Witness" could convincingly argue: "You must admit that things can't go on as they are."[43]

It is rather surprising that the Witnesses (and the Adventists) were not joined by other Biblical literalists in this highly persuasive interpretation of recent history. The "Niagara Group" who instituted the Prophetic Conferences were among the founding fathers of what became, in the twentieth century, Fundamentalism; but the major thrust of that movement, for reasons which have received no adequate historical explanation, turned away from the stress on the Second Coming to a stress on the literal inerrancy of Scripture, and this put them on the path which led them in 1925 to the Scopes "monkey trial"—a conflict between religion and science even more anachronistic than that which plagued the mind of the Gilded Age. The Jehovah's Witnesses, like the Fundamentalists, rejected the theory of evolution on Scriptural proof-text grounds.[44] But they were early recognized by the Fundamentalists as ideological competitors,[45] and the movements went their separate ways. Meanwhile, among the liberals, A. V. G. Allen's dialectics were forgotten, and the puzzling question put by George Santayana was never really answered.

9

High Church, Low Church, Inter-Church: Ecumenical Crosscurrents in the Gilded Age[1]

"We are not divided,
All one body we,
One in hope and doctrine,
One in charity."

Sabine Baring-Gould,
Onward, Christian Soldiers

"The sacrifice of Theology is as deso-
lating for the intellectual minority in a
religious community as the sacrifice of
current myths is for the community at
large. . . . We are all inclined, to some extent,
to assume . . . that we alone have received a
revelation; . . . and that, in consequence,
we ourselves are 'the Chosen People'
and 'the Children of Light,' while the rest of
the Human Race are gentiles sitting in darkness. . . . [But] 'the heart of so great a mystery
cannot ever be reached by following one
road only.' "

Arnold J. Toynbee[2]

177

I   🌀 HE cry of 'Union, Union, the glorious Union!' "
John C. Calhoun declared in his last speech to the Senate, "can no more
prevent disunion than the cry of 'Health, health, glorious health!' . . . can
save a patient lying dangerously ill." The great, grim South Carolinian saw
one symptom of the Union's dangerous illness in the snapping of ties that
had bound two great nationalizing and unifying institutions in America:
the political parties and the Protestant churches. After the War Between
the States the political institutions proved capable of mending such breaks
more quickly than the religious communions. The Democratic Party was
again a national institution at least by 1876, when de facto it won a presidential election; and the Federal Union again became a reality when the
Republican whom an electoral commission declared to have been the winner
of that contest withdrew the troops whose presence in three Southern states
had insured his victory.[3] By way of contrast the General Synod of the South,
a Lutheran body which was a by-product of the Civil War, did not come
back into a national fellowship until 1918, when it merged with the United
Lutheran Church. The Northern and Southern Methodists, whose separation
over the slavery question dated from 1844, began conversations on reunion
in the same year as the Hayes-Tilden electoral contest, but they were unable
to make it a reality until 1939, nearly a century after the original schism.
Formal reunion among Presbyterians was rejected by a close vote in the
Southern presbyteries as late as 1954, and today it seems as far-off as ever.[4]
The Southern Baptist Convention, organized in 1845, has gone its separate
way, growing in membership, wealth, and influence, down to the present
day. Meanwhile, in these and other denominations the normal Protestant
process of division continued, and in spite of all the movements toward
church federation or merger in the twentieth century, there still remained in
1963, according to the *Yearbook of American Churches*, twenty-eight distinct
Baptist bodies, sixteen separate Lutheran synods, twenty-two varieties of
Methodists, ten kinds of Presbyterians (not counting the Reformed churches
of Continental origin), and twelve different denominations each of which
called itself the Church of God.[5] And dozens of religious groups existed
which made no statistical reports, for the *Yearbook* or any other "mainstream" agencies.

Some churches escaped division over the slavery-secession controversy only to fall victim to something else. The Disciples of Christ managed to hold together throughout the War, for example, even though their ministers and members resided primarily in the much-fought-over border South; we are told that after Union armies had occupied middle Tennessee and northern Alabama, General (later President) James A. Garfield, who was an ordained minister of that denomination, preached in an Alabama church at a service with Confederate soldiers in the audience, and that this relaxed relationship between Federal and Rebel coreligionists was quite normal.[6] Yet within a few years that denomination was embroiled in a bitter quarrel over the use of instrumental music in worship, leading to a formal schism. The old inclusive spirit of Barton W. Stone "waned," writes N. Eugene Tester; "Disciples judged each other's loyalty primarily by an attitude toward the organ. . . . Men boasted of the congregations into which they had thrust organs, or of those in which they had thwarted its introduction, as so many scalps dangling from the party belt."[7] By 1889, Disciples opposed to "innovations" were gathered at Sand Creek, Illinois, to take action which amounted to division, and for the Federal church census of 1906 the "Churches of Christ (non-instrumental)" asked to be listed separately.

A similar fate befell the Episcopalians, just as they were beginning to congratulate themselves on having come through the Civil War essentially undivided. It was true that the Anglican bishops of the South had organized their dioceses into an Episcopal Church for the Confederate States of America, and that one of them, Bishop and General Leonidas K. Polk, had died fighting under the Stars and Bars. Nevertheless, when the Southern churchmen reappeared at the parent Church's General Convention of 1865, a convention majority rejoiced at their presence and voted to seat them—in stark contrast to the fate of the Southern political representatives who presented themselves before a wrathful Radical Republican Congress at the end of that same year.[8] But then, as some Episcopalians had privately warned it might,[9] the denomination experienced schism over an entirely different set of issues. By a strange twise of destiny George Cummins, the very delegate to the 1865 General Convention who had offered the motion to accept the representatives sent from Texas, North Carolina, and Tennessee to that body, became in 1873 the leader of the rebels, who named themselves the Reformed Episcopal Church and elected Cummins to be their first Presiding Bishop.

Raymond W. Albright, a modern Anglican historian, following what seems to have been a considerable consensus among the Episcopal clergy in the Gilded Age, has concluded that if Cummins had led his schismatic movement at the General Convention of 1868 "he might easily have had the concurrence of most of the other bishops present," as well as the support of four or five hundred of the clergy, who would inevitably "have been followed by thousands of leading laymen."[10] But schisms, like revolutions, must come when the time is ripe. The secession of 1873 was on a modest scale, involving at the outset only nineteen laymen and eight of the clergy. However, it was an acute manifestation of a chronic disorder in the Episcopal Church; and it may also be studied for insight into the form taken by the age-old conflict of freedom and order in other American churches during the Gilded Age.

    II   It was particularly ironical that the only schism, if the special case of the Confederate Church be excepted, in the one hundred and eighty years of the Protestant Episcopal Church's existence should have been triggered by a call for greater church unity. Counter-tendencies to the divisiveness endemic in American religion have always been present, even at the time when the ties of which Calhoun spoke were breaking. Lefferts A. Loetscher delivered a memorable presidential address to the American Society of Church History on "The Problem of Christian Unity in Early Nineteenth Century America," pointing to the multitude of agencies at work in that age across sectarian lines, planting home missions, distributing tracts and Bibles, working in hospitals and prisons, or agitating for social reforms— temperance, the overthrow of slavery, world peace.[11] The same transdenominational thrust was evident in Western Europe also. Out of these early ecumenical concerns came a desire that this existing unity among Christians be expressed in a more general organization; in 1846, therefore, leaders of the major Protestant denominations met in London to found the Evangelical Alliance.

    Although Americans had played a major if not the decisive role in establishing the Alliance, the slavery issue made it impossible either to organize an American branch or to hold a meeting on American soil until after the Civil War. When that assembly finally took place, in New York City from October 3 to 12, 1873, the *Times* proclaimed it to be "the most remarkable and important religious council which has ever been convened on this continent." These sessions were intensively covered in the secular as well as the religious press, and the general public interest (or at least curiosity) can be gauged from the crowds in attendance; an alert Hartford *Courant* reporter even noticed some ticket scalping.[12]

The sessions of the Evangelical Alliance had the cosmopolitan flavor we have come to associate with such conferences in more recent years. The Alliance represented no churches as such, but against the prevailing sectarian atmosphere its tone was warmly ecumenical. In addition to the kinds of papers theologians enjoy reading to one another on such occasions there were many pulpit exchanges and some interchurch religious services. During the first day's session the Dean of Canterbury read a letter from his Archbishop expressing sympathy with the objectives of the Alliance and a prayer "that God may hasten the time when differences which at present tend too much to keep Christians asunder may be removed." Hopes rose that national as well as sectarian differences might be transcended; at one of the sessions a German delegate exclaimed: " 'I know there are times—and this is one of them—when Germany can extend her hand to France'—and having said this he advanced to where [a French delegate] was sitting and gave him his hand, while the audience rose and cheered tumultuously."[13]

But there seemed little if any incentive to remove one of the most long-standing of these divisions. The great issue for Christians of that day, said the New York *Herald,* was how to meet the challenge of unbelief; but at the meetings of the Alliance that cause had "had but one or two exponents of any ability. For the far narrower and more vulgar fight between Protestantism and Catholicism it could call forth every man on its roll of members." The Chicago *Tribune* concurred; "The Alliance has hitherto been composed of those bodies of Christians . . . who, if they held one thing in greater disesteem than another, it was the Roman Catholic Church," an editorial in that newspaper declared. "We suppose that not one third of the men or women brought up in evangelical churches in this country ever heard a kind word said in their youth concerning the Catholic faith, though they have all heard this church denounced as the 'Scarlet Woman,' and if the Catholic laity escaped like excoriation, it was on the ground that they were too ignorant and too priest-ridden to know any better."[14] Even within the Protestant consensus of the Alliance the centrifugal force of sectarian division proved stronger than the hopes of union; before the conference was over it had touched off yet another denominational schism.

When the Dean of Canterbury was publicly criticized in an open letter from another visiting English churchman for the "grave . . . breach of ecclesiastical order" of having shared in a joint celebration of Holy Communion with Alliance leaders from other denominations, the American Episcopalian George Cummins (who had also participated in one of the Alliance-sponsored joint communion services) decided that this rebuke

THE MENACE OF THE VATICAN.

We suppose that not one third of the men and women
brought up in evangelical churches in this country ever
heard a kind word said . . . concerning the Catholic faith.
—*Chicago Tribune, 1873.*

was the last straw. Within a month Bishop Cummins announced his intention to leave the Protestant Episcopal Church, and on the second of December in a New York City Y.M.C.A. hall the Reformed Episcopal Church was born. Rejecting the "high church" exclusiveness of the parent denomination, the Reformed Episcopalians began to revise the Book of Common Prayer, and they specifically invited "our fellow Christians of other branches of Christ's Church" to share in the Communion service. From the beginning, ministers of other denominations were accepted in the Reformed Episcopal

Church without reordination, and members of other evangelical churches were received without having to be reconfirmed. "We would walk together," W. R. Nicholson wrote in 1874 in concluding one list of *Reasons Why I Became a Reformed Episcopalian*, "through the boundless landscape with our Presbyterian brethren, and Methodist, and Baptist, and all who love the Lord Jesus Christ."[15]

To the ear of a person unfamiliar with liturgical worship, a church service using the new Reformed Episcopal prayer book would not have sounded very different from what the parent church was doing, especially by contrast with the spontaneous style of prayer used by other American Protestants (at Dwight L. Moody's revivals, for example). But Cummins and his associates substituted "low church" language for "high" at a number of strategic points. Thus, the embarrassing words, to most American Protestants, "Grant us . . . so to eat the flesh of thy dear Son Jesus Christ, and to drink His blood" became "Grant us . . . so to commemorate in this breaking of bread the death of thy dear Son;" and the ambiguity of "Take and eat this" and "Drink this" ("This what?" a suspicious Protestant might have asked) was resolved by making it "Take and eat this bread" and "Drink this wine." And afterward, instead of thanking God "that thou dost vouchsafe to feed us, who have duly received these holy Mysteries," the Reformed Episcopalians thanked Him "that thou hast vouchsafed to call us to the knowledge of the truth."[16]

In short, here were a group of men who, in the innovative, science-minded nineteenth century, sought to purge their faith of denominational exclusiveness and "holy mysteries." By contrast with the thought-confining creeds, the antique liturgy, and the medieval sacerdotalism of their High Church adversaries, what could have been more in harmony with the spirit of the age? Surprisingly a twentieth-century Anglican commentator, looking back on the Reformed Episcopalians and on the Low Church movement of which they were the most acute expression, saw them not as progressive in terms of their day but as reactionary: "One can sympathize with these men who seemed to see everything for which they stood swept away," Bishop Edward L. Parsons wrote in 1946. "They did not know that they belonged to a past age."[17]

Anglican special pleading conceivably might be involved in such a statement, but non-Anglicans would be under no such inhibition. In 1963 the editors of a collection of documents in American church history whose own academic affiliations were, respectively, with a Methodist, a Presbyterian, and an interdenominational theological seminary, likewise saw the Reformed Episcopal schismatics as "far more conservative theologically" than some of their contemporary High Church rivals.[18] Conservative in what sense? one is moved to ask. Conservative, the Reformed Episcopalians said themselves in their *Declaration of Principles,* in the sense of "holding 'the faith once delivered unto the saints.' " In his address upon election as leader of the new Church Bishop Cummins told his brethren: "We have not met to destroy, but to restore; not to pull down, but to reconstruct. . . . We are not schismatics . . . we are not disorganizers; we are restorers of the old; repairers of the breaches; reformers."[19]

One might raise the skeptical objection that almost all revolutions, no matter how drastically innovative, seek for some kind of sanction in the past; Marxism, for example, imagines a primitive and uncorrupted age before early man fell into sin by inventing private ownership. But as was pointed out in the previous chapter a kind of Protestant primitivism, which appealed against the religious authority of the sixteenth century back to that of the first, was widespread in Victorian America. Thus, in committing itself to "the Holy Scriptures of the Old and New Testaments as the Word of God, and the sole rule of faith and practice," the Reformed Episcopal Church aligned itself with a broad orthodox-Protestant consensus, save for the quirk of retaining liturgical worship and the historic episcopate; and the latter, the Reformers explained, they recognized not "as of Divine right, but as a very ancient and desirable form of church polity."

By thus in effect rejecting the authority of the historic Church in favor of the authority of the Bible, the Reformed Episcopalians opened themselves to a charge that they were committing themselves not to radical innovation but to its exact opposite: resistance to all change. In March, 1874—scant weeks after the launching of the new sect—Bishop Cummins preached a sermon in which, after arguing that the Roman Catholic Church had been wrong in suppressing Galileo's findings in astronomy, he somewhat inconsistently exhorted his fellow-Christians to resist Darwinism to the last, as a doctrine evidently contrary to Scripture. Andrew Dickson White, the doughty chronicler of the warfare between science and theology, seized upon this sermon for a characteristically tart comment: "The Bishop forgets that Galileo's doctrine seemed to such colossal minds as Bellarmin [sic], and Luther, and Bossuet, 'evidently contrary to Scripture.' "[20]

Criticisms of the more thoroughgoing Low Church clergymen by their religious superiors, such as Bishop Horatio Potter's admonition to one young rebel in 1868 that "we are not at liberty to preach any kind of doctrine which our . . . minds may invent," may thus seem in a sense unfair. Was *sola scriptura,* so vigorously defended by men like Cummins, a doctrine capriciously invented by modern "independent thinkers, free to follow any wayward fancy of our own," as Potter characterized them?[21] Or was it not rather, in modern Darwinian times, a hopeless historical anachronism? Raymond Albright has suggested that even the Reformed Episcopalians' negatives, *e.g.*, the elimination from their worship of words like "body" and "blood"—at first glance so attractive to an antisupernaturalist modern—really came down to a "demand for rigid monolithic uniformity to guarantee the orthodoxy of the true church."

Forty years after the division, the first official historian of the Reformed Episcopal Church prophesied that if the new denomination's *Declarations of Principles* were "boldly, yet reverently carried out in the strength of the Lord," their Church would "withstand all the adverse waves of unbelief and of the 'false doctrine, heresy and schism' from which we plead to be delivered."[22] A canon of falsehood implies a canon of truth; it would seem, then, that High Churchmen and Low were agreed that a Faith transcending history *had* been "once delivered to the saints," and that "false doctrine, heresy, and schism" did have to be combatted in its name—but, each side attributed the true faith to itself and the falsehood to its opponent. Either alternative, that of a medievalist High Churchmanship committed to the values of a tradition-ridden Church, or of a primitivist Low Churchmanship committed to the values of an archaic Scripture, seemed out of the question for any progressive, modern-minded man; for if ritualism seemed a restoration among Episcopalians of "popery," biblicism drew the taunt of the great anticleric Robert Ingersoll: "The Protestants have a book for their pope."[23] To the scientist's view of an ever-growing, ever-changing world, the religionist seemed able to oppose only an incense-swinging obscurantism or an equally sterile Biblical fundamentalism.

III   Still, in a world that has continued to grow and change, both Catholic and Fundamentalist views have shown vitality beyond what a consistent "progressive" might have expected. Fundamentalism was destined to surface with great vigor in the 1920's, to the appalled surprise of many religious liberals,[24] and in 1909 Professor Henry C. Sheldon of Boston University noticed with some alarm that throughout the nineteenth century, for all "the unwonted progress of free thought and scientific investigation" during the same era, "movements toward radical forms of sacerdotalism have been inaugurated, pushed forward with desperate energy" by Roman Catholics, by Eastern Orthodox, by Anglo-Catholics, by "the more radical neo-Lutherans," and by Mormons— "and crowned with large measures of apparent success." To the enlightened modern mind a "profound emphasis on priestly authority and sacramental efficacy" might seem "ridiculously inadequate" to the needs of the times, but Sheldon warned that the opponents of what he termed "sacerdotalism" should not rely upon the spirit of the age to fight their battles for them; "more than one spirit works in the age."

Even more disconcerting to a liberal intellectual than the appeal to men with minds he considers sound of a philosophy he considers outdated is the appeal of such a philosophy to youth. In this respect Henry Sheldon's criticism, at least as applied to High Church Episcopalians, was far wide of the mark. The Anglo-Catholic movement, Sheldon thought, was the kind of ideology which, "once it gets thoroughly engrained into a company of men," becomes extremely difficult for "those who have received it by inheritance and training" to shake off[25]—a judgment which overlooks the historically crucial fact that the nineteenth-century Catholic revival among Episcopalians had been to a great extent the work of younger men in that Church, however "old" may have seemed some of the ideas they shared.

British in origin, the Tractarian or "Oxford Movement" quickly crossed the ocean. By the time of the American Civil War, here and there throughout what was still called the Protestant Episcopal Church in the United States altar candles were burning, Gregorian rather than Anglican chant was sounding, and "ministers" were calling themselves "priests." This movement was so markedly a matter of youth against age that in the flurry of name calling and heresy-hunting in which both sides engaged it sometimes seemed that the measure of one's "Catholicism" was his willingness to defy his bishop— which from the logic of that kind of churchmanship might seem self-contradictory.[26]

After the War, the young men who were doing such things gained a powerful ally among their elders. John Henry Hopkins, Sr., by seniority their Church's Presiding Bishop, published a tract in 1866 entitled *The Law of Ritualism*, a book whose argument commenced on its front cover with a picture of a smoking censer. Practices such as the use of altar lights, incense, and eucharistic (more bluntly, Mass) vestments were not only legally permissible, however "papist" or "Romish" they seemed to Protestant or "low church" Episcopalians, but also, thought Hopkins, the Catholic spirit they symbolized was likely in the long run to carry the day. In all probability this Ritualism would "grow into favor . . . until it [became] the prevailing system." The historical process was working for, not against, liturgical worship.

> The old, the fixed, and the fearful will resist it. But the young, the ardent and
> the impressionable will follow it more and more. The spirit of the age will favor
> it. . . . The lovers of glory and beauty will favor it. . . . The rising generation of
> clergy will favor it.

If the young and ardent were going to embrace a cause which the old and
fearful were bound to resist, then perhaps there was more to the Catholic
movement in the Episcopal Church than simple surrender to a medieval past.
As Ferdinand C. Ewer, a particularly prickly Anglo-Catholic polemicist of
the Gilded Age, wrote in 1883: "If the Catholics swing incense and hear
confessions, they are very apt to startle by affirming that Darwin and evolution are not necessarily wrong."

This was a position not yet very popular among the High Church party in
America. Presiding Bishop John Henry Hopkins for example wanted the
Lambeth Conference of the world's Anglican bishops in 1867 to uphold "the
unerring truth of the Holy Scriptures, as the Divinely inspired rule of faith
and practice, and to condemn as false and heretical all doctrine which is opposed to the same"[27]—the doctrine in dispute at the moment being that favorite battleground of Biblical criticism, the question of whether Moses wrote
the Pentateuch. But most Low Church bishops and clergy of Hopkins's generation had been equally Biblical literalists, whereas High Churchmanship—
as symbolized by the publication in England in 1889 of *Lux Mundi*—Seemed
to offer a possible way out.

The authors of *Lux Mundi*, whose views on sin and the fall of man were
examined in an earlier chapter, had been working and teaching together at
Oxford University for a decade when they published their collection of scholarly essays on the relationship between the Christian faith and "modern intellectual and social problems," including those posed by the theory of
evolution, the modern "higher criticism" of the Bible, and the new social
interdependence of mankind. They represented in effect a second generation
of the group which had sparked the liturgical renewal of the 1830's; their
credentials both in the Anglo-Catholic movement and in the British scholarly world were, in short, unimpeachable. To the old Evangelical and Low
Church view of a static faith "once delivered to the saints" which must be
conserved in Gospel purity against Romanizing or other innovations, these
men counterposed the conviction that the age in which they lived was "one
of profound transformation, intellectual and social, abounding in new needs,
new points of view, new questions." In the words of *Lux Mundi*'s editor and
principal contributor, Charles Gore,

The Church, standing firm in her old truths, enters into the apprehension of the new social and intellectual movements of each age; and because "the truth makes her free" is able to assimilate all new material, to welcome and give its place to all new knowledge, to throw herself into the sanctification of each new social order . . . shewing again and again her power of witnessing under changed conditions to the catholic capacity of her faith and life.[28]

Cummins's Low Church militants, made doubly anxious to maintain their Scriptural purity in the face of the charge of schism, offered no direct answer to the challenge of the new science and scholarship, whereas the rationale of Charles Gore (and of John Henry Newman, in his *Essay on the Development of Christian Doctrine*), by stressing the capacity of the Church for intellectual self-renewal, enabled young churchmen to cease being defensive against the new knowledge and go over to the attack.

A favorite argument of positivists and freethinkers, then as now, was that the historical development of religion is a matter of "less and less"—from Catholicism to the Continental Reformation to Puritanism to Arminianism to Deism to Transcendentalism to Humanism. Francis Ellingwood Abbot, a founder of the Free Religious Association, saw Christianity as "coming to its prime in the Romish, and lying at Death's door in the Unitarian Church."[29] What the new generation of Catholic intellectuals did was in effect to reverse this argument. Rather than shutting out more, as man becomes less superstitious, religion was seen as taking in more, as man becomes more cosmopolitan. Thus High Church Episcopalians of this stamp, like Roman Catholics of Cardinal Newman's sort, were able to assert against the reductionist claims of many secular thinkers that increasing Catholicity was the wave of the future; and against the exclusiveness of the Low Churchmen's Biblical "faith once delivered" they were able to counterpoise the inclusiveness of a protean and ever-maturing Church.

IV   But churchmanship of Ferdinand Ewer's and Charles Gore's kind was distinctly a minority movement within American religion as a whole, and its Roman Catholic equivalent does not seem to have been popular with Catholics in America.[30] Furthermore, Bishop Cummins faulted his opponents in the Church he had quit not only for their Ritualist innovations but also for their spirit of separatism. High Churchmen in the Gilded Age like the John Henry Hopkinses, Senior and Junior, were inclined to regard their persuasion as the party of the future, but if anything on the religious scene in the 1870's looks like a "party of the future" from the standpoint of the twentieth century it is the cause of interdenominational unity. From the Evangelical Alliance of that day there was movement, slowed but not checked by the World Wars, toward ever-increasing Christian union, culminating in the foundation of the World Council of Churches; the subsequent entrance into that Council of the Iron Curtain churches; the dramatic gestures toward "Our separated brethren" by Pope John; and the meetings of his successor with the Archbishop of Canterbury and with the Eastern Orthodox Oecumenical Patriarch. Surely in this light it could be maintained that the Reform Episcopal Church, if more "narrow" than some communicants of the P. E. Church in clinging to a Scripture untempered by history, was more "ecumenical" in its conception of its relationship to other kinds of Christians.

But a curious thing happened. By the end of its first generation the new Church, conceived in revolt against the exclusivism of its parent, had developed an exclusive consciousness of its own. (Very likely in nineteenth-century America this was inevitable; the largest conventional denomination native to the United States, the Disciples of Christ, had been the handiwork of Presbyterian, Methodist, and Baptist come-outers who had wanted only to transcend their partisan sectarian backgrounds and dwell together simply as "Christians," but they ended by creating still another sect—three more sects, as it finally turned out). By 1901 a Reformed Episcopal bishop would be warning a young people's conference in Chicago to be on their guard: "Allow nothing in the Church which can create the impression that you are striving to conceal the impassable gulf separating us from the Anglican Church as it is in the present day." The following year Mrs. Annie Darling Price, writing the official history of the new church, closed with a plea that the children in Reformed Episcopalian Sunday Schools be taught "the distinctive principles of our denomination."[31]

When the Federal Council of Churches was established in 1908 the Reformed Episcopal Church, consistent with its own founding principles, became a charter member, and took enough pride in that affiliation to mention it in the statements subsequently furnished for the Federal census of religious bodies.[32] However, in the struggle during the twentieth century to maintain a constituency with distinctive consciousness, the ecumenical aspiration has been lost. In more recent years the denomination has dropped out of relationship with the Federal (later National) Council. A church which had begun with such high hopes, "like a bugle-blast waking up drowsy thinkers" in the "Old Church," as one early convert put it, "as though it were a *Sursum Corda* pronounced, or sung, or thundered, into that Church's ears," ended by surviving anticlimactically as one of a scatter of obscure and ingrown American remnant sects.[33] This paradoxical outcome had been inherent in the situation of its founding fathers. The one seemingly unanswerable argument of those who remained in the "Old Church" was to point out that Bishop Cummins and his associates, for all the sincerity of their ecumenical intentions, had felt it necessary in the interest of Christian unity to divide Christianity still further.

Phillips Brooks, for example, whose churchmanship was neither "high" nor "low," approved of the Evangelical Alliance and believed in the open pulpit quite as fully as Cummins did, to the extent that he could preach effectively in one of a series of meetings sponsored by the lay revivalist Dwight L. Moody, and could participate in union Good Friday services at Boston's Old South Church with Congregationalist, Baptist, and even Unitarian fellow-clergy; but he did not approve of the Cummins schism. In Brooks's opinion, leaving one's church was no way to achieve the goal of union, and he felt it his duty to work within his denomination for the principle of open fellowship, in a sense playing Erasmus to Cummins's Luther.[34] Less charitably Bishop Alfred Lee, who had ordained George Cummins to the ministry, taunted him with the inconsistency of having divided in order to unite: "Will you add another to the unhappy divisions of Protestant Christendom, and when the Church of Christ is already so broken up, increase the number of fragmentary bodies?"[35]

"Is the great family of man divided by races, and geographical separations, and varying traditions, and habits, and languages? The Christianity which is to remedy this [is] still more divided than the human race itself." The cry could have come out of New York's Union Theological Seminary in the 1950's, but in this case the words are from a Lenten sermon of 1865 by the powerful Anglo-Catholic controversialist James DeKoven. This objection to church division was not merely pragmatic; churchmen who talk of "bodies" and "Body" in such a way mean those words in the most theologically literal sense. "The remedy for the ills of a divided humanity is to be found, and only found," DeKoven went on, "in the uniting together of every human being in the Body of Christ, which Body is the one holy Catholic and Apostolic Church. . . . In it there [is] . . . neither Jew nor Greek, barbarian, Scythian, bond nor free, but Christ [is] . . . all and in all."[36]

The paradox here lies in the fact that the Reformed Episcopalian George Cummins and the Anglo-Catholic James DeKoven were each, from his own point of view, an ecumenicalist, but from the other's point of view a separatist. Each thought of his own position as inclusive and the other's as exclusive, and the irony is that both were right. It is a familiar dilemma to anyone who has followed the Protestant-Roman Catholic dialogue of the twentieth century, but it is surprising to find it in this earlier form, woven into the texture of the spiritual crisis of the Gilded Age.

V   For the Protestant of that age, more consciously and systematically anti-Catholic than his modern equivalent who in 1960 might have voted for John Kennedy, DeKoven's words would have had a suspiciously "Romish" smack. And in any case many Protestants, true to the Reformation tradition as they understood it, would have seen nothing wrong in division. As late in the century as 1898 William Newton Clarke suggested that organic union was foreign to the essential genius of Protestantism: "It does not appear to have been the providential purpose that all Christians should be gathered into one great organization," he declared, and, quite unlike the spirit of some World Council of Churches spokesmen of a later day, Clarke doubted that such an ingathering would ever take place; "organization . . . cannot properly be counted as a part of religion."[37]

For churches no less than for states, union was not to be had by crying "glorious union" any more than health was to be had by crying "glorious health"—with the added complication that for Protestant churches in particular it was not clear that union was necessarily the most health-giving thing possible. Better truth as one sees it in a divided state, perhaps, than false doctrine accepted in the interest of union. Some Southern Presbyterians in the Gilded Age were wont to complain against interdenominational Sunday Schools as "retarding the church's development through a foolish similitude of brotherliness," and in 1888 a Baptist lady, recoiling at the "manifest perversion of God's word" every time she saw a candidate for baptism sprinkled rather than immersed, asserted that she "would rather be a Baptist alone than to pretend to be something else where there were a multitude." Some Disciples outdid even this: "I mean to say distinctly and emphatically," wrote the Rev. Moses E. Lard in 1863, "that Martin Luther, if not immersed, was not a Christian."[38]

Methodists appear to have been slightly more tolerant of the beliefs of their fellows; "the Methodist Church . . . merely held that its denomination was the best—not the only one," one historian of the churches in Alabama's Black Belt concluded. But Methodists in New York City found another argument to raise in favor of frank sectarianism. "The prospect of still another sect or denomination of Protestants is not at all alarming to us," said Methodism's authoritative *Christian Advocate* in an editorial commenting upon the Reformed Episcopal schism. "Believing, as we do, that there is more to be feared from too much consolidation than from the opposite, we are quite willing to witness an increase of independent Church organizations whenever good reasons appear for still another 'sect.' " Writing on the subject "Methodism—A Flash or a Flame?" another contributor to that journal found a defense of sectarian distinctiveness in the character of his own denomination. Methodism theologically "holds the middle ground between Calvinism and Universalism," D. A. Goodsell wrote, and in its form of church government it held "the middle place . . . between ineffective liberty and unjustly effective tyranny."[39]

Henry Ward Beecher told the Evangelical Alliance delegates in New York that if the purpose of their organization were "the extermination of sects, I should not belong to it."[40] Less negatively Henry King Carroll, editor of a statistical survey of "the religious forces of the United States" based on the Federal census of 1890, took positive pride in America's infinite variety. Americans liked "the idea of manufacturing or producing just as many articles of merchandise as possible," Carroll reasoned.

> We have invented more curious and useful things than any other nation. In matters of religion we have not been less liberal and enterprising. . . . There are churches small and churches great, churches white and churches black, churches high and low, orthodox and heterodox, Christian and pagan, Catholic and Protestant, Liberal and Conservative, Calvinistic and Arminian, native and foreign, Trinitarian and Unitarian . . . more brands of religion, so to speak, than are found, I believe, in any other country. This we speak of as "the land of the free." . . . We scarcely appreciate our advantages. Our citizens are free to choose a residence in any one of fifty States and Territories, and to move from one to another as often as they have a mind to. There is even a wider range for choice and change in religion.

In the highly-charged "ecumenical" atmosphere of American Protestant officialdom after the Second World War, more was heard of the urgency of unity than of the liberty of diversity; some ecumenically-minded churchmen even prophesied a "coming Great Church." And from time to time as the Gilded Age wore on this same note began to be sounded. Protestants approached the question of organic union, especially with authoritarian Rome, in a more gingerly fashion than Anglo-Catholics like James DeKoven, but a few delegates to the Evangelical Alliance assembly of 1873 did call for a more comprehensive unity: "Was it not time they should all be sick of denominationalisms?" the secretary of the British Alliance cried.[41]

Shame at the sects' mutual hatreds may have accelerated this process.

"Much as I love Presbyterianism, a love inherited from all my ancestors—if on account of it, it were necessary for me to abate in the least my good will toward all sects," David Swing wrote in 1874, "I should refuse to purchase the Presbyterian name at so dear a price." Charles A. Briggs, a fellow-Presbyterian, wrote in 1889: "The process of dissolution has gone on long enough. . . . The drift in the Church ought to stop. . . . The barriers between the Protestant denominations should be removed and an organic union formed."[42]

In 1893 the same cleric wrote, in a surprisingly modern accent, on "The Alienation of Church and People." "The churches are engaged chiefly in the conservative work of caring for the regular worship of the congregations at the stated times," Briggs charged, in language reminiscent of James A. Pike in the 1960's. "The churches are not churches of the people; they are churches of select religious societies, from which the people as such are excluded." As a result, said Professor Briggs, "the church has lost the confidence of the people in its ability to teach them the truth . . . in its authority as a divine institution . . . in its sanctity." He blamed a great deal of this on denominationalism, "the great sin and curse of the modern Church." By implication, ecumenical union held the hope of redemption from the more generalized anxiety that burdened religious believers during the Gilded Age. By "combining the executive bishop with the legislative presbytery and the electing people in one comprehensive organization . . . in which the official doctrine will be reduced to the simple sentences of the universal catholic faith," Charles Briggs hoped, the Church might expect to regain "the confidence of the people in her divine authority, sanctity, and catholicity." The situation was urgent; "We are living in the ebb-time of the Christian Church," Briggs warned. "The Church is ruled by dogmaticians, ecclesiastics, and traditionalists. But their day is almost over." Little could he have known of the irony that history held in store: that the organized Ecumenical Movement of the twentieth century would itself become, to an uncomfortably great extent, the property of dogmaticians, ecclesiastics, and traditionalists![43]

VI   At the end of the nineteenth century Leonard Woolsey Bacon concluded a history of Christianity in America with a chapter tracing the tendencies toward American church union, from the unitive hopes of colonial figures like Zinzendorf through the trans-sectarian societies of the Age of Jackson, the interdenominational activities of the Evangelical Alliance and the Y.M.C.A., and the international conferences of the denominational families themselves—Anglicans at Lambeth from 1867, Reformed

(Presbyterian) churches after 1877, and the conferences of worldwide Methodism beginning in 1881; culminating in the World's Parliament of Religions in 1893. Bacon implied that all these activities were "great providential preparations as for some divine event, still hidden behind the curtain that is about to rise on the new century,—and here the story breaks off half told."

It has been customary to scoff at the optimistic expectations some Victorians had for the coming century, since we know that unbeknownst to them behind that curtain waited the catastrophe of 1914 and the shock of Hiroshima. But the specific "divine event" which Bacon seemed to anticipate was some kind of ecumenical union of at least the American branch of Christendom; and, judging by the forces set loose in Protestantism by the Faith and Order Movement and in Catholicism by the pontificate of John XXIII, the Congregationalist historian's expectation now seems in retrospect rather less utopian. In fact Leonard Woolsey Bacon may have set his sights too low. "The very principle of inclusiveness which the ecumenical movement has so valiantly upheld promises by the year 2000 to be the standard by which it shall have been found wanting," wrote Willard Gurdon Oxtoby two-thirds of the way through the twentieth century. "For why should one stop with *Christian* unity? . . . Ecumenism—defined in terms of Christianity alone—is about to become old-fashioned, and in three decades it will seem downright reactionary."[44]

The quest for a unity broader than that of Christianity was already under way in the Gilded Age, as the next chapter will show. But a more pressing problem for Protestant ecumenists was how to take account of Protestantism's venerable adversary. Particularly since the World's Parliament of Religions, Bacon declared, "the idea . . . that the only Christian union to be hoped for . . . . must be a union to the exclusion of the Roman Catholic Church and in antagonism to it, ought to be reckoned an idea obsolete and antiquated." American Catholics of Bacon's generation might have been excused for greeting this hope with polite skepticism; they were just going through their ordeal with the American Protective Association, they vividly remembered the Know-Nothing days, and they were destined in the following generation to endure Al Smith's troubles with the Ku Klux Klan. When Roman Catholics in 1885 "were left out in the cold" in the discussions of an ad hoc American Congress of Churches, the *Catholic World* said: "Perhaps this 'Protestant' movement—for we regret to say it was confined to that —was not, in its present stage of development, any of our business."

Still, that Catholic journal concluded, such Protestant seekers after union were on the right track. To be sure the logical place in which to find such

READING THE LATEST NEWS FROM NEW YORK. INFALLIBLE POPE.—"THAT'S A BAD LOOK-
OUT. IF THEY PUT A STOP TO IGNORANCE WHAT IS TO BECOME OF ME?"

American Catholics . . . might have been excused for greeting this [Protestant]
hope with polite skepticism.

unity was the one church which already possessed it, an answer Protestants
have usually found infuriating; but if all roads insistently led to Rome, this
was Rome conceived of not entirely with the rigor of Pius IX but with something of a Johannine breadth, at least by the harshly competitive sectarian
standards of 1885. Conceding that "the church on the human side is always
imperfect," the *Catholic World*'s editor suggested that his own would profit
by the inclusion of a Chinese national among the College of Cardinals, and

MOODY AND SANKEY IN PHILADELPHIA—THE OPENING SERVICE.

by the opening of the Papacy itself to the man most qualified spiritually and temporally, "irrespective of his race or nationality." (We should remember that the Congress of the United States had passed the Chinese Exclusion Act but two years previously, and that up until our own age of Catholic *aggiornamento* it seemed unthinkable that the supreme pontificate itself would ever be anything but an Italian preserve.) As for the Protestant churchmen who took part in or sympathized with the Congress of Churches, said the *Catholic World*, "their authority is greater than they think."[45]

Indeed, some thoughtful Protestants were beginning to ask, how different are we, really? Do "high" churchmen practice a formal liturgy whereas "low" churchmen practice a more spontaneous kind of worship? In 1886 a leading Presbyterian took note of the increasingly liturgical nature of worship in his denomination, for all the cries of alarm against the progress of this "formalism."[46] Do "low" churchmen govern themselves democratically, whereas "high" churchmen submit to the government of bishops? "No small part . . . of the actual, practical work of a bishop is really done among Congregationalists by an irresponsible episcopacy of theological professors, secretaries of societies, 'leading pastors,' etc.," one member of that church family observed.[47] Do "high" churchmen believe in the magic transformation of the

Mass, whereas modern-minded "low" churchmen merely honor their Founder's death by giving a banquet in His memory? Henry Ward Beecher stood before his congregation on July 5, 1874, holding before them the bread and wine for Communion and said: "For whom is it? What is it? It is bread for the hungry. It stands here today saying 'I represent God.' "[48]

Perhaps the doctrine that God "represents Himself by the loaf and the crushed cluster" was not fully "Catholic," but it was a long way from the going "memorialist" interpretation of most of Beecher's Congregationalist colleagues. As usual, Henry Ward Beecher's sensitive antennae had felt a coming trend and articulated it into oratory. Fifteen years later the Presbyterian Charles Briggs declared that he "would rather partake of the Lord's Supper with one who believed in the real presence of Christ, even though he were a Lutheran, than commune with one who denied the real presence, even though he were a Presbyterian."[49] Not long afterward Briggs was ousted from the ministry of his denomination as a liberal, and subsequently he became an Anglican; this was an historical development which, from the conventional understanding we have had of religion in the Gilded Age, would be simply incomprehensible.[50]

10

The Meeting of East and West

"From Greenland's icy mountains, from
    India's coral strand,
Where Afric's sunny fountains roll down
    their golden sand,
From many an ancient river, from many
    a palmy plain,
They call us to deliver their land from
    error's chain.

What though the spicy breezes blow soft
    o'er Ceylon's isle,
Where every prospect pleases and only
    man is vile?
In vain with lavish kindness the gifts of
    God are strown;
The heathen in his blindness bows down
    to wood and stone."

Reginald Heber,
Bishop of Calcutta 1823–1826

"Some of our mail has been about our religious message on Christmas Eve. We
thought a long time about that, and I
personally changed my mind. I first thought
we should use something specifically Christian, something about Christmas. But when
we thought about the vastness of our world,
we decided to read a message that did not
belong to any one religion but which belonged to all men on earth, the story of
our creation."

Astronaut William Anders, of Apollo 8[1]

199

I   "THE nineteenth century has gone into history with an imperishable name and glory." So wrote Judson Smith, corresponding secretary for the American Board of Commissioners for Foreign Missions, in 1901. Our—meaning the Christian West's—knowledge of the world and its peoples had been vastly expanded; the whole domain of the natural sciences had been comprehensively mapped and explored; steam and electricity had revolutionized men's lives and brought them closer together; civil and religious liberty had made solid gains. The development of the foreign missionary enterprise had been no less remarkable. At the beginning of the nineteenth century there had been "a few societies, scantily manned and equipped, prosecuting their work far apart, . . . with very meager results"; by the end of the century these had grown into a movement "of wide reach, conscious of itself, experienced, wisely drilled and led, attempting great things and winning splendid victories." The great religions of the East, which as the century opened had "seemed to stand untouched and strong, firm in their hold upon the people, stout in the opposition they offered to the entrance of a new faith," had ceased by the century's end to be formidable opponents: "Hinduism, Buddhism, Confucianism, are but the shadows of their former strength, and seem on the point of extinction." There were "no backward steps in Christ's march down the centuries and across the nations to universal victory," the missionary executive proclaimed. "We do not now celebrate the triumph, but we are on the march; every foe flees before us, every year makes the cause more resistless; and the end is both certain and near at hand."[2]

Today the end which Judson Smith so confidently prophesied in 1901 seems both less near and less certain. We have seen a renascent Hinduism contributing greatly, in its Gandhist version, toward the liberation of India; we have seen a militant Islam, checked in the Middle East but vigorously expanding in Africa and, in its Black Muslim offshoot, helping perhaps to open a new chapter in the religious history of black America; we have seen a resurgent Buddhism toppling governments in Burma and Ceylon, and a variant of that faith challenging the *pax Americana* in Japan; and if Confucianism on the Chinese mainland is "but a shadow of its former strength," even the most zealous of Christian prophets might balk at forecasting the imminent triumph in China of Christianity. Felicitating Richard Milhouse Nixon upon the favorable horoscope that an astrologer in Viet Nam had cast for his Presidential inauguration on January 20, 1969—on the condition that he bring the war in Viet Nam to an end—Tran Van Dinh, a representative in the United States and Canada of the Vietnamese Overseas Buddhist Association, complimented the American President on the peaceful rhetoric in his Inaugural Address by saying "Here you sound like a Buddhist." To Judson Smith seventy years earlier this praise might have sounded unseemly, coming as it did from a representative of one of the religions Smith had said were "on the point of extinction."[3]

But at the time Smith wrote his triumphant eulogy the statistics of an ever-expanding missionary enterprise appeared fully to support his claim. To the "isolationism" the history textbooks so often have associated with Gilded-Age America the confident and aggressive outreach of foreign missions was an important exception, and the unconverted masses who were the object of that outreach sometimes drew the same mixture of compassion and condescension that was beginning to be accorded to the American Indian. When a half-dozen Methodist ladies in Boston organized in 1869 what later became the Woman's Foreign Missionary Society, they founded a journal which they cozily named *The Heathen Woman's Friend*, and later when the secretary of the Methodist Board of Foreign Missions, John Morrison Reid, undertook the editing of a volume of essays on the major religious faiths with which Christian missionaries could expect to contend as they carried the Gospel to other parts of the world, he had no hesitation in entitling the book *Doomed Religions*.[4]

Involved in such attitudes may have been the bias of sheer ignorance, like the vague anti-Semitism of the prairie farmer who had never seen a Jew, for there was not very much in the way of organized non-Western religion in the United States in the Gilded Age. The census of 1890 listed no more than forty-seven Chinese temples—forty of them in far-off California—ministering to a Chinese population in excess of 100,000. The Theosophical Society, founded in 1875 "to promote the study of Aryan and other Eastern literatures, religions, and sciences" and "to investigate unexplained laws of nature and the psychical powers latent in man," by 1890 stood only in 118th place in the roster of American denominations (out of 143 distinct groups listed), with a scant 695 members, barely edging out the Old Catholics (655).[5] But even lengthy residence among people who practiced those other religions sometimes only reinforced the missionaries' prejudices. In 1884 an American Protestant who lived in Yokohama, assisted by a member of the Yale faculty

A SUGGESTIVE CONTRAST.—THE INDIAN IN THE WILD AND IN THE CIVILIZED STATE. MISS KITTY ROSS, DAUGHTER OF A LEADING OFFICIAL OF THE CHEROKEE NATION; AND CROW FOOT, SON OF SITTING BULL.

who had spent forty years in China and by a former professor at the American college in Beirut, put together a large, sumptuously illustrated treatise on the world's religions, packed with the picturesque encyclopedic detail which Americans in their nonfiction reading have always enjoyed—and called it *Error's Chains: How Forged and Broken.*

Catholic writers sometimes put it less stridently, but they came to the same conclusion. "It must be premised that all of these systems [the Eastern religions] embody portions of the primitive traditions of the race, and are so far true and similar to the Catholic religion," Merwin-Marie Snell acknowledged, but "their special claims have little or no logical foundation, and utterly vanish under a rigid application of the laws of evidence" (which was, of course, precisely what Protestants, Jews, and freethinkers had always said of the special claims of Catholicism).[6] Meanwhile the liberal modernists who had been wrestling with the Higher Criticism and with Darwinism, men presumably less sure of the canons of truth and error than were the more orthodox, found their own subtle ways of condescending to the non-Western religions. Although James Freeman Clarke sought in his monumental *Ten Great Religions: An Essay in Comparative Theology* (1871) "to do equal justice to all the religious tendencies of mankind," he ended by putting all but one of these tendencies firmly in their inferior place: "Christianity is the religion of the most civilized and the only progressive nations of the world." Christians could afford a generous estimate of whatever was excellent "in the feeling of the Japanese, in the morality of the Chinese, or in the thought of the Hindu," George A. Gordon told the American Board of Commissioners for Foreign Missions in 1895, by virtue of "the absolute incomparableness of Christianity," for in the last analysis "there can be no possible competition between the idea of the cross and anything that these natives have to offer."[7]

II   Foreign nationals did not enjoy being called "natives" then any more than they do today, and heirs of the ancient civilizations of Asia in particular resented being grouped among the world's savage "heathen." Had Christians taken the trouble to master Indian philosophy, or to learn the language in which it was written? a native of India demanded. (Indeed to this day, in most of the West, what one word connotes remoteness and obscurity more than the word *Sanskrit*?) To the Western argument that the civilization of India had produced not only magnificent art treasures and profound religious philosophies but also poverty, cruelty toward the Untouchables, and the *suttee*,[8] it was only too easy for a Hindu to lash back at the "Christian" countries with a *tu quoque*. "How has your own nation in the United States treated the [American] Indians?" asked a Brahmin, Purushotam Rao Telang, in *The Forum* for December, 1894.

> Who by force brought the African to your shores? What became of the aborigines of Australia? How was India conquered, and by whom? Who snatched the kingdom of Hawaii from the Queen of those Islands? Who were the Crusaders? Who burned people at the stake and invented torturing-machines? Who were those who wished to burn Galileo for expounding the theory of the earth's motion? . . . Christian history is full of [such] instances, and . . . these facts have much to do with the Hindu prejudices against Christianity.

By a bitter irony, what this Indian national professedly admired most in Christian civilization was the very thing from which the Christians were setting out to redeem it, namely its "worldliness." In material progress the Western peoples had left the East far behind, Telang acknowledged; "You enjoy life better than we do. We eat to live, and you live to eat." The West's railroads and telegraphs were bringing the different Indian nationalities together, and through the influence of the West's newspapers, printing presses, and schools hard lines of caste were slowly passing away. If the object of Americans were truly to improve the condition of India's poor, the writer concluded, "then, instead of teaching them religion, send teachers and open schools; give them education and let them select any religion they like."[9]

In the meantime the consciousness was dawning upon some few in the

Christian West that the "natives" might after all have something to teach them. With his usual open-mindedness Phillips Brooks visited India in 1883, and although the Brahmin from Boston rejected the religion of the Brahmans from Delhi "as a philosophy, or answer to the problems of existence," he conceded to it "a wonderful power of appeal to some moods of almost all our natures . . . sufficient to make us understand how it could have been, and still is, held by multitudes of souls." The sojourn in India seems to have made a lasting impression. Answering a correspondent in that country five years after the visit, Brooks wrote: "Your letter brought me the Indian sunshine and color and strength, and Boston for a moment seemed the unreal thing"—a major concession, for a New England "native"! "The trees are chattering Puritan theology, and I am rejoicing that the world is larger than they know."[10] A different way of discovering that the world was larger than he had known was that of Leighton Parks, who on a visit to Japan in the Eighties had the disconcerting experience of being worsted in argument by a Japanese priest, in a lengthy debate covering creation, transmigration, the authority of the Bible, the nature of God, and (inevitably) the question of historical progress. Parks and his companions left the temple afterward "having much to think of, for in a nation 'very superstitious' we had met a man who was 'working righteousness' "—and who, moreover, had left the American visitor "feeling very much like a *sophomore!*"[11]

Already in 1871 James Freeman Clarke was worried lest the reaction against "the extravagant condemnation of the heathen religions" had gone too far in the opposite direction: "An ignorant admiration of the sacred books of the Buddhists and Brahmins has succeeded to the former ignorant and sweeping condemnation of them." If there were few outright conversions of Americans to non-Western faiths, there was considerable toying with the idea of syncretism. In that same year, 1871, Lydia Maria Child, writing on "The Intermingling of Religions" for the *Atlantic Monthly*, likened the state of the world in her day to that of the West at the beginning of the Christian era, when a framework of Roman roads and Roman laws had drawn the nations into a Cosmopolis wherein the early missionaries could propagate their faith. In the nineteenth century as in the first, "old traditions are everywhere relaxing their hold upon the minds of men," and the ultimate outcome might not be the total Christian conquest that the authors of *Doomed Religions* and *Error's Chains* expected, but rather the fusion of diverse religious traditions into one "Eclectic Church": "Men find there are gems hidden among all sorts of rubbish. These will be selected and combined in that Church of the Future now in process of formation."[12]

There was much in the religions and philosophies of the East to make such a prospect plausible, but just as there were countless committed Christians who believed with Judson Smith in the imminent and inevitable world triumph of their own uniquely genuine revelation, so likewise there were advocates of Buddhism and Hinduism who had no hesitation in proclaiming the positive superiority of their faiths over those of the West. "Christianity boasts of the time-worn saying of the fatherhood of God and the brotherhood of man," observed Virchand R. Gandhi in 1894, "but what is this compared with the universalism of the Bhagavad Gita, which declared that the religiously enlightened looks with equal love upon a Brahmin, a *chandala* (the lowest of castes), a cow, an elephant, or a dog?"[13] Buddhists could be equally as convinced that their own faith was higher than that of the Christians. "The future will see a great spiritual struggle," wrote Philangi Dasa in 1888; "but it will not, as some suppose, be between the growing Materialism and the decaying Christianism of to-day, but between Materialism and Buddhism."

Dasa therefore decided that the time had come to reverse the missionary process, and he undertook a vow to publish for seven years a Buddhist missionary magazine, the first in an occidental language and the first to appear in Christendom. Appropriately enough it lived out its seven-year span in Santa Cruz, California, under the name of *The Buddhist Ray*. Nor was this so exotic a transplant as an American reader might at first have expected. The editor sought to relate its message to that of a religious movement which had already had some intellectual influence in this country, namely Swedenborgianism, and in his lead editorial for Volume I, Number 1, this pioneering evangelist of The Buddha skillfully aligned the philosophical negations of Asian antiquity with the religious doubts of America's Gilded Age. "Why Buddhism?" Dasa asked.

> Because it does not try to define the Undefinable
> Because it does not make itself ridiculous by projecting its own image and calling this the Creator . . .
> Because it does not propagate itself by cheat, torture, sword, and fire . . .
> Because it does not paralyze the Mind by picturing before it an endless hell . . .
> Because it does not insult the Human Soul by placing mediators and priests between it and the Divine Spirit. . . .
> Because it does not affront Reason by teaching that the mystery of life can be solved by it in one incarnation.[14]

Rationalist and skeptic writers since the time of Volney and Voltaire had noted the striking surface resemblances between Buddhism, especially in its Tibetan (Tantric) version, and Catholicism—an infallible "pope," the Dalai

Lama; tonsured monks, confession, the vow of celibacy; veneration of images and relics, bells, incense, and holy water; and especially the story of Buddha's birth to a Blessed Mother named Mayä, a birth celebrated in one passage of the Buddhist scriptures which strikingly parallels Simeon's *nunc dimittis* prayer in Luke 2:25–35. These resemblances were the basis for arguing that Christianity was derivative, not original: "Christ but an ideal Jewish facsimile of Buddha, and the Catholic Church an occidental copy of Eastern Lamaism." As a result, the Roman Catholic Church in America may have been more sensitized to the threat from this quarter than was American Protestantism. Examining a Buddhist catechism primarily intended for circulation in non-Buddhist countries, a writer in the *Catholic World* for January, 1888, (the very month in which Philangi Dasa launched the *Buddhist Ray*) took note of Question 128, dealing with Buddhism's ethic—"goodness without a God; a continued existence without what goes by the name of 'soul'; happiness without an objective heaven; a method of salvation without any vicarious Saviour; a redemption by one's self as the redeemer, and without rites, prayers, penances, priests, or intercessory saints; and a *summum bonum* attainable in this life and in this world"—and the writer asked: is this not just what modern secular man is trying to do?[15]

III   I am not a Hindoo, my Lord; because I cannot believe men can make their own gods. . . . I am not a Buddhist, . . . because I cannot believe the soul goes to nothingness after death. . . . I am not a Confucian; because I cannot reduce religion to philosophy or elevate philosophy into religion. . . . I am not a Jew; because I believe God loves all peoples alike. . . . I am not an Islamite; because when I raise my eyes to Heaven, I cannot tolerate sight of a man standing between me and God—no, my Lord, not though he be a Prophet. . . .
     I am not a Christian; . . . because I believe God is God.

The speaker is "the Prince of India," the protagonist in General Lew Wallace's historical romance of Constantinople's fall. Wallace had come a long way from the orthodox Christian confession he had made in *Ben-Hur*! His fictional advocate of a "religion of the One God," with both Christ and Mahomet demoted approximately to the status of Elijah—and the secret hope that "in fullness of time both Christ and Mahomet would be forgotten"—lays before the court of Constantine Paleologus an exhibit of the sacred books of the world's great religions (the Bible, the Koran, the Kings [*I Ching*], the Avesta, the Sutras, the Vedas) and expounds from them a firmly reductionist philosophy of comparative religion, dwelling in particular upon the innumerable parallels in the traditional accounts of the lives of the Buddha and of the Christ. Since the Prince in the novel is the legendary Wandering Jew, and is therefore himself a product of one of Christ's miracles, Wallace in a remote and far-fetched way may in the end have given the palm to Christianity. But neither the die-hard Orthodox Church of the Empire nor the fanatical worship of the Imams comes off very well in the story, and although Wallace's Prince of India is technically the "villain" of the piece (since he switches sides in mid-narrative, for revenge), he takes command of scene after scene in a way to suggest that the author intended him to have the last word.

In an age and a society intellectually inclined to monism as Wallace's America was, his (or the Prince's) resolution of the problem posed by comparative religion was also monistic: the worship of the One God was itself to become an exclusive religion, with "all other worship to be punishable as heresy." As the Prince imagines the demise of the Church of Rome, and so also "the isms of the Brahman and the Hindoo, so the Buddhist, the Confucian, the Mencian—they would all perish under the hammering of the union," one begins to appreciate the criticism by Wallace's biographer Irving McKee of the Prince of India's religious scheme as a transplanted version of "American 'efficient' management," on the octopus-model of the Standard Oil Company.[16] Yet the proposal has a poignancy that a reader in our own religiously more relativistic age may easily miss.

The Prince is aware of a paradox inherent in all previous attempts at high religion, namely that although the idea of one universal God has been in theory a means of drawing all mankind together, in practice "there has been nothing so fruitful of bickering, hate, murder and war." ("From the Ceylonesian: 'Who is worthy praise but Buddha?' 'No,' the Islamite answers: 'Who but Mahomet?' and from the Parsee: 'No—who but Zarathustra?' 'Have done with your varieties,' the Christian thunders: 'Who has told the truth like Jesus?' Then the flame of swords, and the cruelty of blows—all in God's name!") The fictional Emperor Constantine, presiding over a city torn by rioting subsects of Christians, and besieged by a foe who matches them all in religious fanaticism, admits that "the world is sadly divided with respect to religion, and out of its divisions have proceeded the mischiefs to which you have referred. Your project," he tells the Prince, "is not to be despised." Shortly the Emperor will himself die fighting in a war largely religious in its origins. Both Greek and Turk reject the Prince of India's plan for a uniform syncretistic religion; the ancient great church of Hagia Sophia duly falls to the conquering sword of Islam; and the Prince's perception that "the wrestling of tongues and fighting were not about God, but about forms, and immaterialities" is lost in the bark of a great primitive gun, progenitor of the artillery Wallace himself had heard thundering at Shiloh.[17]

Four decades after the fall of Constantinople, Christopher Columbus sailed to the New World; and four centuries afterward, in 1893—the year, coincidentally, in which *The Prince of India* was published—the fourth centennial of the discovery of America was celebrated by the opening of a "world's fair," the Columbian Exposition, in Chicago. An editorial in Chicago's *Daily Inter Ocean* for September 12, 1893, repeating a traditional historical interpretation, stated that Columbus had urged as a special reason for his voyage that it would "make the Christian world in general and the royal houses of Aragon and Castile so rich that they could at last wage a successful war against the Moslem for the possession of the sepulcher wherein the body of Jesus of Nazareth was supposed to have been buried." In some ways, the newspaper argued, we have undeniably made progress; "Today, instead of trying to gain possession of an empty tomb . . . at the risk of bringing the horrors of war upon the continents," representatives of Christianity and of Islam were participating in a World's Parliament of Religions, which had just opened in Chicago as an adjunct to the World's Fair.

"Christians and Jews, Mohammedans, Buddhists, Brahmans and followers of about every religious creed in the civilized world met in one grand assembly this morning for the first time in the history of the world," said the Chicago *Daily News* on September 11. "The dark-skinned sectarians of the oriental countries in their white and yellow robes and turbans sat side by side with the dark-gowned and hatted prelates of the Greek church and a red cloaked and capped cardinal of the church of Rome."[18] They were welcomed to Chicago by the Columbian Exposition's President, in the hope that their Parliament would prove to be "a golden milestone on the highway of civilization—a golden stairway leading up to the table-land of a higher, grander and more perfect condition, when peace will reign and the enginery of war be known no more forever."[19] Today it is hard to read such editorials and news stories without a sense of pathos. "The flame of swords and the cruelty of blows," if not exactly "in God's name," has tended nevertheless to make the religious and international fraternalisms of the past sound irrelevant. The *Inter Ocean's* implicit prophecy was wrong; twice in a generation the rattle of small-arms fire has been heard in the vicinity of the Holy Sepulcher, the second time quite possibly "at the risk of bringing the horrors of war upon the continents," and neither a Roman Pontiff nor a devout Buddhist U.N. Secretary-General seemed able to do much more to arrest the course of war in Southeast Asia than to wring his hands.

Perhaps all this helps to explain why the 1893 World's Parliament of Religions has received so little recent scholarly attention.[20] Yet the hopes and fears of the past can illuminate the dilemmas of the present. "Time and again the greatest audience which has ever packed the Art palace thundered its approval of the spirit of toleration and liberality which made possible the parliament of the religions of the world," the *Daily News* story continued; rather than smile at the naïveté of that audience and of the anonymous reporter who covered the event, the reader two-thirds of a century later might do better to ask himself where that spirit of toleration and liberality has gone.

IV   The effective achievement of a World's Parliament of Religions was largely the work of the Reverend John Henry Barrows.[21] The credentials for the mover of so cosmopolitan an undertaking were unmistakably and parochially American; Barrows was even born in a log cabin! His father had been a preacher and teacher in the new states of Ohio and Michigan, his mother an early student at Oberlin, and both parents had been active in the antislavery movement. Educated at three different theological seminaries, Yale, Union, and Andover, from none of which he took a degree, Barrows may have had his international perceptions sharpened by a brief period of travel in Europe (1873); but except for six years in a Congregational church in Lawrence, Massachusetts, most of his own parish ministry was spent in the continental heartland—in Kansas (three years), in Springfield, Illinois, and for fifteen years at the First Presbyterian Church in Chicago. He was, wrote Shailer Mathews (himself a Chicagoan) "an effective preacher, an enemy of religious intolerance, and a pioneer in various undertakings looking toward civic and religious advance."

This kind of activism got him the chairmanship of the World's Fair Committee on Religious Congresses and the vigorous support of people like Mrs. Potter Palmer, but the assembling of a worldwide religious congress proved to be no easy task. Barrows himself noted that "the Committee's appeal was usually made to individuals and not to organizations," which meant that he and his associates "could not depend for the successful accomplishment of their plans on the vote and coöperation of religious bodies." And for bringing in the adherents of Confucius and of the Buddha, of Hinduism and of Islam, of Shinto and of Zen, there was not even the tenuous institutional structure that existed for world Protestantism in its Evangelical Alliance. In the end the holding of the conference was a monument to what tireless publicity can accomplish: ten thousand letters and forty thousand documents, sent out to a mailing list in thirty different countries; editorials published in London,

RECEPTION OF QUEEN KAPIOLANI OF HAWAII AT THE WHITE HOUSE, MAY 4TH—THE QUEEN AND SUITE APPROACHING THE BLUE ROOM.

Athens, Constantinople, Berlin, Melbourne, Tokyo, Shanghai, Calcutta, Madras, Mexico City, Budapest, New York, Boston, and Honolulu; prize essays on Confucianism and Taoism, for which more than sixty Chinese scholars competed; word-of-mouth advertising by prominent American travelers overseas; and the quiet support of the U. S. government, from its ministers and consuls abroad to Secretaries of State John W. Foster and James G. Blaine.

There were some important American absences; the Methodist bishops, for example, excused themselves on the ground that they were too busy with their regular appointments (not an unfamiliar excuse, to anyone who knows that denomination!), but on the whole America's religious leadership responded with enthusiasm. Phillips Brooks died before the Parliament convened but one of his last public acts was to send it his blessing. Philip Schaff, sensing one last opportunity to bear witness to the cause of Christian reunion which had been the passion of his life, disregarded the advice of physicians and friends ("They said it would kill me. Well, let it kill me") and went to

Chicago.[22] Lyman Abbott, Charles A. Briggs, and Theodore T. Munger were there to read papers, as were the Social Gospel pioneers Francis Peabody, Richard T. Ely, and Washington Gladden—and also evangelical conservatives like B. Fay Mills. Reform Judaism was represented by men of the stature of Isaac M. Wise, Kaufman Kohler, and Emil Hirsch, and Orthodox Judaism by the Sephardic rabbi H. Pereira Mendes. Roman Catholic clerics as prominent as James Cardinal Gibbons, Bishop John J. Keane, Monsignor Robert Seton (formerly private chamberlain to Pius IX), and Walter Elliott, who had succeeded to Isaac Hecker's post as editor of the *Catholic World*, were participants. W. T. Harris, United States Commissioner of Education and editor of the *Journal of Speculative Philosophy*, addressed one of the sessions, as did the philosopher of science Paul Carus. Daniel Offord, a member of the Shaker sect, came to the Parliament to expound his doctrines, and Mary Baker Eddy held the platform to explain hers.

Internationally, the gathering was considerably less representative. Many of the nominal spokesmen for China, India, and Japan were Christian missionaries to those countries, or persons whom they had converted. So important a world religion as Islam was represented by a Western convert to that faith, Mohammed Alexander Russell Webb, rather than by a native of the Middle East.[23] A prominent Afro-American clergyman, Bishop Benjamin William Arnett of the A.M.E. Church, spoke at the Parliament, but no believer in any of the religions native to Africa was present. Bishop Arnett did his best to represent, in some fashion, both black America and "the African continent, with its millions of acres and millions of inhabitants, with its mighty forests, with its great beasts, with its great men, and its great possibilities"; significantly at that early date he raised the issue of colonial liberation, and to the discomfiture perhaps of some European delegates to the Parliament (*e.g.*, Germany's Count Bernstorff!), he predicted that God would raise up in Africa a Jefferson to write that continent's declaration of independence, and a Washington—or perhaps a Toussaint L'Ouverture—to lead its hosts. But for the present, this black American clergyman ruefully acknowledged, "We come last on the program."[24]

But for all the Parliament's limitations, visitors to Chicago during the Columbian Exposition were exposed to an unprecedented variety of religious opinions. The audiences—and they were large—could hear Serge Wolkonsky enlivening one of the sessions with a Russian folktale, or Professor Max Müller discoursing on "Greek Philosophy and the Christian Religion," or Henry Drummond lecturing on evolution. They could listen to Pung Kwang Yu, First Secretary of the Chinese Legation in Washington, or Chandradat

Chudhadharn, a member of the royal family of Thailand. They could begin to be aware of the rich religious diversity of the Indian subcontinent as they saw the platform occupied in turn by Jinjanji Jamshedji Modi, a Parsee; Manilal Mabhubhai D'Vivedi, an orthodox Hindu; H. Dharmapâla, an "Orthodox Southern" (*Theravada*) Buddhist; C. N. Chakravarti, a Theosophist; P. C. Mozoomdar, of the Brahmo-Somaj; and Virchand A. Gandhi, a Jain. They might weary, as the formal papers which seem inescapably a part of such gatherings droned on, or they might be caught up in the bursts of crowd-feeling that greeted some of the presentations such as that of Reuchi Shibata, President of the Jikko sect of Shintoism: "A wave of applause for the high priest broke forth all over the house," according to the *Daily Inter Ocean*. "The great audience stood up and cheered and waved their handkerchiefs," and began a "mad rush for the platform" that was checked only by a shout that if they persisted the stage would break down.[25]

There were inevitably some objections. Delegate Joseph Cook of Boston was unhappy at the favorable publicity newspapers like the *Inter Ocean* were giving to non-Christian—he almost said non-Protestant!—belief. "With the press of the country applauding the liberal or rational sentiments of the religious congress and especially the advocates of paganism," said Cook before a meeting of five hundred Methodist ministers in Chicago, "what will be the effect on foreign missions collections?"[26] By the time the Parliament was over Cook had decided that on balance it had been "a resplendent service to Truth," but Morgan Dix, rector of Trinity Church in New York City, remained unconvinced; he felt that the Parliament had been "a masterpiece of Satan." A year previously the Northern Presbyterian General Assembly had passed a resolution that emphatically condemned the Parliament, a particularly crippling blow.[27] Some of the denominational congresses which were planned to coincide with the Parliament's sessions had to be cancelled; the Baptists backed out, for example, when the World's Fair committed the sacrilege of opening on Sundays.[28] A letter to Barrows from a clergyman in Hong Kong gave him "credit for the best intentions," but warned him that he was "unconsciously planning treason against Christ."[29] And both the Archbishop of Canterbury and the Sultan of Turkey disapproved.

Moreover, the association between the Parliament and the Exposition inevitably gave the religious deliberations, no matter how serious, somewhat the air of being just another World's Fair sideshow. "The omnipresent photographer couldn't be shut out," said the Chicago *Daily News*, covering the opening exercises. "He squeezed down to the front in the gallery and squared his camera at Cardinal Gibbons as though he were a prize heavy draft horse at a county fair." The *Inter Ocean*'s praise for the Parliament's objectives frequently modulated into boosterism for Chicago, now by virtue of the Fair "a microcosm, a compendium of the world's civilization." That newspaper was observant enough to concede that the crowds attending the Parliament meetings might be moved less by liberality toward new ideas than by the lure of the sensational: "There is a kind of popular curiosity that likes to run after heresy and everything that is not quite orthodox," with the result that people flocked to hear both Professor Charles A. Briggs, the distinguished American exponent of the Higher Criticism, and also that most far-out of Theosophists, Annie Besant.[30] Contemplating the "wild inventions on exhibition in the Chicago Congress of All Religions" ("Some are brand-new, and look very gay; some are made up of scraps of exploded religions clumsily stuck together and varnished"), the New York *Evening Sun* intimated that this assemblage was only what one might have expected of unsophisticated Chicagoans; "We certainly should not like to see them all put on exhibition at once in New York."[31]

And in spite of all the publicity there was also, in some quarters, massive indifference. The New York *Times* Index for 1893 listed thirteen columns of headlines on the Chicago World's Fair, and not one story or editorial specifically on the World's Parliament of Religions. But the *Times* was not the pervasive force then that it has since become. Every morning that the Parliament was in session the delegates could read the long and highly complimentary accounts of their proceedings which appeared locally in the *Inter Ocean*, colorfully illustrated with pen-and ink sketches.[32] Their own mood seems to have been predominantly one of exaltation; "A holy intoxication, it has been said, overcame the speakers as well as the audience," and one attendant was reminded of "the emotions he had felt in the great revival meetings of President Finney and Mr. Moody." Barrows himself was so convinced the Parliament's work was under Providential guidance that he ventured "to express the conviction that, within a hundred years, pilgrims from many lands would flock to the scenes of the World's First Parliament of Religions, in the unhistoric City of Chicago, almost as they have for centuries flocked to Westminster Abbey, St. Peter's Church, and the Holy Shrines of Jerusalem."[33]

V   As is the tendency with all religious revivals, the glow of this one quickly faded. "Seen in retrospect," wrote Shailer Mathews a generation later, "the World's Parliament of Religions appears less resultful than was foretold." As an historic landmark in the meeting of East and West, however, Mathews thought it to have been "of no small significance";

"Whatever else the Parliament may have accomplished, it developed respect for non-Christian religions on the part of intelligent religious persons." But the reader who belongs to a still more recent generation, sensitized to a rhetoric of "confrontation" rather than of "dialogue," may find the hundreds of pages of sweetness-and-light recorded in these proceedings a bit cloying. In their effort to accentuate the positive in their deliberations, the conferees tended to evade any hard-headed grappling with the very real differences in outlook, metaphysically and otherwise, between the faiths of East and West that would have to be faced before any genuine understanding could result.

It is worth noting that John Henry Barrows was also the author of a book on *Henry Ward Beecher, the Shakespeare of the Pulpit*, celebrating a man renowned for his golden vagueness in showdown situations. As we read Barrows's own consciously picturesque language—"This Book [the proceedings of the Parliament] will also be read in the cloisters of Japanese scholars, by the shores of the Yellow Sea, by the watercourses of India and beneath the shadows of Asiatic mountains near which rose the primal habitations of man"[34]—we may turn with something like relief to the Parliament's occasional discordant interruptions, even to one as petty as the hostile reception an American audience, long alerted to the "menace" of Mormonism, accorded to a distinguished Muslim convert when he attempted a mild defense of polygamy.

> There are conditions under which it is beneficial (cries of "no," hisses, and slight applause). . . . I say that a pure-minded man can be a polygamist and be a perfect and true Christian, (cries of "No, No," hisses and groans), but he must not be a sensualist. When it is understood what the Mussulman means by polygamy, what he means by taking two or three wives, any man who is honest and faithful and pure minded will say, "God speed him." (Cries of "No," "Shame," hisses, and applause).

It may be significant that Mohammed Webb eventually won back his audience and carried the day by crying: "Fortunately, Islam has more religion than theology [Applause]."[35]

Underneath the consensus-rhetoric of the Parliament, however, was a subtle but definite cleavage. Some members of the conclave seem genuinely to have sought a least-common denominator among all the religions, upon which could be erected a world faith; others saw the Parliament primarily as a forum for the triumph of their own.

In the Preface to his fifteen-hundred-page account of the World's Parliament, Barrows indicated where his own deepest convictions lay: with the

"Asiatic Peasant who was the Son of God."[36] Some Christian delegates, free from the diplomatic limitations by which Barrows was bound as the Parliament's host and chairman, were more blunt. George F. Pentecost, a popular London evangelist, began his presentation by declaring: "Christianity is a fighting religion. . . . It is not intolerant of other religions, except as light is intolerant of darkness, but will in no case compromise with error." Carried away by his zeal, Pentecost made some gratuitous remarks about temple prostitution in India, which were repeated in the press.[37] Other Christian speakers (Joseph Cook excepted), and leaders of other religions, were less vehement, and generally managed to have their say without making attacks upon their rivals' faiths,[38] but some of them were no less didactic in the claims they made for their own. The Sinhalese Buddhist Dharmapâla, for example, referred to Ancient India's religious revolution of twenty-five centuries ago as "the greatest the world has ever seen"—which at one stroke disposed of the Reformation, the Hegira, the Exodus, and the Crucifixion; and the Muslim convert Mohammed Webb began his speech on "The Spirit of Islam" with the declaration: "There is not a Mussulman on earth who does not believe that ultimately Islâm will be the universal faith."[39]

Some whose claims were far less sweeping were equally clear in the conviction that it was their own specific religion, not some syncretistic mishmash, which they expounded. Thus Isaac Mayer Wise took great satisfaction from having proclaimed "the God of Israel and His ethical law" in a way that was "intensely Jewish, without reference to any other creed, belief, or literature, simply our own from our own sources . . . and yet commanded the respect of the assembled representatives of all religions."[40] The same spirit of living in a traditional faith and finding it good breathed through every line of Jinjanji Jamshedji Modi's winsome exposition of "The Religious System of the Parsees." And Kung Hsien Ho, author of the prize-winning essay on Confucianism, found in that faith "a doctrine of impartiality and strict uprightness, which one may body forth in one's person and carry out with vigor in one's life. Therefore we say, when the sun and moon come forth (as in Confucianism) then let the light of candles be dispensed with."[41]

But there was also the other view, that the parallel paths followed by the diverse faiths of man must one day converge. Quite unexpectedly the English-language interpreter Z. Noguchi, who was present on the platform to translate the speeches of four Japanese Buddhist priests, in his own remarks swung away from sectarian Buddhism altogether: "Geometry teaches us that the shortest line between two points is limited to only one; so we must find out that one way of attaining the truth among the thousands of ways to which the rival religions point us, and if we cannot find that one way among the already established religions, we must seek it in a new one." The American Thomas Wentworth Higginson dusted off an old lecture on "The Sympathy of Religions"[42] and told the Parliament: "The great religions of the world are but larger sects; they come together, like the lesser sects, for works of benevolence; they share the same aspirations; and every step in the progress of each brings it nearer to all the rest." And Swami Vivekananda, whose own spiritual mentor Sri Ramakrishna had already broken a long trail away from orthodox Hinduism, captured the imagination of the crowd in the prayer concluding his major address to the Parliament: "May He who is the Brahma of the Hindus, the Ahura Mazda of the Zoroastrians, the Buddha of the Buddhists, the Jehovah of the Jews, the Father in Heaven of the Christians, give strength to you to carry out your noble idea."[43]

VI   After the World's Fair had closed, Swami Vivekananda—who by all the accounts had been the Parliament's most vivid personality—stayed on, lecturing in and around Chicago and, it is said, giving spiritual counsel to the elder John D. Rockefeller and to the opera singer Emma Calvé.[44] Eventually he signed on with a lecture bureau for a three-year speaking tour. In an age which relished oratory he appears to have been a master of it; he was well informed, transparently sincere, and good-humored, and by the grace of God he had somehow managed to learn English with a bit of Irish brogue.[45] Much of what he said was intended as a correction of erroneous missionary-inspired beliefs about India (it was actually necessary in those days for an Indian national speaking in a large American city to answer questions such as: "Do the people of India throw their children into the jaws of the crocodiles?"), and its effectiveness may be gauged from the ferocity of the Christian rebuttals that followed him wherever he went: "No sooner had Swamiji left Detroit than the orthodox divines began, as one writer put it, "to pound the dust all out of their pulpit cushions.' " By coincidence the Student Volunteer Movement, with its ringing slogan "The Evangelization of the World in This Generation," had scheduled its second international convention to meet in Detroit at about that time, and Swami Vivekananda's appearance on that band of zealous missionaries' own home ground seems to have had the same upsetting psychological effect as a spirited and skillful guerilla attack upon an army from the rear.[46]

It is not clear just when the Hindu visitor ceased to think of his campaign primarily as a good-will and fund-raising tour for the religious and educational work which prior to the Parliament's meetings he had been doing in India, and instead became consciously a missionary to the Americans.[47] He told one Chicago churchwoman "he had had the greatest temptation of his life in America"; when she teasingly asked "Who is she, Swami?" "he burst out laughing and said, 'Oh, it is not a lady, it is Organization!' " explaining that the followers of his own mentor Ramakrishna "had all gone out alone and when they reached a village, would just quietly sit under a tree and wait for those in trouble to consult them. But in the States he saw how much could be accomplished by organizing work." The eventual result was the founding in New York in 1894 of the Vedanta Society, which continues to this day as a mission-station for Eastern religion in America.[48] That same autumn Mrs. Ole Bull, widow of the great Norwegian concert violinist, introduced Vivekananda and his Vedanta philosophy "to her cautious and faintly suspicious Cambridge friends," at her salon on Brattle Street where John Fiske, Thomas Wentworth Higginson, Irving Babbitt, Hugo Munsterburg, Alice Longfellow, Julia Ward Howe, and a Radcliffe undergraduate named Gertrude Stein were wont to discuss the great questions of the day. Here the Swami met William James, and here he held the classes for perplexed Harvard philosophy majors that led eventually to an invitation, on March 25, 1896, to lecture on the Vedanta before the Graduate Philosophical Society of Harvard University—the innermost intellectual citadel of WASP America.[49]

Other non-Christian delegates to the World's Parliament of Religions planted the seeds of their faiths in the United States also. Mohammed Webb, the fez-wearing American convert to Islam, told the Parliament that a Muslim study group had already been established in New York.[50] One relatively modern offshoot of Islam has done still better in this country. Ibrahim Kheirallah, a Babist, gave a course of lectures in conjunction with the Parliament and won about a hundred converts; by 1901 there were reported to be a thousand Babists (or Baha'is) in Chicago, four or five hundred in Kenosha, Wisconsin, another four hundred in New York City, and another thousand scattered across the country from Boston and Washington and Baltimore all the way to Denver and San Francisco. An important early convert was Phoebe Hearst (wife of Senator George Hearst, who founded the nucleus of his son's vast publishing empire); she organized a pilgrimage to the Holy Land in 1898 to visit Abdul-Baha, leader of the predominant faction in that movement, who reciprocated in 1912 by laying the cornerstone for an impressive Baha'i house of worship in Wilmette, Illinois, not far from the scene of the World's Parliament of Religions.[51] In the same hopeful spirit late in 1899 a Japanese priest, perhaps encouraged by the favorable reception the Parliament had given his countrymen, arrived in San Francisco to "spread the Gospel of Buddha among the Americans," out of a conviction that probably no religion other than Buddhism "would satisfy the refined minds of the twentieth century."[52]

It must be said at once, however, that aside from the recent vogue for Baha'i on college campuses there is probably less heard of "the sympathy of religions" today in America than there was at the end of the Gilded Age, Arnold Toynbee to the contrary notwithstanding. In Boston, Thomas Wentworth Higginson's own bailiwick, the venerable Charles Street Meeting House (built 1807, remodeled *ca.* 1850) has within the past decade been rededicated in the service of a "religion of one world," for which a striking and appropriate symbol was found by filling the chancel with a mural of the Great Nebula in Andromeda; but the services held therein prompted one Beacon Hill lady passing by to murmur "Hog-wash," another to remark "This church is simply not in step," and another to say, when she saw a new family entering the Meeting House for the first time, "I am so happy to see *somebody* going in there."[53] As for the Oriental religions themselves, their visible accomplishments in the New World, at least so far, have been small; the modest Buddhist, Muslim, and Hindu houses of worship in America are physically far outmatched by the Mormon Temple in Salt Lake City, the Mother Church of Christian Science in Boston, or the Cathedral of Saint John the Divine.

This would not be important if one could point to a great surge of Eastern spirituality among Americans, but it would be a claim most difficult to prove.[54] Even after fighting three major wars on non-Western ground, few Americans really know much more about Asia than they did when the Parliament of Religions opened three quarters of a century ago. As a result, most of them have not been able to distinguish between the serious mission of a D. T. Suzuki or a Nikhilananda (Vivekananda's heir and successor) and the vulgar counterfeits so frequently offered in the East's name.[55] Yearning for the peace of mind that Oriental religion promises, they have had no stomach for the self-discipline it demands, and so they have resorted to shortcuts: "beat" Zen, or crash courses with a *guru,* or LSD. They have "taken" Yoga in the same way they ingest the latest fads in health foods, and indeed the very words *Swami, Mahatma,* and *Yogi,* evocative of great holiness in their homeland, have acquired in America a bad (or at most a comic) name.

Two modern investigators concluded that "the majority of Western seekers are as little willing to commit themselves to any of the oriental systems as they are to follow the teachings of Christ," and then asked, "Why then do they seek enlightenment from the East? Apparently, because there is empirical evidence (or so they are assured) that Eastern techniques work without supernatural strings." Swami Vivekananda told the Harvard dons in 1896, "The Yogi wants no faith or belief in his science but that which is given to any other science, just enough gentlemanly faith to come and make the experiment."[56] And here perhaps is the heart of the matter. Exotic as seemed the spectacle at the World's Parliament of Religions, its deliberations prove after all to have been conditioned by the same world-wide shock of encounter between science and faith that characterized the spiritual crisis of America's Gilded Age.

That thoroughgoing German scientific materialist Ernest Haeckel, on a visit to Ceylon, is said to have told "a Singhalese gentleman of high birth" that "so far as explained to him, the Buddhistic theory of the eternity of matter and force, and other particulars, were identical with the latest inductions of science," and Thomas Henry Huxley by the time of his Romanes Lectures in 1893 had begun to find compatibilities between science and Indian thought, from which "the supernatural, in our sense of the term, was entirely excluded."[57] It is a viewpoint which from time to time has been shared by other Western scientists, even under the radically revised ground rules for science since the revolution wrought by Planck and Heisenberg,[58] and it is an argument which the men of the East understandably have found polemically attractive. The latest discoveries of science, Vivekananda told the World's Parliament of Religions, seemed "like the echoes from the high spiritual flights of Vedantic philosophy," and the young Sinhalese monk Dharmapâla informed them that the theory of evolution, in 1893 still a raw and traumatic idea for many of the Western Christian and Jewish delegates, was one of the ancient teachings of The Buddha.

But in a sense such arguments were a capitulation to the radical scientific positivism which for a generation had been so ruthlessly preached in the pages of the *Popular Science Monthly*. "Science will not cease to advance with its work, come what may, and let who will be hurt," E. L. Youmans had said. "It cannot pause, it cannot compromise. . . . The only question then is, whether Religion will take its unyielding theology out of the way, or wait to have it crushed and cast aside."[59] If Religion tried to elect a third option, of substituting for its own unyielding theology a different system of ideas that would not be crushed under the scientific juggernaut (whether these comprised the universal "sympathy of religions" Thomas Higginson preached, or came down to the specific tenets of one of the ancient non-Western faiths), still it would be Science, not Religion, that stood as the arbiter of which among the competing schemes of values might be judged acceptable.

The trouble with such a solution to the spiritual crisis was that science was part of the problem—as it still is. It may well still be true, as Sir Edwin Arnold affirmed in *The Light of Asia,* that "between Buddhism and modern science there exists a close intellectual bond," despite the subsequent scientific revolutions of the twentieth century. But what comfort is that to the person who seeks to affirm, against the consciousness-disintegrating forces unleashed in the modern world, not the "self-extinction" Buddhism strives for but rather the self's integrity?[60] If Buddhism and the Vedanta, or Baha'i —or Islam, or Judaism, or Christianity—have anything to offer to "postmodern" man, as he is sometimes called, it will not be on the ground that one of these, or even a "sympathetic" combination of them, is more scientific than the others, necessary though it is for man as a religious being honestly to square his accounts with science. It will be because they do something to or for him that science can not.

Albert Einstein in 1941 had no difficulty in finding a definition for science: it was "the century-old endeavor to bring together by means of systematic thought the perceptible phenomena of this world into as thoroughgoing an association as possible." But, he admitted, "When asking myself what religion is I cannot think of the answer so easily." Einstein thought, however, that scientific reasoning could indirectly aid religion in the course of its own "striving after the rational unification of the manifold." "Whoever has undergone the intense experience of successful advances made in this domain," he said in what was close to a personal *confessio fidei,* "is moved by profound reverence toward the . . . grandeur of reason made manifest in existence, and which, in its profoundest depths, is inaccessible to man."[61] The answer to this twentieth-century physicist-saint's question, "What is religion?", might well be: That which can account, upon its own terms, for Einstein's use of the unscientific word "reverence" to describe his feelings as a human being toward what he as a scientist had found.

Notes

PREFACE

1. William R. Hutchison to the author, March 31, 1969.

2. Robert T. Handy to the author, March 5, 1969.

3. ["Christian Reid," pseud.] "The Doctor's Fee," *The Catholic World*, XLII (February, 1886), p. 610.

4. He further suggests the existence, among Catholics and non-Catholics alike, of a "practical" agnosticism in that period which never became formulated at the level of doctrine; an existential judgment that "God was not dead, simply committed to the marketplace, the polling-booth, and the research laboratory." Robert D. Cross to the author, February 10, 1969.

5. This sentence is a response to a letter to the author from William A. Clebsch, February 26, 1969.

CHAPTER 1

1. Ambrose Bierce, *The Devil's Dictionary* (New York, [1911] 1935), p. 95.

2. Years later, Ward underscored this passage in pencil, as if to indicate that the loss of faith had become irrevocable. Bernhard J. Stern, ed., *Young Ward's Diary* (New York, 1935), p. 50.

3. Perry Miller, *American Thought: Civil War to World War I* (New York, 1954), p. xxvi.

4. John Tyndall, "The Rev. James Martineau and the Belfast Address," Chap. 33 of Tyndall, *Fragments of Science* (New York, n.d.), p. 516. This essay originally appeared in the *Fortnightly Review*, 1875. On Huxley's agnosticism, see A. O. J. Cockshut, *The Unbelievers: English Agnostic Thought, 1840–1890* (New York, 1966), pp. 88–98.

5. Emma Connor, Dedicatory Hymn for Cosmian Hall, Florence, Mass., March 25, 1874. (From mimeographed sheet as sung at the Free Congregational Society of Florence centennial service, Northampton, Mass., May 12, 1963.)

6. Benjamin F. Underwood, "The Practical Separation of Church and State," an address delivered July 2, 1876, at a Centennial Congress of Liberals, as reprinted in Joseph L. Blau, ed., *Cornerstones of Religious Freedom in America* (Boston, 1949), p. 219. The phrase "tough old atheist," used to characterize Underwood, is Blau's.

7. "A Non-Church-Goer," pseud., "Church Attendance," *North American Review*, CXXXVII (July, 1883), p. 76.

8. Horace Bushnell, *Views of Christian Nurture . . .*, 2nd ed. (Hartford, 1848), as cited in Joseph L. Blau, ed., *American Philosophic Addresses, 1700–1900* (New York, 1946), p. 614.

9. William Culp Darrah, *Powell of the Colorado* (Princeton, 1961), p. 375. For the quarrel between father and son, see *ibid.*, pp. 25f., 39, 72.

10. Max Eastman, *Enjoyment of Living* (New York and London, 1948), p. 277.

11. R. Habersham Barnwell to the Reverend William H. Barnwell, from Petersham, Mass., June 14, 1923. Letter in the possession of a grandson, the Reverend Stephen B. Barnwell, a member of the Department of History, Northern Michigan University, Marquette, Mich.

12. "Christopher Crowfield," pseud. (Harriet Beecher Stowe), *The Chimney Corner* (Boston, 1868), p. 192.

13. James Parton, "Henry Ward Beecher's Church," *Atlantic Monthly*, XIX (January, 1867), p. 41. This essay has been reprinted in its entirety in Robert D. Cross, ed., *The Church and the City* (Indianapolis, 1967), pp. 127–153.

14. Rudyard Kipling, *From Sea to Sea* (New York, 1899), as quoted in Charles N. Glaab, ed., *The American City: a Documentary History* (Homewood, Ill., 1963), p. 339.

15. When it was suggested to Ward in 1890 that he was antagonizing the public by the adverse references to religion in his writings and that he ought to tone them down, Ward replied, "I do not write for the feeble minded." Quoted in Samuel Chugerman, *Lester F. Ward: The American Aristotle* (Durham, N.C., 1939), p. 244.

16. Berenice Cooper, *"Die Freie Gemeinde*: Freethinkers on the Frontier," *Minnesota History*, XLI (Summer, 1968), pp. 53–60. My own estimate of the significance of these societies differs somewhat from that of the author of the article.

17. Charles Marion Russell to William Wesley Van Orsdel, March 20, 1918, reproduced in Charles M. Russell, *Good Medicine* (Garden City, [1929]1930), p. 98. Russell's hand-printed letters, almost invariably illustrated with sketches—in this case of a paddle-wheel steamer and of a buffalo—must be seen in order to appreciate their charm.

18. "A Non-Church-Goer," *op. cit.*, pp. 79, 83; Hamilton Wright Mabie, *Footprints of Four Centuries: the Story of the American People* (Philadelphia and Chicago, 1895), p. 413.

19. "In some respects, the civilization of Western Europe was more profoundly moulded by Christianity than at any previous time in that century," Latourette wrote, and "in the United States of America the gains made by Christianity were even more striking than in Europe." Kenneth Scott Latourette, *A History of the Expansion of Christianity*, IV (New York, 1941), pp. 457, 460, 461. Compare Latourette's one-volume *History of Christianity* (New York, 1953), in which the period 1800–1914 is again referred to as "The Great Century"; see in particular Chap. 50. The same author's *Christianity in a Revolutionary Age* (New York, 1961) is perhaps a shade less confident in tone, but the judgment is essentially the same; see in that work Vol. III, Chap. 8.

20. Martin E. Marty, *The Infidel: Freethought and American Religion* (Cleveland, 1961), p. 139; Richard Hofstadter, *Anti-Intellectualism in American Life* (New York, 1963), p. 120, n. 6. Hofstadter further argued that one reason for the "notable freedom from bigotry and militancy" in Dwight L. Moody, in contrast to some of Moody's epigoni in the twentieth century, is that the great Gilded-Age evangelist's "religious style had already been formed by the early 1870's, when the incursions of modernism were still largely restricted to highbrow circles"—and were therefore less threatening than they later became. *Ibid.*, pp. 122, 121.

21. Henry F. May, *Protestant Churches and Industrial America* (New York, 1949), Part II; Julia B. Foraker, *I Would Live It Again: Memories of a Vivid Life*, as quoted in Ari and Olive Hoogenboom, eds., *The Gilded Age* (Englewood Cliffs, N.J., 1967), p. 158.

22. Charles C. Cole, *The Social Ideas of the Northern Evangelists, 1826–1860* (New York, 1954), pp. 239f.

23. Publisher's advertisement for R. G. Ingersoll's *The Gods, and Other Lectures*, facing p. 233 of Robert G. Ingersoll, *The Ghosts, and Other Lectures* (Washington,

1878). For some contemporary assessments, pro and con, of the man's lifetime impact, published at the time of Ingersoll's death, see *Public Opinion*, XXVII (September 14, 1899), p. 337.

24. "It is one of the subjects of common lamentation that the men who write are almost uniformly 'broad', or 'liberal', or 'infidel'." *Scribner's Monthly*, X (June, 1875), p. 241. "The sword of lath with which the prim apologist of former days set out to attack the 'shallow skeptic' must be laid aside for good and all. The leaders of the antichristian movement are among the most distinguished of living scientists, the most richly gifted of contemporary thinkers." W. S. Lilly, "The Present Outlook for Christianity," *The Forum*, II (December, 1886), p. 318.

25. "Treasures New and Old," Sermon XXVIII in James DeKoven, *Sermons Preached on Various Occasions* . . . (New York, 1880), pp. 320ff.; New York *Christian Advocate*, XLVIII (December 4, 1873), p. 386; C. M. Morse, "The Church and the Working-man," *The Forum*, VI (February, 1889), p. 659.

26. Henry King Carroll, *The Religious Forces of the United States, Enumerated, Classified, and Described on the Basis of the Government Census of 1890* ["American Church History Series," I] (New York, 1893; rev. ed., 1896), pp. xxxvi–xxxvii; W. S. Lilly, *op. cit., loc. cit.*

27. "The Music of the Church," *Scribner's Monthly*, X (June, 1875), p. 243.

28. Anon., "The Hymns We Want," a letter to the editor of the New York *Christian Advocate*, L (February 11, 1875), p. 42.

29. "The Decline of Spirituality in the Church," "Editor's Outlook," *The Chautauquan*, V (April, 1885), p. 424.

30. "Editor's Easy Chair," *Harper's New Monthly Magazine*, LII (January, 1876), p. 293.

31. *American Israelite*, XXIV (May 3, 1878), as quoted in James G. Heller, *Isaac M. Wise, His Life, Work, and Thought* (New York, 1965), p. 672; *Jewish Messenger*, as quoted in the New York *Christian Advocate*, XLVIII (December 4, 1873), p. 388. Compare also Rabbi Solomon Schindler, explaining his abandonment of the innovation he had tried as pastor of a Reform congregation of holding religious services on Sunday rather than on the traditional Hebrew Sabbath: "Sunday services are not a failure because they are held on Sunday, but because people do not care for *any* services, and as it is here, it is, I suppose, in other cities." Quoted in Stuart Rosenberg, *The Search for Jewish Identity in America* (Garden City, 1964), p. 198.

32. William Scarlett, ed., *Phillips Brooks: Selected Sermons* (New York, 1949), p. 283.

33. Phillips Brooks, "The Pulpit and Popular Skepticism," as reprinted in Brooks, *Essays and Addresses, Religious, Literary, and Social* (New York, 1894), pp. 65, 67.

34. Washington Gladden, *Who Wrote the Bible? A Book For the People* (Boston, 1891), pp. 5f.; Phillips Brooks, "The Pulpit and Popular Skepticism," previously cited, at p. 67.

35. "A Survey of the Political and Religious Attitudes of American College Students," *National Review*, XV (October 8, 1963), pp. 279–302, esp. p. 296. See also pp. 286f., 291, 294, 297–230.

36. Richard John Neuhaus, "Liturgy and the Politics of the Kingdom," *Christian Century*, LXXXIV (December 20, 1967), p. 1623.

37. Vernon L. Parrington, *Main Currents in American Thought* (New York, 1930), Vol. III, pp. 318, 192.

38. Augustine F. Hewitt, O. S. P., "The Coming International Scientific Congress of Catholics," *Catholic World*, XLVI (January, 1888), pp. 460f.

39. John Burroughs, "The Natural *versus* the Supernatural," *Popular Science Monthly*, XXXI (May, 1887), p. 14; [E. L. Youmans,] editorial in *ibid.*, XI (July, 1877), p. 369.

40. "Men of Understanding," Sermon XXII in James DeKoven, *op. cit.*, pp. 251ff. First preached in 1874.

41. "The Gates of the Invisible," Sermon XV in *ibid.*, p. 157 (first preached in 1878); "Men of Understanding," *ibid.*, p. 258.

42. Isaac M. Wise, "The Martyrdom of Jesus of Nazareth" (Cincinnati, 1874), as quoted in James G. Heller, *op. cit.*, p. 629.

43. "The Ascension," *Catholic World*, XXIII (June, 1876), pp. 377f. (compare Howard Chandler Robins's hymn, "And have the bright immensities," in the [Episcopal] *Hymnal*, 1940); Newman Smyth, *Old Faiths in New Light* (New York, 1879), pp. 344, 345, 347.

44. Thorstein Veblen, "The Place of Science in Modern Civilization," in *The Place of Science in Modern Civilization, and Other Essays* (New York, [1919] 1961), pp. 1, 2 (first published in the *American Journal of Sociology*, XI [March, 1906]); DeKoven, "The Gates of the Invisible," pp. 158f.

45. Henry Drummond, *The Ascent of Man* [The Lowell Lectures, 1894] (New York, 1894), pp. 334, 333.

46. A pointed contemporary comment, which anticipated Parrington's "plateau" metaphor, is in John Burroughs, "The Decadence of Theology," *North American Review*, CLVI (May, 1893), at p. 578.

47. Bernard Jaffe, *Michelson and the Speed of Light* (Garden City, 1960), p. 56; Lowell Lectures quotation from Paul F. Boller, "New Men and New Ideas: Science and the American Mind," Chap. X of H. Wayne Morgan, ed., *The Gilded Age: A Reappraisal* (Syracuse, 1963), p. 226; reference to Morley is in Jaffe, *op. cit.*, p. 80.

48. Bliss Perry, ed., *The Heart of Emerson's Journals* (Boston, 1926), p. 330.

49. Henry Ward Beecher, "The Study of Human Nature," as reprinted in *Popular Science Monthly*, I (July, 1872), pp. 330, 331. The editor's comment on Beecher's article strongly implied that the major battle for science was not going to be fought out in the church in any case: "He [Beecher] presents, with his usual force, the claims of this subject upon students of his profession, but the reader will hardly fail to remark that this argument is much broader than its professional application." The teacher, not the preacher, carried the brunt of scientific enlightenment. Editorial, "Man as an Object of Scientific Study," *ibid.*, p. 366.

50. Quoted in Wilbur L. Cross, *Connecticut Yankee: An Autobiography* (New Haven, 1943), p. 69.

51. [Edward L. Youmans] Editorial, "The Conflict of Ages," *Popular Science Monthly*, VIII (February, 1876) p. 494; replying to the Rev. Charles F. Deems, "Science and Religion," in *ibid.*, pp. 434–449.

52. H. L. Mencken, *Minority Report: H. L. Mencken's Notebooks* (New York, 1956), p. 3.

53. Quoted in Martin E. Marty, *op. cit.*, p. 175. Italics added.

54. Hugh Miller Thompson, *The World and the Man* [Baldwin Lectures, the University of Michigan, 1890] (New York, 1890), p. 22. For a similar view by an eminent Victorian who survived into our own times, see Bertrand Russell to G. Lowes Dickinson, July 16, 1903; printed in Russell, *Autobiography*, I: *1872–1914* (Boston, 1967), p. 303.

55. Brooks, "The Pulpit and Popular Skepticism," at p. 61.

56. DeKoven, "The Gates of the Invisible," pp. 160, 163, 157.

CHAPTER 2

1. Bertrand Russell, *Selected Papers* (New York, 1927), p. 44.

2. "One of the Difficulties of Psycho-Analysis," Chapter XX of Sigmund Freud, *Collected Papers,* Vol. IV (New York, 1959), pp. 350, 355, 352. This essay was first published in 1917.

3. Jacques Barzun, *Darwin, Marx, Wagner: Critique of a Heritage,* rev. 2nd ed. (New York, 1958), p. 3.

4. Dyson Hague, "The Doctrinal Value of the First Chapters of Genesis," Chapter 6 in *The Fundamentals,* VIII (Chicago, n.d.), p. 82.

5. Benjamin Spock, *Baby and Child Care* (New York, 1957), 48th printing, March, 1962, p. 223. The claimed paperback circulation of this book in 1965 was 17 million, outselling even *Peyton Place* and *God's Little Acre.*

6. For example, Dr. Spock carried over from early Darwinism a version of the theory of use and disuse—"Our ancestors stood up because they had found more useful things to do with their hands than walking on them"—which is, from the standpoint of modern evolutionary thought, questionable to say the least.

7. Communicated to the author by the boy's teacher, Leonard Lubinsky, subsequently a graduate student in the University of Massachusetts, 1964–5.

8. Quoted in John Moffatt Mecklin, *The Survival Value of Christianity* (New York, 1926), pp. 9f.

9. Alfred W. McCann, *God—or Gorilla?* (New York, 1922), pp. 273, 271.

10. Minot J. Savage, *The Religion of Evolution* (Boston, 1876), p. 82, as quoted in Ernst Benz, *Evolution and Christian Hope: Man's Concept of the Future from the Early Fathers to Teilhard de Chardin,* tr. by Heinz G. Frank (New York, 1966), p. 149.

11. John Augustine Zahm, *Evolution and Dogma* (Chicago, 1896), as excerpted in R. J. Wilson, ed., *Darwinism and the American Intellectual* (Homewood, Ill., 1967), p. 84.

12. "L. S." [Leslie Stephen], "Darwinism and Divinity," *Popular Science Monthly,* I (June, 1872), pp. 189f.

13. Theodore T. Munger, "Evolution and the Faith," *Century Magazine,* XXXII (New Series, X) (May, 1886), pp. 108, 113.

14. James Freeman Clarke, "Have Animals Souls?" *Atlantic Monthly,* XXXIV (October, 1874), pp. 412, 416.

15. Theodore T. Munger, *The Appeal to Life* (Boston, 1887), pp. 221f.

16. James Thurber, "The Human Being and the Dinosaur," in *Further Fables For Our Time* (New York, 1956), p. 69.

17. The same argument was heard in England during the Darwinian crisis, but one leading biographer of Darwin and Huxley has pointedly doubted its validity: "Between [Darwin] and Newton, as religious influences, there is probably not much to choose." The lucid passage that follows deserves to be studied in its entirety. William Irvine, *Apes, Angels, and Victorians* (Cleveland and New York, 1959), p. 97.

18. Alexander Winchell, *Sketches of Creation* . . . (New York, 1870), Preface, p. vii. (Written in October, 1869).

19. A. Hunter Dupree, *Asa Gray* (Cambridge, Mass., 1959), p. 366. But the biographer comments: "The argument from design was . . . a proper philosophical problem of the eighteenth century. The eighteenth century was gone, and Gray could not single-handedly bring it back." *Ibid.,* p. 369.

20. J. I. D. Hinds, "Charles Darwin," *Cumberland Presbyterian Review,* I (January,

1889), as quoted in "Miscellanies," *Popular Science Monthly,* XXXVI (January, 1890), p. 425.

21. Washington Gladden, *How Much is Left of the Old Doctrines?* (Boston, 1899), p. 44; Gladden to Lyman Abbott, as quoted in Barbara Cross, *Horace Bushnell: Minister to a Changing America* (Chicago, 1958), p. 160.

22. Charles Sanders Peirce, "The Order of Nature" ["Illustrations of the Logic of Science," Fifth Paper], *Popular Science Monthly,* XIII (June, 1878), p. 216.

23. T. T. Munger, "Evolution and the Faith," p. 112; Charles F. Deems, "Our Readers Reply," *Century Magazine,* XXXII (September, 1886), p. 807. Charles Hodge, in his famous polemic *What Is Darwinism?* (excerpts reprinted in R. J. Wilson, *op. cit.,* pp. 47–57), made the same point that the theory of evolution necessarily overthrew the classic argument from design. But many of his contemporaries used Munger's strategy of accepting evolutionist conclusions while denying their premises, a tactic which persists among twentieth-century theists; see for example Langdon B. Gilkey, "Darwin and Christian Thought," *Christian Century,* LXXVII (January 6, 1960), pp. 7–10.

24. Edward Lurie, The Jacob Zisskind Lectures, Smith College, 1965; notes taken by the author, January 8, 1965.

25. Editorial, "The Popular Science Monthly," *Scribner's Monthly,* IV (October, 1872), p. 775; reply in *Popular Science Monthly,* II (November, 1872), p. 116. This attack by *Scribner's* was a body blow at everything for which Youmans and his magazine stood, because, as one modern student has pointed out, "The word which best defines the general concept or outlook which Youmans wanted to persuade his readers to accept is 'nature,' and the natural law which overrode all others was evolution." William E. Leverette, Jr., "E. L. Youmans's Crusade for Scientific Autonomy and Respectability," *American Quarterly,* XVII (Spring, 1965), pp. 12ff.

26. Quoted in John Fiske, "Agassiz and Darwinism," *Popular Science Monthly,* III (October, 1873), pp. 692ff. Fiske was particularly annoyed by this religious adulation of Agassiz since the Harvard professor was in fact not "orthodox"; "It is not many years since these very persons"—Darwin's detractors in theology—"regarded Professor Agassiz with dread and abhorrence, because of his flat contradiction of the Bible in his theory of the multiple origin of the human race." *Ibid.,* p. 697.

27. Oliver Wendell Holmes, Sr., "Agassiz's Natural History," *Atlantic Monthly,* I (January, 1858), p. 320.

28. Louis Agassiz, "Evolution and Permanence of Type," *ibid.,* XXXIII (January, 1874), pp. 92ff. For another specimen of Agassiz's scientific reasoning see his review of *The Origin of Species* in 1860 for the *American Journal of Science and Arts,* an abridged version of which appears in R. J. Wilson, *op. cit.,* pp. 20–37.

29. New York *Christian Advocate,* XLIX (January 1, 1874), p. 4; J. B. Drury, "Darwinism," *Scribner's Monthly,* X (July, 1875), pp. 348–360.

30. See the thoughtful discussion of Wise's views on evolution in James G. Heller, *Isaac M. Wise: His Life, Work, and Thought* (New York, 1965), pp. 510ff.

31. William Irvine, *op. cit.,* pp. 195, 350, discusses Darwin's and Huxley's views of this problem. See also A. O. J. Cockshut, *The Unbelievers: English Agnostic Thought 1840–1890* (New York, 1966), Chap. 4: "Evolution and Ethics."

32. John S. Vaughan, "Evolutionary Theory as Applied to Conscience," *Catholic World,* LI (April, 1890), pp. 64, 66, 69, 73.

33. Quoted in John Rickard Betts, "Darwinism, Evolution, and American Catholic Thought, 1860–1890," *Catholic Historical Review,* XLV (July, 1959), p. 173.

34. *American Israelite,* XIV (January 24, 1868); compare Wise's judgment in *ibid.,*

XLIII (August 13, 1896), that Darwinism remained no more than a "wonderful conglomeration of unfounded hypotheses." Both quotations as in Heller, *op. cit.,* p. 515. Consistent with this position, Wise also continued to reject the "higher criticism" of the Old Testament: "These extraordinary theories must be dropped by all who wish to understand the Bible." *Ibid.,* p. 531, citing the *American Israelite,* XXXIV (October 28, 1887), p. 4.

35. Lewis Henry Morgan, *Ancient Society* (Chicago, n. d. [Preface dated March, 1877]), p. v; compare p. 153 in the same edition.

36. Quoted in Paul F. Boller, Jr., "New Men and New Ideas: Science and the American Mind," Chap. X in H. Wayne Morgan, ed., *The Gilded Age: a Reappraisal* (Syracuse, 1963), p. 237.

37. A. F. Hewitt, "Scriptural Questions," *Catholic World,* XLIV (February, 1887), p. 666; Rudolph Virchow, "The Problems of Anthropology," address at the opening of an international congress of prehistoric archeology and anthropology, Moscow, translated from *Revue Scientifique* for *Popular Science Monthly,* XLII (January, 1893), pp. 374, 376.

38. See for example "Evolutionism in the pulpit," by "an occupant of the pew," *The Fundamentals: a Testimony to the Truth* (Chicago, n. d. [1909–1914]), Vol. VIII, Chapter II; and Alfred W. McCann, *op. cit.,* Chapter I.

39. Willy Ley, *The Days of Creation* (New York, 1941), p. 237. The Virchow tradition persisted in Germany as well as among American Fundamentalists. In 1926 Max Westenhöfer, a pupil of Virchow's, startled the scientific world by inverting Darwin's chronology, and wrote on *Man as the Oldest Form of Mammal.* Herbert Wendt, *In Search of Adam,* tr. by James Cleugh (Boston, 1956), p. 222.

40. Phillips Brooks, sermon preached in Andover, Mass., January 4, 1887, as quoted in A. V. G. Allen, *Life and Letters of Phillips Brooks* (New York, 1901), Vol. III, p. 244; James Woodrow, *Evolution: an address delivered May 7th, 1884, before the Alumni Association of the Columbia Theological Seminary, Columbia, S. C., 1884,* text reprinted in Joseph L. Blau, ed., *American Philosophic Addresses, 1700–1900* (New York, 1946), pp. 486ff. (this quotation at p. 499).

41. George Henslow, "Genesis, Geology, and Evolution," *Popular Science Monthly,* IV (January, 1874), pp. 324, 328; Theodore T. Munger, *The Freedom of Faith* (Boston, 1883), pp. 19ff.

42. One relatively early attempt to explain away that fourth day is Hugh Miller, *The Testimony of the Rocks; or, Geology in its Bearings on the Two Theologies, Natural and Revealed* (Boston, 1857), pp. 200ff.

43. Willy Ley, *op. cit.,* p. 112; George Daniels, ed., *Darwinism Comes To America* (Waltham, Mass., 1968), pp. 94, 95.

44. On the transit of the "higher criticism" of the Bible to the United States see Jürgen Herbst, "German Theological Science and American Religion," Chapter IV in Herbst, *The German Historical School in American Scholarship: a Study in the Transfer of Culture* (Ithaca, 1965).

45. William North Rice, "Darwinian Theory of the Origin of Species," *New Englander,* 1867, pp. 607ff., as excerpted in George Daniels, *op. cit.,* p. 44. This judgment is particularly significant inasmuch as Rice himself had not yet accepted the Darwinian theory; his doctoral dissertation, published in 1867, explicitly rejected it. Daniels, *op. cit.,* p. 42.

46. Karl Marx and Friedrich Engels, *On Religion* ([Moscow, 1957] New York, 1964), pp. 192f.

47. #458 in *Hymns of the Spirit* (Boston, 1937). Compare a letter from Gannett to

John W. Chadwick, December 12, 1885: "Shall the name [Unitarian] be denied to persons saying what we do of 'Christianity,' and 'God'? . . . The discussion which in Parker's day was at the miracle-line,— . . . in 1880 at the 'Christian' line,—[is] now . . . verging toward the 'God'-word line. . . . The deeper question will be over this thought of 'God,'—and all involved." Quoted in William H. Pease, "Doctrine and Fellowship: William Channing Gannett and the Unitarian Creedal Issue," *Church History,* XXV (September, 1956), p. 218.

48. "The chief voices of Unitarianism thus far . . . have made Unitarians say they believe in the Bible and Christ in the sense of church and creed . . . ; but the real fact is that their fundamental view, and their whole direction, are otherwise—humanistic and rationalistic." Anon., "Confessions of a Unitarian," *The Forum,* II (October, 1886), p. 163.

49. For an example of this point of view see Karl Barth, *The Word of God and the Word of Man,* tr. by Douglas Horton (New York, [1928] 1957), Chapters II and III, esp. pp. 60–62.

50. The reformulation of this doctrine in the nineteenth century by Carl Ferdinand Wilhelm Walther, who helped to make it definitive for the powerful branch of Lutheranism he had been instrumental in establishing in the United States, and in which he remained the dominant figure until his death midway through the Gilded Age, is discussed in Robert D. Preus, "Walther and the Scriptures," *Concordia Theological Monthly,* XXXII (November, 1961), pp. 669–691. For a stimulating interpretation of American Lutheran history I am indebted to William E. Magney, "Confessionalism, Americanism, and the Road to the Lutheran Ghetto," unpublished seminar paper, the University of California, 1964.

51. *Lutheran Witness-Reporter,* I (July 11, 1965), p. 3. As an example of the intellectual dilemma this has posed for scholars who are members of the Missouri Synod see Norman C. Habel, *The Form and Meaning of the Fall Narrative: a Detailed Analysis of Genesis 3* (St. Louis, 1965). Arthur Carl Piepkorn, a colleague of Professor Habel in that denomination's Concordia Theological Seminary, has argued that American Lutherans have misunderstood the European roots of their own tradition of Biblical interpretation. Piepkorn, "What Does Inerrancy Mean?" *Concordia Theological Monthly,* XXXVI (September, 1965), pp. 577–593.

52. John W. Klotz, *Genes, Genesis, and Evolution* (St. Louis, 1955; 2nd printing, 1959), p. 389.

53. A classic and definitive statement of the "WASP" version of this doctrine is Archibald A. Hodge and Benjamin B. Warfield, "Inspiration," *Presbyterian Review,* II (1881); excerpts reprinted in H. Shelton Smith, Robert T. Handy, and Lefferts A. Loetscher, eds., *American Christianity: an Historical Interpretation with Representative Documents,* Vol. II: *1820–1960* (New York, 1963), pp. 324–332.

54. Some of them attempted such an intellectual reconciliation by way of the philosophic school known as Scottish Realism, but this device only riveted them more tightly to a dogmatic scholasticism. Sydney E. Ahlstrom, "The Scottish Philosophy and American Theology," *Church History,* XXIV (September, 1955), pp. 257–272.

55. L. T. Townsend, *The Bible and Other Ancient Literature in the Nineteenth Century* (New York, 1889); Francis Darwin, ed., *Life and Letters of Charles Darwin,* as quoted in Irvine, *op. cit.,* p. 109.

56. P. B. Warring, "Genesis and 'Science,' " New York *Christian Advocate,* March 7, 1878, as quoted in George Daniels, *op. cit.,* p. 103. Compare Anon., "The Sixth Day of Creation," *Boston Review,* III (1863), as quoted in *ibid.,* p. 102: "Wherever there

is an actual contradiction between the facts of geology and the words of inspiration properly interpreted, geology is wrong, and needs to reconsider its facts."

57. "I was there and heard it, although I believe the brother was entirely sincere in his denial." Francis J. McConnell, "Borden Parker Bowne," *Methodist Review* (Fifth Series, Vol. XXXVIII), May–June, 1922, p. 345. The "brother" McConnell referred to in this passage was not Bowne, who clearly belonged in the modernist camp.

58. Raymond W. Albright, *A History of the Protestant Episcopal Church* (New York, 1964), pp. 287, 308, 309.

59. H. L. Mencken, *Treatise on the Gods* (New York, 1930), pp. 338ff.

60. Quoted in John Rickard Betts, *op. cit.,* p. 178. In a *Literary Digest* article published in 1899, cited in *ibid.,* p. 183, Father Zahm wrote that he had had to withdraw his book *Evolution and Dogma* from circulation even though he knew "that every eminent man of science throughout Europe is in perfect sympathy with my views."

61. Fred Hoyle, *Frontiers of Astronomy* (New York, 1955; paper, 1957).

62. Clarence A. Walworth, "The Days of Genesis," *Catholic World,* XLII (February, 1886), pp. 641ff.

63. Quoted in James G. Heller, *op. cit.,* p. 656; compare n. 34, above.

64. Andrew Dickson White, *Autobiography* (New York, [1905] 1922), Vol. II, pp. 543, 549; Peter Gregg Slater, "Andrew Dickson White and the Battle of Science with Religion," unpublished seminar paper, the University of California, Berkeley, 1964, p. 25.

65. *Introduction to Contemporary Civilization in the West: a Source Book* (New York, 1946), Vol. II, p. 997; Walter Lippmann, *A Preface to Morals* (New York, 1929), p. 36.

CHAPTER 3

1. Walt Whitman, "Animals," in Oscar Williams, ed., *F. T. Palgrave's The Golden Treasury of the Best Songs and Lyrical Poems: A Modern Edition* (New York, 1953), p. 345.

2. John Wise, *Vindication of the Government of New England Churches,* excerpts as reprinted in Perry Miller, ed., *The American Puritans: Their Prose and Poetry* (New York, 1956), pp. 127, 125.

3. William Ellery Channing, "Likeness to God," from Channing, *Works* (Boston, 1849), Vol. III, pp. 227ff., as reprinted in Joseph L. Blau, ed., *American Philosophic Addresses 1700–1900* (New York, 1946), pp. 563ff.

4. Barbara Cross, *Horace Bushnell: Minister to a Changing America* (Chicago, 1958), p. 19.

5. Phillips Brooks, "The Mitigation of Theology," 1878; reprinted in William Scarlett, ed., *Phillips Brooks: Selected Sermons* (New York, 1949), pp. 267–279.

6. Even the rigorous Princeton Theology, Ernest Sandeen has argued, was quite a different phenomenon from what since Edwards's time had been called the "New England Theology." Its doctrine of the Bible in particular was in the nineteenth century something quite new, even though it would be seized upon by Fundamentalists in the twentieth century as a defense of the "old-time religion." Ernest R. Sandeen, "The Princeton Theology: one source of Biblical literalism in American Protestantism," *Church History,* XXXI (September, 1962), pp. 307ff.

7. Washington Gladden, *How Much Is Left of the Old Doctrines?* (Boston, 1899), p. 211.

8. Editorial in *The Independent,* 1873, as quoted in Washington Gladden, *Recollections* (Boston, 1909), p. 224. Compare Henry Ward Beecher, "The Progress of Thought in the Church," *North American Review,* CXXXV (August, 1882), 99–117, esp. p. 112.

9. Oliver Wendell Holmes, Sr., *"Mechanism in Thought and Morals," an address delivered before the Phi Beta Kappa Society of Harvard University, June 29, 1870* . . . (Boston, 1882), as reprinted in Blau, *American Philosophic Addresses,* pp. 415ff.; this citation at p. 449.

10. Mary Baker Eddy, *Retrospection and Introspection* (Boston, 1891, 1892), p. 13. See the discussion of this episode in Robert Peel, *Mary Baker Eddy: the Years of Discovery* (New York, Chicago, San Francisco, 1966), p. 23 and *passim.*

11. Editorial, "The Roots of Our Present Evils," *Catholic World,* XXIII (May, 1876), pp. 150, 152, 149.

12. Henry Van Dyke, *The Gospel for an Age of Doubt,* in *The Works of Henry Van Dyke* ["Avalon Edition"], Vol. XIV (New York, 1921), pp. 226f.

13. Isaac M. Wise, *The Essence of Judaism* (Cincinnati, 1861), p. 8; Wise, *Judaism and Christianity* (Cincinnati, 1883), p. 64; both as quoted in Betsey Rosten, "Isaac Mayer Wise: a Jew in Transition," unpublished seminar paper, the University of California, Berkeley, 1964, pp. 18, 27.

14. Henry Ward Beecher, *Evolution and Religion* (New York, 1885), p. 92, as quoted in Robert Johnson, "The Harmonization of Evolution and Religion in Nineteenth Century America," unpublished seminar paper, Northern Illinois University, 1967, p. 26. The reader should bear in mind that Beecher's record on anti-Semitism was rather *better* than that of his Christian colleagues in general; (see below, Chapter 6, n. 4) so that this remark becomes a measure of the desperate lengths to which a Christian clergyman could go in his effort to live down the heritage of Calvinism.

15. Reinhold Niebuhr, *Reflections on the End of an Era* (New York, 1934), p. 48.

16. Frances Perkins, *The Roosevelt I Knew* (New York, 1946), pp. 146–148.

17. Harry Emerson Fosdick, *The Living of These Days: an Autobiography* (New York, 1956), pp. 250, 35f., 51, 66.

18. J. I. D. Hinds, "Charles Darwin," *Cumberland Presbyterian Review,* I (January, 1889), as cited in "Miscellanies," *Popular Science Monthly,* XXXVI (January, 1890), p. 425. As a Cumberland Presbyterian Hinds may have had a specifically denominational anti-Calvinist axe to grind; see Hubert W. Morrow, "Cumberland Presbyterian Theology: a Nineteenth Century Development in American Presbyterianism," *Journal of Presbyterian History,* XLVIII (Fall, 1970), 203–220.

19. Isaac M. Wise, *A Defense of Judaism* versus *Proselytizing Christianity* (Cincinnati, 1889), p. 40, as quoted in James G. Heller, *Isaac M. Wise: His Life, Work, and Thought* (New York, 1965), p. 655.

20. Andrew Dickson White, *A History of the Warfare of Science with Theology in Christendom* (New York, 1898), Vol. I, p. 312.

21. John M. Tyler, *The Whence and Whither of Man: a Brief History of his Origin and Development through Conformity to Environment* (New York, 1896), p. 308.

22. Quoted in John Rickard Betts, "Darwinism, Evolution, and American Catholic Thought, 1860–1900," *Catholic Historical Review,* XLV (July, 1959), p. 171.

23. William Newton Clarke, *An Outline of Christian Theology* (New York, 1898), p. 245.

24. The Predestination Controversy (*Gnadenwahlstreit*) came to a head in 1881, when the Missouri Synod adopted C. F. W. Walther's Thirteen Theses on election. To this quarrel, writes the Lutheran historian Carl S. Meyer, "as much as to any other

single factor . . . may be ascribed the divisions within American Lutheranism for many decades." Meyer, *Log Cabin to Luther Tower: Concordia Seminary During One Hundred and Twenty-five Years* (St. Louis, 1965), p. 78.

25. John Fiske, *The Destiny of Man Viewed in the Light of his Origin* (Boston, 1884), p. 103; Lyman Abbott, *The Evolution of Christianity* (Boston, 1892), p. 227; Abbott, *The Theology of an Evolutionist* (Boston, 1897), p. 48. Other examples of this antianimal bias are quoted in Robert Johnson, *op. cit.,* esp. pp. 24–27.

26. Theodore T. Munger, "Man the Final Form in Creation," from *The Appeal to Life* (Boston, 1887), pp. 283ff.; reprinted in Blau, *American Philosophic Addresses,* pp. 709ff.; this citation at p. 724.

27. Edward Eggleston, *The Hoosier Schoolmaster* (Library Edition, New York, 1892; first copyright 1871), pp. 111f.

28. William Ellery Channing, *op. cit.,* p. 582; Perry Miller, ed., *Margaret Fuller, American Romantic* (Garden City, 1963), p. xviii.

29. A. F. Hewitt, "The Radical Fault of the New Orthodoxy," *Catholic World,* XLVI (December, 1887), p. 363; Lyman Abbott, *The Evolution of Christianity,* p. 255.

30. Joseph LeConte, *Evolution: its Nature, its Evidences, and its Relation to Religious Thought,* rev. 2nd ed.(New York, [1891] 1899), pp. 374–375.

31. Gertrude Himmelfarb, *Victorian Minds* (New York, 1968), p. 305; Howard Phillips Lovecraft to Reinhardt Kleiner, September 14, 1919, as printed in Lovecraft, *Selected Letters,* Vol. I, *1911–1924* (Sauk City, Wisconsin, 1965), p. 87; Lovecraft to Frank Belknap Long, October 8, 1921, in *ibid.,* p. 158.

32. Theodore T. Munger, *The Freedom of Faith* (Boston, 1883), p. 62, as cited in H. Shelton Smith, *Changing Conceptions of Original Sin: a Study in American Theology since 1750* (New York, 1955), p. 168. Smith's judgment on Munger was informed by the "neo-orthodox" theological developments described in Part II, above, and was quite harsh: "There is little evidence to show that Munger held a serious view of the human predicament."

33. Munger, "Man the Final Form in Creation," as cited in n. 26, above; John M. Tyler, *op, cit.,* p. 222.

34. Evelyn Hubbard, "A Survey of the Hymnary of the Gilded Age," unpublished seminar paper, Northern Illinois University, 1967, pp. 9f., quoting Lester Hostetler, *Handbook to the Mennonite Hymnary* (Newton, Kansas, 1940), p. 275.

35. One vehement British atheist indicted the Church of England for the language of its marriage service, which "contains things no bride could hear without a blush *if she understood them*"; and the Mills, father and son, were agreed that sexual preoccupation was "one of the deepest seated and most pervading evils in the human mind," which man in the course of his upward progress would outgrow. Gertrude Himmelfarb, *op. cit.,* p. 306.

36. Barbara Cross, *op. cit.,* p. 160, synthesizing the thought of Lyman Abbott, Minot J. Savage, and Henry Ward Beecher; H. Shelton Smith, Robert T. Handy, and Lefferts A. Loetscher, eds., *American Christianity: An Historical Interpretation with Representative Documents,* II: *1820–1960* (New York, 1963), p. 260.

37. William Irvine, *Apes, Angels, and Victorians: Darwin, Huxley, and Evolution* (Cleveland and New York, 1959), pp. 196f.

38. Charles Darwin, *The Descent of Man, and Selection in Relation to Sex* [a reprint of the second revised and augmented edition, first published in 1874] (New York, 1898), pp. 620, 608, 618.

39. Sigmund Freud, "One of the Difficulties of Psycho-Analysis," Chapter XX in Freud, *Collected Papers* (New York, 1959), Vol. IV, p. 351.

40. Theodore T. Munger, "Man the Final Form in Creation," as cited in notes 26 and 33, above; this quotation at p. 721.

41. Charles Gore, ed., *Lux Mundi: a Series of Studies in the Religion of the Incarnation,* 10th edition (London, 1890), Appendix II, pp. 527f., 534f.

42. *Ibid.,* pp. xvii, xxxiv and following; Reinhold Niebuhr, "As Deceivers, Yet True," in *Beyond Tragedy* (New York, 1937), pp. 3–24, as reprinted in Smith, Handy, and Loetscher, eds., *American Christianity,* Vol. II, pp. 455–465.

43. J. R. Illingworth, "The Incarnation in Relation to Development," in Charles Gore, *op. cit.,* pp. 193, 208f.

44. Borden Parker Bowne, *Philosophy of Theism* (New York, 1887), as quoted in William R. Hutchison, "Liberal Protestantism and the 'End of Innocence'," *American Quarterly,* XV (Summer, 1963), p. 137; Lewis F. Stearns, *Present-Day Theology* (New York, 1893), as cited in H. Shelton Smith, *Changing Conceptions of Original Sin,* p. 184; William Newton Clarke, *op. cit.,* pp. 245, 232.

45. For example, he told the Harvard graduating class of 1884: "The first secret of all effective and happy living is a true reverence for the mystery and greatness of your human nature, for the things which you and your brethren are, in simply being men." Quoted in Alexander V. G. Allen, *Life and Letters of Phillips Brooks* (New York, 1901), Vol. III, p. 123.

46. *Ibid.,* p. 113; Phillips Brooks, "The Mitigation of Theology," as cited in n. 5, above, pp. 272f.

47. *Fortnightly Review,* n.s., LVIII (1892), 569, as quoted in William Irvine, *op. cit.,* p. 326. Compare also the quotation from Huxley in *ibid.,* p. 322.

48. Quoted in Morris Kline, *Mathematics in Western Culture* (New York, 1953), p. 255.

49. "Jean Meslier," pseud. [Paul Henri Thiry, Baron d'Holbach], *Superstition in All Ages,* tr. by Anna Knoop (New York, 1920; this translation first published in 1878), pp. 110, 113.

50. Morris Kline, *op. cit.,* p. 321; Lynde Phelps Wheeler, *Josiah Willard Gibbs: the History of a Great Mind* (New Haven, 1951), p. 82.

51. Significantly Isaac Mayer Wise, who was holding out for free will (compare note 13, above), denied this materialistic conception: "Memory is the function of a non-material substance which we call soul." *American Israelite,* XXXIV (October 7, 1887), as quoted in James G. Heller, *op. cit.,* p. 516.

52. Oliver Wendell Holmes, Sr., "Mechanism in Thought and Morals," as cited in note 9, above, pp. 441, 443, 418, 438ff.; Holmes to Noah Porter, December 13, 1879, as printed in George S. Merriam, ed., *Noah Porter: A Memorial by Friends* (New York, 1893), p. 187.

53. Oliver Wendell Holmes, Sr., *Elsie Venner: a Romance of Destiny* (Boston, [1861] 1886). Serialized in *The Atlantic* in 1859 as "The Professor's Story."

54. Benjamin Kidd, *Social Evolution* (New York and London, 1894), pp. 32f.; John M. Tyler, *op. cit.,* p. 175, and compare in the same work Chapter VII, pp. 177ff.

55. Carl Resek, *Lewis Henry Morgan: American Scholar* (Chicago, 1960), pp. 152f.

56. Harriet Beecher Stowe, *Oldtown Folks* (Boston, 1869), p. 26.

57. William James, "The Dilemma of Determinism," an address to the Harvard Divinity Students, published in the *Unitarian Review* for September, 1884; reprinted in James, *The Will to Believe and Other Essays in Popular Philosophy* (New York and London, [1897] 1910), pp. 145–183; this quotation at p. 162.

58. Washington Gladden, *How Much Is Left of the Old Doctrines?* p. 227. Gladden conceded the force of the new argument from eugenics; of the much-discussed Jukes

family he wrote, "Blood tells; and no kind of blood has a more impressive story to tell than this kind." But this had nothing to do with *moral* determinism, Gladden argued; such people "deserve, instead of wrath, the tenderest pity of all good men." *Ibid.,* p. 124.

59. William Newton Clarke, *op. cit.,* p. 213. But Clarke protected the Christian orthodoxy of his argument with a Calvinist, or at least with a Lutheran, hedge: "The ideal freedom of the will exists only in a morally perfect life . . . but in man this does not occur." The man who has fallen into sin really does have "moral inability" of his own volition to get out again (compare Edwards), and therefore requires "the in-breathing of a holy, spiritual energy"—the Grace of God, in more traditional termi-nology—"that shall enable the will to reassume and hold its normal place."

60. Mark Twain, *What Is Man?,* in Albert Bigelow Paine, ed., *The Writings of Mark Twain,* Vol. XXVI (New York, [1917] 1929), pp. 82, 73, 90. (*What Is Man?* was first copyrighted in 1906.)

CHAPTER 4

1. Leslie A. Fiedler, "Adolescence and Maturity in the American Novel," Chapter 13 in *An End to Innocence: Essays in Culture and Politics* (Boston, 1955), pp. 197f.

2. Mary McCarthy, "The Fact in Fiction," in *The Humanist in the Bathtub* (New York, 1964), p. 190.

3. Ambrose Bierce, "What I Saw of Shiloh," as quoted in Richard O'Connor, *Ambrose Bierce: a Biography* (Boston and Toronto, 1967), p. 27; Irving McKee, *"Ben-Hur" Wallace: the Life of General Lew Wallace* (Berkeley and Los Angeles, 1947), p. 49.

4. Quoted in Richard O'Connor, *op. cit.,* p. 72. A persuasive suggestion as to why Bierce was able to get away with this sort of thing in San Francisco in the Seventies—with the implication that it might not have gotten by in Boston or even in New York at that same period may be found in Larzer Ziff, *The American 1890's: Life and Times of a Lost Generation* (New York, 1966; paper, 1968), p. 167.

5. O'Connor, *op. cit.,* p. 83; Lew Wallace, "How I Came to Write *Ben-Hur,*" *Youth's Companion,* LXVI (February 2, 1893), p. 57. McKee, on the basis of the General's private correspondence, accepted this self-assessment—and also the genuineness of Wallace's religious conversion when it came. Irving McKee, *op. cit.,* pp. 164 and 167n.

6. *Harper's Weekly,* March 6, 1886. On this same point see Willard Thorp, "The Religious Novel as Best-seller in America," in James Ward Smith and A. Leland Jamison, eds., *Religious Perspectives in American Culture* ["Religion in American Life," II] (Princeton, 1961), p. 205.

7. McKee, *op. cit.,* quoting Carl Van Doren, *The American Novel* (New York, 1921).

8. McKee, *op. cit.,* p. 227; *Atlantic Monthly,* XLVII (May, 1881), p. 710.

9. McKee, *op. cit.,* pp. 190, 174.

10. *Ibid.,* pp. 177–188. McKee reprinted a generous selection of early playbills for *Ben-Hur,* of intrinsic interest to the student of the history of the theater quite apart from their documentation of the play's success.

11. *Ibid.,* p. 187; Willard Thorp, *op. cit.,* p. 206, n. 6.

12. Ben Ray Redman, Introduction to Lew Wallace, *Ben-Hur: a Tale of the Christ* (New York, 1960), p. xvii.

13. Commenting on "the degree to which the popular works of the Gilded Age clung to the values and beliefs of an earlier time," Robert R. Roberts concluded: "In-deed, the insistent celebration of these virtues of an earlier America leads to the

conclusion that there was an awareness of the forces that were transforming the nation and a fierce resistance to them." Roberts, "Gilt, Gingerbread, and Realism: the Public and Its Taste," Chapter 8 in H. Wayne Morgan, ed., *The Gilded Age: a Reappraisal* (Syracuse, 1963), p. 194.

14. "Biblical religion grew up in protest against the fertility cults of the ancient Near East. Could it have coped with the subtler perversions of our Far West?" in "Movies: the Bible Against Itself," lead editorial in the *Christian Century*, LXXVI (October 28, 1959), p. 1235.

15. Compare the "boundless preoccupation with the minutiae of technical perfection, with ersatz authenticity (*e.g.*, rebuilding Palestine in Southern California) and in the mere piling up of detail upon detail" during the filming of *The Big Fisherman*, *Solomon and Sheba*, *Ben-Hur*, and other Biblical motion-picture extravaganzas. The editors of the *Christian Century* ended by urging readers, instead of attending such pictures, to see instead "the coming film version of *Elmer Gantry*, Sinclair Lewis's stinging study of hypocrisy." *Ibid.*, p. 1236.

16. Lew Wallace, "How I Came to Write *Ben-Hur*," as cited in n. 4, above.

17. Apart from the Biblical set-pieces—the Nativity, the baptism by John, the last hours on the Cross—Christ was "not present as an actor in any scene of my creation," Wallace wrote (in *ibid.*), except for one short scene in which He gives a cup of water to Ben-Hur at the well near Nazareth.

18. Lew Wallace, "The Boyhood of Christ," *Harper's New Monthly Magazine*, LXXIV (December, 1886), pp. 3–18.

19. For "muscular Christianity" and its possible relationship to nineteenth-century imperialism and militarism, see William E. Winn, *"Tom Brown's School Days* and the Development of 'Muscular Christianity,' " *Church History*, XXIX (March, 1960), pp. 64–73.

20. Evelyn Hubbard, "A Survey of the Hymnary of the Gilded Age," unpublished seminar paper, Northern Illinois University, 1967, pp. 47f., citing Lloyd Lewis, "Hymn From an Abattoir," *American Mercury*, XXIV (October, 1931), pp. 221–229. Compare Fletcher Pratt, *A Short History of the Civil War* (New York, 1952), pp. 348f.

21. Irving McKee, *op. cit.*, pp. 231, 233; Richard O'Connor, *op. cit.*, pp. 162, 163.

22. This could have been the result merely of Eastern literary provincialism. In *The Forum*, XVI (October, 1893), pp. 156–166, Hamlin Garland asked: "Shall our literature . . . be only as large as the conception of New York and Boston critics?" If at that time Chicago was still struggling for parity, as Hamlin charged, a book printed in far-off San Francisco after it had been rejected by all the Eastern publishers was presumably beneath such critics' notice.

23. *Harper's New Monthly Magazine*, LXXXVI (January, 1893), p. 317; Larzer Ziff, *op. cit.*, p. 170.

24. "A Horseman in the Sky," "Chickamauga," "An Affair of Outposts," "A Son of the Gods," in *The Collected Works of Ambrose Bierce*, Vol. II: *In the Midst of Life (Tales of Soldiers and Civilians)* (New York and Washington, 1909), pp. 15–26, 46–57, 146–164, 58–70; definition of "extinction" as in *Collected Works*, Vol. VII; *The Devil's Dictionary* (New York and Washington, 1911), p. 94.

25. "Parker Adderson, Philosopher," in Bierce, *Collected Works*, Vol. II, pp. 133–145; this at p. 139.

26. O'Connor, *op. cit.*, p. 168.

27. Elizabeth Stuart Phelps, *The Silent Partner* (Boston, [1871] 1899), p. 296.

28. Unsigned review of *The Silent Partner* in *Harper's New Monthly Magazine*, XLIII (July, 1871), p. 301.

29. Elizabeth Stuart Phelps, *Chapters From a Life* (Boston, 1897), as quoted in Willard Thorp, *op. cit.,* p. 225.

30. Helen Sootin Smith, Introduction to Elizabeth Stuart Phelps, *The Gates Ajar* (Cambridge, Mass., 1964), p. xix.

31. Elizabeth Stuart Phelps, "A Sacrifice Consumed," *Harper's New Monthly Magazine,* XXVIII (January, 1864), pp. 235–240.

32. Wallace, *Ben-Hur* (1960), p. 394; Bierce, in the story "One Kind of Officer," *Collected Works of Ambrose Bierce,* Vol. II, p. 180.

33. Elizabeth Stuart Phelps, *The Gates Ajar,* (Cambridge, Mass., 1964; first published in 1868), pp. 5, 6.

34. She quoted effectively a letter from Martin Luther to one of his children, describing in simple, graphic language the joys of heaven awaiting "the children that love to pray and to learn, and are good"—but Miss Phelps's translation of this letter seems to have been a very free one. *Ibid.,* p. 125, n. 17.

35. Elizabeth Stuart Phelps, "A Plea for Immortality," *Atlantic Monthly,* XLV (February, 1880), p. 279.

36. Elizabeth Stuart Phelps, "Since I Died," reprinted as a chapter in Phelps, *Sealed Orders* (tenth ed., Boston, 1897; copyright 1879), pp. 168–175.

37. Elizabeth Stuart Phelps, *Beyond the Gates* (thirty-second edition, Boston, 1898; copyright 1883), p. 51.

38. *Ibid.,* p. 191. Compare A. E. Coppard's delightful treatment of this same problem in his short story "Clorinda Walks in Heaven," in Alexander Laing, ed., *Great Ghost Stories of the World* (New York, 1939), pp. 717–722.

39. Mark Twain did in fact write a lampoon on Elizabeth Phelps's work, and he made the most of his opportunities; *e.g.,* since the afterworld includes all persons who have ever died, the American sector of Heaven is populated chiefly by Indians! But Mrs. Clemens thought this kind of irreverence was improper, and so *Extract From Captain Stormfield's Visit to Heaven* was not published until the twentieth century. Willard Thorp, *op. cit.,* p. 226, n. 25.

40. The most recent editor of *The Gates Ajar* falls into this kind of judgment in spite of a strenuous scholarly effort to understand and appreciate Miss Phelps's point of view: "*The Gates Ajar* portrays the spiritual world as wish-fulfilling extension of the material world. . . . Elizabeth Stuart Phelps invests heavenly society with a stability that perhaps only a Victorian could conceive." Helen Sootin Smith, *op. cit.,* p. xxii.

41. Sigmund Freud, "Thoughts for the Times on War and Death" (1915), in Freud, *Collected Papers* (New York, 1959), Vol. IV, Chapter XVII; this quotation at p. 317.

42. *Overland Monthly,* III (September, 1869), p. 293. A quarter-century afterward Elizabeth Phelps stated that she had received ten thousand personal letters from readers of *The Gates Ajar,* and quoted from a few of them in a way that suggests that the reception accorded her first novel may have been in part a subtle rejection of the official cult of optimism and success associated with the Gilded Age: "In these days when culture and religion are both forced to an exotic warmth which it is the fashion to call optimism, it requires some courage to say, point blank, that this life is, so far as this world goes, taken as a whole, a failure." Elizabeth Stuart Phelps Ward, " 'The Gates Ajar'—Twenty-Five Years Later," *North American Review,* CLVI (May, 1893), pp. 567–576; this quotation at p. 571.

43. [H. F. Scudder] "The Annexation of Heaven," *Atlantic Monthly,* LIII (January, 1884), p. 143.

44. *The Complete Writings of Walt Whitman* [Paumanok Edition] (New York and London, 1902), Vol. II, p. 221.

45. William Irvine, *Apes, Angels, and Victorians: Darwin, Huxley, and Evolution* (Cleveland and New York, 1959), p. 12.

46. Richard O'Connor, *op. cit.,* p. 95.

47. "The Famous Gilson Bequest," in Bierce, *Collected Works,* Vol. II, pp. 266–280; this quotation at pp. 279f. For a classic example of the power that deliberate ambiguity of this sort can give to a short story, see Guy de Maupassant's *Le Horla.* In his more restrained fashion Henry James was a master of the same technique.

48. Howard Phillips Lovecraft, *Supernatural Horror in Literature* (New York, 1945), p. 13. Compare the musings on this same point by one of Bierce's fictional characters— typically, for him, a soldier on picket—in the story "A Tough Tussle," *Collected Works of Ambrose Bierce,* Vol. III: *Can Such Things Be?* (New York and Washington, 1910), pp. 106–120, and esp. p. 113.

49. "Christian Reid," pseud., "The Doctor's Fee," *Catholic World,* XLII (February and March, 1886), pp. 608–634 and 732–756, and XLIII (April, 1886), pp. 35–47.

50. E. P. Roe, *Barriers Burned Away* (New York, [1872] 1906).

51. William Dean Howells, *The Minister's Charge* (Boston, 1887). For the evolution of Howells's own religious views see Arnold B. Fox, "Howells as a Religious Critic," *New England Quarterly,* XXV (June, 1952), pp. 199–216.

52. Mark Twain and Charles Dudley Warner, *The Gilded Age: a Tale of To-Day* (New York, [1873] 1890), Vol. II, Chapter xxii.

53. Harriet Beecher Stowe, *Oldtown Folks* (Boston, 1869), Preface, p. vi.

54. Mary McCarthy, reviewing Graham Greene's drama *The Potting Shed,* has called its religious references "sly and suggestive." To the extent that a novel-reading and play-going public accepts the "monotonously bootleg fashion in which God is sneaked into the works of this fairly popular writer," she concludes, "religion . . . has become the new pornography." McCarthy, "Sheep in Wolves' Clothing," *Partisan Review,* XXIV (Spring, 1957), pp. 273, 274. To illustrate what she meant, imagine what Greene or T. S. Eliot would have done with the situation confronting Ralph Hartsook in Chapter VIII of *The Hoosier Schoolmaster*—a situation about which Eggleston was able to write with quite unselfconscious piety.

55. Robert T. Handy in a letter to the author, June 9, 1969.

56. *The Forum,* XII (February, 1892), p. 815; Vernon Louis Parrington, *Main Currents in American Thought* (New York, 1930), Vol. III, p. 64.

57. Harriet Beecher Stowe, *Oldtown Folks* (as cited in n. 52), p. 378; Stowe, *The Minister's Wooing* (Boston, [1859] 1896), p. 247.

58. Edward Eggleston, *The Hoosier Schoolmaster* (New York, [1871] 1892), Chap. XII.

59. Johanna Johnston, in *Runaway to Heaven: the Story of Harriet Beecher Stowe* (Garden City, 1963), p. 387, hints at "some hidden streak of jealousy" in Henry Ward Beecher toward his sister for her literary successes, even though he was offered a higher price for *Norwood* than anything she had received for a serial story. At the same time that he was writing *Norwood,* Harriet was working on *Oldtown Folks,* and it may be significant that Beecher thought it better if they kept their respective manuscripts to themselves until done.

60. Stowe, *Oldtown Folks,* p. 266; Henry Ward Beecher, *Norwood; or, Village Life in New England* (New York, 1868), p. 120.

61. Howells found the hero and heroine in particular so insipid that while they might easily be believed to be models of dull virtue, "that they are young and handsome seems doubtful; and we should not believe it but that we have Mr. Beecher's

word for it." [William Dean Howells] Review of *Norwood* in the *Atlantic Monthly,* XXI (June, 1868), p. 761.

62. Stowe, *Oldtown Folks,* p. 386.

63. Margaret Deland, *John Ward, Preacher* (Boston, 1888), pp. 98, 245.

64. See Grier Nicholl, "The Image of the Protestant Minister in the Christian Social Novel," *Church History,* XXXVII (September, 1968), pp. 319–334.

CHAPTER 5

1. John Boyle O'Reilly, "The Infinite," in Stanton A. Coblentz, ed., *Unseen Wings: the Living Poetry of Man's Immortality* (New York, 1949), pp. 258f. A lively sketch of O'Reilly's career can be found in Arthur Mann, *Yankee Reformers in the Urban Age* (Cambridge, Mass., 1954), pp. 27–44.

2. William B. Hesseltine, *Ulysses S. Grant: Politician* (New York, 1935), p. 452.

3. [F. Bruce Morgan] "Is This the Post-Christian Era?" lead editorial, *Theology Today,* XVIII (January, 1962), pp. 399–405.

From either an historical or a sociological point of view all such judgments are impressionistic and to some degree subjective: "Despite the importance of the topic, empirical studies of the individual's relationship to death have been comparatively few and recent. Great obstacles to research are posed by people's reluctance to discuss so private a matter, as well as by their underlying ambivalence toward death itself." John W. Riley, Jr., "Death," in David L. Sills, ed., *International Encyclopedia of the Social Sciences* (New York, 1968), Vol. IV, p. 23. If people are in fact more willing to talk to investigators in personal terms about sexual matters than they are about death, considering that both of these subjects were taboo areas in polite society not so long ago, we may be less "emancipated" in our attitude toward personal extinction than Professor Morgan's essay implies.

4. John J. McMahon, "Catholic Students Look at Death," *Commonweal,* LXXXVIII (January 26, 1968), pp. 491–494. By 1968 the only surprising feature of such testimony was its occurrence in a church-controlled classroom. Half a century earlier, questionnaires on the belief in God and in personal immortality among American college students and among natural and social scientists had shown what was coming. See James H. Leuba, *The Belief in God and Immortality: a Psychological, Anthropological and Statistical Study* (Boston, 1916), esp. pp. 185–213.

5. A. V. G. Allen, *Life and Letters of Phillips Brooks* (New York, 1901), Vol. II, p. 481. Conversely, there remained many in the "activist" 1960's who thought of life after death not as activity but as repose. "In a public lecture I once remarked, quite incidentally, that Christ did not promise us eternal rest but *eternal life* and that the concept of 'life' is scarcely synonymous with 'rest.' Many in the audience were troubled and did not understand." Ignace Lepp, *Death and its Mysteries* (New York, 1968), p. 183.

6. Sidney E. Mead has a penetrating comment on America's Protestant folk-hymns (such as this one, which he quotes) in his seminal essay "The American People: Their Space, Time, and Religion," Chapter I of *The Lively Experiment: the Shaping of Christianity in America* (New York, 1963), esp. p. 12.

7. For the dating of the composition of these hymns I am indebted to a study by Evelyn Hubbard, "A Survey of the Hymnary of the Gilded Age," unpublished seminar paper, Northern Illinois University, 1967.

8. Henry Ward Beecher, *Yale Lectures on Preaching* (three volumes in one, New

York, 1887), Third Series, Chapter XII, p. 320. Perhaps Beecher was unaware of the Feuerbachian implications of that last line!

9. Washington Gladden, *How Much Is Left of the Old Doctrines?* (Boston, 1899), pp. 314, 316; William Scarlett, ed., *Phillips Brooks: Selected Sermons* (New York, 1949), p. 369.

10. Charles A. Briggs, *Whither? A Theological Question for the Times* (New York, 1889), p. 285; Elizabeth Stuart Phelps, "The Psychical Wave," *The Forum,* I (June, 1886), pp. 380, 381, 388.

11. William Osler, *Science and Immortality* [The Ingersoll Lecture, 1904] Boston, 1904, p. 25. For a characteristic contemporary statement of this position, see the quotation from E. Dühring's *Der Werth des Lebens* in William James, *Human Immortality: Two Supposed Objections to the Doctrine* [The Ingersoll Lecture, 1898], 2nd edition, Boston, 1899, p. 11, n. 2.

12. In 1932, contemplating a new wave of discoveries in neurophysiology (popularly expressed in books with titles like *The Wisdom of the Body* and *The Physical Basis of Mind*) which seemed to overthrow completely any dualistic concept of "mind" and "body" as separate entities, the philosopher Roy Wood Sellars commented: "It is upon this rock that all theories of immortality break to pieces." Sellars, *The Philosophy of Physical Realism* (New York, 1932), p. 304, as quoted in Ashley Montagu, *Immortality* (New York, 1955), p. 25. See also the discussion of the destructive monistic implications of physiology and medicine for the concept of survival after death in Corliss Lamont, *The Illusion of Immortality* (London, [1935] 1936), pp. 58–112.

13. Lovecraft to Frank Belknap Long, July 17, 1921, in H. P. Lovecraft, *Selected Letters,* Vol. I, *1911–1924* (Sauk City, Wis., 1965), p. 141.

14. Paul Carus, *The Religion of Science* (Chicago, [1893] 1896), pp. 48, 39, 56; Samuel Chugerman, *Lester F. Ward, the American Aristotle* (Durham, N. C., 1939), pp. 249f.

15. Quoted in Ashley Montagu, *op. cit.,* p. 67, and in Philip S. Moxom, *The Argument for Immortality* (Cambridge, Mass., 1894), p. 4. Montagu's and Moxom's own comments upon this widely-anthologized poem may be read as a debate in miniature on the merits of George Eliot's position on the immortality question. Moxom's paper is more readily available to the modern reader in John Henry Barrows, ed., *The World's Parliament of Religions* (Chicago, 1893), pp. 466–479.

16. Corliss Lamont, *op. cit.,* p. 239; Junius Henry Browne, "The Dread of Death," *The Forum,* VI (October, 1888), p. 220; Alan Lomax, ed., *The Folk Songs of North America* (Garden City, 1960), p. 350.

17. "Confessions of a Skeptic," *The Forum,* II (November, 1886), p. 290.

18. A. V. G. Allen, *op. cit.,* Vol. III, p. 370; James DeKoven, "The Christian Struggle," Sermon XIX in *Sermons Preached on Various Occasions . . .* (New York, 1880), p. 203.

19. Quoted in "Editor's Easy Chair," *Harper's New Monthly Magazine,* LII (March, 1876), pp. 612f.

20. Francis Darwin, ed., *Life and Letters of Charles Darwin* (London, 1888), Vol. I, p. 312; Harry Emerson Fosdick, *The Living of These Days: an Autobiography* (New York, 1956), p. 241. Compare the very similar argument of Lyman Abbott in *The Theology of an Evolutionist* (Boston, 1897), pp. 170f.

21. John Fiske, *Through Nature to God* (Boston, [1899] 1900), p. 170; Theodore T. Munger, "Immortality and Modern Thought," *Century Magazine,* XXX [n. s., VIII] (May, 1885), p. 76.

22. Blaise Pascal, *Pensées,* tr. by W. F. Trotter (New York, 1941), pp. 81, 82, and *passim* in Section III, "On the Necessity of the Wager."

23. Robert G. Ingersoll, "Address at the Funeral of His Brother," as reprinted in Ingersoll, *The House of Death, Being Funeral Orations and Addresses, etc.* (London, 1897), pp. 72f.

24. Orvin Larson, *American Infidel: Robert G. Ingersoll* (New York, 1962), p. 143.

25. Robert G. Ingersoll, *The House of Death,* pp. 36, 64, 87f.

26. Ingersoll, *The Ghosts, and Other Lectures* (Washington, 1878), p. 14.

27. Quoted in C. H. Cramer, *Royal Bob: the Life of Robert G. Ingersoll* (Indianapolis, 1952), p. 264.

28. Munger, "Immortality and Modern Thought," as cited in n. 21, above, p. 68; Minot J. Savage, "Experiences with Spiritualism," *The Forum,* VIII (December, 1889), p. 451. Compare Alexander Winchell, *Sketches of Creation* (New York, 1870), p. 371: "There must be a substratum that has not yet been sounded lying beneath the confused and apparently capricious phenomena of clairvoyance, mesmerism, dreams, and spiritual manifestations. With much imposition, there is much which can not be scientifically ignored. It remains to resolve the mystery of these sporadic phenomena—to reduce them to law . . .."

29. More recently it has been possible for at least one well known and highly articulate American clergyman to combine the most radical skepticism toward all the traditional doctrines of the Church with a heightened belief in immortality. James A. Pike, "Why I'm Leaving the Church," *Look,* April 29, 1969, pp. 54–58; James A. Pike with Diane Kennedy, *The Other Side: an Account of My Experiences with Psychic Phenomena* (New York, 1969).

30. E. A. Sears, "The Transparencies of Nature," New York *Christian Advocate,* XLIX (January 1, 1874), p. 1; Sir James Jeans, *The Mysterious Universe,* new rev. ed. (New York and Cambridge, [1932] 1935), p. 186.

31. "Miracle, in the sense of violation of law, is simply impossible. . . . It is as impossible for God to perform a miracle in this sense as it is for him to lie. . . . In what sense, then, is a miracle possible? I answer, only as an occurrence or a phenomenon *according to a law higher than any we yet know."* Joseph LeConte, *Evolution: its Nature, its Evidences, and its Relation to Religious Thought,* 2nd rev. ed. (New York, [1891] 1899), p. 356. Italics in the original.

32. Compare Chapter I, Part V, above. For an example of the speculative difficulties people got themselves into in their efforts to answer this question literally, see Andrew Jackson Davis, *Views of our Heavenly Home* (Rochester, N. Y., [1878] 1910), pp. 64–87, and esp. p. 165, where Davis attempted an estimate of the distance between Earth and Heaven in miles.

33. Newman Smyth, *Old Faiths in New Light* (New York, 1879), pp. 377, 375. See the expansion of this idea in the same author's *The Place of Death in Evolution* (New York, 1897).

34. Thomson Jay Hudson, *A Scientific Demonstration of the Future Life* (1895; 8th edition, Chicago, 1904), p. 255. But for a powerful contemporary rebuttal to this reasoning, see Chauncey Wright, "Evolution of Self-Consciousness," an abridgment of which appears in Perry Miller, ed., *American Thought: Civil War to World War I* (New York and Toronto, 1954), pp. 28–45. Wright argued that those aspects of man's psyche which he had been pleased to think of as peculiarly his own can be accounted for by natural evolutionary processes; see esp. pp. 31–38.

35. Drummond's work with Moody went so far as helping in the personal ministry

to those who came to the "inquiry-room" after Moody's sermons; Ernst Benz, *Evolution and Christian Hope: Man's Concept of the Future, from the Early Fathers to Teilhard de Chardin* (New York, 1966), p. 156. For an example of Drummond's public lectures on evolution, see *The Ascent of Man* (New York, 1894); for an example of his more purely devotional writing—the kind that would have made him congenial to Dwight L. Moody, in spite of the latter's rejection of the theory of evolution—see Drummond's often-reprinted essay on I Corinthians 13, *The Greatest Thing in the World.*

36. Henry Drummond, *Natural Law in the Spiritual World* (Philadelphia, 1893), p. 218.

37. Munger, "Immortality and Modern Thought," as cited in notes 21 and 28, above, pp. 72, 74; "L. S." [Leslie Stephen], "Darwinism and Divinity," *Popular Science Monthly,* I (June, 1872), pp. 199, 200. Evolutionary theists really could elect neither option, for to have granted souls to "lower" animals would have undermined their denial of man's basically animal nature, so crucial to their optimism about his future potential; compare the discussion of the "man-animal" problem in Chapters II and III. Nevertheless at least one of them, who had affirmatively answered the question of whether animals had souls, proceeded to the logical next question "Are they immortal?" and, after a bit of verbal hemming and hawing, concluded with a tentative "yes"; if ours persist after death, so in all fairness ought theirs. James Freeman Clarke, "Have Animals Souls?" *Atlantic Monthly,* XXXIV (October, 1874), p. 421.

38. H. T. Pledge, *Science Since 1500* (London, [1939] 1947), p. 222. A readable and still fairly accurate popular account of DeVries's work is in Willy Ley, *The Days of Creation* (New York, 1941), pp. 97–102.

39. Joseph LeConte, *op. cit.,* p. 318. A variant on this hypothesis of immortality as "emergent" is that of Henri Bergson, in his *Creative Evolution* (New York, 1937); another, popular among twentieth century immortalists who have read Freud, posits a "death-trauma" comparable to the "birth-trauma" of psychoanalytic theory, thereby neatly resolving the paradox that man should suffer anxiety at the prospect of moving on to a world which by definition is better than this one. Ignace Lepp, as cited in n. 5, above, pp. 168f.

40. An argument against the usual liberal-theist concept of human immortality as being in violation of the unity of the space-time continuum is in Arthur S. Eddington, *The Nature of the Physical World* (Cambridge, 1928; Ann Arbor, 1958), p. 351.

41. *Proceedings of the Tenth Annual Convention of the American Association of Spiritualists, held at Grow's Opera Hall, Chicago, on Tuesday, September 16* [1873], p. 35. Hereafter cited as American Association of Spiritualists, *Proceedings* (1873).

42. Robert W. Delp, "Andrew Jackson Davis: Prophet of American Spiritualism," *Journal of American History,* LIV (June, 1967), p. 44; Joseph McCabe, *Spiritualism: a Popular History from 1847* (London, 1920), p. 105. The 1890 U. S. Census listed 334 organized Spiritualist congregations, with 45,000 (living) communicants; in short, there were a few more Spiritualists in the United States than there were Mennonites (41,541, divided into twelve bodies), and a few less than there were Universalists (49,194). There were three times that many Mormons and Jews, twelve times that many Episcopalians, and thirty times that many Colored Baptists. Henry King Carroll, *The Religious Forces of the United States, Enumerated, Classified, and Described on the Basis of the Government Census of 1890* ["American Church History Series," I] (New York, 1893), General Statistical Summaries, Table II, pp. 390f., and Table IV, p. 394.

43. The confession in 1888 by one of the original Fox sisters of Hydesville that the "spirit rappings" which had made her famous were no more than the cracking of her

own knuckle bones was a particularly crushing blow. New York *Herald,* September 24 and October 10, 1888, as quoted in McCabe, *op. cit.,* pp. 44 and 45.

44. *Religio-Philosophical Journal,* XV (January 24, 1874), p. 1; William Jay Youmans, "The Everlasting Ghost," *Popular Science Monthly,* XLII (March, 1893), pp. 701–703; editorial, "Katie King," *Harper's Weekly,* XIX (January 9, 1875), p. 26.

45. John Fiske, *The Unseen World* (Boston, 1876; 16th impression, 1899), p. 43; Robert Peel, *Mary Baker Eddy: the Years of Discovery* (New York, 1966), p. 133. Peel concludes, incidentally, after careful examination of the evidence (*ibid.,* p. 133, n. 40, and p. 221) that Mrs. Eddy was never herself a Spiritualist, and labels as false the assertion (by Spiritualists) that for a time she was a practicing medium in Boston. Compare B. F. Austin, *The A.B.C. of Spiritualism* (Summit, N.J., n.d.; first published in 1920), pages not numbered, Questions 73, 74, 75, and 76.

46. See for example *Religio-Philosophical Journal,* XXVI (March 8, 1879), p. 4: "Bores and imbeciles and poetasters are not at once converted into sages and geniuses by slipping off this physical husk; . . . we must judge of their utterances precisely as one would of those from human beings in the flesh." Was this a hint, perhaps, that the only ghosts who took the trouble to come back and talk to us were those with nothing better to do?

47. Robert Dale Owen, "How I Came to Study Spiritual Phenomena," *Atlantic Monthly,* XXXIV (November, 1874), p. 580. But Owen's credulity may be inferred from the kind of information he admitted as evidence, in, *e.g., Footfalls on the Boundary of Another World* (3rd English edition, reprinted from the 10th American edition, London, 1875). See also the highly skeptical review of Owen's book *The Debatable Land Between This World and the Next* which appeared in the *Overland Monthly,* VIII (April, 1872), pp. 388–391.

48. See for example *Religio-Philosophical Journal,* XXV (January 18, 1879). Gresham's Law seems to have operated as effectively in the spiritual as in the fiscal world; a letter to the editor in that same issue complained that "Honest Mediums Cannot Earn Their Bread."

49. William James, "What Psychical Research Has Accomplished," *The Forum,* XIII (August, 1892), p. 727.

50. "Professor Wundt on Spiritualism," *Religio-Philosophical Journal,* XXVII (September 13, 1879), pp. 4f., replying to Wilhelm Wundt, "Spiritualism as a Scientific Question," *Popular Science Monthly,* XV (September, 1879), 577–593; William James, "What Psychical Research Has Accomplished," p. 737. Compare the article on "Spiritualism" in the present edition of the *Encyclopedia Britannica,* Vol. XXI, p. 241: "There were strong emotional involvements in both the rejection and the acceptance of spiritualism that have made difficult an impartial appraisal of the evidence."

51. Oliver Wendell Holmes, *The Professor at the Breakfast-Table* (Boston, [1859] 1882), pp. 15f.; Robert Dale Owen, "Some Results From My Spiritual Studies," *Atlantic Monthly,* XXXIV (December, 1874), pp. 719, 729, 721, 722, 726.

52. Quoted in Robert W. Delp, *op. cit.,* p. 48. See also Andrew Jackson Davis, *op. cit.,* p. 256, "Evils in the Social Structure."

53. Robert Dale Owen, "Some Results From My Spiritual Studies," p. 726. Modern Spiritualism, at least in its "high-church" form (so to speak) as organized into the National Spiritualist Association of Churches, has been far less heterodox and far more Biblicist than Robert Dale Owen, arguing for the truth of its doctrines in "fundamentalist" fashion by citing Scriptural proof-texts. See National Spiritualist Association of Churches in the United States of America, *Yearbook, 1963* (Milwaukee, 1963),

pp. 13f. But some of its spokesmen still engage in skeptical rebuttal of the standard Christian legends, as for example the Nativity stories; see Converse E. Nickerson, "The Origin of the Christmas Festival," *The National Spiritualist,* XLV (December, 1963), pp. 3–5. I am indebted to my colleague, Professor Thomas B. Jones of Northern Illinois University, for the loan of materials from his personal collection of the literature of Spiritualism.

54. Hamlin Garland, *The Tyranny of the Dark* (London and New York, 1905); *Forty Years of Psychic Research: a Plain Narrative of Fact* (New York, 1936). In his later years Garland seems to have become more skeptical, both about spiritualism and about immortality—and at the same time more socially and politically conservative. John E. Higgins, "A Man From the Middle Border: Hamlin Garland's Diaries," *Wisconsin Magazine of History,* XLVI (Summer, 1963), p. 300.

55. William Dean Howells, *The Undiscovered Country* (Boston, 1880). Like Hamlin Garland, Howells in his late years seems to have become more agnostic about the future life. See Arnold B. Fox, "Spiritualism and the 'Supernatural' in William Dean Howells," *Journal of the American Society for Psychical Research,* LIII (October, 1959), pp. 121–130. Howells's *A Hazard of New Fortunes,* perhaps his greatest novel— or, at any rate, his most meaningful for the modern reader—also raises some issues bearing upon the concerns of the present chapter. See William Dean Howells, *A Hazard of New Fortunes* (New York, paper, 1965; first published in 1890), pp. 370, 376, 386, 392, 395, 423, 431.

56. Arthur Mann, *op. cit.,* p. 166.

57. As a matter of fact Ingersoll did address the somewhat Chautauqua-like camp meetings the Spiritualists held annually at Lily Dale, New York. Eva Wakefield Ingersoll, *The Letters of Robert G. Ingersoll* (New York, 1951), p. 271.

58. American Association of Spiritualists, *Proceedings* (1873), pp. 4, 83, 105, 27, 10, 9, 48, 139, 190, 191.

59. The Spiritualists re-elected Mrs. Woodhull as their President less than a year after she had openly published her charges against Beecher in *Woodhull & Claflin's Weekly.* The *Religio-Philosophical Journal,* even though it opposed The Woodhull, published some of these Beecher stories, apparently in order to show to what lengths of scurrility she and her associates were capable of going. See J. K. Bailey, "The Real Issue," *Religio-Philosophical Journal,* XIII (March 31, 1873).

60. *Ibid.,* XIV (September 27, 1873), p. 4; *ibid.,* XIII (August 23, 1873), p. 4; *ibid.,* August 9, 1873, p. 2.

61. On The Woodhull's recantation, see Emanie Sachs, *The Terrible Siren: Victoria Woodhull, 1838–1927* (New York, 1928), Chapter 13, and Johanna Johnston, *Mrs. Satan: the Incredible Saga of Victoria C. Woodhull* (New York, 1967), pp. 241–245.

62. Elizabeth Stuart Phelps, "The *Décolleté* in Modern Life," *The Forum,* IX (August, 1890), pp. 670–684; this quotation at p. 673. Compare the same writer's contribution to a symposium on "Women's Views of Divorce" in the *North American Review,* CL (January, 1890), pp. 128–131, in which she argued that divorce should be justified only as one would a surgical operation, and that even when permitted it should be made "unenviable, unpopular, unlikely . . . as disgraceful as crime . . . as hard as death."

63. Norman O. Brown, *Life Against Death: the Psychoanalytical Meaning of History* (Middletown, Conn., 1959), p. 309; "Articles of Religion, as Established by the Bishops, the Clergy, and the Laity of the Protestant Episcopal Church . . . in the Year of our Lord 1801," in *The Book of Common Prayer* (New York, 1945), p. 603.

64. Isaac Wise, for example, went on record as opposed to the doctrine of physical

resurrection as early as 1851, and thereafter maintained a rigorous dualism between the "physical" and the "spiritual"; see James G. Heller, *Isaac M. Wise: His Life, Work, and Thought* (New York, 1965), pp. 218, 516, 527. William Newton Clarke interpreted the Pauline concept of a "spiritual body" (as in I Cor. 15:35–54) as "a body that has no identity with flesh," and missed the point (according to more recent scholarship) of what Paul meant by "flesh." "As to the body of man, theology is not concerned with it. . . . Of personality, [the body] is no necessary part. Personality might exist without it." In death, "the spirit leaves the material body, but lives on." Clarke, *An Outline of Christian Theology* (New York, 1898), pp. 455, 184, 187, 449.

65. See, for example, A. Cleveland Coxe, 'Vulcan, or Mother Earth?" *The Forum,* I (March, 1886), pp. 64–74, and in reply John W. Chadwick, "Cremation, Nevertheless," *ibid.,* May, 1886, pp. 273–283.

66. Junius Henri Browne, "The Silent Majority," *Harper's New Monthly Magazine,* XLIX (September, 1874), p. 486.

CHAPTER 6

1. Wilbur L. Cross, *Connecticut Yankee: an Autobiography* (New Haven, 1943), p. 40.

2. Message reconvening the Second Vatican Council, Sunday, September 29, 1963 (United Press dispatch, September 30, 1963).

3. New York *Times,* March 20, 1887, p. 8; Edward W. Bok, ed., *Beecher Memorial: Contemporaneous Tributes to the Memory of Henry Ward Beecher* (Brooklyn, 1887).

4. New York *Times,* March 17, 1887, p. 8; Lyman Abbott, *Silhouettes of My Contemporaries* (Garden City, 1921), p. 239.

5. Rabbi [Kaufman] Kohler of Synagogue (properly, Temple) Beth-El, as quoted in New York *Times,* March 13, 1887, p. 3. See also the testimony to the same point by the Ethical Culturist Felix Adler, in Bok, *op. cit.,* pp. 96f.; it is a comment upon the Brooklyn of a century ago that Adler praised Beecher for having risen "so high above the social prejudices of his surroundings."

6. This poem was printed in *ibid.,* pp. 23f. Four other verse-eulogies of Beecher appeared in the Bok volume, but leading poets of the day—Joaquin Miller, John Greenleaf Whittier—confined their tributes to prose.

7. Editorial, "The Jackals and the Lion," New York *Times,* March 8, 1887, p. 2; editorial, "Bigotry At the Grave," Chicago *Times,* as cited in *ibid.,* March 9, 1887, p. 3; *National Cyclopedia of American Biography,* III (New York, 1893), p. 130.

8. This and similar posters were reproduced in Henry Ward Beecher, *Patriotic Addresses in America and England, from 1850 to 1885, on Slavery, the Civil War, and the Development of Civil Liberty in the United States* (New York, [1887] 1891), facing p. 653. (Hereafter cited as *Patriotic Addresses.*)

9. Jonathan Blanchard, "The Spirit of the Cynosure," *The Christian Cynosure,* IV (July 11, 1872), p. 2; Blanchard, "Henry Ward Beecher," *ibid.,* May 9, 1872, p. 3. A sympathetic but perceptive study of Blanchard's thought is Richard A. Taylor, "Jonathan Blanchard: 19th Century Evangelical," unpublished Master's thesis, Northern Illinois University, 1971. I am indebted also to Mr. Taylor for generously having made available to me Xeroxed copies of editorials from Blanchard's newspaper, *The Christian Cynosure,* a complete file of which is on deposit at Wheaton College, Wheaton, Illinois.

10. New York *Herald,* July 23, 1874, p. 6.

11. Johanna Johnston, *Mrs. Satan: the Incredible Saga of Victoria C. Woodhull* (New York, 1967), p. 154.

12. *Ibid.*, p. 159; Emanie Sachs, *The Terrible Siren: Victoria Woodhull, 1838–1927* (New York, 1928), pp. 171–175.

13. Mrs. L. E. Drake, "Progression; or, I Wish It Were Respectable," as read by Mrs. Rhoda Loomis at the *Proceedings of the Tenth Annual Convention of the American Association of Spiritualists, Held at Grow's Opera Hall, Chicago, on Tuesday, September, 16* [1873], pp. 4–5. (Hereafter cited as *Proceedings*.)

14. New York *Herald*, July 23, 1874, p. 3.

15. See for example New York *Times*, July 28, p. 4, col. 1, and *ibid.*, p. 5, col. 3. But compare also the tepid headlines the *Times* gave to Tilton's detailed charges against Beecher: "An Extraordinary Story—Private Letters of the Parties Implicated" with those of its morning competitor the *Herald*: "Adultery Charged Against the Plymouth Pastor—Bedroom and Parlor Scenes—Mr. Tilton's Description of His Wife Before and After the Fall." New York *Times*, July 22, 1874, p. 1; New York *Herald*, same date, p. 3.

16. The official minutes of that convention began with complaints from the delegates of unfair treatment by the newspapers of Chicago; one said that they had accused her in print of telling "dirty stories." *Proceedings*, pp. 2–3.

17. E. P. Buffett, "An Afternoon at the Beecher Trial," *Overland Monthly*, XV (August, 1875), pp. 194, 191.

18. New York *Times*, January 6, 1875, p. 1; Austin Abbott, ed., *Official Report of the Trial of Henry Ward Beecher* (New York, 1875), Vol. I, pp. 139ff. (Hereafter cited as *Trial*.)

19. *Ibid.*, p. 184. The New York *Times* discussed this incident in its issue for January 7, 1875, p. 1.

20. The New York *Times* suggested that the participants might have been the victims of the rigor of Anglo-Saxon jurisprudence, which forces a court to find a man unequivocally "Guilty" or "Not Guilty"; a canny Scottish jury given such a case might properly have brought in a verdict of "Not Proven." *The Beecher Trial: a Review of the Evidence* (New York: pamphlet, 1875; expanded from a story in the New York *Times*, July 3, 1875), p. 1. (Hereafter cited as *Review of the Evidence*.)

21. Chicago *Tribune*, April 17, 1878, p. 4. But the New York *Herald*, same date, p. 5, although expressing regret "that the vile thing should ever have been disinterred," maintained that the Brooklyn scandal was of such significance that it could not be lightly ignored, "in spite of its ill savor and of the universal nausea it produces." Throughout the controversy the rewrite men on James Gordon Bennett's *Herald* were prone to let themselves go. Even astronomy was summoned to set the stage; "At this epoch," the lead for one *Herald* story began, "when the tail of Coggia's comet is so near the beaming face of the Man in the Moon and the busy tongue of scandal is waving a tale of unwonted length . . ." *Ibid.*, July 2, 1874, p. 4.

22. Paxton Hibben, *Henry Ward Beecher: an American Portrait* (New York, [1927] 1942), p. 273; New York *Herald*, April 17, 1878, p. 5. The New York *Times*, same date, p. 2, gave the substance of this interview in quotation so indirect as to exasperate the historian; for all its sensationalism, I have consciously used the *Herald* as a corrective on the *Time*'s pedestrian reporting.

23. Opening address of Mr. Samuel D. Morris for Plaintiff, *Trial*, Vol. I, p. 269; *The Case of Henry Ward Beecher: Opening Address by Benjamin F. Tracy, of Counsel for the Defendant* (New York, 1875), p. 2. (Hereafter cited as Tracy, *Opening Address*.)

24. Editorial, the New York *Times,* March 9, 1887, p. 4. For all its obituary praise of Beecher, the *Times* stuck by its "Not Proven" verdict of 1875: "He had the defect of his qualities—vitality, emotionalism, and intellectual inconsistency—or he could never have permitted his reputation to be clouded by the scandal of 1874, in which his part, whether innocent or not, was most pitiful."

25. Anecdote by Moorfield Storey, cited as not previously published by James Ford Rhodes in his *History of the United States* (New York, 1920), Vol. VIII, pp. 221–223; reprinted in Ray A. Billington et al., *The Making of American Democracy: Readings and Documents* (New York, 1950), Vol. II, p. 81.

26. "Notes From Havana," New York *Times,* August 7, 1874, p. 2; editorial, "The Root of our Present Evils," *Catholic World,* XXIII (May, 1876), pp. 149, 154.

27. Chicago *Tribune,* July 1, 1874, p. 2.

28. "An Episcopalian," letter to the New York *Herald,* July 18, 1874, p. 8 (my italics); "An Actor Replies," *ibid.,* July 22, 1874, p. 4.

29. Quoted in Paxton Hibben, *op. cit.,* p. 92. By the end of his life Beecher seems to have mellowed considerably on the theater, judging from a conversation the well known actor-director-playwright Dion Boucicault reported he had had with Beecher in 1884: "I remarked that many sincere and good people objected to the stage because its very soul was a fiction, and its art was a moral conveyed in a falsehood. After a reflection of a moment, he remarked, almost to himself, 'And the parables of our Savior?' " Edward Bok, *op. cit.,* p. 40.

30. *Review of the Evidence,* p. 5; Hartford *Courant* as quoted in the New York *Herald,* July 23, 1874, p. 3; Springfield *Republican* as quoted in the New York *Times,* August 3, 1874, p. 4; New York *Times,* July 30, 1874, p. 4. Compare also the editorial in the New York *Christian Advocate,* XLIX (July 9, 1874), p. 220.

31. The Baltimore *Gazette* said that Tilton had told his story "with such circumstantiality of detail as almost to force conviction"; the Chicago *Times* claimed he had "substantiate[d] his charges by incontrovertible proofs." On the other hand the Baltimore *American* called Beecher's accuser a "wretched egotist who could write the story of his wife's seduction and ruin in a style that rivals the worst of sensational novels," and the Troy (N.Y.) *Times* declared: "The World Can Afford the Extinction of Tilton." Press sampling from these and many other newspapers commenting on the case is in the New York *Herald,* July 23, 1874, p. 3.

32. Hibben, *op. cit.,* p. 243. Compare also *The Nation,* XXI (July 8, 1875), p. 22: "It can hardly be said that this is a victory for anybody, but it is something very like a defeat for Mr. Beecher."

33. *Harper's Weekly,* XIX (July 17, 1875), p. 574; *Scribner's Monthly,* X (September, 1875), p. 637. Another journal that stuck with Beecher for reasons described in the chapter just previous was the Spiritualists' *Religio-Philosophical Journal;* see the editorial "Mr. Beecher as a Great Reformer," in Vol. XVIII (July 31, 1875), p. 156.

34. Indeed Tilton's own leading counsel, William A. Beach, was later said to have believed Beecher innocent after having seen his performance on the witness stand. To the inevitable question of professional integrity thus raised Irving Browne, editor of the *Albany Law Journal,* replied: "He [Beach] simply went on after Mr. Beecher's testimony, and made the best he could of a poor case." Quoted in John R. Howard, "Review of Mr. Beecher's Personality and Political Influence," in Beecher, *Patriotic Addresses,* p. 151.

35. Quoted in the New York *Herald,* July 3, 1874. Compare the editorial in Vol. XLIX (July 30, 1874), p. 244, of the New York *Christian Advocate,* which hitherto had assumed Beecher would be acquitted, but now considered the pastor and his

friends to be acting as they would be expected to if Tilton's charges were true: "With deepest sorrow and alarm at what has transpired, we wait further developments, determined to cease to hope only when compelled to do so." See further n. 41, below.

36. *Harper's Weekly,* XIX (July 24, 1875), p. 595. Be it remembered that Presidents of the United States did not begin receiving annual salaries this large until the late 1960's—and then, of course, in greatly depreciated dollars by the standards of 1875.

37. Soon after Tilton had made his accusation public, in fact, a libel action was entered on the Plymouth pastor's behalf which, had it been pressed, would have made it the case of *Beecher* v. *Tilton* rather than the other way around. See *People* v. *Tilton,* as discussed in the New York *Times,* July 29, 1874, p. 5; July 30, p. 5; August 4, p. 5. The case never got past a preliminary hearing; Justice Riley dismissed it on the ground that the complainant was a "private person" rather than a friend of the alleged libellee. Beecher's failure to press this matter became one more debating point in the attempt to sift the evidence: was he magnanimous, or was he guilty?

38. New York *Herald,* July 24, 1874, p. 3; New York *Times,* same date, p. 1, slightly different wording (omitting for example the aside to "Mr. Stenographer").

39. This radical position was one that Tilton had come to only slowly. Compare the high Christology implicit in his poem "The True Church," in *Atlantic Monthly,* XI (March, 1863), pp. 350–353.

40. Tracy, *Opening Address,* p. 8; *ibid.,* p. 32; New York *Times,* February 26, 1875, p. 3.

41. *Trial,* Vol. I, pp. 174f.; another example, *ibid.,* p. 239. What we can not now know at this distance is how many people declined to accept the argument by counsel for both sides that the outcome of the trial was crucial for organized religion. Midway through the trial, in the course of explaining why it had refrained from printing any correspondence it had received in the case, the New York *Christian Advocate* declared: "Christianity is not on trial at the Brooklyn court-house." But then it somewhat smugly covered itself by the sectarian observation that if Christianity was not on trial, perhaps Congregationalism was: "Happily, that affair [*Tilton* v. *Beecher*] is quite outside of our ecclesiastical fold," the Methodist weekly declared, "and, indeed, a good way further than some have fancied." New York *Christian Advocate,* Vol. L (March 18, 1875), p. 84.

42. James Morris Williams, interviewed by the New York *Herald,* July 2, 1874.

43. Tracy, *Opening Address,* p. 32; "Future Punishment," a sermon preached Sunday morning, October 16, 1870, and reprinted in Henry Ward Beecher, *Two Sermons* (New York, 1871), p. 102; New York *Times,* December 17, 1877, p. 8; editorial in *ibid.,* p. 4; *ibid.,* December 18, 1877, p. 4; *ibid.,* January 1, 1878, p. 4.

44. *The Christian Cynosure,* XIX (March 17, 1887), p. 8. Blanchard thought this inaction particularly damning inasmuch as Edward Beecher, one of Henry's brothers, was at that time already active in the abolitionist movement. In fairness to Henry, however, it should be noted that in the discussion preceding the Compromise of 1850 the pastor of Plymouth Church stood well to the Left of what was to become the Clay consensus of that year. See "Shall We Compromise?" *The Independent,* February 21, 1850, as reprinted in Henry Ward Beecher, *Patriotic Addresses,* pp. 167–177. John C. Calhoun is supposed to have had this article read to him shortly before his death and to have commented: "That man understands the thing. He has gone to the bottom of it." *Ibid.,* p. 167n.

45. Andrew Carnegie, *Autobiography* (Boston, 1920), p. 336; New York *Herald,* July 6, 1874, p. 6. The *Times,* on July 8, 1874, p. 8, carried a slightly different version

of what Beecher had said: "He did not by this mean to commit himself to the statement that men had sprung from the brute creation. He did not propose that theory at all."

46. As has already been observed, Ingersoll was one of the contributors to the Beecher memorial volume of 1887. "Born in a Puritan penitentiary, of which his father was one of the wardens," Ingersoll wrote, Henry Ward Beecher had freed himself from that prison, and thereafter had "taught the Church to think and doubt." Bok, op. cit., pp. 28, 32. See also Robert G. Ingersoll, *The House of Death, being Funeral Orations and Addresses, etc.* (London, 1897), pp. 11–16.

47. Jonathan Blanchard, in *The Christian Cynosure,* IV (July 11, 1872), p. 2; James Parton, "Henry Ward Beecher's Church," *Atlantic Monthly,* XIX (January, 1867), pp. 43, 50, 44.

48. Joseph R. Brandon, *Some Thoughts on Judaism: Two lectures delivered May, 1879 before the Y.M.H.A.* (San Francisco, 1881), p. 3. But Isaac Wise considered Beecher not yet sufficiently emancipated from Christian dogmas, particularly that of the Trinity, a doctrine Wise considered "the unfinished business of Christianity, which will turn up and annoy the house so long, until finally disposed of as a useless burden." *American Israelite,* XV (April 23, 1869), as quoted in James G. Heller, *Isaac M. Wise: His Life, Work, and Thought* (New York, 1965), p. 628.

49. *Atlantic Monthly,* XXVI (July, 1870), p. 118.

50. *Webster's Collegiate Dictionary,* 5th ed. (Springfield, Mass., 1947), p. 515. This was the largest abridgment of *Webster's New International Dictionary,* 2nd ed., copyright 1934.

51. Allan Nevins and Milton Halsey Thomas, eds., *The Diary of George Templeton Strong,* Vol. IV: *Post-war years, 1865–1875* (New York, 1952), entry for July 23, 1874, p. 531.

52. Letter to the editor, dated June 29, 1874, published in the New York *Herald,* July 3, 1874, p. 3. The writer (under the pen name "Sic Semper") was described by the *Herald* as "a frequent attendant at Plymouth Church and on speaking terms with both Mr. Beecher and Mr. Tilton."

53. *Woodhull & Claflin's Weekly,* November 2, 1872, as quoted in Emanie Sachs, op. cit., pp. 174f. See also the biased but possibly accurate account of another speech by The Woodhull, made after Tilton had published his charges, in the San Francisco *Chronicle,* as quoted in the New York *Herald,* July 12, 1874, p. 3.

54. *Harper's Weekly,* XIX (July 17, 1875), p. 574.

55. His texts were Matthew 20:28 and Philippians 2:1–11, both of which were painfully relevant. New York *Herald,* July 6, 1874, p. 6. (This was the same sermon which carried the cautious reference to evolution, cited in n. 44, above.)

56. New York *Times,* January 16, 1875, p. 5; *ibid.,* January 25, 1875, p. 2.

57. Lewis O. Brastow, *Representative Modern Preachers* (Freeport, N.Y., [1904] 1968), p. 103, citing an article by Immanuel Christlieb in "The History of Preaching," *Real Encyklopädie,* XVIII (1888), p. 644.

58. Phillips Brooks, "Address at the Installation of Rev. Lyman Abbott, D.D., over Plymouth Church, Brooklyn, New York, January 16, 1890," in Brooks, *Essays and Addresses, Religious, Literary, and Social* (New York, 1894), p. 178. The quotation from Brooks's father is in A. V. G. Allen, *Life and Letters of Phillips Brooks* (New York, 1901), Vol. I, p. 522.

59. Nevins and Thomas, *op. cit.,* entry for January 12, 1871, p. 341. For a striking example of Beecher's comic showmanship in the pulpit see John R. Howard, as cited in n. 33 above, at p. 139.

60. New York *Herald,* July 6, 1874, p. 6; Theodore Parker, quoting from *Life Thoughts, Gathered from the Extemporaneous Discourses of Henry Ward Beecher by a Member of his Congregation* (Boston, 1858), in a review for the *Atlantic Monthly,* I (May, 1858), p. 869.

61. Lyman Abbott, *Reminiscences* (Boston, 1915), p. 130; John R. Howard, as cited in notes 33 and 58, p. 64; James Parton, *op. cit.,* p. 47.

62. *Harper's New Monthly Magazine,* LXXIV (May, 1887), p. 981; Lyman Abbott, *Silhouettes of My Contemporaries,* p. 229.

63. New York *Christian Advocate,* XLIX (May 21, 1874), p. 164. A more moderate view was expressed in *ibid.,* L (March 11, 1875), p. 76: "God would never have given us the faculty of mirth and the muscles for laughter if it were sinful to use them." But the writer maintained that "on this side of our nature lie special perils of ruinous excess," a position still a long way from that of Henry Ward Beecher.

64. See for example Hibben, *op. cit.;* Robert D. Cross, *op. cit.,* pp. xxiii, xxiv, xxxiii; Harvey Wish, *Society and Thought in Modern America,* rev. 2nd ed. (New York, 1962), p. 153.

65. Robert T. Handy, "The Protestant Quest for a Christian America," *Church History,* XXII (March, 1953), p. 13. This essay has been reprinted as *The Protestant Quest for a Christian America, 1830–1930* [Facet Books Historical Series, #5] (Philadelphia, 1967).

66. For this exact phrase "qualitative hedonism" I am indebted to my father, the Rev. Manfred A. Carter, now deceased, of Hampden, Maine, who was using it in his pastoral thinking and writing in the early 1940's, well before the current moral debate in the Church had begun.

67. Sinclair Lewis, Foreword to Paxton Hibben, *op. cit.,* p. ix.

68. Vernon L. Parrington, *Main Currents in American Thought* (New York, 1930), Vol. III, p. 75. Another exception to the general adverse posthumous consensus on Beecher is Frank Hugh Foster's unduly neglected *The Modern Movement in American Theology* (New York, 1939), Chap. V: "The School of Henry Ward Beecher." It is interesting that even after Hibben's belittling biography had seemingly demolished Beecher's reputation altogether, Foster—who had lived through part of the Beecher era—could still write of "the freedom and breadth of his great personality," and call the first sermon in Beecher's *Evolution and Religion* "a truly noble utterance, which needs careful attention in our own day."

69. See the discussion by the present writer of the ambivalences in those mental and moral liberations—which had in them a disguised "Puritanism" of their own—in *The Twenties in America* (New York, 1968), pp. 59ff.

70. Abbott, *Silhouettes of My Contemporaries,* p. 214; New York *Times,* September 12, 1874, p. 2; *Proceedings,* pp. 236, 235; Emanie Sachs, *op. cit.,* p. 173.

71. Editorial in the New York *Times,* September 12, 1874, p. 6; *Review of the Evidence,* p. 34. This mental climate is typically expressed in the chapter on Beecher in Lewis O. Brastow, *op. cit.,* p. 110: "This emotional exuberance, this passionate intensity, this irrepressible energy of physical and psychical personality, this irresistible impulse of nature" came in for praise as the root cause of Beecher's genius; on the other hand, "His powers were not co-ordinated . . . he was so many-sided, so kaleidoscopic . . . , so subject to inward revulsions and changes of mood, so impulsive and emotional, that a disturbance of balance was inevitable." Significantly, Brastow assumed Beecher's innocence in the Tilton affair; would he have praised the "full and free play of individuality" in Beecher if the verdict had gone the other way?

CHAPTER 7

1. James H. Smylie, "Thanksgiving Amid Arrogance of Prosperity," *Theology Today*, XXIII (October, 1966), pp. 327–35.

2. Quoted in A. V. G. Allen, *Life and Letters of Phillips Brooks* (New York, 1901), Vol. III, pp. 279, 280. But it may also be typical of the period that in a year or two Brooks would recover his "cool": "The thing which grows on me is the splendid sense of liberty which is everywhere . . . so let us rejoice and hope great things of 1890."

3. Editorial, "Cause and Cure," *The Catholic World*, XLIII (April, 1886), p. 6.

4. Washington Gladden, "Is It Peace Or War?" *Century Magazine*, XXXII (August, 1886), pp. 576, 565. This was originally an address delivered at a mass meeting of workingmen and employers in Cleveland. It was repeated several times in Boston that same year, and eventually reprinted in Gladden's book *Applied Christianity*; it is in print today in Robert T. Handy, ed., *The Social Gospel in America 1870–1920* (New York, 1966), pp. 49–71.

5. H. L. Hastings, *The Signs of the Times: or a Glance at Christendom as it is* (Boston, 1862), p. 25 (compare also p. 377); James DeKoven, "The Church of the Living God," in *Sermons Preached on Various Occasions . . .* (New York, 1880), pp. 40, 42.

6. Hastings, *op. cit.*, p. 408; De Koven, *op. cit.*, p. 48.

7. See the discussion in Henry F. May, *Protestant Churches and Industrial America* (New York, 1949), esp. Part II.

8. I am here in partial dissent from the view expressed by R. J. Wilson in *Darwinism and the American Intellectual* (Homewood, Ill., 1967), and by Edward Kirkland in *Dream and Thought in the Business Community* (Ithaca, 1956; paper, Chicago, 1964). Although Kirkland was no doubt right in saying that the influence of "social Darwinism" in the Gilded Age has been exaggerated by intellectual historians, perhaps because of a professional tendency to over-value intellectual history, and although the American businessman's lionizing of the social Darwinist Herbert Spencer may have been, as Wilson argues, merely an attempt at cultural veneer (like supporting a symphony orchestra), we cannot neglect the force of Richard Hofstadter's observation: "The generation that acclaimed Grant as its hero took Spencer as its thinker." Richard Hofstadter, *Social Darwinism in American Thought*, rev. ed. (Boston, 1955), p. 34.

9. It is worth noting in this connection that Charles A. Briggs, subject of a famous heresy trial in the Gilded Age and a major figure in the transmission to America of the Higher Criticism, seems to have "remained conservative . . . on nearly all social issues." William R. Hutchison, ed., *American Protestant Thought: the Liberal Era* (New York, 1968), p. 27.

10. *Motorman and Conductor* (January, 1899); *United Mine Worker's Journal*, June 15, 1893, both as quoted in Herbert Gutman, "Protestantism and the American Labor Movement: the Christian Spirit in the Gilded Age," in Alfred F. Young, ed., *Dissent: Explorations in the History of American Radicalism* (DeKalb, Ill., 1968), pp. 150, 149.

11. Vincent Harding, "Religion and Resistance Among Ante-Bellum Negroes," a paper read before the Organization of American Historians, Chicago, April 27, 1967.

12. Gutman, *op. cit.*, p. 161; May, *op. cit.*, pp. 91–111.

13. C. M. Morse, "The Church and the Working-man," *The Forum*, VI (February, 1889), pp. 654, 659; James Parton, "Henry Ward Beecher's Church," *Atlantic Monthly*, XIX (January, 1867), p. 41.

14. H. P. Smyth, "Archdeacon Farrar's Advice," *Catholic World*, XLIII (April, 1886), p. 119; editorial, "The Typical Men of America," *ibid.*, XXIII (July, 1876), p. 486.

15. *The Christian Cynosure*, IV (February 15, 1872), p. 1; Patrick F. McSweeney, "The Church and the Classes," *Catholic World*, XLVII (July, 1888), pp. 471, 473.

16. "Great Cities," *Christian Pioneer*, VII (August 1, 1867); "The Problems of the Cities," *Christian Evangelist*, XIX (April 28, 1882), both as quoted in David Edwin Harrell, Jr., "The Agrarian Myth and the Disciples of Christ in the Nineteenth Century," *Agricultural History*, XLI (April, 1967), pp. 185, 192.

17. Walter Elliott, O. S. P., "The Evangelical Conference at Washington," *Catholic World*, XLVII (August, 1888), pp. 641ff.; editorial, "The Root of our Present Evils," *ibid.*, XXIII (May, 1876), p. 151; *ibid.*, XLVII (August, 1888), pp. 645f.

18. The following section of this chapter is adapted from a comment read by the author before a joint meeting of the Mississippi Valley Historical Association with the American Catholic Historical Association, Omaha, May 2, 1963.

19. *Catholic World*, XLIV (January, 1887), p. 567; "The Catholic Church in the United States, 1776–1876." *ibid.*, XXIII (July, 1876), pp. 452, 451.

20. Archbishop John Ireland, as quoted in Patrick J. Ahern, "Nationalism and Religion: John Ireland," a paper read before the Mississippi Valley Historical Association and the American Catholic Historical Association, Omaha, May 2, 1963, p. 2.

21. *Ibid.*, pp. 4, 9, quoting from Ireland.

22. *Ibid.*, p. 11 (Father Ahern's own judgment on Ireland).

23. *Ibid.*, p. 2, quoting Ireland; Dorothea Muller, "The Social Philosophy of Josiah Strong," *Church History*, XXVIII (June, 1959), pp. 183–201.

24. *Catholic World*, XL (February, 1885), p. 708.

25. Robert D. Cross, *The Emergence of Liberal Catholicism in America* (Cambridge, Mass., 1958), pp. 110, 105; see also pp. 39, 102.

26. McSweeney, *op. cit.*, p. 480.

27. On McGlynn, see Robert D. Cross, *op. cit.*, pp. 120–124. For a contemporary American Catholic reaction to the silencing of McGlynn in 1886 by his ecclesiastical superiors, see "Galileo Galilei and Dr. McGlynn," *Catholic World,* XLVI (October, 1887), pp. 110ff.

28. Robert Kelley, "Presbyterianism, Jacksonianism and Grover Cleveland," *American Quarterly*, XVIII (Winter, 1966), p. 630. Kelley blamed the subsequent lack of concrete accomplishment by the Cleveland Administrations (1885–89 and 1893–97) upon a "disparity between diagnosis and prescription," rather than upon Cleveland's having been "a front man for the moneyed interests" as historians had usually assumed.

29. An important pioneering study of the Social Justice movement in American Judaism is Leonard J. Mervis, "The Social Justice Movement and the American Reform Rabbi," *American Jewish Archives*, VII (June, 1955), pp. 171–230.

30. Henry Steele Commager, *The American Mind: An Interpretation of American Thought and Character since the 1800's* (New Haven, 1950), p. 167; Sidney E. Mead, *The Lively Experiment: The Shaping of Christianity in America* (New York, 1963), p. 178.

31. But we must overly condescend to these men. Martin Marty has wisely reminded us that when the early Social Gospel writers are judged afresh from their own writings rather than from our own second-hand epithets about them ("naive, optimistic, progressivistic, even utopian"), they "reveal just enough of a hard edge and of pragmatic attention to detail to mar the stereotypes." Marty, "Redeeming the Poor," a review of R. T.

Handy, ed., *The Social Gospel in America* (previously cited), in *Book Week*, July 3, 1966, p. 4.

32. See the forceful argument—itself a major revision of previous historians' generalizations about the rise of the Social Gospel—in Timothy L. Smith, *Called Unto Holiness, The Story of the Nazarenes: The Formative Years* (Kansas City, 1962), p. 200.

33. Chicago City Missionary Society, *Annual Report*, 1888, p. 12, as cited in David Ramis, "The Work of the Chicago City Missionary Society of the Chicago Congregational Churches, 1882–1892: a Study of Attitudes Toward Immigrant and Labor During the Period of the Emergent Social Gospel," unpublished seminar paper, Northern Illinois University, 1967, p. 17; C.C.M.S. *Annual Report*, 1884, pp. 5–6, as cited in *ibid.*, p. 1. In ten such Annual Reports Ramis found only one instance of what might be termed a "social gospel" diagnosis of the condition of the people to whom the Society ministered, and that was a reference to the least controversial of the Progressive issues, poisoned food. C.C.M.S. *Annual Report*, 1888, p. 12.

34. "Why Does Crime Increase?" *Christian Evangelist,* XXII (May 28, 1885), p. 339, as cited in David Edwin Harrell, Jr., *op. cit.,* p. 190; *ibid.,* p. 192.

35. James H. Findlay, "Moody, 'Gap-Men,' and the Gospel: the Early Days of the Moody Bible Institute," *Church History,* XXXI (September, 1962), p. 327. See also Dennis L. Olenik, "The Social Philosophy of Dwight L. Moody," unpublished Master's thesis, Northern Illinois University, 1964, esp. pp. 20f., 31f.

36. This analogy was made by Reinhold Niebuhr in his earliest written work, *Leaves From the Notebook of a Tamed Cynic* (New York, [1929] 1957), p. 134, quoting from a ms. diary entry in 1926.

37. Gladden elaborated these views in his book *Tools and the Man: Property and Industry under the Christian Law* (Boston, [1893] 1896), Chap. VI, in which he argued that cooperation was "the logic of Christianity."

38. Charles Taze Russell, *The Divine Plan of the Ages* ["Studies in the Scriptures," I] (East Rutherford, N. J., 1954 [first published in 1886]), pp. 325, 332f., 335, 312, 339, 341.

39. Russell, *The Battle of Armageddon* ["Studies in the Scriptures," IV] (East Rutherford, N. J., 1953 [first published in 1897]), *passim,* esp. pp. 633f.

40. C. Howard Hopkins, *The Rise of the Social Gospel in American Protestantism, 1865–1915* (New Haven, 1940), p. 19.

41. From one point of view this act of resistance could itself be construed as a kind of "social gospel," in its denial of the totalitarian claims of the secular state; secular liberals who would reject all or most of the theological claims of the Jehovah's Witnesses—*e.g.,* the typical activist in the American Civil Liberties Union—have seen the Witnesses' stand in the flag-salute question as a major assertion of the rights of the free citizen. See also the dissent by Mr. Justice Stone in *Minersville School District* v. *Gobitis,* 310 U.S. 586, and the majority opinion delivered by Mr. Justice Jackson in *West Virginia Board of Education* v. *Barnette,* 319 U.S. 624.

42. A case study is H. Peers Brewer, "The Protestant Episcopal Freedman's Commission, 1865–1878," *Historical Magazine of the Protestant Episcopal Church,* XXVI (December, 1957), 361–381. That this neglect—not so much racist as simply heedless —was not solely a reaction to the supposed excesses of Southern Reconstruction is shown by Lionel D. Ridout in "The Church, the Chinese, and the Negroes in California, 1849–1893," *ibid.,* XXVIII (June, 1959), 115–138.

43. A careful statistical study of Northern denominational aid to the freedmen in the immediate postwar years is Willie D. Gaither, "A Fool's Errand, a Drop in the

Bucket, or In *His* Steps?" unpublished seminar paper, Northern Illinois University, 1967. In sharp contrast to much historical writing on this aspect of Reconstruction— *e.g.,* R. E. Morrow, *Northern Methodism and Reconstruction* (East Lansing, Mich., 1956)—Gaither does not consider freedmen's aid of this private and voluntary sort as merely another form of carpetbagging. He compares the mentality of the Northern religious workers who went South during the period that ended in 1876 with that of Peace Corpsmen in the 1960's: "Their letters to the North read like today's *Peace Corps Volunteer* magazine." Gaither, p. 33.

44. *Voice of Missions,* I (January, 1893), p. 2. Edwin S. Redkey quite frankly calls Turner a "black nationalist" who "urged neither integration nor accommodation with white society." Redkey, "Bishop Turner's African Dream," *Journal of American History,* LIV (September, 1967), p. 290.

45. Rt. Rev. Francis Janssens, "The Negro Problem and the Catholic Church," *Catholic World,* XLIV (March, 1887), pp. 725, 722. Janssens wrote, of course, out of his church's wide experience with other non-European peoples: "Wherever the church has sent her missionaries, one of the great cares, after the first preaching of the faith, has ever been to erect seminaries to train a native priesthood."

46. Quoted in Wesley J. Gaines, *African Methodism in the South, or Twenty Five Years of Freedom* (Atlanta, 1890), p. 71, as cited in Vivian Narehood, "Pride Against Prejudice," unpublished seminar paper, the University of California, 1964, p. 32. I am indebted to Mrs. Narehood for first having called my attention to the existence of black nationalism in the Gilded Age; in 1964, when the historiographic and sociological consensus was still (rather dogmatically) that the Negro church throughout its history had been by definition "Uncle Tom," this was a highly original and independent judgment for a white graduate student in American history to make. Subsequent scholarship, as in Redkey, *op. cit.,* and Vincent Harding, *op. cit.,* has abundantly confirmed it.

47. *Voice of Missions,* I (January, 1893), p. 1; *ibid.,* May, 1893, p. 1. I am indebted to my colleague Otto Olsen of Northern Illinois University for the loan of a microfilm reel of this journal.

48. Even then there seem to have been rural-urban cleavages among American Negroes. See Turner's editorial that castigated the big-city churches of his denomination for having given proportionately less to the cause than the rural parishes. *Ibid.,* August, 1893, p. 2.

49. *Ibid.,* September, 1893, p. 2; letter of July 18, 1893, printed in *ibid.,* August, p. 3.

50. Needless to say Turner disagreed with Washington's premise that social equality for the Negro would have to wait on economic achievement: "With all due respect to Professor Washington personally, . . . he will have to live a long time to undo the harm he has done our race." *Voice of Missions,* October, 1895; Redkey, *op. cit.,* p. 288.

51. Unlike some of the more thoroughgoing black nationalists of the later 1960's Turner did not think the Negro could or should *start* this war of redress, pitting his eight or ten millions against sixty million whites and his pittances against the white man's billions of dollars. "To talk about physical resistance is literal madness."

52. *Voice of Missions,* I (December, 1893), p. 3.

CHAPTER 8

1. J. B. Bury, *The Idea of Progress: an Inquiry into its Growth and Origin* (New York, [1932] 1955), p. 2; Robert Benchley, "Isn't It Remarkable?" (copyright 1936),

in Henry C. Carlisle, Jr., *American Satire in Prose and Verse* (New York, 1962), p. 432.

2. Edward L. Youmans, "Introduction— . . . Mental Discipline in Education," in E. L. Youmans, ed., *The Culture Demanded by Modern Life* (New York, 1867), p. 1; [Finley Peter Dunne,] *Mr. Dooley in Peace and War* (Boston, 1899), p. 172.

3. Bury, *op. cit.,* pp. 335, 344, 336, 338. Georg Iggers, in a comment upon a paper by the present writer, pointed out that Spencer "was also the author of the extremely pessimistic *Man Versus the State,"* and that "a strong pessimistic note entered English and French liberal thought in the nineteenth century" [*Church History,* XXXII (March, 1963), pp. 92, 91].

4. Andrew Dickson White, *A History of the Warfare of Science with Theology in Christendom* (New York, 1898), Vol. I, p. 310; *The Praeger Picture Encyclopedia of Art* (New York and Washington, 1958), p. 549. This latter judgment is especially striking, coming from editors whose conception of the history of art remained at least tentatively developmental: "There may be a law of evolution in art corresponding to what has been found to occur in Nature." *Ibid.,* p. 12. On the same point see Herbert Read, *Art and the Evolution of Man* (London, 1951).

5. Herbert Wendt, *In Search of Adam,* trans. James Cleugh (Boston, 1956), p. 329. Compare the statement attributed to the French prehistorist Emile Cartailhac in *ibid.,* p. 335.

6. E. L. Youmans, "The Accusation of Atheism," *Popular Science Monthly,* XI (July, 1877), pp. 367ff.; George Santayana, *Character and Opinion in the United States* (Garden City, [1920] 1956), p. 10.

7. "The Dead in Christ," Sermon VII in James DeKoven, *Sermons Preached on Various Occasions* . . . (New York, 1880), p. 66; "Lost Opportunities," Sermon XXVI in *ibid.,* p. 306; Chicago *Tribune,* July 4, 1876.

8. Winthrop Hudson so summarizes a modern biographer's judgment on one prominent religious "progressive," Lyman Abbott, and concludes that the logical outcome of so rigorously pursued an evolutionary theology was the complete secularization of Abbott's thinking. Winthrop S. Hudson, reviewing Ira V. Brown, *Lyman Abbott: Christian Evolutionist* (Cambridge, Mass., 1953), in *Church History,* XXIII (December, 1954), p. 383.

9. "The Catholic Church in the United States, 1776–1876," *Catholic World,* XXIII (July, 1876), p. 439; "The Typical Men of America," *ibid.,* p. 479; "The Root of Our Present Evils," *ibid.,* May, 1876, pp. 146, 150, 151; *ibid.,* July, 1876, p. 487; Syllabus of Pius IX, annexed to the encyclical *Quanta Cura,* 1864, in Anne Fremantle, ed., *The Papal Encyclicals in their Historical Context* (New York, 1956), p. 152.

10. As late as 1932 an American Protestant liberal concluded that the Catholic "loves the glamor of feudalism and cannot bear to give it up." On this point see the present writer's *The Idea of Progress in American Protestant Thought, 1930–1960* ["Facet Books Historical Series," #11] (Philadelphia, 1969), pp. 3, 19.

11. Quoted in Will Herberg, *Protestant-Catholic-Jew: an Essay in American Religious Sociology,* new rev. ed. (Garden City, N. Y., 1960), p. 164, n. 164.

12. Sidney E. Mead, *The Lively Experiment: the Shaping of Christianity in America* (New York, 1963), p. 108; Hugh Wamble, "Old Landmarkism: Doctrinaire Ecclesiology Among Baptists," *Church History,* XXXIII (December, 1964), pp. 429–447.

13. Quoted in N. Eugene Tester, "Schisms Within the Disciples of Christ Denomination, 1809–1909" (unpublished Master's thesis, Northern Illinois University, 1969), p. 60. See also the quotations on p. 69.

14. For all their conscious quest for relevance to the problems of their own day, in the words of one of their own most distinguished scholars "Friends undertook

seriously to revive and restore primitive Christianity, a way of life . . . which seemed to them to have largely disappeared from the world." Rufus M. Jones, *The Later Periods of Quakerism* (London, 1921), Vol. II, p. 713. See also *ibid.,* p. 980.

15. Fred C. Luebke, "The Origins of Thomas Jefferson's Anti-Clericalism," *Church History,* XXXII (September, 1963), p. 351; L. T. Townsend, *The Bible and Other Ancient Literature in the Nineteenth Century* (New York, 1889), pp. 190, 193.

16. H. H. Wyman, "Creeds, Old and New," *Catholic World,* XLIV (February, 1887), pp. 691, 693. Jaroslav Pelikan has argued that this "faith once delivered" position has been outflanked, in the modern Catholic Church, by such actions as the proclamation by Pius XII in 1950 of the bodily assumption of the Virgin Mary—a dogma that grew out of "a tradition for which there is . . . no positive evidence until long after the apostolic age," and which therefore represented, in some sense, creedal evolution; for "what can it mean for a doctrine to 'become' part of the Catholic faith, which is, by definition, universal both in space and time?" Pelikan, "An Essay on the Development of Christian Doctrine," *Church History,* XXXV (March, 1966), p. 3.

17. A few of these iconoclasts retained a concept of the nature of man which was curiously static, "progressive" though their theology was. See for example Benjamin F. Underwood, "The Practical Separation of Church and State," as reprinted in Joseph L. Blau, ed., *Cornerstones of Religious Freedom in America* (Boston, 1949), pp. 220, 221.

18. Ralph Waldo Emerson, "Divinity School Address," as reprinted in Joseph L. Blau, ed., *American Philosophic Addresses, 1700–1900* (New York, 1946), p. 601; Francis Ellingwood Abbot, "The Genius of Christianity and Free Religion," as reprinted in *ibid.,* p. 708.

19. *American Israelite,* May 14, 1875, as quoted in James G. Heller, *Isaac M. Wise: His Life, Work, and Thought* (New York, 1965), p. 536; Isaac Mayer Wise, *Judaism: Its Doctrines and Duties* (Cincinnati, 1872), pp. 3f., as quoted in Betsey Rosten, "Isaac Mayer Wise: a Jew in Transition," unpublished seminar paper, the University of California, 1964, p. 23.

20. *American Israelite,* I (December 29, 1854), p. 196, as quoted in Heller, *op. cit.,* p. 520; compare in *ibid.,* pp. 364, 537. But not all liberal American Jews agreed; Solomon Schindler for example argued that "the religion of the future will be neither specifically Jewish nor Christian nor Mohammedan." Quoted in Arthur Mann, *Yankee Reformers in the Urban Age* (Cambridge, Mass., 1954), p. 60.

21. Joseph R. Brandon, *Some Thoughts on Judaism: Two Lectures Delivered in May, 1879 before the Y.M.H.A.* (San Francisco, 1881), pp. 12, 24, 26; Washington Gladden, *How Much Is Left of the Old Doctrines?* (Boston, 1899), p. 247.

22. Robert Peel, *Mary Baker Eddy: the Years of Discovery* (New York, 1966), p. 275; Henry Ward Beecher, "The Study of Human Nature," as reprinted in W. R. Hutchison, ed., *American Protestant Thought: the Liberal Era* (New York, 1968), pp. 40, 41.

23. New York *Christian Advocate,* XLIX (June 11, 1874); American Baptist Publication Society, *Annual Reports,* 1899 and 1900, and pamphlet, n. d., "On the Rails with the Gospel," as cited in Paul C. Kurtz, "Northern Baptists on the Frontier," unpublished seminar paper, Northern Illinois University, 1969, pp. 17–21. Mr. Kurtz included with this paper two color photographs of the chapel car "Grace," built in 1915, which was retired in 1946 to the American Baptist Assembly Grounds, Green Lake, Wisconsin. *Ibid.,* pp. 18, 19.

24. *Millennial Harbinger,* 1868, p. 140, as cited in N. Eugene Tester, *op. cit.,* p. 61; Herbert L. Willett, *Our Plea For Union and the Present Crisis* (Chicago, 1901), pp. 7,

8, as quoted in Tester, pp. 95f. For an example of the same adaptive process at work in one of the older Eastern-seaboard denominations, see David E. Swift, "Conservative versus Progressive Orthodoxy in Latter 19th-Century Congregationalism," *Church History*, XVI (March, 1947), 22f. The border-South Cumberland Presbyterians went through a similar adaptation, adopting a new Confession of Faith in 1883 to show that "ours is not a fixed and changeless, but a progressive creed; and that through all the decades we are to seek a more and more nearly exact statement of the truth revealed in Scripture, and believed by our own people." Rev. J. M. Howard, as quoted in Hubert W. Morrow, "Cumberland Presbyterian Theology: A Nineteenth Century Development in American Protestantism," *Journal of Presbyterian History*, XLVIII (Fall, 1970), p. 220.

25. Chapman, "The Idea of the Kingdom of God," *Bibliotheca Sacra*, LIV (July, 1897), p. 541, as quoted in W. R. Hutchison, "Liberal Protestantism and the 'End of Innocence,' " *American Quarterly*, XV (Summer, 1963), p. 129.

26. Alexander V. G. Allen, *Religious Progress* (Boston and New York, 1894), pp. 13, 14, 15, 24, 28, 43, 58, 91, 65, 105, 93.

27. See the discussion of the Second Vatican Council's action setting up a special Secretariat for Nonbelievers (*noncredenti*), in J. Robert Nelson, "Lord, I Don't Believe; Help My Belief!", Editorial Correspondence, *The Christian Century*, LXXXVI (April 16, 1969), pp. 501f.

28. Clarke, *An Outline of Christian Theology* (New York, 1898), p. 116. Compare the prophecy, in Benjamin Kidd, *Social Evolution* (New York and London, 1894), p. 329, that man would achieve the completest expression of his highest ethical qualities in the twentieth century, rather than in the apostolic age. In the context of the rest of Kidd's book, the means of achievement of these qualities is implicitly biological, which raises the ancient Gnostic heresy in a new guise, and plays havoc with any of the usual formulations of the doctrine of the Incarnation.

29. The question was put in this blunt way by John W. Buckham in 1909, in a document reproduced in H. Shelton Smith, Robert T. Handy, and Lefferts A. Loetscher, eds., *American Christianity: an Historical Interpretation with Representative Documents*, Vol. II: *1820–1860* (New York, 1963), p. 303.

30. Ralph Waldo Emerson, "Divinity School Address," as cited in Blau, *American Philosophic Addresses*, p. 593; Emerson, *Complete Works*, Vol. XI: *Miscellanies* (Boston, 1904), pp. 490f.

31. George Santayana, *op. cit., loc. cit.* That Protestant liberals have never fully worked their way out of this difficulty is implied in, *e.g.*, Morton T. Kelsey, "Is the World View of Jesus Outmoded?" *Christian Century*, LXXXVI (January 22, 1969), pp. 112–115.

32. Lyman Abbott, *The Evolution of Christianity* (Boston, 1892), p. 240; Abbott, *The Theology of an Evolutionist* (Boston, 1897), pp. 75f.

33. James Whiton, *Gloria Patri* (New York, 1892), p. 54, as quoted in Frank Hugh Foster, *The Modern Movement in American Theology: Sketches in the History of Protestant Thought from the Civil War to the World War* (New York, 1939), p. 75.

34. William Newton Clarke, *op. cit.*, Part IV, pp. 260–368, esp. pp. 261, 292, and the tacitly Monophysite position he came to on p. 302.

35. Washington Gladden, *How Much Is Left of the Old Doctrines?* (Boston, 1899), p. 168. Frank Hugh Foster, himself a "modernist," claimed that Washington Gladden "presented the same view of the person of Christ as Lyman Abbott," and argued that 1892, the year Abbott's *Evolution of Christianity* and Whiton's book on the Trinity, *Gloria Patri*, were published was "the date at which the Liberal theology

became largely unitarian." As to Gladden, from my own reading in the polemical literature of the period I am unable to agree. While Washington Gladden concurred in Abbott's judgment that the difference between the human and the divine was one of degree, not of kind, Gladden managed to work his way back to a Christology that would have been "high" by Foster's standards; see Gladden, *How Much Is Left of the Old Doctrines?* pp. 162, 172.

36. Henry Drummond, *Natural Law in the Spiritual World* (Philadelphia, n. d.), p. 281; Joseph LeConte, *Evolution: its Nature, its Evidences, and its Relation to Religious Thought* (New York, 1899), p. 360; Newman Smyth, *Old Faiths in New Light* (New York, 1879), pp. 185, 278.

37. William Newton Clarke, *op. cit.,* p. 444; Ernest R. Sandeen, "Towards a Historical Interpretation of the Origins of Fundamentalism," *Church History,* XXXVI (March, 1967), p. 75. This essay has also been published as *The Origins of Fundamentalism: Toward a Historical Interpretation* ["Facet Books Historical Series," #10] (Philadelphia, 1968).

38. *Prophetic Studies of the International Prophetic Conference* (New York and Chicago, 1886), p. 216, as quoted in Janice Brandon, "Millennialism in America," unpublished research paper, Northern Illinois University, 1969, p. 10.

39. A beginning is Timothy White, *A People For His Name: a History of Jehovah's Witnesses and an Evaluation* (New York, 1968); see the brief anonymous review of this work in *Church History,* XXXVIII (March, 1969), p. 128. A useful study of the Witnesses in terms of their developed ideology rather than of their history is Roylston Pike, *Jehovah's Witnesses* (New York, 1954); and see also Werner Cohn, "Jehovah's Witnesses as a Proletarian Movement," *American Scholar,* XXIV (Summer, 1955), pp. 281–298.

40. [Charles Taze Russell,] *Studies in the Scriptures, I: The Divine Plan of the Ages* (East Rutherford, N. J., 1954), p. 12. (Originally published in 1886 under the title *Millennial Dawn.*)

41. Washington Gladden, *Tools and the Man: Property and Industry Under the Christian Law* (Boston, [1893] 1896), p. 307.

42. See "The Battle of the Sand Belt," Chap. 43 of Mark Twain, *A Connecticut Yankee in King Arthur's Court* (New York: paperback, 1960), pp. 291–304. Few nineteenth-century American novels have been more massively misinterpreted than this one; Van Wyck Brooks, taking the anti-chivalric Philistinism of the body of the tale as containing all of its message, was typical of literary critics in quite missing the point.

43. Quoted by Sidney E. Mead, reviewing Roylston Pike, *op. cit.,* in *Church History,* XXIV (December, 1955), p. 384.

44. Russell conceded "creation-epochs" to Lyell, but not an inch to Darwin. Charles Taze Russell, *The New Creation* ["Studies in the Scriptures," VI] (East Rutherford, N. J., [1904] 1955), p. 22: "The devout child of God . . . will soon be able to see the sophistry of Mr. Darwin's theory." See in particular the caricature of the theory of natural selection by the survival of the fittest in *ibid.,* p. 21, and other attacks on Darwin and evolution throughout Chap. I, "In The Beginning."

45. See for example the vitriolic essay by William G. Moorehead, "Millennial Dawn: a Counterfeit of Christianity," the concluding essay in Vol. VII of *The Fundamentals: a Testimony to the Truth* (Chicago, [1909–1914]). Moorehead considered, and denied, the possibility that the founder of the Jehovah's Witnesses "is self-deceived, and . . . believes that what he has published is the truth of the Bible"; it

followed logically, therefore, "that Mr. Russell is being used by the Evil One to subvert the truth of God." *Ibid.,* p. 107.

CHAPTER 9

1. This chapter is based (after substantial revision) upon an article entitled "The Reformed Episcopal Schism of 1873: an Ecumenical Perspective," which appeared in the *Historical Magazine of the Protestant Episcopal Church,* XXXIII (September, 1964), pp. 225–238. It is reprinted here with the kind permission of that journal.

2. Arnold J. Toynbee, *An Historian's Approach to Religion* [The Gifford Lectures, 1952 and 1953] (London, New York, and Toronto, 1956), pp. 284, 253.

3. A standard monograph on the compromise of 1877 is C. Vann Woodward, *Reunion and Reaction: the Compromise of 1877 and the End of Reconstruction* (Boston, 1951). Details, for example, describing exactly what happened on election night, have been modified somewhat by subsequent research [see *Journal of Southern History,* XXXII (August, 1966), pp. 351ff.], but in its general outlines the Woodward interpretation still holds.

4. On the rejection of Presbyterian union in 1954 at the grassroots level in the Southern church, after its General Assembly had approved a proposed plan of union with the Northern Presbyterians, see David M. Reimers, "The Race Problem and Presbyterian Union," *Church History,* XXXI (June, 1962), esp. p. 212. For evidence of continuing strife over this and related issues, see James H. Smylie, "Ecclesiological Storm and Stress in Dixie," *The Christian Century,* LXXXV (March 13, 1968), pp. 321–25.

5. This count of the separate denominations was taken from Benson Y. Landis, ed., *Yearbook of American Churches* (1963). I have left this count as it stood in 1963, before the impact of COCU and of the inter-Lutheran confederation of 1965—both somewhat problematical—could be felt.

6. Forrest F. Reed, "Background of Division—Disciples of Christ and Churches of Christ," an address delivered at the Tennessee Assembly of Christian Churches, Disciples of Christ Historical Society Breakfast, April 22, 1967, in Memphis (Nashville: pamphlet, 1968), p. 14.

7. N. Eugene Tester, "Schisms Within the Disciples of Christ Denomination, 1809–1909" (unpublished Master's thesis, Northern Illinois University, 1969), pp. 71f. Tester suggests that the War itself may have exacerbated the Disciples' sectarian tendency, despite the wartime fraternalism noted by Reed (n. 6, above); see *ibid.,* p. 12.

8. The 1865 General Convention is described by the son of its most prominent participant in [John Henry Hopkins, Jr.] *The Life of the Late Right Reverend John Henry Hopkins, First Bishop of Vermont and Seventh Presiding Bishop, by one of his sons* (New York, 1873), Chapter XIX.

9. Allan Nevins and Milton Halsey Thomas, eds., *The Diary of George Templeton Strong,* IV: *Post-War Years, 1865–1875* (New York, 1952), p. 190. I am indebted to Professor Kenneth Stampp, of the University of California, Berkeley, for having called my attention to this diary as an important source for church history.

10. Raymond W. Albright, *A History of the Protestant Episcopal Church* (New York, 1964), p. 277. I am indebted to the late Professor Albright also for an illuminating conversation about the Reformed Episcopal schism shortly after publication of the magazine version of this chapter.

11. Lefferts A. Loetscher, "The Problem of Christian Unity in Early Nineteenth

Century America," *Church History,* XXXII (March, 1963), pp. 3–16. [This essay has since been reprinted, under the same title, in the Facet Books Historical Series, #12, Richard C. Wolf, ed. (Philadelphia, 1969).] On the same point see also Timothy L. Smith, *Revivalism and Social Reform in Mid-Nineteenth Century America* (New York, 1957).

12. New York *Times,* October 2, 1873, p. 8; Hartford *Daily Courant,* October 9, 1873, p. 2, as cited in George E. Moore, "The Sixth General Conference of the Evangelical Alliance, New York, 3–12 October, 1873," unpublished research paper, the University of California, 1964, p. 52, n. 53. On attendance at the sessions see *ibid.,* pp. 19–24.

13. New York *Tribune,* October 4, 1873, p. 2; Hartford *Daily Courant,* October 4, 1873, p. 1. A slightly different version of the Franco-German incident appeared in the Boston *Evening Transcript,* October 3, 1873, p. 1. George E. Moore, *op. cit.,* p. 50, notes 14, 19.

14. New York *Herald,* October 9, 1873, p. 6; Chicago *Tribune,* October 10, 1873, p. 4.

15. W. R. Nicholson, *Reasons Why I Became a Reformed Episcopalian* (Philadelphia, 1875), p. 22.

16. *The Book of Common Prayer . . . as revised and proposed for the use of the Protestant Episcopal Church, 1785,* which was considered a less "Catholic" book than that of 1789 which the P. E. Church was using, was reprinted late in 1873 for use by the Reformed Episcopal Church, without revision except for the insertion of that Church's *Declaration of Principles,* pending the issuance of their own *Book of Common Prayer of the Reformed Episcopal Church* (Philadelphia, 1874). Compare in these respective versions the Order for Holy Communion, pp. 39–63 in the 1785 reprint and pp. 76–99 in the Reformed Episcopalians' revision.

17. Edward L. Parsons, retired Bishop of California, reviewing E. Clowes Chorley, *Men and Movements in the American Episcopal Church* (New York, 1946), in the *Historical Magazine of the Protestant Episcopal Church,* XV (January, 1946), p. 7.

18. H. Shelton Smith, Robert T. Handy, and Lefferts A. Loetscher, eds., *American Christianity: an Historical Interpretation with Representative Documents,* Vol. II: *1820–1960* (New York, 1963), p. 310.

19. Some non-Episcopalian admirers concurred. See, for example the *Methodist Recorder,* as cited in Annie Darling Price, *A History of the Formation and Growth of the Reformed Episcopal Church, 1873–1902* (Philadelphia, 1902), p. 113: "No new tenets are attempted. It is a restoration rather than a reformation."

20. Andrew Dickson White, "The Warfare of Science," *Popular Science Monthly,* VIII (March, 1876), p. 568, n. 1.

21. Quoted in "The Tyng Case," pp. 79–83 of George E. DeMille, "The Episcopate of Horatio Potter . . . Sixth Bishop of New York," *Historical Magazine of the Protestant Episcopal Church,* XXIV (March, 1955), pp. 66–92; this citation at p. 82.

22. Albright, *op. cit.,* p. 287; Annie Darling Price, *op. cit.,* p. 300.

23. Quoted in Martin E. Marty. *The Infidel: Freethought and American Religion* (Cleveland, 1961), p. 153.

24. P. A. Carter, "The Fundamentalist Defense of the Faith," in John Braeman et al., eds., *Change and Continuity in Twentieth-Century America: the 1920's* ["Modern America," II] (Columbus, 1968), pp. 179–214, esp. pp. 184–87.

25. Henry C. Sheldon, *Sacerdotalism in the Nineteenth Century: a Critical History* (New York and Cincinnati, 1909), pp. vii, 448, 428. A less alarmist view of "sacerdotalism" was taken by Henry King Carroll, who was in charge of the Division of

Churches for the 11th U. S. Census, in *The Religious Forces of the United States* ["American Church History Series," I] (New York, 1893), p. lxi: "Evangelical Christianity is the dominant religious force of the United States. . . . There has been an increase of what some call churchliness, and confessionalism has developed to a remarkable degree among the Lutherans, but these are limited movements, and do not give character to the Christianity of the day. The Catholic revival in the Protestant Episcopal Church is spending itself within that denomination, and probably repels as many as it attracts to that communion."

26. See George E. DeMille, *The Catholic Movement in the American Episcopal Church,* 2nd edition, rev. and enl. (Philadelphia, 1950).

27. Hopkins, Sr., as quoted in E. Clowes Chorley, *op. cit.,* pp. 373f.; Ewer, as quoted in *ibid..* p. 318; Hopkins, Sr., as quoted in Hopkins, Jr., *op. cit.,* p. 415.

28. Charles Gore, ed., *Lux Mundi: A Series of Studies in the Religion of the Incarnation* (London, 1889), pp. vii and following. Gore and his associates of course took their cue in these essays from one who had not stayed with the Anglicans, John Henry Cardinal Newman, in his *Essay on the Development of Doctrine.* On the significance for European intellectual history of Newman's having written that essay, see Alfred North Whitehead, *Science and the Modern World* [The Lowell Lectures, 1925] (New York, [1925] 1947), p. 262.

29. Francis Ellingwood Abbot, "The Genius of Christianity and Free Religion," as reprinted in Joseph L. Blau, ed., *American Philosophic Addresses, 1700–1900* (New York, 1946), p. 690.

30. Compare for example the essay by H. H. Wyman, "Creeds, Old and New," in the *Catholic World,* XLIV (February, 1887), discussed above in Chapter VIII, Part III.

31. Charles E. Cheney, as quoted in A. D. Price, *op. cit.,* p. 212; *ibid.,* p. 300.

32. See United States Department of Commerce, Bureau of the Census, *Religious Bodies, 1906* (Washington, 1910), Vol. II, p. 598; *ibid., 1916* (Washington, 1919), Vol. II, p. 641; *ibid., 1926* (Washington, 1929), Vol. II, p. 1252. Doctrinal statements were omitted from all denominational reports for the religious census of 1936.

33. W. R. Nicholson, *op. cit., loc. cit.*

34. Stephen Tyng, Jr., to Phillips Brooks, as quoted in A. V. G. Allen, *Life and Letters of Phillips Brooks* (New York, 1901), Vol. II, pp. 275ff.; Phillips Brooks to the Rev. John C. Brooks, May 27, 1891, in *ibid.,* Vol. III, p. 438; *ibid.,* Vol. II, p. 205. In an address in 1881 Brooks argued that if his Church had met the dissidents halfway, and allowed them to "disuse one word in one service of the Prayer-book, and say that they meant by that disuse a doctrine which our Church by no means excommunicates persons for believing . . . they would have continued in membership with us to this day." Brooks, "Liturgical Growth," Address at the Seventh Congress of the Protestant Episcopal Church, Providence, Rhode Island, 1881, reprinted in Phillips Brooks, *Essays and Addresses, Religious, Literary, and Social* (New York, 1894), pp. 86ff.; this quotation at p. 100.

35. Quoted in E. Clowes Chorley, *op. cit.,* p. 423.

36. James DeKoven, "The Church of the Living God," reprinted in DeKoven, *Sermons Preached on Various Occasions* (New York, 1880), pp. 43f. DeKoven was of course quoting and paraphrasing Colossians 3:11.

37. William Newton Clarke, *An Outline of Christian Theology* (New York, 1898), pp. 38lf.

38. Glenn N. Sisk, "Churches in the Alabama Black Belt 1875–1917," *Church History,* XXIII (June, 1954), pp. 161, 156 (quoting the *Alabama Baptist,* Nov. 1,

1888); N. Eugene Tester, *op. cit.,* p. 83, quoting *Lard's Quarterly,* September, 1863. That this extreme sectarianism was no mere Southern or border-South regional quirk is evident from Wilbur L. Cross's report of a public debate on infant baptism in his home town of Mansfield, Connecticut, in the 1870's; Cross, *Connecticut Yankee: An Autobiography* (New Haven, 1943), p. 56.

39. Sisk, *op. cit.,* p. 159; Editorial, "Bishop Cummins and his 'schism,' " New York *Christian Advocate,* XLIX (January 22, 1874), p. 28; D. A. Goodsell, "Methodism— a Flash or a Flame?" *ibid.,* XLVIII (October 2, 1873), p. 313.

40. Boston *Evening Transcript,* October 9, 1873, p. 2, as quoted in George E. Moore, *op. cit.,* p. 11. Many delegates seem to have concurred; the New York *Tribune,* October 4, 1873, p. 7, quoted one of them as having said that "it was not possible except by despotism to put an end to variety."

41. Henry King Carroll, *op. cit.,* pp. xiv, xv; Boston *Evening Transcript,* October 4, 1873, p. 2, as cited in George E. Moore, *op. cit.,* p. 9.

42. David Swing, "Declaration in Reply to the Charges of Professor Patton," May 4, 1874, as reprinted in William R. Hutchison, ed., *American Protestant Thought: the Liberal Era* (New York, 1968), p. 53; Charles A. Briggs, *Whither? A Theological Question For the Times* (New York, 1889), p. xi.

43. Charles A. Briggs, "The Alienation of Church and People," *The Forum,* XVI (November, 1893), pp. 375, 369, 377, 378, 366.

44. Leonard Woolsey Bacon, *A History of American Christianity* ["American Church History Series," XIII] (New York, 1897), p. 419; Willard Gurdon Oxtoby, "The Post-Ecumenical Era," *Theology Today,* XXIII (October, 1966), p. 379.

45. Leonard Woolsey Bacon, *op. cit., loc. cit.;* editorial, "The American Congress of Churches," *Catholic World,* XLII (December, 1885), pp. 409, 411, 415.

46. Samuel M. Hopkins, "Christian Union," a letter to the editor of *Century Magazine,* XXXII (June, 1886), p. 322.

47. George Fisher, letter to the editor in *ibid.,* July, 1886, p. 487. Like James De-Koven twenty years earlier, Fisher drew a secular parallel and made it a rationale for ecumenicalism: "As nations . . . would aspire after a 'federation of mankind,' so the churches of the nations might have their forms of union."

48. New York *Herald,* July 6, 1874. For the "existential" context of this particular communion service, see above, Chapter VI, Part V. Was it also significant that in the course of that Sunday's sermon Beecher had cautiously broached the theory of evolution?

49. Charles A. Briggs, *Whither?* p. 270.

50. Somewhat similar to Briggs's spiritual pilgrimage was that of Newman Smyth, one of the pioneer liberal theists who sought accommodation with Darwinism (*Old Faiths in New Light,* 1879; *The Place of Death in Evolution,* 1897). By 1908 Smyth was writing on the topic *Passing Protestantism and Coming Catholicism,* and for the rest of his life he worked diligently for Anglican-Congregationalist *rapprochement.* See Peter G. Gowing, "Newman Smyth and the Congregational-Episcopal Concordat," *Church History,* XXXIII (June, 1964), pp. 175–91.

CHAPTER 10

1. "The Astronauts Write Their Stories of the Flight," *Life,* LXVI (January 17, 1969), p. 31. At the time this manuscript was completed a lawsuit was pending under the "establishment clause" of the First Amendment, seeking to enjoin NASA from authorizing any more such religious goings-on in outer space at the taxpayer's expense.

2. Judson Smith, "Protestant Foreign Missions: a Retrospect of the Nineteenth Century," *North American Review*, CLXXII (March, 1901), pp. 394, 395, 400, 402. But see Mark Twain's savage essay "To the Person Sitting in Darkness," *ibid.*, February, 1901, pp. 161–76; his "To My Missionary Critics," *ibid.*, April, 1901, pp. 520–34; and Judson Smith's "The Missionaries and their Critics," *ibid.*, May, 1901, pp. 724–33.

3. Tran Van Dinh, "An Open Letter to President Nixon," *Christian Century*, LXXXVI (March 5, 1969), p. 314.

4. Theodore L. Agnew, "Reflections on the Woman's Foreign Missionary Movement in Late 19th-century American Methodism," *Methodist History*, VI (January, 1968), p. 4; *ibid.*, p. 6, n. 25.

5. Henry King Carroll, *The Religious Forces of the United States, Enumerated, Classified, and Described on the Basis of the Government Census of 1890* ["American Church History Series," I] (New York, 1893; revised Jan. 1, 1896, with additional tables of statistics for the five years since the census of 1890), pp. 87, 353, 396.

6. Frank S. Dobbins, assisted by S. Wells Williams and Isaac Hall, *Error's Chains: How Forged and Broken* (New York, 1884); Merwin-Marie Snell, "Parseeism and Buddhism," *Catholic World*, XLVI (January, 1888), p. 451.

7. James Freeman Clarke, *Ten Great Religions*, Vol. I: *An Essay in Comparative Theology* (Boston, 1871; eighteenth edition, 1882), p. 3; *ibid.*, Vol. II: *A Comparison of All Religions* (Boston, 1883), p. 353; George A. Gordon, "The Gospel for Humanity," as reprinted in William R. Hutchison, ed., *American Protestant Thought: The Liberal Era* (New York, 1968), p. 101

8. Virchand R. Gandhi, "Why Christian Missions Have Failed in India," *The Forum*, XVII (April, 1894), p. 166; Fred. Perry Powers, "The Success of Christian Missions in India" [replying to Gandhi], *ibid.*, June, 1894, pp. 475–483.

9. (Purushotam Rao Telang) "Christian Missions as Seen by a Brahman," *ibid.*, XVIII (December, 1894), p. 487.

10. Phillips Brooks, "Impressions of Indian Religion," unpublished mss. quoted in A. V. G. Allen, *Life and Letters of Phillips Brooks* (New York, 1901), Vol. II, p. 534; letter dated July 6, 1888, as reprinted in *ibid.*, Vol. III, p. 273.

11. Leighton Parks, "A Bōzŭ of the Monto Sect," *Century Magazine*, XXXII (July, 1886), pp. 477–81. The entire article should be read for its period flavor; it is a classic meeting of East and West.

12. James Freeman Clarke, *op. cit.*, Vol. I, p. 13; Lydia Maria Child, "The Intermingling of Religions," *Atlantic Monthly*, XXVIII (October, 1871), p. 395.

13. Virchand R. Gandhi, *op. cit.*, p. 163. This defense of Brahmanism was all the more striking, considering that V. R. Gandhi was himself not a Brahman but a Jain.

14. *The Buddhist Ray*, I (February, 1888); *ibid.*, January, 1888, p. 1. In true self-extinguishing Buddhist fashion the editor did not reveal his own identity until the last paragraph of the last issue published [VII (November–December, 1894), p. 16]: "As the seven years have now elapsed, and my vow has been fulfilled, I now extinguish *The Buddhist Ray.*"

15. John Gmeiner, "The Light of Asia and the Light of the World," *Catholic World*, XLII (October, 1885), p. 5; "Was Christ a Buddhist?" *ibid.*, LIII (May, 1891) [a reply to an article in *The Arena* on the same theme]; Merwin-Marie Snell, *op. cit.*, p. 456.

16. Irving McKee, *"Ben-Hur" Wallace* (Berkeley, 1947), p. 241. But compare the quotation from Meredith Nicholson on Wallace, as having been at heart "an Oriental," in *ibid.*, p. 268.

17. Lew Wallace, *The Prince of India; or, Why Constantinople Fell*, 2 vols. (New York, [1893]1898), Vol. I, pp. 392f., 401; Vol. II, pp. 54–65, 71, 79.

18. Chicago *Daily News*, September 11, 1893, p. 1. The *Inter Ocean*'s account of the Parliament's opening, under the headline "Creeds in Council," was even more colorful: "From the snow-capped mountains of Norway, from sunny France and the German Fatherland came the representatives of Christianity to meet in friendly conference with the swarthy sons of India." Chicago *Inter Ocean*, September 12, p. 1.

19. Address of H. N. Higinbotham, as reprinted in John Henry Barrows, ed., *The World's Parliament of Religions, an Illustrated and Popular Story of the World's First Parliament of Religions, held in Chicago in connection with the Columbian Exposition of 1893* (Chicago, 1893), Vol. I, p. 83.

20. An exception is Egal Feldman, "American Ecumenicism: Chicago's World Parliament of Religions in 1893," *Journal of Church and State*, IX (Spring, 1967), pp. 180–199.

21. Shailer Mathews, "Barrows, John Henry," in Allen Johnson, ed., *Dictionary of American Biography*, Vol. I (New York, 1928), pp. 651f.

22. Barrows, *op. cit.*, Vol. I, p. 60; Phillips Brooks's statement as printed in *ibid.*, p. 25; Philip Schaff as reported in *ibid.*, p. 138. Schaff's address to the Parliament, "The Reunion of Christendom"—a major landmark in the subsequent history of the Ecumenical Movement—is in Vol. II, pp. 1192–1201.

23. There was also a brief letter addressed to the Parliament on "The Koran and Other Scriptures" from J. Sanua Abou Naddara, a resident of Paris. *Ibid.*, Vol. II, pp. 1146–1148.

24. *Ibid.*, Vol. I, pp. 107, 108, 109.

25. Chicago *Inter Ocean*, September 14, 1893, p. 1. That newspaper's interest in the Parliament may be gauged by the fact that it regularly gave the proceedings top coverage: front page, far right-hand column, and continuing to all of page 2, sometimes going on for several columns on p. 3 as well.

26. According to the *Daily News*, Cook said that the religious weeklies would have to be depended on to counteract "the bad effect of the liberal daily press"—and he hit home with that audience by claiming that "the Catholic church was noted by the press ten times more than the Methodist church." Chicago *Daily News*, September 18, 1893, p. 1.

27. Brief quotations from Joseph Cook and Morgan Dix as reported in Barrows, *op. cit.*, Vol. II, p. 1557; the Presbyterian resolution as reported in *ibid.*, Vol. I, p. 19. But Barrows noted that "this resolution was adopted without debate in the hurried closing hours of the Assembly," a not unfamiliar denominational (and secular!) procedure, and that leading Presbyterian churchmen and journals endorsed the Parliament.

28. *Ibid.*, p. 58. Compare *The Chautauquan*, XVII (July, 1893), p. 478: "The question of keeping the World's Fair open on the Sabbath is still a matter of national concern. . . . It rests upon the law-abiding and respectable elements of our population to check the advance of a spirit which is manifestly in opposition to the improvement of our civilization." On a proposed Methodist boycott of the World's Fair (but not, specifically, of the Parliament), see the New York *Times*, February 21, 1893, p. 1; May 23, p. 1; June 19, p. 5.

29. Barrows, *op. cit.*, Vol. I, p. 26. The Parliament's Chairman carefully bracketed this letter with another from a minister in Tientsin who approved.

30. Chicago *Daily News*, September 11, 1893, p. 1; Chicago *Inter Ocean*, September 13, 1893, p. 3; *ibid.*, September 17, p. 1. The *Daily News*, whose coverage of the Parliament after the first day was perfunctory, gave front-page treatment to both Miss Besant (September 15) and Briggs (September 16), noting in the case of the former

that "curiosity seekers fairly climbed over each other this morning in their wild efforts to get into the theosophical congress at the art palace," and referring to the latter as a "celebrity."

31. New York *Sun*, as quoted in "Editor's Outlook: The Talking Side of the Chicago Exposition," *The Chautauquan*, XVIII (November, 1893), p. 226.

32. A typical newspaper page layout for the day's Parliament of Religions story included a picture of the hall, with speakers, bunting, the ushers in cutaways with hands folded on their stomachs, and the ladies in bustles and impressive hats; and pen-portraits of Ganendra Chakravarti, the portly theosophist; Reuchi Shibata, the Shinto high priest; Bishop B. W. Arnett, the black American; Zitsuzen Ashitsu, a Japanese Buddhist; a "delegate from India"; the young Sinhalese monk, Dharmapâla—and, inevitably, Mrs. Potter Palmer. Chicago *Inter Ocean*, September 12, 1893, p. 2.

33. Barrows, *op. cit.*, Vol. II, p. 1566; *ibid.*, Vol. I, p. 60.

34. Shailer Mathews, *op. cit.*, p. 652; Barrows, *op. cit.*, Vol. I, p. ix.

35. Chicago *Inter Ocean*, September 21, p. 2. Barrows's own comment on this episode, in *op. cit.*, Vol. I, pp. 126f., is most revealing of his own conception of the limits of the Parliament's objectives.

36. *Ibid.*, Vol. I, p. ix. Further on, Barrows made his own Christian commitment even more clear: "When on the third of September, in the First Presbyterian Church of Chicago [*i.e.*, the church of which Barrows himself was pastor], the Buddhist delegation sat and reverently listened to a sermon on 'Christ the Wonderful,' a discourse preceded by the baptism and reception of three Chinese converts, and followed by an impressive address from the Archbishop of Zante, it appeared as if the Parliament had already opened beneath the splendor of the Cross." *Ibid.*, p. 61.

37. George F. Pentecost, "The Invincible Gospel," *ibid.*, Vol. II, pp. 1166–1172; impromptu remarks reported in Vol. I, p. 143. Outside the meeting halls, of course, the sniper fire could be even more intense. Bishop J. P. Newman of the Methodist Church, whose Indiana Conference happened to be in session, took the occasion to attack all the major Asian religions: Buddhism had given to the world "no literature, no system of free government, no social system, no heroic virtues"; the teachings of Confucius "had kept China at a standstill for 2,500 years"; and "India was a vast pantheon in which everything was worshiped, even the vilest beasts." Chicago *Inter Ocean*, September 19, 1893, p. 6.

38. Philangi Dasa's missionary paper expressed satisfaction that the "heathens" at the World's Parliament of Religions had behaved better than Joseph Cook. *Buddhist Ray*, VI (November–December, 1893), p. 1.

39. H. Dharmapâla, "The World's Debt to Buddha," in Barrows, *op. cit.*, Vol. II, p. 862; Mohammed Webb, "The Spirit of Islam," *ibid.*, p. 989.

40. Isaac M. Wise to William Stix, September 22, 1893, as quoted in James G. Heller, *Isaac M. Wise: His Life, Work, and Thought* (New York, 1965), p. 488; text of Wise's address is in Barrows, *op. cit.*, Vol. I, pp. 290–295.

41. Modi's essay is in *ibid.*, Vol. II, pp. 898–920; Kung Hsien Ho's in *ibid.*, Vol. I, pp. 596–604, this quotation at p. 604.

42. But see the criticism of this earlier essay in James Freeman Clarke, *op. cit.*, Vol. I, pp. 490f. Flatly denying several of Higginson's generalizations (*e.g.*, "Every race believes in a Creator," "Every race believes in immortality," "Every race recognizes in its religious precepts the brotherhood of man"), Clarke asserted: "Nothing is gained for humanity by such statements, which are refuted immediately by the most evident facts. The true 'sympathy of religions' does not consist in their saying the same thing."

43. Z. Noguchi, "The Religion of the World," Barrows, *op. cit.*, Vol. I, p. 442; Thomas Wentworth Higginson, "The Sympathy of Religions," *ibid.*, p. 782; Narendranath Datta ("Swami Vivekananda"), "Hinduism," *ibid.*, Vol. II, p. 978.

44. Marie Louise Burke, *Swami Vivekananda in America: New Discoveries* (Calcutta, 1958; rev. 2nd ed., 1966), pp. 120–124. Of these the Calvé story seems the better founded; "There is nothing in the published accounts of his [Rockefeller's] life to corroborate the story that he was inspired by Swamiji." *Ibid.*, p. 123.

45. He probably got this from a professor in India who was a graduate of Trinity College, Dublin. *Ibid.*, p. 104.

46. *Ibid.*, pp. 242, 289, and all of Chapter VII, "The Christian Onslaught."

47. Vivekananda's biographers seem to disagree sharply on this point. Burke's judgment, that "the idea of teaching Vedanta to the West did not fully evolve in his mind until the last of 1894," is based on unpublished letters which did not come to light until comparatively recently; *ibid.*, pp. 365–376.

48. The Vedanta Society marked its seventy-fifth anniversary in 1969 by undertaking to raise five million dollars for a monastery and retreat center. The campaign was launched with a benefit concert in Orchestra Hall, Chicago, by the well-known Indian sitar player Ravi Shankar. Chicago *Tribune*, August 24, 1969.

49. Cornelia Conger, "Memories of Swami Vivekananda," reprinted in Burke, *op cit.*, p. 103; *ibid.*, pp. 492, 519. The Harvard lecture was reprinted under the title *Vedanta Philosophy at the Harvard University* (Calcutta, 1946).

50. Barrows, *op. cit.*, Vol. II, p. 994. See also New York *Times*, August 6, 1893, p. 8; December 11, 1893, p. 16.

51. E. Denison Ross, "Bābism," *North American Review*, CLXXII (April, 1901), p. 622; Shoghi Effendi, *God Passes By* (Wilmette, Ill., 1944), pp. 257, 259, as quoted in Allan Eickelmann, "A World Faith in America," unpublished research paper, Northern Illinois University, 1969, pp. 12f. See also the obituary of Abdul-Baha in the New York *Times*, December 1, 1921, p. 17.

52. Quoted in M. L. Gordon, "Shall We Welcome Buddhist Missionaries to America?" *Open Court*, XIV (May, 1900), p. 301. The author moralistically disapproved of the mission, but the *Open Court's* editor, Paul Carus, welcomed it. *Ibid.*, p. 303.

53. Kenneth L. Patton, *A Religion for One World* (Boston, 1964), pp. ix, x. The iconography of that church, drawn literally from all of the planet's religions—"primitive" and "civilized," ancient and modern, Eastern, African, and Western—is most impressive.

54. Donald Meyer, in *The Positive Thinkers: a Study of the American Quest for Health, Wealth, and Personal Power from Mary Baker Eddy to Norman Vincent Peale* (Garden City, 1965; paper, 1966), argues that the vogue for "New Thought" was not as Eastern-influenced as it has sometimes been judged to be: "The East shimmered in circles beyond our ken, among theosophists, Vedantists, followers of Swami Ramakrishna. Breaking free of old creeds and dogmas, New Thought expressed no instinct to embrace still older ones." Meyer, p. 16.

55. Even Vivekananda, although he carefully and consistently disentangled his message from the faddish occultism which it superficially resembled, and never compromised with the Christians, came to feel that he had to soften his stern Vedantic views for his American hearers. Burke, *op. cit.*, p. 603.

56. Swami Vivekananda, *op. cit.*, p. 26. See also Vivekananda, *Yoga Philosophy: Lectures delivered in New York, Winter of 1895–6 on Râja Yoga, or Conquering the Internal Nature*, 4th ed. (London and Bombay, 1897).

57. Haeckel as quoted in Merwin-Marie Snell, *op. cit.*, p. 454; T. H. Huxley, *Evolution and Ethics, and Other Essays* (New York, 1896), p. 61.

58. A startling example is Erwin Schrödinger, *What Is Life? The Physical Aspect of the Living Cell* (Cambridge and New York, 1946), pp. 87–89.

59. "Religion and Science at Vanderbilt," *Popular Science Monthly*, XIII (August, 1878), p. 492; quoted in Steven D. Gotham, "A New Chapter in the History of the Warfare of Science with the Forces of Tradition," unpublished seminar paper, Northern Illinois University, 1969, p. 3; Barrows, *op. cit.*, Vol. II, pp. 968, 868.

60. Arnold as quoted in *ibid.*, p. 877. See Edward Conze, *Buddhism: its Essence and Development* (New York, 1959), pp. 18–21. For a typical argument that the Buddhist theory of consciousness more closely parallels modern dynamic psychology than the Graeco-Western one, see U Thittila, "The Fundamental Principles of Theravada Buddhism," Chap. II in Kenneth W. Morgan, ed., *The Path of the Buddha* (New York, 1953).

61. Albert Einstein, *Out of My Later Years* (New York, 1950), p. 24.

Bibliography

(Nelson Burr, *A Critical Bibliography of Religion in America* ["Religion in American Life," IV], 2 vols., Princeton University Press, 1961, has now become an indispensable research tool in the study of American religious history. Books which have appeared since its publication have been regularly reviewed in the journal *Church History*, and pertinent articles have been conveniently cross-indexed in the quarterly listings of recent historical articles in American journals by the *Mississippi Valley Historical Review*, now re-named the *Journal of American History*.)

I. COLLECTIONS OF HISTORICAL DOCUMENTS.

Billington, Ray A., Loewenberg, Bert J., and Brockunier, S. Hugh, *The Making of American Democracy: Readings and Documents.* 2 vols. New York: Rinehart, 1950.

Blau, Joseph L., ed., *American Philosophic Addresses, 1700–1900.* New York: Columbia University Press, 1946.

————, *Cornerstones of Religious Freedom in America.* Boston: Beacon Press, 1949.

Cross, Robert D., ed., *The Church and the City.* Indianapolis: Bobbs-Merrill, 1967.

Daniels, George, ed., *Darwinism Comes To America.* Waltham, Mass.: Blaisdell, 1968.

Fremantle, Anne, ed., *The Papal Encyclicals in their Historical Context.* New York: G. P. Putnam, 1956.

Glaab, Charles N., ed., *The American City: a Documentary History.* Homewood, Ill.: Dorsey Press, 1963.

Handy, Robert T., ed., *The Social Gospel in America, 1870–1920: Gladden, Ely, and Rauschenbusch.* New York: Oxford University Press, 1966.

Hoogenboom, Ari, and Hoogenboom, Olive, eds., *The Gilded Age.* Englewood Cliffs, N. J.: Prentice-Hall, 1967.

Hutchison, William R., ed., *American Protestant Thought: the Liberal Era.* New York: Harper & Row, 1968.

Introduction to Contemporary Civilization in the West: a Source Book, Vol. II. New York: Columbia University Press, 1946.

Miller, Perry, ed., *The American Puritans: Their Prose and Poetry.* New York: Doubleday, 1956.

————, *American Thought: Civil War to World War I*. New York: Rinehart, 1954.

————, *Margaret Fuller, American Romantic*. Garden City: Doubleday, 1963.

Smith, H. Shelton, Handy, Robert T., and Loetscher, Lefferts A., eds., *American Christianity: an Historical Interpretation with Representative Documents*. 2 vols. New York: Charles Scribner's Sons, 1960 and 1963.

Wilson, R. J., ed., *Darwinism and the American Intellectual*. Homewood, Ill.: Dorsey Press, 1967.

II. NEWSPAPERS AND PERIODICALS PUBLISHED DURING THE GILDED AGE.

Atlantic Monthly.
The Buddhist Ray.
The Catholic World.
Century Magazine.
The Chautauquan.
Chicago *Daily News.*
Chicago *Inter Ocean.*
Chicago *Tribune.*
The Christian Cynosure.
The Forum.
Harper's New Monthly Magazine.
Harper's Weekly.
The Nation.
New York *Christian Advocate.*
New York *Herald.*
New York *Times.*
North American Review.
Overland Monthly.
Popular Science Monthly.
Religio-Philosophical Journal.
Scribner's Monthly. Succeeded in 1881 by *Century Magazine.*
Voice of Missions.

III. WORKS FIRST WRITTEN IN (OR NEAR) THE GILDED AGE.

A. Literary.

Beecher, Henry Ward, *Norwood; or, Village Life in New England*. New York: C. Scribner & Company, 1868.

Bierce, Ambrose, *Collected Works*, Vols. II, III, VII. New York and Washington: Neale Publishing Company, 1909, 1910, 1911.

Deland, Margaret, *John Ward, Preacher*. Boston: Houghton, Mifflin, 1888.

[Dunne, Finley Peter] *Mr. Dooley in Peace and War*. Boston: Small, Maynard, & Co., 1899.

Eggleston, Edward, *The Circuit Rider: a Tale of the Heroic Age*. New York: J. B. Ford, 1874.

—————, *The Hoosier Schoolmaster*. Library Edition. New York: Orange Judd, 1892 (first copyright 1871).

Emerson, Ralph Waldo, *Complete Works*, Vol. XI: *Miscellanies*. Boston: Houghton, Mifflin, 1904.

Garland, Hamlin, *The Tyranny of the Dark*. London and New York: Harper & Brothers, 1905.

Holmes, Oliver Wendell, Sr., *Elsie Venner: a Romance of Destiny*. Boston: Houghton, Mifflin, 1886 (serialized in the *Atlantic Monthly* in 1859; first published in book form in 1861).

—————, *The Professor at the Breakfast-Table*. Boston: Houghton, Mifflin, 1882 (first copyright 1859).

Howells, William Dean, *A Hazard of New Fortunes*. With an Afterword by Benjamin DeMott. New York: New American Library, 1965 (first published in 1890).

—————, *The Minister's Charge, or, the Apprenticeship of Lemuel Barker*. Boston: Ticknor & Company, 1887.

—————, *The Undiscovered Country*. Boston: Houghton, Mifflin, 1880.

Perry, Bliss, ed., *The Heart of Emerson's Journals*. Boston: Houghton, Mifflin, 1926.

Phelps (Ward), Elizabeth Stuart, *Beyond the Gates*. Thirty-second edition. Boston: Houghton, Mifflin, 1898 (copyright 1883).

—————, *The Gates Ajar*. With an Introduction by Helen Sootin Smith. Cambridge, Mass.: Harvard University Press, 1964 (first published in 1868).

—————, *Sealed Orders*. Tenth edition. Boston: Houghton, Mifflin, 1897 (first published in 1879).

—————, *The Silent Partner*. Boston: Houghton, Mifflin, 1899 (first published in 1871).

Roe, E. P., *Barriers Burned Away*. New York: Dodd, Mead, 1906 (first published in 1872).

Stowe, Harriet Beecher ["Christopher Crowfield," pseud.], *The Chimney Corner*. Boston: Ticknor & Fields, 1868.

—————, *The Minister's Wooing*. Boston: Houghton, Mifflin, 1896 (first published in 1859).

—————, *Oldtown Folks*. Boston: Fields, Osgood & Company, 1869.

"Twain, Mark," pseud. [Samuel Langhorne Clemens] *The Writings of Mark Twain*, Vols. I–II, V–VI, XII, XIII, XIV, XXVI. New York: Harper & Brothers, 1929 (first published in this edition 1917).

Wallace, Lew, *Ben-Hur: a Tale of the Christ*. With an Introduction by Ben Ray Redman. New York: Heritage Press, 1960 (first published in 1881).

—————, *The Prince of India; or, Why Constantinople Fell*. 2 vols. New York: Harper & Brothers, 1898 (first published in 1893).

Whitman, Walt, "Whispers of Heavenly Death." In *The Complete Writings of*

Walt Whitman ["Paumanok Edition"], Vol. II. New York and London: G. P. Putnam's Sons, 1902.

Williams, Oscar, ed., *F. T. Palgrave's The Golden Treasury of the Best Songs and Lyrical Poems: A Modern Edition.* New York: Pocket Books, 1953.

B. Books Dealing with the Impact of Science upon Religion.

Abbott, Lyman, *The Evolution of Christianity.* Boston: Houghton, Mifflin, 1892.

————, *The Theology of an Evolutionist.* Boston: Houghton, Mifflin, 1897.

Carus, Paul, *The Religion of Science.* Chicago: Open Court, 1896 (first published in 1893).

Darwin, Charles, *The Descent of Man, and Selection in Relation to Sex.* New York: D. Appleton & Co., 1898 (a reprint of the second revised and augmented edition, first published in 1874).

Drummond, Henry, *The Ascent of Man* [The Lowell Lectures, 1894]. New York: J. Pott & Co., 1894.

————, *Natural Law in the Spiritual World.* Philadelphia: Henry Altemus, 1893 (first published in 1883).

Fiske, John, *The Destiny of Man Viewed in the Light of his Origin.* Boston: Houghton, Mifflin, 1884.

————, *Through Nature to God.* Boston: Houghton, Mifflin, 1900 (copyright 1899).

————, *The Unseen World, and Other Essays.* Tenth impression. Boston: Houghton, Mifflin, 1899 (first published in 1876).

Gladden, Washington, *How Much is Left of the Old Doctrines? A Book for the People.* Boston: Houghton, Mifflin, 1899.

————, *Who Wrote the Bible? A Book for the People.* Boston: Houghton, Mifflin, 1891.

Hudson, Thomson Jay, *A Scientific Demonstration of the Future Life.* 8th edition. Chicago: A. C. McClurg, 1904 (copyright 1895).

Huxley, Thomas Henry, *Evolution and Ethics, and Other Essays.* New York: D. Appleton & Co., 1896.

James, William, *Human Immortality: Two Supposed Objections to the Doctrine.* [The Ingersoll Lecture, 1898] 2nd edition. Boston: Houghton, Mifflin, 1899.

————, *The Will to Believe and Other Essays in Popular Philosophy.* New York and London: Longmans, Green, 1910 (first published in 1897).

Kidd, Benjamin, *Social Evolution.* New York and London: Macmillan, 1894.

LeConte, Joseph, *Evolution: its Nature, its Evidences, and its Relation to Religious Thought.* 2nd edition, revised. New York: D. Appleton & Co., 1899 (first published in 1891).

Marx, Karl, and Engels, Friedrich, *On Religion.* With an Introduction by Reinhold Niebuhr. New York: Schocken Books, 1964. [Exact reprint of edition published in the U.S.S.R. (Moscow: Foreign Languages Publishing House, 1957).]

"Meslier, Jean" (Paul Henri Thiry, Baron d'Holbach), *Superstition in All Ages.*

Tr. by Anna Knoop. New York: P. Eckler, 1920. (This translation was first published in 1878.)

Miller, Hugh, *The Testimony of the Rocks; or, Geology in its Bearings on the Two Theologies, Natural and Revealed.* Boston: Gould & Lincoln, 1857.

Morgan, Lewis Henry, *Ancient Society.* Chicago: Charles H. Kerr, 1877.

Munger, Theodore T., *The Appeal to Life.* Boston: Houghton, Mifflin, 1887.

————, *The Freedom of Faith.* Boston: Houghton, Mifflin, 1883.

Osler, Sir William, *Science and Immortality.* [The Ingersoll Lecture, 1904] Boston: Houghton, Mifflin, 1904.

Smyth, Newman, *Old Faiths in New Light.* New York: Scribner's, 1879.

————, *The Place of Death in Evolution.* New York: Scribner's, 1897.

Townsend, Luther Tracy, *The Bible and Other Ancient Literature in the Nineteenth Century.* New York: Chautauqua Press, 1889 (copyright 1885).

Tyler, John M., *The Whence and Whither of Man: a Brief History of his Origin and Development through Conformity to Environment.* New York: Scribner's, 1896.

Tyndall, John, *Fragments of Science: a Series of Detached Essays, Addresses, and Reviews.* ["The Home Library"] New York: A. L. Burt, n. d.

Van Dyke, Henry, *The Gospel for an Age of Doubt.* In *The Works of Henry Van Dyke* ["Avalon Edition"], Vol. IV. New York: Scribner's, 1921 (first published in 1896).

White, Andrew Dickson, *A History of the Warfare of Science with Theology in Christendom.* 2 vols. New York: D. Appleton, 1898 (copyright 1896).

Winchell, Alexander, *Sketches of Creation: A Popular View of Some of the Grand Conclusions of the Sciences in Reference to the History of Matter and of Life, together with a Statement of the Intimations of Science Respecting the Primordial Condition and the Ultimate Destiny of the Earth and the Solar System.* New York: Harper & Brothers, 1870.

Youmans, Edward L., ed., *The Culture Demanded by Modern Life; a Series of Addresses and Arguments on the Claims of Scientific Education.* New York: D. Appleton, 1867.

C. Other Works Dating from the Period.

Allen, Alexander V. G., *Religious Progress.* Boston: Houghton, Mifflin, 1894.

Bacon, Leonard Woolsey, *A History of American Christianity* ["American Church History Series," XIII]. New York: Christian Literature Company, 1897.

Barrows, John Henry, ed., *The World's Parliament of Religions: an Illustrated and Popular Story of the World's First Parliament of Religions, held in Chicago in connection with the Columbian Exposition of 1893.* 2 vols. Chicago: Parliament Publishing Company, 1893.

Beecher, Henry Ward, *defendant. Official Report of the Trial of Henry Ward Beecher,* with notes and references by Austin Abbott. 2 vols. New York: G. W. Smith & Co., 1875.

Beecher, Henry Ward, *Patriotic Addresses in America and England, from 1850 to 1885, on Slavery, the Civil War, and the Development of Civil Liberty in the United States.* New York: Fords, Howard, & Hulbert, 1891 (copyright 1887).

————, *Two Sermons, "The Heavenly State" and "Future Punishment."* New York: pamphlet, 1871.

————, *Yale Lectures on Preaching.* 3 vols. in 1. New York: Fords, Howard, and Hulbert, 1887.

Bok, Edward W., ed., *Beecher Memorial: Contemporaneous Tributes to the Memory of Henry Ward Beecher.* Brooklyn: privately printed, 1887.

The Book of Common Prayer . . . as revised and proposed for the use of the Protestant Episcopal Church, 1785. Reprinted with the *Declaration of Principles of the Reformed Episcopal Church.* Philadelphia: James A. Moore, 1873.

The Book of Common Prayer of the Reformed Episcopal Church. Philadelphia: James A. Moore, 1874.

Brandon, Joseph R., *Some Thoughts on Judaism: Two Lectures delivered May, 1879 before the Y. M. H. A., San Francisco.* San Francisco: pamphlet, 1881.

Brastow, Lewis O., *Representative Modern Preachers.* Freeport, N. Y.: Books for Libraries, 1968 (first published in 1904).

Briggs, Charles A., *Whither? A Theological Question for the Times.* New York: Scribner's, 1889.

Brooks, Phillips, *Essays and Addresses, Religious, Literary, and Social.* New York: E. P. Dutton, 1894.

Carroll, Henry King, *The Religious Forces of the United States, Enumerated, Classified, and Described on the Basis of the Government Census of 1890* ["American Church History Series," I]. New York: Christian Literature Company, 1893; rev. ed., 1896.

The Case of Henry Ward Beecher. Opening Address by Benjamin F. Tracy, of Counsel for the Defendant. New York: pamphlet, 1875.

Clarke, James Freeman, *Ten Great Religions.* 2 vols. Boston: Houghton, Mifflin, 1871 and 1883.

Clarke, William Newton, *An Outline of Christian Theology.* New York: Scribner's, 1898.

Davis, Andrew Jackson, *Views of Our Heavenly Home.* Rochester, N. Y.: Austin Publishing Co., 1910 (first published in 1878).

DeKoven, James, *Sermons Preached on Various Occasions.* New York: D. Appleton and Company, 1880.

Dobbins, Frank S., assisted by S. Wells Williams and Isaac Hall, *Error's Chains: How Forged and Broken.* New York: Standard Publishing House, 1884.

Drummond, Henry, *The Greatest Thing in the World.* Philadelphia: Henry Altemus, n. d. [Author's personal copy; a family memento.]

Gladden, Washington, *Tools and the Man: Property and Industry Under the Christian Law.* Boston: Houghton, Mifflin, 1896 (copyright 1893).

Gordon, M. L., "Shall We Welcome Buddhist Missionaries to America?" *Open Court*, XIV (May, 1900), pp. 301–303.

Gore, Charles, ed., *Lux Mundi: a Series of Studies in the Religion of the Incarnation*. 10th edition. London: John Murray, 1890.

Hastings, Horace Lorenzo, *The Signs of the Times; or, a Glance at Christendom as it Is*. Boston: H. L. Hastings, 1864.

Ingersoll, Robert G., *The Ghosts, and Other Lectures*. Washington: C. P. Farrell, 1878.

————, *The House of Death, Being Funeral Orations and Addresses, Etc.* London: Forder, 1897.

Mabie, Hamilton Wright, *Footprints of Four Centuries: the Story of the American People*. Philadelphia and Chicago: International Publishing Company, 1895.

Nevins, Allan, and Thomas, Milton Halsey, eds., *The Diary of George Templeton Strong*, Vol. IV: *Post-war years, 1865–1875*. New York: Macmillan, 1952.

[The New York *Times*] *The Beecher Trial: A Review of the Evidence*. New York: pamphlet, 1875.

Nicholson, W. R., *Reasons Why I Became a Reformed Episcopalian*. Philadelphia: pamphlet, 1875.

Owen, Robert Dale, *Footfalls on the Boundary of Another World*. 3rd English edition, reprinted from the 10th American edition. London: Trübner, 1875.

Price, Annie Darling, *A History of the Formation and Growth of the Reformed Episcopal Church, 1873–1902*. Philadelphia: J. M. Armstrong, 1902.

Proceedings of the Tenth Annual Convention of the American Association of Spiritualists, held at Grow's Opera Hall, Chicago, on Tuesday, September 16 [1873]. Chicago: privately printed, n.d.

Russell, Charles Taze, *The Battle of Armageddon* ["Studies in the Scriptures," IV]. East Rutherford, N. J.: Dawn Bible Students Association, 1954 (first published in 1897).

————, *The Divine Plan of the Ages* ["Studies in the Scriptures," I]. East Rutherford, N. J.: Dawn Bible Students Association, 1954 (first published in 1886 under the title *Millennial Dawn*).

————, *The New Creation* ["Studies in the Scriptures," VI]. East Rutherford, N. J.: Dawn Bible Students Association, 1955 (1904).

Scarlett, William, ed., *Phillips Brooks: Selected Sermons*. New York: E. P. Dutton, 1949.

Sheldon, Henry C., *Sacerdotalism in the Nineteenth Century: A Critical History*. New York: Eaton & Mains, 1909.

Stern, Bernhard J., ed., *Young Ward's Diary*. New York: G. P. Putnam, 1935.

Thompson, Hugh Miller, *The World and the Man* [Baldwin Lectures, the University of Michigan, 1890]. New York: T. Whittaker, 1890.

Vivekānanda, Swami (Narendranātha Datta), *The Vedanta Philosophy at the Harvard University*. Calcutta: Advaita Ashrama, 1946.

————, *Yoga Philosophy: Lectures delivered in New York, Winter of 1895–6 on Râja Yoga, or Conquering the Internal Nature.* 4th edition. London and Bombay: Longmans & Company, 1897.

IV. BIOGRAPHIES AND AUTOBIOGRAPHIES.

Abbott Lyman, *Reminiscences.* Boston: Houghton, Mifflin, 1915.

————, *Silhouettes of My Contemporaries.* Garden City: Doubleday, Page, 1921.

Allen, Alexander Viets Griswold, *Life and Letters of Phillips Brooks.* 3 vols. New York: E. P. Dutton, 1901.

"Beecher, Henry Ward." *National Cyclopedia of American Biography*, Vol. III. New York: James T. White, 1893. P. 130.

Burke, Marie Louise, *Swami Vivekananda in America: New Discoveries.* Rev. 2nd. ed. Calcutta: Advaita Ashrama, 1966.

Carnegie, Andrew, *Autobiography.* Boston: Houghton, Mifflin, 1920.

Chugerman, Samuel, *Lester F. Ward: The American Aristotle.* Durham, N. C.: Duke University Press, 1939.

Cramer, C. H., *Royal Bob: the Life of Robert G. Ingersoll.* Indianapolis: Bobbs-Merrill, 1952.

Cross, Barbara, *Horace Bushnell: Minister to a Changing America.* Chicago: University of Chicago Press, 1958.

Cross, Wilbur L., *Connecticut Yankee: An Autobiography.* New Haven: Yale University Press, 1943.

Darrah, William Culp, *Powell of the Colorado.* Princeton, N. J.: Princeton University Press, 1951.

Delp, Robert W., "Andrew Jackson Davis: Prophet of American Spiritualism." *Journal of American History*, LIV (June, 1967), pp. 43–56.

Dupree, A. Hunter, *Asa Gray.* Cambridge, Mass.: Harvard University Press, 1959.

Eastman, Max, *Enjoyment of Living.* New York and London: Harper, 1948.

Eddy, Mary Baker, *Retrospection and Introspection.* Boston: W. G. Nixon, 1891, 1892.

Fosdick, Harry Emerson, *The Living of These Days; an Autobiography.* New York: Harper, 1956.

Garland, Hamlin, *Forty Years of Psychic Research: a Plain Narrative of Fact.* New York: Macmillan, 1936.

Gladden, Washington, *Recollections.* Boston: Houghton, Mifflin, 1909.

Heller, James G., *Isaac M. Wise, His Life, Work, and Thought.* New York: Union of American Hebrew Congregations, 1965.

Hibben, Paxton, *Henry Ward Beecher: an American Portrait.* With a Foreword by Sinclair Lewis. New York: Readers Club, 1942 (first published in 1927).

[Hopkins, John Henry, Jr.] *The Life of the Late Right Reverend John Henry Hopkins, First Bishop of Vermont and Seventh Presiding Bishop, by one of his sons.* New York: F. J. Huntington, 1873.

Irvine, William, *Apes, Angels, and Victorians: Darwin, Huxley, and Evolution.* Cleveland: World Publishing Company, 1959.

Jaffe, Bernard, *Michelson and the Speed of Light.* Garden City: Doubleday, 1960.

Johnston, Johanna, Mrs. *Satan: the Incredible Saga of Victoria C. Woodhull.* New York: G. P. Putnam, 1967.

————, *Runaway to Heaven: the Story of Harriet Beecher Stowe.* Garden City: Doubleday, 1963.

Larson, Orvin, *American Infidel: Robert G. Ingersoll.* New York: Citadel Press, 1962.

McConnell, Francis J., "Borden Parker Bowne." *Methodist Review*, Fifth Series, Vol. XXXVIII (May–June, 1922), pp. 341–357.

McKee, Irving, *"Ben-Hur" Wallace: the Life of General Lew Wallace.* Berkeley and Los Angeles: University of California Press, 1947.

Mathews, Shailer, "Barrows, John Henry." Allen Johnson, ed., *Dictionary of American Biography*, Vol. I. New York: Scribner's, 1928. Pp. 651–652.

Merriam, George S., ed., *Noah Porter: a Memorial by Friends.* New York: Scribner's, 1893.

Niebuhr, Reinhold, *Leaves From the Notebook of a Tamed Cynic.* New York: Meridian Books, 1957 (first published in 1929).

O'Connor, Richard, *Ambrose Bierce: a Biography.* Boston and Toronto: Little, Brown, 1967.

Peel, Robert, *Mary Baker Eddy: the Years of Discovery.* New York, Chicago, San Francisco: Holt, Rinehart, & Winston, 1966.

Perkins, Frances, *The Roosevelt I Knew.* New York: Viking Press, 1946.

Resek, Carl, *Lewis Henry Morgan: American Scholar.* Chicago: University of Chicago Press, 1960.

Russell, Bertrand, *Autobiography*, Vol. I: *1872–1914.* Boston: Little, Brown, 1967.

Sachs, Emanie, *"The Terrible Siren;" Victoria Woodhull, 1838–1927.* New York: Harper, 1928.

Wallace, Lew, "How I Came to Write *Ben-Hur.*" *Youth's Companion*, LXVI (February 2, 1893), p. 57.

Wheeler, Lynde Phelps, *Josiah Willard Gibbs: the History of a Great Mind.* New Haven: Yale University Press, 1951.

White, Andrew Dickson, *Autobiography.* 2 vols. New York: the Century Company, 1922 (first published in 1905).

V. OTHER HISTORICAL STUDIES.

A. Books and Pamphlets.

Albright, Raymond W., *A History of the Protestant Episcopal Church.* New York: Macmillan, 1964.

Barzun, Jacques, *Darwin, Marx, Wagner: Critique of a Heritage.* Revised 2nd edition. New York: Doubleday, 1958.

Benz, Ernst, *Evolution and Christian Hope: Man's Concept of the Future from the Early Fathers to Teilhard de Chardin.* Tr. by Heinz G. Frank. New York: Doubleday, 1966.

Boller, Paul F., Jr., *American Thought in Transition: the Impact of Evolutionary Naturalism, 1865–1900.* Chicago: Rand McNally, 1969.

Brown, Norman O., *Life Against Death: the Psychoanalytical Meaning of History.* Middletown, Conn.: Wesleyan University Press, 1959.

Bury, J. B., *The Idea of Progress: an Inquiry into its Growth and Origin.* With an Introduction by Charles A. Beard. New York: Dover Publications, 1955 (first published in the United States in 1932).

Carter, Paul A. *The Idea of Progress in American Protestant Thought, 1930–1960* ["Facet Books Historical Series," #11]. Philadelphia: Fortress Press, 1969.

————, *The Twenties in America.* New York: Thomas Y. Crowell, 1968.

Chorley, E. Clowes, *Men and Movements in the American Episcopal Church.* New York: Scribner's, 1946.

Cockshut, A. O. J., *The Unbelievers: English Agnostic Thought, 1840–1890.* New York: New York University Press, 1966.

Cole, Charles C., *The Social Ideas of the Northern Evangelists, 1826–1860.* New York: Columbia University Press, 1954.

Commager, Henry Steele, *The American Mind: an Interpretation of American Thought and Character Since the 1880's.* New Haven: Yale University Press, 1950.

Cross, Robert D., *The Emergence of Liberal Catholicism in America.* Cambridge, Mass.: Harvard University Press, 1958.

DeMille, George E., *The Catholic Movement in the American Episcopal Church.* 2nd edition, revised and enlarged. Philadelphia: Church Historical Society, 1950.

Foster, Frank Hugh, *The Modern Movement in American Theology: Sketches in the History of Protestant Thought from the Civil War to the World War.* New York: Fleming H. Revell, 1939.

Gabriel, Ralph H., *The Course of American Democratic Thought: an Intellectual History since 1815.* 2nd edition. New York: Ronald Press, 1956 (originally published in 1940).

Handy, Robert T., *The Protestant Quest for a Christian America, 1830–1930.* ["Facet Books Historical Series," #5]. Philadelphia: Fortress Press, 1967.

Herbst, Jürgen, *The German Historical School in American Scholarship: a Study in the Transfer of Culture.* Ithaca, N.Y.: Cornell University Press, 1965.

Himmelfarb, Gertrude, *Victorian Minds.* New York: Alfred Knopf, 1968.

Hofstadter, Richard, *Anti-Intellectualism in American Life.* New York: Alfred Knopf, 1963.

————, *Social Darwinism in American Thought,* rev. ed. Boston: Beacon Press, 1955 (first published in 1944).

Hopkins, C. Howard, *The Rise of the Social Gospel in American Protestantism,*

1865–1915 ["Yale Studies in Religious Education," XIV]. New Haven: Yale University Press, 1940.

Jones, Rufus M., *The Later Periods of Quakerism*. 2 vols. London: Macmillan, 1921.

Kirkland, Edward, *Dream and Thought in the Business Community, 1860–1900*. Chicago: Quadrangle Books, 1964 (first published in 1956).

Kline, Morris, *Mathematics in Western Culture*. New York: Oxford University Press, 1953.

Latourette, Kenneth Scott, *A History of the Expansion of Christianity*. 7 vols. New York: Harper, 1937–1945.

Loetscher, Lefferts A., *The Problem of Christian Unity in Early Nineteenth Century America* ["Facet Books Historical Series," #12]. Philadelphia: Fortress Press, 1969.

Lovecraft, Howard Phillips, *Supernatural Horror in Literature*. With an Introduction by August Derleth. New York: Ben Abramson, 1945.

McCabe, Joseph, *Spiritualism: a Popular History from 1847*. London: T. Fisher Unwin, 1920.

Mann, Arthur, *Yankee Reformers in the Urban Age*. Cambridge, Mass.: Harvard University Press, 1954.

Marty, Martin E., *The Infidel: Freethought and American Religion*. Cleveland: World, 1961.

May, Henry F., *Protestant Churches and Industrial America*. New York: Harper, 1949.

Mead, Sidney E., *The Lively Experiment: the Shaping of Christianity in America*. New York: Harper & Row, 1963.

Meyer, Carl S., *Log Cabin to Luther Tower: Concordia Seminary During One Hundred and Twenty-five Years*. St. Louis: Concordia, 1965.

Meyer, Donald, *The Positive Thinkers: a Study of the American Quest for Health, Wealth, and Personal Power from Mary Baker Eddy to Norman Vincent Peale*. Garden City: Doubleday, 1966 (copyright 1965).

Morgan, H. Wayne, ed., *The Gilded Age: A Reappraisal*. Syracuse, N. Y.: Syracuse University Press, 1963.

Mott, Frank Luther, *A History of American Magazines*, Vol. III: *1865–1885*. Cambridge, Mass.: Harvard University Press, 1938.

Parrington, Vernon L., *Main Currents in American Thought*. 3 vols. New York: Harcourt, Brace, 1930.

Persons, Stow, *American Minds*. New York: Henry Holt, 1958.

Pledge, H. T., *Science Since 1500*. London: H. M. Stationer's Office, 1947 (copyright 1939).

Pratt, Fletcher, *A Short History of the Civil War*. New York: Pocket Books, 1952.

Randall, James G., and Donald, David. *The Civil War and Reconstruction*. 2nd edition. Boston: D. C. Heath, 1961.

Read, Sir Herbert, *Art and the Evolution of Man*. London: Freedom Press, 1951.

Rosenberg, Stuart, *The Search for Jewish Identity in America.* Garden City: Doubleday, 1964.

Sandeen, Ernest R., *The Origins of Fundamentalism: Toward a Historical Interpretation* ["Facet Books Historical Series," #10]. Philadelphia: Fortress Press, 1968.

Santayana, George, *Character and Opinion in the United States.* Garden City: Doubleday, 1956 (first published in 1920).

Schlesinger, Arthur M., Sr., *A Critical Period in American Religion, 1875–1900* ["Facet Books Historical Series," #7]. Philadelphia: Fortress Press, 1967.

Smith, H. Shelton, *Changing Conceptions of Original Sin: a Study in American Theology since 1750.* New York: Scribner's, 1955.

Smith, James Ward, and Jamison, A. Leland, eds., *Religious Perspectives in American Culture* ["Religion in American Life," II]. Princeton, N. J.: Princeton University Press, 1961.

Smith, Timothy L., *Called Unto Holiness, the Story of the Nazarenes: the Formative Years.* Kansas City: Nazarene Publishing House, 1962.

————, *Revivalism and Social Reform in Mid-Nineteenth Century America.* New York: Abingdon, 1957.

Toynbee, Arnold J., *An Historian's Approach to Religion* [The Gifford Lectures, 1952 and 1953]. London, New York, Toronto: Oxford University Press, 1956.

Veblen, Thorstein, *The Place of Science in Modern Civilization, and Other Essays.* New York: Russell & Russell, 1961 (first published in 1919).

Wendt, Herbert, *In Search of Adam.* Tr. by James Cleugh. Boston: Houghton, Mifflin, 1956.

Whitehead, Alfred North, *Science and the Modern World* [The Lowell Lectures, 1925]. New York: Macmillan, 1947 (first published in 1925).

Wish, Harvey, *Society and Thought in Modern America*, rev. 2nd ed. New York: David McKay, 1962.

Woodward, C. Vann, *Reunion and Reaction: the Compromise of 1877 and the End of Reconstruction.* Boston: Little, Brown, 1951.

Young, Alfred F., ed., *Dissent: Explorations in the History of American Radicalism.* DeKalb: Northern Illinois University Press, 1968.

Ziff, Larzer, *The American 1890's: Life and Times of a Lost Generation.* New York: Viking Press, 1968 (first published in 1966).

B. Articles and Papers.

Agnew, Theodore L., "Reflections on the Woman's Foreign Missionary Movement in Late 19th-century American Methodism." *Methodist History*, VI (January, 1968), pp. 1–14.

Ahern, Patrick J., "Nationalism and Religion: John Ireland." A paper read before a joint meeting of the Mississippi Valley Historical Association with the American Catholic Historical Association, Aaron I. Abell, presiding. Omaha, May 2, 1963.

Betts, John Rickard, "Darwinism, Evolution, and American Catholic Thought, 1860–1890." *Catholic Historical Review*, XLV (July, 1959), pp. 161–185.

Brandon, Janice I., "Millennialism in America." Northern Illinois University: unpublished research paper, 1969.

Brewer, H. Peers, "The Protestant Episcopal Freedman's Commission, 1865–1878." *Historical Magazine of the Protestant Episcopal Church*, XXVI (December, 1957), pp. 361–381.

Carter, Paul A., "The Fundamentalist Defense of the Faith." In John Braeman, et al., *Change and Continuity in Twentieth-Century America: the 1920's* ["Modern America" Series, II]. Columbus: Ohio State University Press, 1968, pp. 179–214.

————, "The Reformed Episcopal Schism of 1873: An Ecumenical Perspective." *Historical Magazine of the Protestant Episcopal Church*, XXXIII (September, 1964), pp. 225–238.

Church History, XXI–XXXVIII (1952–1969). All articles and reviews dealing with England or the United States in the nineteenth century were read and indexed. Fourteen articles are cited in the Notes.

Cooper, Berenice, *"Die Freie Gemeinde:* Freethinkers on the Frontier." *Minnesota History*, XLI (Summer, 1968), pp. 53–60.

DeMille, George E., "The Episcopate of Horatio Potter (1802–1887), Sixth Bishop of New York, 1854–1887." *Historical Magazine of the Protestant Episcopal Church*, XXIV (March, 1955), pp. 66–92.

Eickelmann, Allan, "A World Faith in America." Northern Illinois University: unpublished research paper, 1969.

Feldman, Egal, "American Ecumenicism: Chicago's World's Parliament of Religions of 1893." *Journal of Church and State*, IX (Spring, 1967), pp. 180–199.

Fox, Arnold B., "Howells as a Religious Critic." *New England Quarterly*, XXV (June, 1952), pp. 199–216.

————, "Spiritualism and the 'Supernatural' in William Dean Howells." *Journal of the American Society for Psychical Research*, LIII (October, 1959), pp. 121–130.

Gaither, Willie D., "A Fool's Errand, a Drop in the Bucket, or In *His* Steps?" Northern Illinois University: unpublished seminar paper, 1967.

Gotham, Steven D., "A New Chapter in the History of the Warfare of Science with the Forces of Tradition." Northern Illinois University: unpublished seminar paper, 1969.

Harding, Vincent, "Religion and Resistance Among Ante-bellum Negroes." A paper read before the Organization of American Historians, Chicago, April 27, 1967.

Harrell, David Edwin, Jr., "The Agrarian Myth and the Disciples of Christ in the Nineteenth Century." *Agricultural History*, XLI (April, 1967), pp. 181–192.

Higgins, John E., "A Man From the Middle Border: Hamlin Garland's Diaries." *Wisconsin Magazine of History*, XLVI (Summer, 1963), pp. 294–302.

Hubbard, Evelyn, "A Survey of the Hymnary of the Gilded Age." Northern Illinois University: unpublished seminar paper, 1967.

Hutchison, William R., "Liberal Protestantism and the 'End of Innocence'." *American Quarterly*, XV (Summer, 1963), pp. 126–139.

Johnson, Robert, "The Harmonization of Evolution and Religion in Nineteenth Century America." Northern Illinois University: unpublished seminar paper, 1967.

Kelley, Robert, "Presbyterianism, Jacksonianism and Grover Cleveland." *American Quarterly*, XVIII (Winter, 1966), pp. 615–636.

Kurtz, Paul C., "Northern Baptists on the Frontier." Northern Illinois University: unpublished seminar paper, 1969.

Leverette, William E., Jr., "E. L. Youmans's Crusade for Scientific Autonomy and Respectability." *American Quarterly*, XVII (Spring, 1965), pp. 12–32.

Magney, William, "Confessionalism, Americanism, and the Road to the Lutheran Ghetto." University of California: unpublished seminar paper, 1964.

Mervis, Leonard J., "The Social Justice Movement and the American Reform Rabbi." *American Jewish Archives*, VII (June, 1955), pp. 171–230.

Moore, George E., "The Sixth General Conference of the Evangelical Alliance, New York, 3–12 October 1873." University of California: unpublished research paper, 1964.

Morrow, Hubert W., "Cumberland Presbyterian Theology: A Nineteenth Century Development in American Presbyterianism." *Journal of Presbyterian History*, XLVIII (Fall, 1970), pp. 203–220.

Narehood, Vivian, "Pride Against Prejudice." University of California: unpublished seminar paper, 1964.

Olenik, Dennis L., "The Social Philosophy of Dwight L. Moody." Northern Illinois University: unpublished Master's thesis, 1964 (Robert Schneider, director).

Piepkorn, Arthur Carl, "What Does Inerrancy Mean?" *Concordia Theological Monthly*, XXXVI (September, 1965), pp. 577–593.

Preus, Robert D., "Walther and the Scriptures." *Ibid.*, XXXII (November, 1961), pp. 669–691.

Ramis, David, "The Work of the Chicago City Missionary Society of the Chicago Congregational Churches, 1882–1892: a Study of Attitudes Toward Immigrant and Labor During the Period of the Emergent Social Gospel." Northern Illinois University: unpublished seminar paper, 1967.

Redkey, Edwin S., "Bishop Turner's African Dream." *Journal of American History*, LIV (September, 1967), pp. 271–290.

Reed, Forrest F., "Background of Division—Disciples of Christ and Churches of Christ." An address delivered at the Tennessee Assembly of Christian Churches, Disciples of Christ Historical Society Breakfast, April 22, 1967, in Memphis, Tennessee. Nashville: pamphlet, 1968.

Ridout, Leonard D., "The Church, the Chinese, and the Negroes in California, 1849–1893." *Historical Magazine of the Protestant Episcopal Church,* XXVIII (June, 1959), pp. 115–138.

Rosten, Betsey, "Isaac Mayer Wise: A Jew in Transition." University of California: unpublished seminar paper, 1964.

Slater, Peter Gregg, "Andrew Dickson White and the Battle of Science With Religion." University of California: unpublished seminar paper, 1964.

Smylie, James H., "Thanksgiving Amid Arrogance of Prosperity." *Theology Today,* XXIII (October, 1966), pp. 327–335.

Swift, David E., "Conservative versus Progressive Orthodoxy in Latter 19th-century Congregationalism." *Church History,* XVI (March, 1947), pp. 22–31.

Taylor, Richard S., "Jonathan Blanchard: 19th-Century Evangelical." Northern Illinois University: unpublished Master's thesis, 1971.

Tester, N. Eugene, "Schisms Within the Disciples of Christ Denomination, 1809–1909." Northern Illinois University: unpublished Master's thesis, 1969.

VI. OTHER WORKS CONSULTED.

Austin, B. F., *The A. B. C. of Spiritualism.* Summit, N. J.: Stow Memorial Foundation, n. d. (first published in 1920).

Barth, Karl, *The Word of God and the Word of Man.* Tr. by Douglas Horton. New York: Harper, 1957 (first published in 1928).

Bergson, Henri, *Creative Evolution.* Tr. by Arthur Mitchell. New York: Henry Holt, 1937.

The Bible. (Citations throughout the manuscript are from the King James Version.)

The Book of Common Prayer, and Administration of the Sacraments and Other Rites and Ceremonies of the Church, According to the Use of the Protestant Espiscopal Church in the United States of America. Together with the Psalter, or Psalms of David. New York: Church Pension Fund, 1945.

Carlisle, Henry C., Jr., *American Satire in Prose and Verse.* New York: Random House, 1962.

The Christian Century, 1959–1969. Pertinent articles were clipped and filed as they appeared (see Notes).

Cohn, Werner, "Jehovah's Witnesses as a Proletarian Movement." *American Scholar,* XXIV (Summer, 1955), pp. 281–298.

Conze, Edward, *Buddhism: Its Essence and Development.* With a Preface by Arthur Waley. New York: Harper, 1959 (first published in 1951).

Derleth, August, and Wandrei, Donald, eds., *Selected Letters of H. P. Lovecraft,* Vol. I: *1911–1924.* Sauk City, Wis.: Arkham House, 1965.

Eddington, Arthur S., *The Nature of the Physical World.* Ann Arbor: University of Michigan Press, 1958 (first published in 1928).

Einstein, Albert, *Out of My Later Years.* New York: Philosophical Library, 1950.

Encyclopedia Britannica. Chicago, London, Toronto, Geneva, Sydney: Encyclo-
    pedia Britannica, Inc., 1964.
Freud, Sigmund, *Collected Papers.* Edited by Sir Ernest Jones, 5 vols. New York:
    Basic Books, 1959.
The Fundamentals: a Testimony to the Truth. 12 vols. Chicago: privately printed,
    n. d. [1909–1914].
Habel, Norman C., *The Form and Meaning of the Fall Narrative: a Detailed
    Analysis of Genesis 3.* St. Louis: Concordia, 1965.
Herberg, Will, *Protestant-Catholic-Jew: an Essay in American Religious Sociol-
    ogy,* new rev. ed. Garden City: Doubleday, 1960.
Hoyle, Fred, *Frontiers of Astronomy.* New York: New American Library, 1957
    (first published in 1955).
Jeans, Sir James, *The Mysterious Universe.* New revised edition. New York:
    Macmillan; Cambridge: at the University Press, 1935 (copyright 1932).
Klotz, John W., *Genes, Genesis, and Evolution.* St. Louis: Concordia, 1955; sec-
    ond printing, 1959.
Laing, Alexander, ed., *Great Ghost Stories of the World: The Haunted Omnibus.*
    New York: Garden City Publishing Company, 1939.
Lamont, Corliss, *The Illusion of Immortality.* London: Watts & Co., 1936 (first
    published in 1935).
Landis, Benson Y., ed., *Yearbook of American Churches: 1963.* New York: As-
    sociation Press, 1963.
Lepp, Ignace, *Death and its Mysteries.* New York: Macmillan, 1968.
Leuba, James H., *The Belief in God and Immortality: a Psychological, Anthro-
    pological and Statistical Study.* Boston: Sherman, French & Co., 1916.
Ley, Willy, *The Days of Creation.* New York: Modern Age Books, 1941.
Lippmann, Walter, *A Preface to Morals.* New York: Macmillan, 1929.
Lomax, Alan, ed., *The Folk Songs of North America.* Garden City: Doubleday,
    1960.
McCann, Alfred W., *God—or Gorilla? How the monkey theory of evolution
    exposes its own methods, refutes its own principles, denies its own in-
    ferences, disproves its own case.* New York: Devin-Adair, 1922.
McMahon, John J., "Catholic Students Look at Death." *Commonweal,*
    LXXXVIII (January 26, 1968), pp. 491–494.
Mecklin, John Moffatt, *The Survival Value of Christianity.* New York: Harcourt,
    Brace, 1926.
Mencken, Henry L., *Minority Report: H. L. Mencken's Notebooks.* New York:
    Alfred Knopf, 1956.
————, *Treatise On the Gods.* New York: Alfred Knopf, 1930.
Montagu, Ashley, *Immortality.* New York: Grove Press, 1955.
Morgan, Kenneth W., ed., *The Path of the Buddha: Buddhism Interpreted by
    Buddhists.* New York: Ronald, 1953.
[Morgan, F. Bruce] "Is This the Post-Christian Era?" *Theology Today,* XVIII
    (January, 1962), pp. 399–405.

National Spiritualist Association of Churches in the United States of America, *Yearbook, 1963.* Milwaukee: published by the Association, 1963.

Nickerson, Converse E., "The Origin of the Christmas Festival." *The National Spiritualist,* XLV (December, 1963), pp. 3–5.

Niebuhr, Reinhold, *Reflections on the End of an Era.* New York: Scribner's, 1934.

Oxtoby, Willard Gurdon, "The Post-Ecumenical Era." *Theology Today,* XXIII (October, 1966), pp. 374–385.

Pascal, Blaise, *Pensées.* Tr. by W. F. Trotter. New York: Modern Library, 1941.

Patton, Kenneth L., *A Religion For One World.* Boston: Beacon Press and Meeting House Press, 1964.

The Praeger Picture Encyclopedia of Art. New York and Washington: Frederick A Praeger; Brunswick, Germany: Georg Westerman Verlag, 1958.

Riley, John W., Jr., "Death and Bereavement." In David L. Sills, ed., *International Encyclopedia of the Social Sciences.* New York: Macmillan and Free Press, 1968. Vol. III, pp. 19–25.

Russell, Bertrand, *Selected Papers.* New York: Modern Library, 1927.

Russell, Charles Marion, *Good Medicine: the Illustrated Letters of Charles Marion Russell.* With an introduction by Will Rogers. Garden City: Doubleday, Doran, 1930 (first published in a limited edition in 1929).

Schrödinger, Erwin, *What Is Life? The Physical Aspect of the Living Cell.* Cambridge: at the University Press; New York: Macmillan, 1945.

Spock, Benjamin, *Baby and Child Care.* New York: Pocket Books, 1962 (forty-eighth printing).

"A Survey of the Political and Religious Attitudes of American College Students." *National Review,* XV (October 8, 1963), pp. 279–302.

Thurber, James, *Further Fables For Our Time.* New York: Simon and Schuster, 1956.

United States Department of Commerce, Bureau of the Census, *Religious Bodies, 1906.* Washington: Government Printing Office, 1910.

————, *Religious Bodies, 1916.* Washington: Government Printing Office, 1919.

————, *Religious Bodies, 1926.* Washington: Government Printing Office, 1929.

Webster's Collegiate Dictionary, 5th edition. Springfield, Mass.: G. & C. Merriam, 1947.

Index

Abbot, Francis Ellingwood, 165, 189
Abbott, Lyman, 28, 50–51, 52, 55, 57, 131, 171, 172, 212, 255n
Abdul-Baha, 218, 266n
Abolitionism, *see* Antislavery movement
Adams, Henry, 160
Adler, Felix, 245n
Africa, 152, 201, 212
African Methodist Episcopal Church, 123, 150–152, 212
Agassiz, Louis, 31, 36, 228n
Agnosticism, 4, 19, 47, 90, 98, 223n
Albright, Raymond W., 180–181, 186, 259n
Allen, Alexander V. G., 167–169, 175
American Association of Spiritualists, 99, 104–106, 114, 131
American Society for Psychical Research, 101
Anders, William, 199
Anglicanism, 39, 41, 57, 58, 91, 136, 145, 166, 169, 170, 184, 190, 194, 198, 219; Anglo-Catholicism, 186–189, 191. *See also* Protestant Episcopal Church
Animals, 27, 43, 45, 242n; *see also* Man, animal origins of
Anti-Catholicism, 144, 182, 183, 192, 195, 196, 255n
Anticlericalism, ix, 7–8, 10, 91, 102, 105
Anti-Semitism, 111, 202, 232n, 245n
Antislavery movement, 3, 5, 103, 113, 122, 123–124, 136, 157, 248n
Ape, as progenitor of man, 22, 24, 89, 98; *see also* Man, animal origins of
Archbishop of Canterbury, 182, 190, 213
Armstrong, J. C., 146, 147
Arnett, Benjamin W., 212, 264n
Arnold, Sir Edwin, 221
Arnold, Matthew, 4, 6
Art, history of, 157, 158, 255n
Asia, 204, 215, 216, 219; *see also* China; India; Japan; Thailand
Astronomy, 16, 40, 45, 92, 185, 199

Atheism, 4, 5, 89, 99; *see also* Anticlericalism; Materialism; Positivism; Science, religion of
Atlantic Monthly, 27, 31, 40, 66, 77, 81, 102, 205

Babbitt, Irving, 218
Bacon, Leonard Woolsey, 194–195
Baha'i (Bahism), 218, 219, 221
Baptists, 163, 166, 179, 191, 192, 213, 242n, 256n
Baring-Gould, Sabine, 177
Barnwell, R. Habersham, 5, 224n
Barrows, John Henry, 210, 213, 214, 215–216, 264n, 265n
Barth, Karl, 36, 48
Beecher, Edward, 248n
Beecher, Eunice (Mrs. Henry Ward), 112, 115, 118
Beecher, Henry Ward, 18, 47, 57, 80–81, 83, 88, 105, 109–132, 139, 166, 193, 198, 215, 226n, 238n, 240n, 250n; *see also* Stowe, Harriet Beecher
Beecher, Lyman, 81, 83
Bell, Alexander Graham, 111
Benchley, Robert, 157
Ben-Hur, see Wallace, Lew
Bernstorff, Johann-Heinrich von, 212
Besant, Annie, 214, 264n
Bhagavad Gita, 206
Bible, 23, 34–35, 37, 38, 45, 56, 103, 133, 137, 138, 151, 164, 165, 173, 185, 186, 188, 205, 207, 228n, 231n, 243n; King James Version, 69, 81, 283. *See also* "Higher Criticism"
Bierce, Ambrose, 1, 65–66, 72–73, 74, 78–79, 238n
Blacks, American, 3, 88, 111, 123, 137, 157, 204, 212; "black nationalism," 150–153, 254n
Blackwell, Elizabeth, 111
Blaine, James G., 10, 119, 143, 211
Blake, William, 27, 29

287